The Great Game in the Indo-Pacific

A Pivot to India

The Great Game in the Indo-Pacific

A Pivot to India

Edited by
Air Marshal Anil Chopra

Associate Editors
Air Commodore Savinder Pal Singh
Mahima Duggal

KW Publishers Pvt Ltd
New Delhi

in association with

Centre for Air Power Studies
New Delhi

Reprint 2024

The Centre for Air Power Studies is an independent, non-profit, academic research institution established in 2002 under a registered Trust to undertake and promote policy-related research, study and discussion on the trends and developments in defence and military issues, especially air power and the aerospace arena, for civil and military purposes. Its publications seek to expand and deepen the understanding of defence, military power, air power and aerospace issues without necessarily reflecting the views of any institution or individuals except those of the authors.

Centre for Air Power Studies
P-284, Arjan Path
Subroto Park
New Delhi 110010

Tele: (91-11) 25699131

E-mail: capsnetdroff@gmail.com
website: www.capsindia.org

ISBN 978-93-91490-38-6 Hardback
ISBN 978-93-91490-49-2 ebook

Published in India by Kalpana Shukla

KW Publishers Pvt Ltd
4676/21, First Floor, Ansari Road
Daryaganj, New Delhi 110002
Phone: +91 11 43528107
Marketing: kw@kwpub.in
Editorial: production@kwpub.in
Website: www.kwpub.in

Printed and bound in India
Quiinkit Infotech Pvt. Ltd., Gurugram

Contents

PART III: Moving Beyond the Quad

Acknowledgements

A book of such a comprehensive nature would not have been possible without an abundance of support and assistance. As a defence-focused research and analysis body, the Centre for Air Power Studies (CAPS) has four core verticals: aerospace power, Indo-Pacific, India's neighbourhood and nuclear security. Amongst these research areas, the Indo-Pacific has rapidly become a strategically critical region where much of the geopolitical activity and flux is focussed. This book has evolved from such a changing landscape in the Indo-Pacific. It originates from CAPS' Indo-Pacific research focus and presents a cross-section of authors who are experts in their respective domains.

First, the chapter authors featured in this volume deserve much appreciation for their outstanding contributions, rich expertise, sincere effort and timely submissions. However, it must be mentioned that the views, facts and figures presented in this book are those of the individual authors. The editors have extended an academic platform to all the experts to express their arguments and viewpoints freely and unreservedly.

Second, I extend my special appreciation to Air Commodore Savinder Pal Singh VSM (Retd.), Senior Fellow at CAPS, and Ms Mahima Duggal, Research Associate at CAPS, for their dedicated hard work and editorial assistantship to successfully accomplish this project. From conceiving the project to reading and reviewing the early chapter drafts, their contributions were indispensable.

Third, I would like to thank the entire team at CAPS for their support to this academic exercise. A special note of acknowledgement goes to the CAPS Indo-Pacific research faculty—Dr Joshy Paul, Dr Poonam Mann, Ms Anu Sharma and Ms Neha Mishra—who helped shape the book from its inception. Our thanks to Group Captain TH Anand Rao for support as the head of the Research Coordination Cell. Thanks to Aditya Hazarika for the copyediting support. Also, particular commendation to the most supportive CAPS library staff—Ms Sushma Zutshi, Ms Surbhi Sareen Sharma, and Mr Rohit Singh Rajput—for their tireless help throughout the entire book project, and especially the publication process.

Last, but not the least, I must appreciate the excellent team at KW Publishers, led by Ms Kalpana Shukla, for their meticulous copy-editing, splendid cover design, ever-patient support, and swift and smooth execution of the project on an extremely tight deadline.

Preface

The global geopolitical equilibrium has shifted from Central Asia to the Indo-Pacific, where the next "Great Game" is evolving. The 18th and 19th centuries belonged to the British Empire, the 20th to the Americans, and now, with the rise of China, some are terming the 21st as the Chinese century. While the USA wants to maintain a unipolar world with a bipolar Asia, China wants a bipolar world and a unipolar Asia, with clear dominance and a sphere of influence. With these two differing global dominance ambitions, the area of competition and strategic showdown has shifted to the Indo-Pacific.

In its quest to checkmate the Soviet Union, the USA had befriended China in the early 1970s. China made full use of that relationship to become a significant economic and, later, military power. After the dissolution of the Soviet Union, its successor, Russia, was considerably weakened. Meanwhile, the US got busy in Iraq and later in its "War against Terror" in West and Central Asia. Meanwhile, China's rise was being monitored on the sidelines, and in 2008, a Quadrilateral Security Dialogue, also called the Quad, evolved among the USA, Japan, Australia, and India. After the more aggressive Xi Jinping took over all instruments of power in China around 2013, China began openly displaying its global dominance ambitions. His two most important initiatives were claiming and building a large number of islands in the South China Sea (SCS) and the Belt and Road Initiative (BRI). Both these initiatives have geostrategic implications.

More aggressive initiatives to confront and compete with China were initiated by the Trump Administration and are now being followed by President Biden's foreign policy through what is being called the "Biden

Doctrine". The key elements of this are to counter China. This is proposed to be done by strengthening Quad engagement and creating a British, Australian, and US team with the AUKUS submarine deal. Biden has ended the "forever wars" like in West Asia. He has recommitted the USA to the North Atlantic Treaty Organisation (NATO). Biden hosted a "Summit for Democracy" in December 2021, seeking concrete action for the defence of the global democratic system and highlighting the "global contest between democracies and autocracies". The USA's latest National Defence Strategy, which is expected to be released this year, is likely to place a sharp focus on strategic competition, particularly with Russia and China. The USA also ratcheted up human rights issues, accusing China of both genocide and crimes against humanity for its treatment of the Uyghurs. The Biden Doctrine also means better alignments in West Asia. He is also strengthening the "America First" policies of his predecessor. On China, the US presidents now have the backing of the American people. A large percentage of them regard China as a competitor or an enemy, and the opinion is nearly as strong and high as during the 1989 Tiananmen Square massacre.

Clearly, the technology-driven 21st century brings new path-breaking disruptive challenges. It requires bolder, new, calibrated approaches. The USA has often had short-term thinking and switched sides between friends and adversaries. China is a case in point. After having fought the Chinese in Korea and Vietnam, the USA became closer to them in the 1970s, at its own peril. Now it is beyond just a grouping of democracies. Today, an "all of society" approach is required in the heavily networked world. Obama's "Pivot to Asia" is perhaps very relevant and, at best, requires a fresh look and impetus. Freedom of navigation, fair trade practices, intellectual property rights, cyber security and human rights are all issues requiring a rule-based global order. Only then can a democratic, free world function in cohesion. China has been trying to exploit the divided American democracy, which it calls chaotic. On the other hand, the challenge for the USA is to reverse China's capability to win or coerce other nations, especially the poorer and smaller ones. The free world needs to evolve new, more realistic inducements like the BRI to support the economic growth of less developed nations. Economic dependence on the global factory, 'China' , has also to be neutralised. US relations with allies in Asia and Europe need to be more predictable and time-tested. There has to be a universal condemnation of human rights violations and sinicisation in Xinjiang and Tibet.

While India continues to engage with the Western nations, it has maintained strategic autonomy as it watches how the US is moving forward on its Indo-Pacific approach and commitments. India is looking at how it would benefit from the US' investment in the Indo-Pacific. Some more European powers, like the UK and France, have an interest in Southeast Asia. The Indo-Pacific is no longer just a two-player chess-board but more like Chinese Checkers, with many players joining in.

China is extensively using its state-controlled media for "wolf warrior" coercive, confrontational, and combative diplomacy to denounce foreign criticism and to build domestic nationalistic fervour. President Xi is being projected as a cult figure to surpass even Mao Zedong. The Communist Party's control over the nation is being strengthened to keep Xi in a position of power. Xi is conscious that China is facing serious demographic issues and an economic slow down, yet he has aggressively antagonised many countries in the region, and that needs to be harnessed for the free world's response.

For a long time, the West has been fixated on Russia. Some of the Russian concerns about the eastward expansion of NATO are perhaps genuine. To compete squarely with China, Russia needs the assurance of the West for its own security. It was not difficult to wean it back from China. The USA and European nations had to be on the same page on this account. Unfortunately, Russia was pushed against the wall and then the Ukraine conflict erupted. Clearly, the way to take on China is to get its neighbours into their own fold. Japan and India, being sizeable economies, with common interests and goals, can cooperate and offer many projects to the smaller Asian countries.

The Indian Ocean region will now see a tripolar competition among New Delhi, Beijing, and Washington. Currently, China is aggressive, the USA is still recovering from the Afghanistan pull-back and the showdown in Ukraine, and India remains more inward-focussed. India's vision, announced by Prime Minister Modi in 2015, of "Security and

Growth for All in the Region," or SAGAR, was meant to benefit all the nations of the region, from the Gulf of Aden in the west to Thailand in the east. However, the stand-off in eastern Ladakh has brought more strategic angles to the vision.

India's Look East and Act East policies have both economic and geopolitical interests. Meanwhile, India has bypassed Pakistan to build closer relations with most countries in West and Central Asia. India has also been investing more in the air and maritime domains to build reach and influence. India is also strengthening its military assets in the island territories that are very strategically located. The signing of enabling security agreements with the USA has improved interoperability. The United States has been more open to selling high-end defence platforms and sharing intelligence inputs. The Indian armed forces are exercising much more with their partners in the Indo-Pacific region. The China-Pakistan nexus will remain a sore issue for India for some time. Unfortunately, the USA still sees Pakistan as a part of its South Asia policy. It is hoped that this too will see a change. Indo-Russia relations will also have to be factored in as an independent pillar.

The reunification of Taiwan with mainland China is the first priority for China currently. China's claims on parts of India's Arunachal Pradesh and the Japanese Senkaku Islands are its next areas of interest. These remain the immediate and critical flashpoints. How the free world reacts to the Chinese aggression on any of these will decide the future course of events. The Indo-Pacific concept can succeed only if Japan, Australia and India are strategically strong. It will work as a significant deterrent when many of the Southeast Asian nations get integrated into the plan.

Whether the Quad or the other trilaterals will one day become military alliances like NATO is still not clear and will depend on how aggressive a hegemon China becomes. The smaller countries may get sandwiched between the money-lending China and the rule-based Western system and the more open and supportive US-led security architecture.

The strategic location of India in the Indian Ocean is important if China has to be squeezed between the Pacific and Indian Oceans. India and the Indian Ocean region are also important for China's economic growth. Any Indo-Pacific strategy must include both military and economic measures to counter China's influence and pressure on the smaller Asian nations. There is also a need for the USA and India to have congruence as to the area that geographically constitutes the Indo-Pacific. For India, it is also time to watch and monitor the emerging new trilateral and other groupings. Surely India needs to build its own conventional military power as a deterrence. For this to happen, the economy has to see continued high growth for at least a decade or two. In the not so distant future, India is expected to be the third-largest economy after China and the USA.

Beijing, Washington, and New Delhi will, thus, emerge as important sides of the global geostrategic triangle. Some think that India could even play an influencing or balancing role between the two competing hegemons, using its strategic autonomy. China will have to understand Indian border sensitivities for that to happen. In all the scenarios, Beijing's neo-colonialism in the Indian Ocean region needs to be checked. India, being the largest country in the Indian Ocean region, is better positioned to control the air and sea lines of communication and can, thus, dominate the area. India's aerospace and maritime modernisation need a major push. It is action time in the region. India will be a major player and so cannot be a quiet spectator. It will have to play its cards based on its own national and geostrategic interests.

This book entitled *The Great Game in the Indo-Pacific: A Pivot to India* looks at a wide variety of subjects and dynamics. It first looks at India's rise, the growing strategic competition in the Indo-Pacific, and the challenges and opportunities for India in the Western Pacific. The aspirations and limitations of India's maritime strategy will decide the power equations in the Indian Ocean region. The balance of competing aerospace assets in the Indo-Pacific region would decide the reach and level of deterrence.

The other important area is the evolving strategic partnerships. The Quad is the most important, comprising the major regional players that carry significant economic and military weightage. The AUKUS brings the UK into the regional strategic connection. India-France-Australia comprise another major trilateral. Clearly, India remains a centrepiece in the region.

Finally, the book looks at moving beyond the Quad. There is a discussion about the Association of Southeast Asian Nations (ASEAN) countries and how they have had serious negative fallouts from China's aggressive push in the South China Sea (SCS). Some of them are contenders to join an extended Quad. The India-Taiwan greater engagement is now more in the open. India's close relations with Russia and the unequal but burgeoning closeness with China have their own dynamics. The book is centred on the India related narrative. India's dominating position at the head of the Indian Ocean, its historic cultural linkages with the West and Southeast Asia, its growing economic and military power, and its respected democratic and secular credentials give India its own place in the world. The book looks at India's aspirations and challenges, and tries to set the direction of India's compass.

Air Marshal **Anil Chopra**
Director-General
Centre for Air Power Studies

List of Tables and Figures

Tables

Figures

List of Abbreviations

4IR	Fourth Industrial Revolution
A2/AD	Anti-Access/Area-Denial
A&N	Andaman and Nicobar
AAM	Air to Air Missiles
ABMS	Air Battle Management System
ACD	Asia Cooperation Dialogue
ACP	African, Caribbean and Pacific
ACSA	Acquisition of Cross Services Agreement
AD	Air Defence
ADIZ	Air Defence Identification Zone
ADMM-Plus	ASEAN Defence Ministers Meeting Plus
AEW&C	Airborne Early Warning and Control
AI	Artificial Intelligence
AIIB	Asian Infrastructure Investment Bank
AIFFP	Australian Infrastructure Financing Facility for the Pacific
AIP	Air Independent Propulsion
AJI	Australia, Japan and India
ALBM	Air-Launched Ballistic Missile
AMTI	Asia Maritime Transparency Initiative
ANU	Australian National University
AOIP	ASEAN Outlook on the Indo-Pacific
APEC	Asia-Pacific Economic Cooperation
APR	Asia-Pacific Region
ARF	ASEAN Regional Forum
ASAT	Anti-Satellite

ASCM	Anti-Ship Cruise Missiles
ASEAN	Association of Southeast Asian Nations
ASEM	Asia-Europe Meeting
ASW	Anti-Sea Warfare
AU	African Union
AUKUS	Australia-United Kingdom-United States
AUSINDEX	Australia-India Exercise
AVIC	Aviation Industry Corporation of China
AWACS	Airborne Warning and Control Systems
B3W	Build Back Better World
BECA	Basic Exchange and Cooperation Agreement
BIMSTEC	Bay of Bengal Initiative for Multi-Sectoral and Economic Cooperation
BJP	Bharatiya Janata Party
BRI	Belt and Road Initiative
BRICS	Brazil, Russia, India, China, and South Africa
CAATSA	Countering America's Adversaries Through Sanctions Act
CAI	Comprehensive Agreement on Investment
CATOBAR	Catapult Assisted Take-Off Barrier Arrested Recovery
CBGs	Carrier Battle Groups
CCP	Chinese Communist Party
CCS	Cabinet Committee on Security
CECA	Comprehensive Economic Cooperation Agreement
CEPA	Comprehensive Economic Partnership Agreement
CICA	Conference on Interaction and Confidence Building Measures in Asia
CIWS	Close-in Weapon System
COMCASA	Communications Compatibility and Security Agreement
COP26	Conference of Parties-26
CPEC	China-Pakistan Economic Corridor

CPTPP	Comprehensive and Progressive Agreement for Trans-Pacific Partnership
CSAR	Combat Search and Rescue
CSG	Carrier Strike Group
CSIS	Centre for Strategic and International Studies
CSP	Comprehensive Strategic Partnership
CUES	Code for Unplanned Encounters at Sea
CWG	Climate Working Group
DAE	Department of Atomic Energy
DCS	Direct Commercial Sales
DEWs	Directed Energy Weapons
DJWG	Defence Joint Working Group
DPG	Defence Policy Group
DPJ	Democratic Party of Japan
DPPG	Defence Procurement and Production Group
EAMF	Expanded ASEAN Maritime Forum
EAS	East Asia Summit
e-CNY	Digital Yuan
ECS	East China Sea
EEU	Eurasian Economic Union
EEZ	Exclusive Economic Zone
EIA	US Energy Information Administration
EMALS	Electromagnetic Aircraft Launch System
EPA	Economic Partnership Agreement
EPQI	Expanded Partnership for Quality Infrastructure
ESGs	Service-to-Service Executive Steering Groups
EU	European Union
EW	Electronic Warfare
FAS	Favourable Air Situation
FDI	Foreign Direct Investment
FMS	Foreign Military Sales
FOIP	Free and Open Indo-Pacific
FONOP	Freedom of Navigation Operation
FRA	Flight Refuelling Aircraft
FTA	Free Trade Agreement

G7	Group of Seven
GCC	Gulf Cooperation Council
GDP	Gross Domestic Product
GMS	Greater Mekong Sub-region
GSOMIA	General Security of Military Information Agreement
HCl	Hydrochloride Acid
HREE	Heavy Rare Earth Elements
HVAA	High Value Air Assets
IAEA	International Atomic Energy Agency
IAF	Indian Air Force
IAFTA	India-ASEAN Free Trade Agreement
ICBM	Intercontinental Ballistic Missiles
ICDP	Integrated Capability Development Plan
ICJ	International Court of Justice
ICP	Industrial Cooperation Programme
ICT	Information and Communication Technology
ICWA	Indian Council of World Affairs
IDSA	Institute for Defence Studies and Analyses
IFANS	Institute of Foreign Affairs and National Security
IIR	Institute of International Relations
IN	Indian Navy
INC	Indian National Congress
INS	Indian Naval Station
IONS	Indian Ocean Naval Symposium
IOR	Indian Ocean Region
IORA	Indian Ocean Rim Association
IOR-IFC	Indian Ocean Region-Information Fusion Centre
IoT	Internet of Things
IOZP	Indian Ocean as a Zone of Peace
IPE	International Political Economy
IP MSI	Indo-Pacific Maritime Security Initiative
IPMZ	Indo-Pacific Maritime Zone
IPOI	Indo-Pacific Oceans Initiative
IR	International Relations

IREL	Indian Rare Earth Limited
ITA	India Taipei Association
IUPAC	International Union of Pure and Applied Chemistry
IUU	Illegal, Unreported and Unregulated
JADC2	Joint All Domain Command and Control
JAI	Japan-America-India
JASDF	Japan Air Self-Defence Force
JCPOA	Joint Comprehensive Plan of Action
JIMEX	Japan-India Maritime Exercise
JMSDF	Japan Maritime Self-Defence Force
J-STARS	Joint Surveillance and Target Attack Radar System
JSF	Joint Strike Fighters
JTG	Joint Technical Group
KMT	Kuomintang
LAC	Line of Actual Control
LACM	Land Attack Cruise Missiles
LAMP	Lynas Advanced Materials Plant
LC	Lanthanide Concentrate
LCA	Light Combat Aircraft
LCH	Light Combat Helicopter
LDP	Liberal Democratic Party
LEMOA	Logistics Exchange Memorandum of Agreement
LREE	Light Rare Earth Elements
MALSIDO	Malaysia-Singapore-Indonesia
MCG	Military Cooperation Group
MDA	Maritime Domain Awareness
MEA	Ministry of External Affairs
MIIT	Ministry of Industry and Information Technology, China
MoU	Memorandum of Understanding
MRBM	Medium-Range Ballistic Missiles
MRT	Mass Rapid Transit
MSG	Mono Sodium Glutamate

MSR	Maritime Silk Road
NAFTA	North American Free Trade Agreement
NAM	Non-Aligned Movement
NATO	North Atlantic Treaty Organisation
NCHC	National Centre for High-performance Computing (Taipei)
NDA	National Democratic Alliance
NDPG	National Defence Programme Guidelines
NFDC	New Framework for Defence Cooperation
NPT	Non-Proliferation Treaty
NSA	National Security Advisor
NSS	National Security Strategy
NWFZ	Nuclear Weapon Free Zone
OBOR	One Belt One Road
ODA	Official Development Assistance
OPV	Offshore Patrol Vessels
Open-RAN	Open Radio Access Networks
ORF	Observer Research Foundation
PACAF	Pacific Air Forces
PASSEX	Passing Exercise
PCA	Permanent Court of Arbitration
PIF	Pacific Island Forum
PLA	People's Liberation Army
PLAAF	People's Liberation Army Air Force
PLAN	People's Liberation Army Navy
PM	Prime Minister
PRC	People's Republic of China
Quad	Quadrilateral Security Dialogue
R&D	Research and Development
RAAF	Royal Australian Air Force
RAN	Royal Australian Navy
RCEP	Regional Comprehensive Economic Partnership
REE	Rare Earth Elements
REO	Rare Earth Element Oxide
RIC	Russia-India-China

RIMPAC	Rim of the Pacific
ROC	Republic of China (Taiwan)
ROK	Republic of Korea
ROKN	Republic of Korea Navy
SAARC	South Asian Association for Regional Cooperation
SAGAR	Security and Growth for All in the Region
SAM	Surface to Air Missile
SIDS	Small Island Developing States
SIMBEX	Singapore-India Maritime Bilateral Exercise
SIPRI	Stockholm International Peace Research Institute
SCO	Shanghai Cooperation Organisation
SCRI	Supply Chain Resilience Initiative
SCS	South China Sea
SDGs	Sustainable Development Goals
SLBM	Submarine Launched Ballistic Missile
SLOCs	Sea Lines of Communication
SSBNs	Submersible Ship Ballistic Missile Nuclear
SSF	Strategic Support Force
STSG	Senior Technology Security Group
TAICS	Taiwan Association of Information and Communication Standards
TAIPEI Act	Taiwan Allies International Protection and Enhancement Initiative Act
TECC	Taipei Economic and Cultural Centre
TPP	Trans-Pacific Partnership
TSDSI	Telecommunications Standards Development Society, India
TSMC	Taiwan Semiconductor Manufacturing Company
TST	Taiwan Strait Transits
UAE	United Arab Emirates
UAV	Unmanned Aerial Vehicle
UCAVs	Unmanned Combat Aerial Vehicles
UK	United Kingdom
UMC	United Microelectronics Corporation

UN	United Nations
UNCLOS	United Nations Convention on the Law of the Sea
UNSC	United Nations Security Council
UPA	United Progressive Alliance
US	United States
USA	United States of America
USAF	US Air Force
USGS	US Geological Survey
USINDOPACOM	United States Indo-Pacific Command
USMCA	US-Mexico Canada Agreement
USPACFLT	United States Pacific Fleet
USN	United States Navy
USSR	Union of Soviet Socialist Republics
VSTOL	Very Short Take-Off and Landing
WHO	World Health Organisation
WTO	World Trade Organisation
ZTE	Zhong Xing Telecommunication Equipment

PART I

India's Emerging Power and the Rise of the Indo-Pacific

1. US-China Strategic Competition in Indo-Pacific

Anil Chopra

The Indo-Pacific has become the new arena for great power rivalry. The region generally comprises the Indian Ocean, the Western and Central Pacific Oceans, and the seas that interlink the two near the Indonesia archipelago. This region saw some great battles between the United States of America (USA) and the Japanese military after the Japanese attacked Pearl Harbour in December 1941, pulling the United States into World War II. China's emergence as a global economic and military power in the last few decades brought new attention to this Indo-Pacific region. "China's rise and increased activism in South Asia and the Indian Ocean region is an uncontested reality even as Asian countries worry about the new cold war which the US and China are locked (in)", writes Rajiv Bhatia.[1] The Japanese suggestion to create a grouping of some of the major democracies in the region in the form of the Quadrilateral Security Dialogue, or "Quad", comprising the United States, Australia, Japan, and India, also shifted the security focus to check the unbridled actions of China in the region.

The 3.5 million sq km large South China Sea[2] (SCS), as the name suggests, is to the south of China. It has on its periphery the islands of Taiwan, parts of the Philippines, Vietnam, Borneo, and Indonesia. The sea has economic significance as major sea lanes pass through it and is, thus, crucial for livelihoods and security in Southeast Asia. However, the hundreds of islands, reefs, atolls and seamounts in the sea, many uninhabited, are claimed by the nations on the periphery. Hence, the disputes.

Since around 1947, the People's Republic of China (PRC-China) and the Republic of China (ROC-Taiwan) have been laying claims to the area within the nine-dash line.[3] These are major islands contested between the surrounding nations. Meanwhile, China began reclaiming land by building islands on small reefs. Subsequent Chinese claims went beyond the nine-dash line. The arbitral tribunal constituted under the United Nations Convention on the Law of the Sea (UNCLOS) gave its ruling on July 12, 2016, stating that China had no historical basis for its claims.[4] UNCLOS does not grant signatories the right to make claims based on historical legacy, as this lacks basis in international law. The ruling further clarified that neither did the nine-dash line have any validity nor did China's claims have any basis. China did not agree with the arbitration tribunal, and continues to claim sovereignty over "virtually all SCS islands and their adjacent waters.[5]" China has used selective historical references to make claims in all the disputes on its borders. It has disputes with most of its neighbours, which include Mongolia, Taiwan, Japan, South Korea, North Korea, the Philippines, Vietnam, Laos, Brunei, Indonesia, Singapore, Myanmar, Nepal, Bhutan, India, and Tibet.[6] It has been belligerent and aggressive in its boundary expansion in recent years. This has strategic implications. The SCS has now emerged as the area of a US-China strategic competition. Fig 1.1 below shows the Chinese claim line and the UNCLOS 200 nautical mile (nm) Exclusive Economic Zone (EEZ).

Fig 1.1: China's Claim Line and UNCLOS 200 nm EEZ

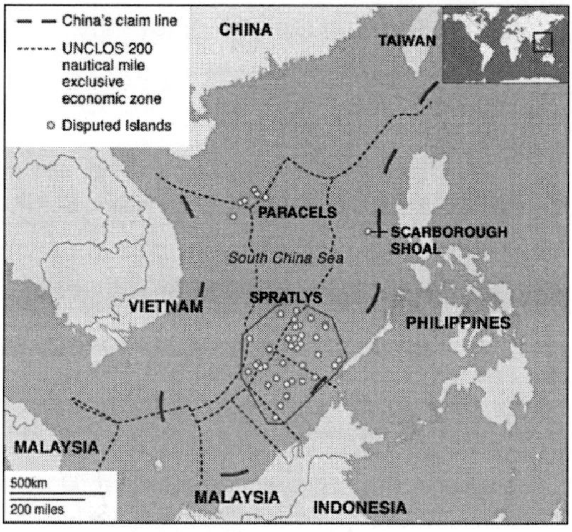

Source: UNCLOS, CIA

Great Wall of Sand: Chinese Island Building in SCS

In the recent years, China has engaged in extensive island-building and base construction in the SCS. It has built 20 outposts in the Paracel Islands and seven in the Spratlys. Earlier, in 2012, it had seized the Scarborough Shoal. Since 2013, China has been carrying out unprecedented dredging and artificial island-building in the Spratlys, and generated nearly 3,200 acres of new land. China has also done significant expansion in the Paracels. All this has been at the cost of neighbours like Vietnam and the Philippines. The James Shoal is an entirely submerged feature, roughly 20 metres (m) below the surface, only 90 km from Malaysia but nearly 1,850 km far from China's coast. Yet China calls it the "southernmost territory of China." The Asia Maritime Transparency Initiative (AMTI) of the Washington-based Centre for Strategic and International Studies (CSIS) has been tracking and monitoring activities on the islands. Pictures of a few of the islands with larger infrastructure have been reproduced below.

Fig 1.2: A Planet Skysat captured this image of Fiery Cross Reef in the South China Sea on May 3, 2020. Fiery Cross Reef is one of China's seven artificial islands in the Spratly Islands and represents a continued military presence in the region

Source: Skysat, https://www.planet.com/gallery/#!/post/fiery-cross-reef

Fig 1.3: Johnson Reef: Usable surface area of 27 acres, with a military base with radar, anti-aircraft guns, a Close-in Weapon System (CIWS) missile-defence system, and a small harbour

Source: CSIS/AMTI

Fig 1.4: Subi Reef, at Spratly Islands is a full military base, with a significant harbour, and a 3,000 m (9,800 ft) airstrip

Source: *The Japan Times*

Fig 1.5: James Shoal

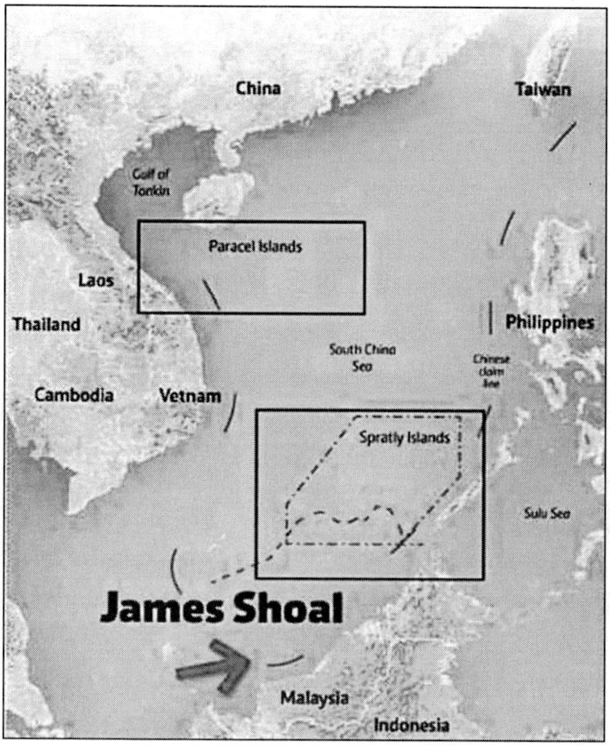

Source: *New Straits Times*

From the pictures above, it can be seen that China is making significant military facilities on artificial islands and developing them as launch pads to gain full control of the SCS.

East China Sea

The East China Sea (ECS) is towards the east of China and covers the area between Taiwan, Japan and South Korea. Territorial sovereignty over the Japanese administered Senkaku Islands in the ECS and the maritime boundary around them are disputed among China, Taiwan, and Japan. Both Taiwan and Japan are close American allies, and any Chinese action against Taiwan or Japan in the ECS would have strategic, political, and economic implications in the region.

Fig 1.6: Senkaku Islands

Source: Wikipedia

Chinese Inroads into Western Pacific

Taking a leaf from its success in the SCS, and the Indian Ocean, China began focussing on influence across the Western Pacific. It has been, literally, trying to buy influence through growing aid and infrastructure investments. The ground reality is that eight countries of Oceania, the region of the Western Pacific, recognise China, and six recognise Taiwan, resulting in continuous diplomatic competition. On the sidelines of the Asia-Pacific Economic Cooperation (APEC) Summit at Papua New Guinea, in 2018, Chinese President Xi Jinping met most of the Pacific Islands leaders,[7] offered partnerships and induced them to join China's Belt and Road Initiative (BRI) by offering them financial assistance. Since these were to be loans and not grants, many were concerned about unsustainable debts, and political strings attached to the Chinese aid. The hidden unsaid agenda of China is to use the ports and airport projects to gain military access to the region. Many Pacific countries are small in size and have structural vulnerabilities, and most are already heavily indebted to China.

As per the Lowy Institute study and analysis,[8] six Pacific countries that owe a significant debt to China include Papua New Guinea, Fiji, Samoa, Tonga, Vanuatu and the Cook Islands. Some of them are large beneficiaries of BRI. The Solomon Islands and Kiribati, which had recognised and maintained diplomatic relations with Taiwan, have now switched recognition to China.[9] As per the Lowy Institute study, Chinese commitments to the region were $5.4 billion in 2017—a substantial jump from just $374 million in 2016. The United States, and its allies, including Australia, New Zealand and Japan, are renewing their diplomatic linkages in the region to counter China's influence and cautioning against debt traps.[10]

Australia also began debt-financing initiatives as part of its broader Pacific 'step-up'. It started a $2 billion Australian Infrastructure Financing Facility for the Pacific (AIFFP). Despite the Chinese initiatives, Australia and New Zealand still provide more than half the aid in the region and have committed to more engagement. China was to commence building the Vaiusu wharf, a China-funded project, in Samoa, but the $100 million Chinese-backed port development has since been cancelled.

China wants to establish 'strategic pivot ports' in Suva, Apia, Port Moresby and Luganville (Vanuatu).[11] It has approached Vanuatu,[12] 2,000 km east of Australia, to build a port-cum-base to host cruise ships, but which also has the potential to service naval vessels and become a military base. In 2019, a Chinese enterprise made an attempt to lease the small Tulagi Island belonging to the Solomon Islands. However, it was vetoed by the local government.

The People's Liberation Army Navy (PLAN) ships have been making repeated port calls to the Pacific Islands. Over the years, China has been giving military aid to the island nations. It donated military trucks to Tonga; gave hydrographic and surveillance vessels, 47 military vehicles, and offered military aid and training to Fiji. China's space-tracking ships that support both civilian and military launches, repeatedly sail to the region. China has reportedly deployed acoustic sensors to monitor US submarines in the island regions. The People's Liberation Army (PLA) is also known to be using fishing vessels for military surveillance. Guam and the Northern Mariana Islands, which sit along the second island chain, are considered by the PLA to be of high military relevance.

PLAN's Expanding Reach

The PLAN has the largest number of surface vessels and submarines, and is second only to the United States Navy (USN) in terms of tonnage. The PLAN has one operational aircraft carrier[13] (another is under sea trials) compared to the USN's 11. The fleet air-arm has nearly 690 aircraft for undertaking various maritime roles. The PLAN inducted its first aircraft carrier, the *Liaoning* (refurbished *Varyag*) in 2012. The first fully indigenous aircraft carrier, the *Shandong* (70,000 tonnes), was commissioned on December 19, 2019. It uses conventional steam turbines with diesel generators as propulsion. The next two that are under construction will be the Type 003 (85,000 tonnes). These will have an Electromagnetic Aircraft Launch System (EMALS) and a steam-powered catapult and could possibly be Catapult Assisted Take-Off Barrier Arrested Recovery (CATOBAR) carriers, thus, allowing heavier fighters to operate from them. China may finally have five or six aircraft carriers by around 2035. It is already working towards building carrier battle group-focussed blue water capabilities. At any given time, it plans to have two carrier groups in the Pacific and one in the Indian Ocean.

In addition, the PLAN[14] has 54 attack/guided missile submarines (the USN has 53), 83 cruisers, destroyers and frigates (the USN has 110), and 6 principal amphibious ships (the USN has 32). Clearly, the PLAN is fast catching up with the USN on many counts but is still far behind in aircraft carriers.

People's Liberation Army Air Force's Expanding Reach

The People's Liberation Army Air Force (PLAAF) is the largest air force in Asia and the second largest in the world. As per the *Military Balance 2020*, it has 1,976 fighter/ground-attack aircraft,[15] 211 bombers, 278 attack-helicopters, 395 heavy/medium transport helicopters, 88 heavy/ medium transport aircraft, 18 aerial refuellers, 29 airborne early warning and control aircraft, and 29 heavy unmanned aerial vehicles. The PLAAF is catching up with the more modern Western air forces across many aircraft and technological capabilities. The PLAAF is in transition from a tactical air force to one with a global reach. The state-owned Aviation Industry Corporation of China (AVIC) is developing and producing state-of-the-art airborne platforms and is fast catching up with the best in the world. The PLAAF has also reoriented its flying training and tactics. There is a greater emphasis on technological support, even for operations. The PLAAF is evolving its operational doctrine, missions and roles, including concentrating on long-range precision strikes. It is working on integrated air and space capabilities and coordinated offensive and defensive operations in conjunction with the Strategic Support Force (SSF).

Nearly 50 J-20 fifth generation fighter aircraft have been inducted, and other fourth generation-plus aircraft are fast replacing the ageing J-7s. The second fifth generation aircraft, the J-31, is under development. The PLAAF is training for the hybrid nature of warfare, including precision and effect-based operations, network-based operational planning, and flexibility. The PLAAF has had low exposure to military conflict and modern air exercises but is trying to compensate through powerful platforms and weapons.

For long range reach, the PLAAF already has a 66-tonne payload class Xi'an Y-20 large military transport aircraft with a maximum range of 7,800 km. Over twenty have been inducted. It also has around 150 Xian H-6 twin-engine bombers (licence-built version of the Soviet Tupolev Tu-16). These can carry 12,000 kg bombs or six cruise or anti-shipping missiles. The PLAAF also has indigenous flight refuellers and Airborne Warning and Control Systems (AWACS), but these numbers are still small. The locally developed Xian H-20 subsonic stealth bomber is expected to enter service by 2025. Clearly, the PLAAF is being built for strategic reach. The nearest major American bomber air base, Guam is around 3,300 km from the mainland. It will be closer to some of the island air bases in the SCS.

US Strategic Goals in the Region

In the SCS and ECS, the US goals would be to secure freedom of the seas and navigation operations, meet its treaty commitments to Japan, Taiwan, and the Philippines, manage the interests of other partner nations like Australia, Association of Southeast Asian Nations (ASEAN) and others. The US would also be interested in securing the Western Pacific from Chinese forays and build-up while preventing China from using the "might-makes-right" approach and becoming a regional hegemon. The US aims to prevent China from its unabated construction of artificial islands and military bases and from using its debt-diplomacy to wean away the small island nations into its fold. The US is conscious that China's domination of its near-seas region would significantly affect US strategic, political, and economic interests across geographic regions. The SCS also borders many nations that are either existing partners of the US or are potential partners, such as Singapore, Vietnam, and Indonesia.

Strategic Implications of China Dominating the SCS

It shall be China's endeavour to use its network of islands, including the newly created ones, for Anti-Access/Area-Denial (A2/AD). It is militarily important for China to keep the US forces away from the first island chain to secure its mainland and prevent intervention in a Taiwan contingency. China is also trying to build a significant sea and air-based deterrent: it has a significant force of nuclear-powered ballistic missile submarines (SSBNs). China would certainly like to exercise full control over the SCS and prevent or delay US advances of any kind. It should be the US' target to destroy the Chinese military bases on the small artificial islands.

Meanwhile, China will exploit the economic benefits of the SCS in terms of fishing, and oil and gas exploration activities. China will also exercise political influence on the countries bordering the SCS. It is already trying to enforce an Air Defence Identification Zone (ADIZ) over the entire SCS. One day, it might try a blockade around Taiwan. The SCS would then become a launchpad for China to project military force in the Western Pacific. This would pose a challenge to the United States and other regional powers. It will also become more difficult for the USA to defend its allies like Japan and Taiwan, among others. A weakened USA could force some countries to switch allegiance to a more powerful China, thus, weakening the US-led regional security architecture.

Weakening US Global Position

After a major victory in World War II, the USA had seen a stalemate in the Korean War, a loss of face in Vietnam, and not so great success in Kosovo. The USA also left Iraq, Syria, and Libya in a general mess. Russia's annexation of Crimea from Ukraine and the inability of the USA to intervene or prevent it also reflected on its power projection limitations. After a 20-year presence and the war against terror in Afghanistan, it had to withdraw, leaving the country in turmoil. For some time now, the USA has not been able to convince all its European allies to stand against China. The USA could not prevent Russia from attacking Ukraine. The US' ability to intervene in Iran has also weakened due to Russian and Chinese support of Iran. While the USA was busy behaving like the global policeman in the "war against terror", China was using the time for building up its economic and military might. China has made significant forays into Africa through its debt diplomacy. The Chinese BRI is also helping it extend its influence in Central and West Asia and the Indian Ocean region. China was among the first to engage with the Taliban in Afghanistan.

For long, China followed Deng Xiaoping's foreign policy guiding philosophy of "hide your strength, bide your time", which he had adopted from the ancient master strategist Sun Tzu's advice to "appear weak when you are strong, and strong when you are weak." However, the Chinese strongman Xi Jinping seems like a man in a hurry. While the USA wants to have a unipolar world and a bipolar Asia, China wants a bipolar world and a unipolar Asia.

The US is a democracy wherein the nation is nearly equally divided between the two major political parties. The long presidential election campaigns are watched by the whole world, and invariably the fissures get exposed. On the other hand, China is relatively autocratically controlled by the Chinese Communist Party (CCP). There is poor connectivity for the Chinese people with the rest of the world. Allegiance to the CCP is more important than the nation. Undoubtedly, the expanding economy has brought up the living standards of the Chinese people. Because of years of humiliation meted out to China by Japan and other powers, the Chinese Communist leader, Mao Zedong, coined the phrase, "political power grows out of the barrel of a gun". China has followed this to build its economic and military power. Autocratic China is, thus, getting to a position to be able to challenge the United States. As the 18th and 19th centuries were considered "British centuries", and the 20th the "American century", the 21st is being called the "Chinese century". In another decade, China will overtake the economy of the United States to become the largest in the world.

The Russian Factor

Immediately after the collapse of the Soviet Union, the Russian economy had crumbled. The then President Boris Yeltsin, was looking for support from the West. But the USA's and its European allies' priority was to get the erstwhile Warsaw Pact countries into their fold. This made Russia insecure. Finally, when the Russian economy recovered a little and the strongman Putin became all-powerful, Russia began flexing its muscle. It again began investing in the military, and especially pushed ahead with development of aircraft and hypersonic weapons. The USA and Europe always had security concerns about Russia. The West kept imposing economic sanctions, off and on. After Russia annexed Crimea in a very smooth and well-orchestrated action, the West became concerned and reacted with further sanctions. After the Russian invasion of Ukraine, the sanctions were tightened further. It also invoked the "our enemy's friend is an enemy" approach. In 2017, the Countering America's Adversaries Through Sanctions Act (CAATSA) federal law was passed by the United States, which then imposed sanctions on Iran, North Korea, and Russia.

Russia realised early that it was being snubbed and pushed away by the Western countries. It then moved closer to China. After the dissolution of the Soviet Union in 1991, US-China relations began to deteriorate. On the other hand, a China-Russia rapprochement began. Initially begun as a "constructive partnership" in 1992, later, it became a "strategic partnership" in 1996, and a treaty of "friendship and cooperation" in 2001. This treaty was renewed in June 2021 for five more years. The two countries have been supporting each other on various global issues and have maintained military, economic, and political relations.

However, the relationship is somewhat unequal and unreal. China has a very dominating and powerful economy. In the initial years, it flooded Russia with cheap copies of Russian artefacts and household goods, to the detriment of the Russian economy. The 4,133-km-long Russia-China border is among the longest between countries. There are boundary disputes between them and they have fought wars in the past. China has ambitions and is increasing its influence in Central Asia, an area historically under Russian influence. The trade between the two is highly in favour of China. China's main interest from Russia comprises natural resources, including minerals and petroleum. For a long time, China was importing weapon platforms and other arms from Russia, but it has now become fairly independent by having created an indigenous industry. In fact, Russia has repeatedly accused China of stealing Russian designs or reverse-engineering them. China is also becoming a significant arms exporter in Asia, Africa and Latin America and has taken away some of the Russian markets.

The current relationship between the two is one of convenience as both are being driven into each other's arms due to the Western pressure. In the long-term, it may be in Russia's interest to be closer to Europe. Many commentators are of the view that the American allies should not overplay the Russian threat but instead, must wean Russia away from the Chinese fold, just as they had done in the 1970s to cause a split between the Communist Soviet Union and China.

Deployable US Military Naval and Air Assets

The US Air Force (USAF) and US Navy (USN) are the largest in the world. As per the *Military Balance 2020,*[16] the USAF has 3,311 fighter/ground-attack aircraft, 157 bombers, 889 attack-helicopters, 3,058 heavy/medium transport helicopters, 675 heavy/medium transport aircraft, 555 aerial refuellers, 113 airborne early warning and control aircraft, and 495 heavy unmanned aerial vehicles. Clearly, on most counts, the USAF's total assets are much larger than those of the PLAAF. However, how many can be physically deployed in the Indo-Pacific region depends on the availability of air bases in the region. The US Navy has 11 aircraft carriers, 53 attack/guided missile submarines, 110 cruisers, destroyers and frigates, and 32 principal amphibious ships. The USN also has a huge air power carrying capability.

US Air and Naval Power in Western Pacific

The United States Indo-Pacific Command (USINDOPACOM) is responsible for the Indo-Pacific region. Manned by nearly 375,000 personnel, it saw major action in the Korea and Vietnam Wars. The Pacific Air Forces (PACAF) is the air component of the command. The PACAF has 334 aircraft and 31,299 airmen. The PACAF includes the Fifth Air Force for USAF operations in Japan, with a primary role to defend Japan and work closely with the Japanese forces. There are three major air bases. The 18 Wing, Kadena, has the F-15C/D Eagle, the E-3B/C Sentry, the HH-60G Pave Hawk, and the KC-135R Stratotanker. The 35 Wing, Misawa, has F-16 fighter aircraft variants. And the 374 Airlift Wing, Yokota, has C-12J and C-130J Hercules transport aircraft and UH-1N Iroquois helicopters. The 18th Expeditionary Air Wing at Kadena also has an E-8C Joint Surveillance and Target Attack Radar System (J-STARS).

The Seventh Air Force is in Korea to maintain the armistice between the two Koreas. The main air bases there are at Kunsan and Osan. The US aircraft housed in South Korea are the F-16C/D and the A-10C Thunderbolt II. The Eleventh Air Force handles all USAF operations in the Pacific Ocean, and includes Alaska, Hawaii and Guam. With headquarters in Alaska, it operates all the aircraft in the USAF inventory, including the F-35, F-22A Raptor, C-17 Globemaster III, C-130, among many others. The PACAF also has expeditionary units in New Zealand and Antarctica. The PACAF also has a large reserve component stationed at air bases in mainland USA, Hawaii and Guam. The United States Pacific Fleet (USPACFLT) includes 250,000 Navy sailors and Marines, 2,000 aircraft, and 200 ships. There are at least two carrier battle groups in the area around Taiwan. These are large nuclear-powered aircraft carriers of the Nimitz class with over 100,000 tonnes displacement and can house nearly 90 fixed wing aircraft and helicopters. The US has twelve similar large carriers that can easily be brought into action. It also has nine 45,000-tonne carriers that can operate Very Short Take-Off and Landing (VSTOL) aircraft, including F-35. The US, thus, has significant air power in the region.

The USPACFLT includes the United States 3rd and 7th Fleets, the naval surface and air assets in the Pacific, US naval forces in Japan and Korea, joint forces in the Marianas and naval forces in the Hawaii region. The 3rd Fleet looks after the Eastern and Northern Pacific, which includes Alaska, the Bering Sea, and part of the Arctic. The 3rd Fleet includes the USS *Nimitz* aircraft carrier with the 11th Carrier Strike Group; aircraft carrier USS *Carl Vinson* with the 1st Carrier Strike Group; aircraft carrier USS *Theodore Roosevelt* with the 9th Carrier Strike Group; and aircraft carrier USS *Abraham Lincoln* with the 3rd Carrier Strike Group. Clearly, it is the most powerful USN fleet. The 7th Fleet is based at Yokosuka, Japan, and is the largest of all the forward-deployed US fleets. It has nearly 70 ships, and over 300 aircraft, with its 5th Carrier Strike Group having the USS *Ronald Reagan* aircraft carrier.

America's Major Friendly Military Assets in Pacific Region

The Japan Air Self-Defence Force (JASDF) operates around 740 aircraft, including approximately 330 fighters. It has a well networked air defence radar chain for early warning and supporting combat air patrols. Of late, the JASDF has been under increasing pressure to intercept PLAAF warplanes that have been attempting to enter the air space around the Senkaku Islands. In just one year ending March 2020, the JASDF had to scramble over 900 times in response to PLAAF aircraft incursions. The JASDF operates the F-15J (155), Mitsubishi F-2 (62) and F-35 (129 on order) fighter aircraft. It has 10 air refuellers and a significant number of Airborne Early Warning and Control (AEW&C) aircraft. The Japan Maritime Self-Defence Force has a fleet of over 150 ships and 350 aircraft, for control over the sea lanes and to patrol territorial waters. It is currently the world's fourth largest navy by total tonnage.

The Royal Australian Air Force (RAAF) has 259 aircraft, of which 110 are combat aircraft. The RAAF has had great combat experience over the last 100 years. Its main combat aircraft are 69 Boeing F/A-18, 24 F/A-18E/F (multi-role), and 37 F-35 Lightning II. It has 18 dedicated electronic warfare aircraft, 14 Boeing P-8 maritime patrol aircraft, and seven Airbus A330 MRTT air refuellers. Ultimately, it will have nearly 100 F-35. It has a sizeable Unmanned Aerial Vehicle (UAV) force and is working on the loyal Wingman unmanned force. Like the Japanese, the RAAF has a high commonality of assets with the USA. The Australian Army and Royal Australian Navy also operate a few aircraft in various specific operational roles.

The Indian Air Force (IAF), and Indian Navy (IN) are among the top few in the world. The IAF has an estimated 1,800 aircraft (900 fighter/attack). The IN has a fleet of around 150 ships and submarines and 300 aircraft. It has one operational aircraft carrier and the second is undergoing sea trials. The IN also has one each nuclear-powered attack and ballistic missile submarine in addition to nearly 15 conventionally-powered attack submarines. It is a blue-water navy with the ability to project power beyond the Indian Ocean. Currently, the influence of the IAF and the IN is mainly restricted to the Indian Ocean. Both have been exercising along with other friendly navies in the Indian and Pacific Oceans. While India is still not part of any military alliance, it will be a major player in the region from the Gulf of Aden to the Malacca Strait, covering some of the major trade routes.

Principle of Freedom of the Seas

One of the key goals of the US is also related to freedom of the seas and treating them as the global commons. The United States considers this to be of key national interest and is willing to use military force to protect that interest. China has chosen its own interpretation of the law of the sea that is not commensurate with general international understanding. Its unilateral actions in the SCS have upset the status quo and challenged the accepted principle of freedom of the seas. China also believes that it has the right to regulate and restrict the movements of foreign military vessels and aerial platforms in its EEZs. This approach is meant to curtail the reach of the US military to carry out reconnaissance and possible offensive operations to support smaller democracies like Taiwan and others in the case of belligerent Chinese actions. If China gets away with its views or actions, it would have an impact on power equations in the

Indo-Pacific. The USA has been trying to rally all the countries that have been affected by China's claims in the SCS. Many ASEAN countries are conscious and a little on the defensive about having a large, powerful and belligerent neighbour like China. China also uses its economic muscle to keep these countries in its fold. Beijing's stubborn position and claims based on its nine-dash line have serious implications for many ASEAN countries.

Freedom of Navigation Operation (FONOP)

The USN has carried out an increasing number of Freedom of Navigation Operations (FONOPs) in the SCS and Taiwan Strait Transits (TST) since 2012. Of late, the PLA has been claiming that it has been driving the USN away. The US 7th Fleet continues its operations in the region as the American commitment to upholding the freedom of navigation and lawful uses of the sea as a principle. It continues to fly, sail and operate as per international laws.[17] In each case, China raises protests, and the PLAN ships and/or aircraft keep issuing warnings to the US Navy ships. The Pentagon has cautioned that China's military challenges to the US in the SCS have attendant risks.[18] There are others who feel there is an increasing risk of serious confrontation. China often quotes many countries which have restrictions inconsistent with the UNCLOS, and do not allow freedom of exercise in the high seas by foreign navies even beyond 12 nautical miles (nm) from the coast. These include Bangladesh, Brazil, Myanmar, India, Iran, Pakistan, and Vietnam among many others. Interestingly, the United States itself is not a party to UNCLOS.

China's "Salami-Slicing" Approach

For a long time, China has been using the salami-slicing approach. It did this to India in eastern Ladakh, where it has been nibbling in the Aksai Chin area. Also, it is trying to do the same in Doklam and along their border in Bhutan. Earlier, China tried the same with Russia. Clearly, the greatest success of this strategy of creeping annexation has been in the SCS, where it has been gradually changing the status quo. China has also been unholy and provocative in using COVID-19 to pursue its strategic goals while the world has been busy saving lives from the widespread pandemic.

How China used the USA for Decades

Mao was no stranger to strategic necessities that would override ideological imperatives.[19] While the USA was trying to wean away Communist China in its strategy to counter-balance the Soviet Union in the 1970s, it was China that benefitted the most in the long run. Many top US technology companies had set up their bases in China, thus, giving it greater access to modern trade practices and technology. Also, China was able to import modern systems from the USA. Many Chinese migrated to the USA and became a powerful diaspora who would not only send remittances and industrial intelligence but also act as a pressure group. While the USA was spending trillions of dollars around the world as a global policeman to counter terrorism, China was gaining time and becoming a major power.

Vulnerability of SCS Islands

Most of the islands in the SCS are on very small parcels of land. They have very limited air defences. These can easily be targeted using cruise missiles launched from ships or aircraft. Only a few have runways on them. These could be targeted first. Most islands also have a very limited capability to launch amphibious operations. So effectively, they do not give China much military reach, but are being used only to reinforce territorial claims.

US Politics: Need for Greater Bipartisanship

The recent elections in the USA have exposed the country as being highly divided. Even though the decision to pull out of Afghanistan has been supported across party lines, the Biden Administration is under severe attack. Internal politics apart, it gives a poor impression to the world and also weakens the global leadership position of the United States. The country needs to maintain and display total unity in its actions to contain China.

US Strategy and Options

While the Quadrilateral Security Dialogue (Quad) began evolving during President Obama's tenure, it was President Trump who accelerated the actions to evolve and develop an aggressive competing strategy and confrontational approach toward China. The Biden Administration continues to maintain that approach. The US has security treaty commitments with many countries in the Western Pacific, including Japan, Taiwan, and the Philippines. It has to maintain the US-led security architecture in the Western Pacific and a favourable regional balance of power; and stop autocratic Communist China from following the "might-makes-right" approach and becoming the world leader, displacing the democratic USA. The USA has to stop and prevent further salami-slicing.

To achieve that, the USA has to prevent intellectual property rights and high technology from being stolen or transferred to China. The USA has to defend its strategic networks from Chinese eavesdropping or cyber attacks. It would have to build anti-China alliances with democracies, and free thinking, law abiding nations, and ensure universal adoption of the Western understanding of the definition of freedom of the seas. It needs an integrated approach, including diplomatic, economic, military, informational, paramilitary, and law enforcing elements. To break the American dollar's dominance over global markets, China has been trying to introduce a digital currency, the digital Yuan (e-CNY).[20] China's attempts to get the digital yuan[21] to become an alternate currency to the US dollar are being countered by promoting alternative crypto-currencies like the digital dollar[22] or equivalent currency. The free world must impose reputational and other costs for China's actions.

The USA must try and isolate China globally. The time has come to woo Russia away from the Chinese fold. After Crisis in Ukraine, this move would get significantly postponed. The USA must thwart Chinese moves in the Arctic, the next area of action. It must make defence and strategic investments here primarily to build its global power and counter China rather than fight other countries' regional wars. Countering the Chinese influence through the BRI would be critical. An alternative to the BRI is a strategic necessity if the United States and its allies desire to slow down Beijing's expanding access and influence.[23]

The USA will require close coordination, first, with the countries around the SCS, such as Japan, South Korea, the Philippines, Vietnam, and Indonesia. Australia, the UK, France, and Germany also have regional interests and are building alliances. India is a major regional power and the main contestant and bulwark against China. Many of these countries have an axe to grind against China. The Philippines has been challenging Chinese warships in the SCS.[24] Canada has many, very vocal, reasons to increase its naval presence in the SCS.[25] Vietnam has already expanded its Maritime Militia off its southern coast.[26] Indonesia has bolstered its navy as China steps up incursions around ASEAN.[27] The Philippines has planned a military hub with sea cameras amid rows with China in the SCS.[28] Australian warships are regularly conducting transits through the SCS, including in the more contested areas as tensions increase with China.[29] Meanwhile, the Philippines has told its fishermen to ignore Beijing's ban on fishing in the South China Sea.[30] Also, Malaysia and Vietnam have decided to sign an agreement on maritime security to take steps to settle distracting bilateral disputes between the Southeast Asian nations in the South China Sea.[31] The US has been vocally encouraging allies in Southeast Asia to take stronger steps to challenge China in the SCS. In March 2021, the Philippines sent fighter aircraft over Chinese vessels in the SCS.[32] The European Navies have also been increasing their Indo-Pacific presence as concerns about China increase.[33] The US has also asked the ASEAN countries to reconsider deals with blacklisted Chinese firms.[34] Southeast Asia would stand to gain as the US hardens its stand in the SCS. Yet many countries are playing safe, as was the case when Indonesia discovered an underwater spy drone.[35] In some counts, the US has been struggling to build a coalition against China.[36] There are some others who believe in avoiding taking sides with the US or China.[37]

The Trump Administration had followed a plan of openly exposing and criticising China's actions in the SCS. It had begun imposing severe economic sanctions on Chinese firms and officials. Is the cost-imposing strategy of the USA working? There is a need for assessment and review. The US and its allies are having a greater naval presence and conducting FONOPs, including in the Taiwan Strait using operational US Navy and Coast Guard ships. The Philippines has been building up its naval fleet in the SCS. The US Air Force bombers have been conducting overflight operations in the SCS and ECS. The US has also bolstered its military presence and operations in the Indo-Pacific region. The USA must prevent China from turning the SCS into a zone of Anti-Access/Area Denial (A2/AD), thus, keeping other militaries out of the region.

The Indo-Pacific Maritime Security Initiative (IP MSI)[38] has been evolved to enhance maritime security and domain awareness in the SCS and the Indian Ocean region. The initiative also includes significant financial assistance for maritime security for countries in the region. The United States is also increasing defence and intelligence interaction with two key players, Vietnam and Indonesia. The US led Rim of the Pacific (RIMPAC) multilateral naval exercises in the Pacific with nearly two dozen countries are held every alternate year. Interestingly, even China had participated in 2014 and 2016. But the invitation was retracted in 2018.[39] Since January 2021, the USA has imposed additional sanctions against a large number of Chinese officials who were reportedly responsible for, or complicit in, the reclamation and militarisation of disputed islands in the SCS.[40] President Biden also assured the Japanese prime minister of the US' commitment and support to defend the uninhabited Japanese islands claimed by China. There are fears that China's continued deployment of maritime assets near the islets could lead to escalation or a skirmish, Department of Defence spokesperson John Kirby said in February 2021.[41] Though in 2014, the navy leaders of many countries, including China and the USA, agreed to a "Code for Unplanned Encounters at Sea" (CUES) at the 14th Western Pacific Naval Symposium.[42] The US and Chinese Coast Guards had committed to following an arrangement for rules-based behaviour and confidence-building measures through the November 2014 Memorandum of Understanding (MoU).

The USA has 2+2 ministerial meetings with Japan, India, Australia, and some other allies. These meetings include the ministers of defence and external affairs. The Indo-Pacific has been an important area of discussion, among others. The USA would have to readjust its economic model to be able to once again accelerate ahead. In view of the strategic competition, is there a need for increased annual appropriations and prioritisation by the State Department and Pentagon? Shouldn't the focus shift to Asian security compared to Europe and West Asia? Can the US lower its threat assessment of Russia? Can the USA galvanise private investments to counter China's growth and influence? Can the USA get the ASEAN into its fold through mature diplomacy? The USA will have to stop being seen as an arm-twisting, sometimes unreliable, friend? Can the US support make international organisations like the UN more relevant to resolving international disputes?

The USA has to catch up with the Chinese on some crucial defence technologies, such as hypersonic and Directed Energy Weapons (DEWs). The USA will have to become more active in cyber warfare and grey zone operations. Ultimately, the USA must now turn away from the war against terror and concentrate on its strategic completion with autocratic, Communist China, which is rising at the cost of freedom and liberty to its people, and undermining the rule-based world. China must realise that instability and military tensions in the SCS and ECS are detrimental for its own security and world position, and it needs to tread cautiously. The USA has military bases in many countries, therefore, China will find it difficult to target them. The backing of the US allies and partners for both military and non-military stances is crucial. "Prepare now for war in the Pacific. The window to prepare for war in the Western Pacific is closing quickly. The United States must build and prepare naval forces that can deter China or defeat it if necessary. We must build a battle force that is ready for war—not in 2045, but by 2025", says Congressman Michael Gallagher (R-Wisconsin).[43] Till now, diplomacy has not been able to stop China in the SCS. As Beijing is trying to expel the US from the SCS, it is time for Washington to join Beijing for a salami-themed picnic, as some analysts believe.[44]

Challenges and Options: India

The rise of China's hard power in the SCS and its overt desire to dominate Asia and ultimately the globe, has implications for India. There is an uneasy hostility in India about China's rise. A powerful China makes it difficult for India to negotiate on equal terms. It also forces India to commit larger sums towards defence. China's assertive behaviour in the Indian Ocean is also threatening for India. China wants to settle the boundary dispute with India on its own terms, selectively quoting old historic documents that suit its narrative. China also wants to put India in its place as a distant No. 2 in the Asian power equation. The Natuna Island, which is claimed by China, is just 570 km east of Singapore, bringing China very close to India even from the sea. China's investments in ports in the Indian Ocean include Gwadar (Pakistan), Djibouti, Lamu (Kenya), livestock terminal of Sudan Port, Hambantota (Sri Lanka) among many others. Most of these countries are already heavily indebted to China. Kenya, Pakistan, Myanmar, Sri Lanka and Djibouti have significant Chinese debt.[45]

India has to befriend the large number of ASEAN nations that have serious territorial differences with China. It needs to highlight to the smaller nations how China has managed to transform a legal defeat into a politico-military strategic victory through aggression in the SCS and that a similar fate can await them one day through high debt. India must increase defence cooperation with many of the ASEAN and South Asian countries. It needs to win back or retain Nepal, Bangladesh, and Sri Lanka in its zone of influence. It must act big brotherly in the Indian Ocean region, offering economic support with no strings attached. India, along with Japan, can take on joint developmental projects. India has to use its historical friendship with Russia to rein in China. It must try to reduce its trade dependence on China through a planned national strategy and alternative sourcing. It has to continue to use its close linkages in the Quad to put tacital pressure on China. India must actively support FONOPs in the SCS, and must not forget that it is the fourth largest military power, with a significant nuclear deterrent in place, and is no pushover. Meanwhile, as it strengthens economically and militarily, India must bide its time, and engage in neutral constructive engagement while giving clear signals of displeasure at the Chinese behaviour. A Maritime Coordination Cell may be created with like-minded nations to prevent losing strategic control of the Indian Ocean. Exercises to increase maritime interoperability must continue and involve other countries in the region.

India's engagement with the USA should remain calibrated. Undoubtedly, the USA could act as insurance against a stronger China, but physical commitments and limitations must be clearly understood and factored in. No one is likely to physically enter combat in a war between China and India. Yes, intelligence and surveillance support would be forthcoming. India should pressurise the USA to transfer critical and high-end technologies in return for global strategic alignment. The USA has a history of switching sides based on its changing global interests. Ultimately, India must build its own strength. *Atmanirbharta* (indigenisation) will be crucial. Long-range surface-to-surface missiles are an important component of deterrence and India must build a significant arsenal, including hypersonic weapons.

Notes

1. Rajiv Bhatia, "Indo-Pacific, The Contested Theatre", *Gateway House*, February 26, 2019. https://www.gatewayhouse.in/indo-pacific-contested/. Accessed on August 20, 2021.
2. "South China Sea", Lowy Institute, Sydney. https://www.lowyinstitute.org/issues/south-china-sea. Accessed on August 21, 2021.
3. Jacob Rutzick and Jonathan Chen, "The Validity of the 9-Dash Line", *Story Maps Arc GIS*, March 16, 2021. https://storymaps.arcgis.com/stories/4791710315c54e6fb963e10496faa4db. Accessed on August 21, 2021.
4. Law of the Sea, *Bulletin No. 91*, United Nations Division for Ocean Affairs and the Law of the Sea, Office of Legal Affairs, p. 28. https://www.un.org/depts/los/doalos_publications/LOSBulletins/bulletinpdf/LOS_91_WEB.pdf. Accessed on August 20, 2021.
5. Oriana Skylar Mastro, "How China is Bending the Rules in the South China Sea", *The Interpreter*, Lowy Institute, February 17, 2021. https://www.lowyinstitute.org/the-interpreter/how-china-bending-rules-south-china-sea. Accessed on August 20, 2012.
6. Pia Krishnankutty, "Not just India, Tibet — China has 17 Territorial Disputes with its Neighbours, on Land and Sea", *The Print*, July 15, 2020. https://theprint.in/theprint-essential/not-just-india-tibet-china-has-17-territorial-disputes-with-its-neighbours-on-land-sea/461115/. Accessed on August 20, 2021.
7. Liangyu, "Xi Meets Leaders of Pacific Island Nations to Further BRI Cooperation", *Xinhua*, November 17, 2021. http://www.xinhuanet.com/english/2018-11/17/c_137612228.htm. Accessed on August 22, 2021.
8. Roland Rajah, Alexandre Dayant, and Jonathan Pryke, "Ocean of Debt? Belt and Road and Debt Diplomacy in the Pacific", Lowy Institute, October 21, 2019. https://www.lowyinstitute.org/publications/ocean-debt-belt-and-road-and-debt-diplomacy-pacific. Accessed on August 22, 2021.
9. Natalie Whiting, Christina Zhou and Kai Feng, "What Does It Take for China to Take Taiwan's Pacific Allies? Apparently, $730 Million", *ABC News*, September 19, 2019. https://www.abc.net.au/news/2019-09-20/kiribati-to-switch-diplomatic-ties-from-taiwan-to-china/11532192. Accessed on August 22, 2021.
10. Jonathan Barrett, "Sink or Swim: Chinese Port Plans Put Pacific Back in Play", Reuters, August 7, 2019. https://www.reuters.com/article/us-pacific-samoa-china-insight-idUSKCN1UX01I. Accessed on August 22, 2021.

11. Denghua Zhang, "China's Military Engagement with Pacific Island Countries", *Asia and Pacific Policy Society*, August 17, 2020. https://www.policyforum.net/chinas-military-engagement-with-pacific-island-countries/. Accessed on August 22, 2021.
12. David Wroe, "China Eyes Vanuatu Military Base in Plan with Global Ramifications", *The Sunday Morning Herald*, April 9, 2018. https://www.smh.com.au/politics/federal/china-eyes-vanuatu-military-base-in-plan-with-global-ramifications-20180409-p4z8j9.html. Accessed on August 22, 2021.
13. *The Military Balance* 2020, Published February 13, 2020, Chapter 2, p. 27. https://doi.org/10.1080/04597222.2020.1707959. Accessed on August 27, 2021.
14. Ibid.
15. Ibid.
16. Ibid.
17. Chief of Information, "7th Fleet Conducts Freedom of Navigation Operation", US Navy Office of Information, July 12, 2021. https://www.navy.mil/Press-Office/News-Stories/Article/2690226/7th-fleet-conducts-freedom-of-navigation-operation/. Accessed on August 29, 2021.
18. Ryan Pickrell, "Pentagon Says China's Military is Challenging the US with 'Risky' Run-ins in the South China Sea During the Pandemic", *Business Insider*, May 21, 2020. https://www.businessinsider.in/politics/world/news/pentagon-says-chinas-military-is-challenging-the-us-with-risky-run-ins-in-the-south-china-sea-during-the-pandemic/articleshow/75857200.cms. Accessed on August 29, 2021.
19. Bleddyn E. Bowen, "Why was China Receptive to American Overtures During the Early 1970s?," *E International Relations*, March 11, 2010. https://www.e-ir.info/2010/03/11/why-was-china-receptive-to-american-overtures-during-the-early-1970s/. Accessed on August 28, 2021.
20. Frank Lavin, "China's Digital Currency Strategy", *Forbes*, August 1, 2021. https://www.forbes.com/sites/franklavin/2021/08/01/chinas-digital-currency-strategy/?sh=1a99384973ca. Accessed on August 28, 2021.
21. Deutsche Bank, "Digital Yuan: What is it and How Does it Work?," July 14, 2021. https://www.db.com/news/detail/20210714-digital-yuan-what-is-it-and-how-does-it-work?language_id=1. Accessed on August 28, 2021.
22. Daren Fonda, "The US Needs a Digital Dollar to Counter China's Threat, Lawmaker Says", *Barrons*, June 3, 2021. https://www.barrons.com/articles/the-us-needs-a-digital-dollar-51622675067. Accessed on August 28, 2021.
23. William C. Pacatte, "Competing to Win a Coalition Approach to Countering the BRI", Centre for Strategic and International Studies (CSIS), December 2019. https://csis-website-prod.s3.amazonaws.com/s3fs-public/publication/191219Pacatte_Countering_BRI_WEB_FINAL.pdf?ivg8369pub0VTUmhYbJgfbVLTaK4HXL8. Accessed on August 28, 2021.
24. News Desk, "Philippines Challenges Chinese Warship in South China Sea", *Livemint*, July 19, 2021. https://www.livemint.com/news/world/philippines-

challenges-chinese-warship-in-south-china-sea-11626705757074.html. Accessed on August 28, 2021.

25. Jacob Benjamin, "Look for an Increasingly Active Canada in the South China Sea", *The Diplomat*, June 12, 2021. https://thediplomat.com/2021/06/look-for-an-increasingly-active-canada-in-the-south-china-sea/. Accessed on August 28, 2021.
26. Tomoya Onishi, "Vietnam Expands Maritime Militia off Southern Coast", *Nikkei Asia*, June 12, 2021. https://asia.nikkei.com/Politics/International-relations/South-China-Sea/Vietnam-expands-maritime-militia-off-southern-coast#:~:text=Establishing%20a%20new%20maritime%20militia,and%20transportation%20in%20the%20area. Accessed on August 28, 2021.
27. Shotaro Tani, "Indonesia Bolsters Navy as China Steps Up Incursions Around ASEAN", *Nikkei Asia*, June 11, 2021. https://asia.nikkei.com/Business/Aerospace-Defence/Indonesia-bolsters-navy-as-China-steps-up-incursions-around-ASEAN. Accessed on August 28, 2021.
28. Andreo Calonzo, "Philippines Plans Military Hub, Sea Cameras Amid China Row," *Bloomberg*, May 10, 2021. https://www.bloomberg.com/news/articles/2021-05-10/philippines-plans-military-hub-cameras-at-sea-amid-china-spat. Accessed on August 28, 2021.
29. Andrew Tillett, "Navy Goes Full Speed Ahead on South China Sea Transits", *Australian Financial Review*, May 10, 2021. https://www.afr.com/politics/federal/navy-goes-full-speed-ahead-on-south-china-sea-transits-20210507-p57pru. Accessed on August 28, 2021.
30. Karen Lema, "Philippines Tells Fishermen to Ignore Beijing's Ban on Fishing in South China Sea", Reuters, May 5, 2021. https://www.reuters.com/world/asia-pacific/philippines-tells-fishermen-ignore-beijings-ban-fishing-south-china-sea-2021-05-05/. Accessed on August 28, 2021.
31. Sebastian Strangio, "Malaysia, Vietnam Set to Pen Agreement on Maritime Security", *The Diplomat*, April 7, 2021. https://thediplomat.com/2021/04/malaysia-vietnam-set-to-pen-agreement-on-maritime-security/. Accessed on August 28, 2021.
32. Karen Lema, "Philippines Sends Fighter Aircraft Over Chinese Vessels in South China Sea," Reuters, March 28, 2021. https://www.reuters.com/article/us-philippines-china-southchinasea-idUSKBN2BK031. Accessed on August 28, 2021.
33. Masaya Kato, "European Navies Build Indo-Pacific Presence as China Concerns Mount," *Nikkei Asia*, March 4, 2021. https://asia.nikkei.com/Politics/International-relations/Indo-Pacific/European-navies-build-Indo-Pacific-presence-as-China-concerns-mount. Accessed on August 28, 2021.
34. Hau Dinh and Yves Dam Van, "US to ASEAN: Reconsider Deals with Blacklisted China Firms", Associated Press, September 10, 2020. https://apnews.com/article/beijing-global-trade-south-china-sea-international-news-asia-d55e0c17498a09112216412a3f891bc2. Accessed on August 28, 2021.

35. "Indonesia Plays it Safe in US-China Conflict", *Asia Sentinel*, January 18, 2021. https://www.asiasentinel.com/p/indonesia-plays-it-safe-in-us-china?r=yrto&utm_campaign=post&utm_medium=web&utm_source=twitter. Accessed on August 28, 2021.
36. Misha Ketchell, "After all its Posturing, the US is Struggling to Build a Coalition Against China," *The Conversation*, August 18, 2020. https://theconversation.com/south-china-sea-after-all-its-posturing-the-us-is-struggling-to-build-a-coalition-against-china-144533. Accessed on August 28, 2021.
37. Bhavan Jaipragas, "South China Sea: Avoid Siding with US or China, Malaysia Urges Asean," *South China Morning Post*, August 5, 2020. https://www.scmp.com/week-asia/politics/article/3096205/south-china-sea-avoid-siding-us-or-china-malaysia-urges-asean. Accessed on August 28, 2021.
38. Policy Memorandum, Defence Security Cooperation Agency, DSCA Policy 19-49, October 30, 2019. https://samm.dsca.mil/policy-memoranda/dsca-19-49. Accessed on 28 August 2021.
39. Megan Eckstein, "China Disinvited from Participating in 2018 RIMPAC Exercise," *USNI News*, May 23, 2018. https://news.usni.org/2018/05/23/china-disinvited-participating-2018-rimpac-exercise. Accessed on August 28, 2021.
40. Matthew Lee (Associated Press), "US Imposes Sanctions on Chinese Defence Firms over Maritime Dispute," *Defence News*, August 26, 2020. https://www.defencenews.com/industry/2020/08/26/us-sanctions-chinese-defence-companies-over-south-china-sea-dispute/. Accessed on August 28, 2021.
41. John Feng, "Pentagon Warns China About 'Miscalculation' Over Actions in Japanese Waters", *Newsweek*, February 24, 2021. https://www.newsweek.com/pentagon-warns-china-about-miscalculation-over-actions-japanese-waters-1571552. Accessed on August 28, 2021.
42. Chief of Naval Operations Public Affairs, Navy Leaders Agree to Code for Unplanned Encounters at Sea at 14th Western Pacific Naval Symposium, US Indo-Pacific Command, April 23, 2014. https://www.pacom.mil/Media/News/Article/564121/navy-leaders-agree-to-code-for-unplanned-encounters-at-sea-at-14th-western-paci/. Accessed on August 29, 2021.
43. Congressman Michael Gallagher, "Prepare Now for War in the Pacific", US Naval Institute, Vol. 147/7/1,421, July 2021. https://www.usni.org/magazines/proceedings/2021/july/prepare-now-war-pacific. Accessed on August 30, 2021.
44. Michael Rubin, "The US Must Beat China at its Own Game in South China Sea", *The National Interest*, May 13, 2020. https://nationalinterest.org/feature/us-must-beat-china-its-own-game-south-china-sea-153716. Accessed on August 30, 2021.
45. Saeed Faridi, "China's Ports in the Indian Ocean", *Gateway House*, August 19, 2021, https://www.gatewayhouse.in/chinas-ports-in-the-indian-ocean-region/. Accessed on August 30, 2021.

2. India and the Western Pacific: Challenges and Opportunities

Joshy M Paul

The Western Pacific region, comprising the countries bordering the Eastern Indian Ocean and the Western Pacific Ocean, which include Southeast Asia, East Asia, the US, and Australia, has gathered greater traction in India's security strategy in recent times. India's strategic direction towards the Western Pacific region is a sub-set of India's overall policy towards the Indo-Pacific region. The end of the Cold War has provided a greater opportunity for India to enhance its strategic presence beyond its traditional sphere of influence in the region of South Asia. During the Cold War, India consciously decided not to be enmeshed in a bipolar competition, while most Asia-Pacific countries were part of either the East or the West bloc. After the end of the Cold War, New Delhi's interactions with the Western Pacific countries have gradually evolved from economic interactions under the 'Look East' policy to the 'Extended Neighbourhood' strategy. This expanded India's strategic engagement with the East Asian countries, and under the 'Act East' policy, India has become an indispensable power on regional security matters. Besides, the growing India-US strategic partnership has also been a catalyst in India's enhanced strategic partnership with the Western Pacific countries. Economically and security-wise, India's engagement with the Western Pacific countries such as Japan, South Korea, and the Association of Southeast Asian Nations (ASEAN) increased phenomenally during this period. As a result, India became a member of all the multilateral security mechanisms formed to address the problems of the Asia-Pacific region.

Indeed, China's rise and the attendant concerns generated by it among the elite stakeholders in the region have also contributed to India's increased engagement with the West Pacific regional countries.

India's enhanced engagement with the Western Pacific countries can be seen in the way the regional countries have looked to India as a strategic balancer to maintain peace and stability in the region. This is a major shift from their earlier approach to India. When the Asia-Pacific Economic Cooperation (APEC) came into being, India did not find a place in it. However, since the 2000s, India has become an original member of all multilateral fora formed to preserve peace and stability in the region, such as the East Asia Summit, the ASEAN Defence Ministers Meeting Plus, and the major power security initiative called Quadrilateral Security Dialogue (Quad). The emergence of the Indo-Pacific as a single entity, combining both the Western Pacific and the Indian Ocean, also reflects the growing salience of India's economic and security profile, extending beyond the Indian Ocean and going into the South China Sea and East Asian waters. It indicates that developments in one part of the region will have a direct bearing on the other side, so India considers that it has a responsibility to contribute to maintaining peace and security beyond its immediate neighbourhood. The most significant security situation that would affect India is how the US-China relations pan out and the role China is going to play in the future in the Indo-Pacific.

India's interest in the Western Pacific has been driven by both strategic and economic logic, and for that, India acts both independently and in collaboration with like-minded countries. Economically, India's trade and investment partnerships with the region have progressed phenomenally. Security-wise, it is a combination of defensive and offensive realism: the former represents India's need for ensuring freedom of navigation east of the Indian Ocean region, while the latter underlies balancing tactics against China. In other words, it can be argued that India pursues active defensive realism and passive offensive realism. The primary objective of India's Indo-Pacific strategy is to ensure that the region is free from conflict and competition, a repercussion of the US-China conflict. New Delhi's interest is in maximising its security rather than projecting its power in the Indo-Pacific region. As a responsible power in the Indo-Pacific, New Delhi seeks to secure its economic and political interests and military security, instead of power projection tactics.[1] It also aims to prevent China from dominating the region as a hegemonic power.[2] Also, India's policy towards the Western Pacific is linked to Sino-Indian relations. Scholars give varied theoretical interpretations of India's China policy, mostly in the category of realist versions of hedging or balancing; India's strategy towards the Western Pacific can also be seen in the category of counter-containment against China's 'encirclement' strategy of India in the Indian Ocean Region (IOR).[3] In this regard, India has built strategic partnership agreements with regional countries such as South Korea, Japan, the Philippines, Vietnam, as well as with the US and Australia. India's strategic presence in the Western Pacific would ameliorate India's strategic profile from simply being a South Asian power into a pan-Asian power.

Before New Delhi looked at the Western Pacific strategically, it had a long cultural relationship with the regional countries. However, that had not been converted into political or strategic purposes. During the Cold War, India viewed the region as a playground of power politics between two ideological blocs: Capitalism and Communism. India chose a mid-path of mixed economy and kept a distance from the regional countries as the region had no strategic value for New Delhi. Similarly, when the regional countries formed the Asia-Pacific Economic Cooperation (APEC) in 1987, they found no significance in incorporating India into the grouping because India's engagement with the member countries as a whole was minimal. Also, the developments in the East Asian waters had seemingly not posed any direct threat to India's security interest. However, this changed when China launched an ambitious maritime agenda with creeping assertiveness in the South China Sea and set its eyes on the Indian Ocean to emerge as a regional hegemon in the entire Indo-Pacific region. This prompted India to strengthen its strategic cooperation with the regional countries and make its naval presence felt in the East Asian waters in a consistent manner. In short, India's policy towards the Western Pacific is a combination of its growing profile of power status and to balance China in the Indo-Pacific region.

Drivers of India's Approach Towards the Western Pacific

The main drivers of India's policy towards the Western Pacific are: expanding India's footprint beyond the Indian Ocean periphery, a balancing strategy against China, and protecting India's trade and energy interests. Firstly, India emerged as a middle power in the international system at the beginning of the present century. Middle powers are security seekers because their chief concern is to safeguard their sovereignty vis-à-vis the greater (emerging) power.[4] They are status-quoists rather than challengers of the existing system, as the status quo would provide assurance for their security while uncertainty could prevail in the new order. At the same time, they prefer to expand their power and influence beyond their regional system and promote more partnerships with other regional countries. When their economy grows steadily, there would be a conviction among the elites that a robust foreign policy is needed based on the depth of the economic success and convert it into taking geostrategic advantage.[5] India's desire to widen its profile was reflected in the address given by former Indian Prime Minister Atal Bihari Vajpayee at the 2003 Combined Services Conference, "The strategic frontiers of today's India, grown in international stature, have expanded well beyond the confines of South Asia... Our security environment ranges from the Persian Gulf to the Straits of Malacca across the Indian Ocean... and Southeast Asia. Our strategic thinking has also to extend to these horizons."[6] The South China Sea has consistently been depicted as 'secondary areas of interest' in the Indian Navy's Maritime Doctrines since 2007.[7] Eventually, economic growth and geostrategic orientation go hand-in-hand, and this will mostly be visible in the region where the economic interaction is strong. The Look East policy, launched in the early 1990s, which later expanded from Southeast to East Asia, has helped New Delhi strengthen its economic interactions with the Asia-Pacific region, and has transformed India's image from a poor developing country to a rising economic power in Asia. Subsequently, the relationship has progressed from an economic one into a strategic partnership—India is a strategic partner of all major countries from the Western Pacific, except China.

Secondly, India's policy towards the Western Pacific can be seen as a counter-containment strategy against China's expansionism towards the

IOR. China has sought a firm naval presence in the Indian Ocean region since the launching of its military modernisation in the 1990s to become a 'maritime great power'. Initially, Beijing pursued a 'string of pearls' strategy and then the 21st century Maritime Silk Route, popularly known as MSR, to establish its strong strategic presence in the IOR. Besides, the People's Liberation Army Navy (PLAN) has been operating throughout the year since its first distant water operations in 2008 in the Gulf of Aden to participate in anti-piracy operations, occasionally with submarines and advanced destroyers.[8] Its 'places' at Gwadar in Pakistan, Hambantota in Sri Lanka, Lamu in Kenya and Bagamoyo in Tanzania on the east coast of Africa, apart from its naval base at Djibouti, can be utilised for China's security interests in both peace-time and during a conflict.[9] This will make China an indisputable power in the IOR. Its land corridor connecting the Indian Ocean with mainland China through its close friends Pakistan and Myanmar under the Belt and Road Initiative (BRI) will potentially encircle India. To counter this, India is also forging friendship with South and Southeast Asian countries, especially those that consider China's long-term interests to be inimical to them, such as Japan, South Korea, Vietnam, the Philippines, Singapore, Indonesia, and Australia by means of strategic partnership agreements and regular naval arrangements.

India's balancing strategy can be seen under the realist soft balancing in which the threatened states form strategic partnership arrangements with similar countries instead of forming hard military alliances.[10] Countries like Japan, Australia, and South Korea secure their sovereignty under their mutual defence agreements with the US, while New Delhi has always turned a blind eye to military alliances. Its focus has been on an independent posture to deal with emerging threats. When the Chinese threat was looming large, India focussed on building a strong strategic partnership agreement with the US,[11] followed by countries from the Western Pacific region too, such as Japan, Australia, Vietnam, and South Korea, to ensure that the threat was managed. India signed the Strategic Partnership Agreement with Japan in 2006, then with other countries. Today, bilateral strategic partnership agreements signed among the regional countries have become the hallmark of the Indo-Pacific security construct.

Thirdly, it is imperative for New Delhi to get free and uninterrupted access to the regional waters (East and South China Seas) on which India's trade flows up to the Russian Far East. After the 1991 liberalisation, India's trade with the Southeast Asian and East Asian regions has increased phenomenally: India's annual trade with East Asia (Oceania) increased from US$1.68 billion in 2000-01 to $13.45 billion in the 2020-21 period; in the case of Southeast Asia, it increased from $7.06 billion to $78.9 billion during the corresponding period.[12] Besides, India has committed millions of dollars of investments in oil exploration in areas in Russia's Sakhalin and in the South China Sea of Vietnam's Exclusive Economic Zone (EEZ). Protecting these interests is undoubtedly a priority area in India's security calculations.

The trade flows with East Asia pass through disputed waters, so protecting the Sea Lines of Communication (SLOCs) is a major objective of India's security strategy. This has been clearly emphasised as one of the primary mission objectives in the Indian Navy's 2009 Indian Maritime Doctrine.[13] Importantly, China is a party to the maritime disputes in the East and South China Seas: China claims 90 per cent of the South China Sea water body, and if it goes ahead unilaterally with its claims, it will hurt India's trade and energy security interest badly.

From Look East to Act East Policy

India's Look East/Act East policy is one of the successful foreign policy initiatives of the post-Cold War period. Former Prime Minister PV Narasimha Rao was the progenitor of the Look East policy, which he launched in the early 1990s, aimed at reactivating India's links with its Southeast Asian neighbours as part of his economic liberalisation programme. Successive governments have followed the initiative to enhance India's relations with the Asia-Pacific region, indicating how important the region is in India's foreign and security policies. While the initial incentive was mostly economic, as India wanted to attract East Asian investments and technology, the Look East policy acquired a strategic dimension by the late 1990s and extended to Japan and South Korea.[14] Since then, the Association of Southeast Asian Nations (ASEAN) has become a major economic and diplomatic partner of New

Delhi. India's economic resilience was shown when the Western countries and Japan imposed economic sanctions on India after its 1998 nuclear test; however, these did not affect India's economic growth much. Since then, the relationship has progressed to the strategic level. In this context, the Indian Navy and Coast Guard have became increasingly active in the Bay of Bengal while making regular forays in the Western Pacific to promote maritime cooperation with Japan and Vietnam. The Look East policy has helped India get admission into a number of ASEAN-led regional organisations such as the ASEAN Regional Forum (ARF) in 1996 and the East Asia Summit (EAS) in 2002.

The Vajpayee administration (1999-2004) took forward the Look East concept, and the region was brought under the 'extended neighbourhood' strategy, giving as much emphasis to the East and Southeast Asia regions as to the South Asia region.[15] According to the Indian Ministry of External Affairs, the 'extended neighbourhood' "stretches from the Suez Canal to the South China Sea and includes within it West Asia, the Gulf, Central Asia, South-East Asia, East Asia, the Asia-Pacific, and the Indian Ocean Region.[16]" This aligned with India's growing strategic profile as a major power in Asia, as New Delhi started expanding its influence beyond the immediate neighbourhood. India's intention to expand its influence beyond the neighbouring region was explained by the then Minister for External Affairs, Yashwant Sinha, in 2004, "This government, over the last six years, has assiduously promoted the idea that India is a major power ... We have articulated the concept of an extended neighbourhood for India."[17] Similarly, the 1998 nuclear test and India's recovery from the economic sanctions showed India's internal material capacity to withstand external pressure, which led to recognition by the elites from the East and Southeast Asia regions of India's power potential, and that along with China, India also is a rising power in Asia.[18]

The Manmohan Singh government focussed on institutionalising India's engagement with the Western Pacific countries and signed strategic partnership agreements with them. It not only focussed on strategic matters but widened into other areas such as space, nuclear energy, and economic and commercial sectors. Mutual high dignitary visits increased, and today the Indian prime minister visits Tokyo every alternative year.

India-Japan relations have become one of the most important foreign policy achievements that New Delhi has pursued in the post-Cold War era. The bilateral relationship has turned into minilaterals and quadrilateral. The first quadrilateral naval exercise of navies from India, Japan, the US, Australia, and Singapore took place in 2007 in the Bay of Bengal. However, the Quad had to be shelved after its first attempt due to the resistance of China as it branded the Quad as an Asian North Atlantic Treaty Organisation (NATO), but it has been resuscitated in 2017 and now has the potential to grow as a regional balancing mechanism against the Chinese assertiveness in the Indo-Pacific.

The 'Act East' policy, declared by Prime Minister Narendra Modi in 2014, has emphasised for India to become an 'active player' in regional political and security matters.[19] At a brainstorming session of 15 Indian heads of mission in Southeast and East Asia held in August 2014, India's External Affairs Minister Sushma Swaraj urged the diplomats to "Act East and not just Look East" and declared a new direction in India's relations with the East and Southeast Asian countries.[20] Although Act East is a continuation of the Look East policy, the main objective of the former was to enhance economic cooperation with Southeast Asia while later expanding the scope in terms of structure and content. Structurally, Act East is not restricted to any particular region; it comprises the entire east of India, which includes Southeast Asia, East Asia, Australia, New Zealand, and the Pacific island states. The main objective of the Act East policy is to enhance India's strategic profile in these regions and to become an active participant in regional security matters. Even though New Delhi is not a party to any of the maritime disputes in the East Asian waters, with the new policy, India has conveyed that the outcome of developments in these regions could affect India's security interests, and it shall not remain an outsider on regional security matters. For instance, when China rejected the verdict of the International Court of Justice (ICJ) proclaimed in 2016 on the dispute between the Philippines and China over the Chinese nine-dash line claim in the South China Sea, India took a firm position and stated that "all parties must abide by UNCLOS, which establishes the international legal order of the seas and oceans", an apparent reference of disproval to China's position on the dispute.[21]

There has been continuity in India's diplomatic interest towards the Asia-Pacific region since the 1990s due to economic dynamism and strategic interests. Private investments from these countries have poured into India, and it has signed free trade agreements/comprehensive partnership agreements with a number of regional countries. The India-ASEAN Free Trade Agreement (FTA) was signed in 2010; with South Korea, India signed the Economic Partnership Agreement (EPA) in 2009; and a Comprehensive Economic Partnership Agreement with Japan in 2011. Japanese annual Foreign Direct Investment (FDI) to India increased from US$ 1.18 billion in 2009-2010 to US$ 3.2 billion in the 2019-2020 period.[22] Besides, India and Japan proposed the Asia-Africa Growth Corridor (AAGC) to facilitate trade and investment opportunities in the East African region, a counterweight to China's aggressive economic expansion into Africa under the famed 21st Century Maritime Silk Route. Both India and Japan are mulling for joint investment in defence production, an area both countries have not exploited so far. In a way, the Look East/Act East policy has helped India to become a major stakeholder in the security dynamics of the Western Pacific.

India and Regional Security Mechanisms

In security studies, the regional security mechanism means cooperation of countries from a particular region for security purposes.[23] They form a common identity against an imminent or perceived threat. The cooperation becomes necessary because individual countries cannot deter the threat by themselves, while their combined strength would help them overcome the material power of the threatening states. However, it is not necessary that they must form a military alliance; instead, a realist soft balancing strategy can be followed in which countries form strategic arrangements against a perceived threat, and if the threat becomes real, these can be converted into hard military alliances.[24] The 'Delhi Dialogue' between India and the Southeast Asian countries is a major platform for discussing common security issues.[25]

In the Asia-Pacific region, the hub-and-spoke model bilateral military arrangements stitched by the US had been the stabilising factor during the Cold War period. However, this system proved ineffective in the post-Cold War period because of the new emerging power China that is economically integrated with all the regional countries, despite being considered a security threat. In this regard, the regional countries are involved in different levels of strategic partnership arrangements between themselves as well as with external powers. The various levels of arrangements are bilateral, minilateral, and quadrilateral.

Bilaterals

India has signed bilateral strategic cooperation agreements with the Western Pacific countries with the aim of strengthening India's strategic presence in the region. This will enhance bilateral relationships as well as work as a balancing mechanism against Chinese assertiveness. Important among them are India-US, India-Japan, India-South Korea, India-Vietnam, India-Philippines, and India-Australia (Table 2.1). The India-US strategic partnership has a wider scope than the Western Pacific, while Australia is getting increasingly involved in East Asian security matters in recent times. The recently concluded Australia, United Kingdom, United States (AUKUS) treaty has China in its objectives as a major targeting state.[26] Similarly, all the countries with which India has signed strategic partnership agreements from the region also see China as their long-term security threat. They see that such partnerships with other countries would help stabilise the region.[27] Importantly, defence cooperation, especially the joint production of defence systems, is gaining momentum in India's bilateral engagement with the West Pacific regional countries.

Important among such agreements is the India-Japan Strategic Partnership Agreement signed in 2008, a first-ever strategic partnership agreement with a US ally in the region. It heralded a new chapter in India's engagement with the Western Pacific region. India's "Act East" Policy and Japan's "Free and Open Indo-Pacific Vision" have a smooth synergy in promoting a free and open Indo-Pacific.[28] The "Acquisition and Cross-Servicing Agreement" or ACSA that was signed in September 2020, enables Indian warships to access facilities at Japanese ports for replenishment, making longer duration of naval deployment possible in the Western Pacific.[29] Indeed, the China factor helped in strengthening

India-Japan relations, and the growing India-US relations also acted as a catalyst because Washington wanted the regional powers to take more responsibility for the security of the region.[30] The US expects that India, Japan, and like-minded countries will fill the vacuum that emerged when the US decided to close down some of its bases in Southeast Asia in the 1990s and gradually reduce its military presence in the region. The India-Japan bilateral relationship, thus, has culminated in creating minilaterals and quadrilaterals shaping the regional balancing mechanisms in the Indo-Pacific region.

Table 2.1: India's Bilateral Agreements with the West Pacific Countries

Country	Name	Year	Components
Japan	Joint Declaration on Security Cooperation between Japan and India	2008	Security and defence dialogues at Foreign and Defence Ministers level (2+2 meeting); Annual Defence Ministerial Dialogue. NSA-Level Dialogue; FOC Consultations; Coast Guard-to-Coast Guard dialogue; and other bilateral dialogue mechanisms at the higher level, including service chiefs
South Korea	India-Republic of Korea Joint Statement for Special Strategic Partnership	2015	Foreign ministers' level Joint Commission; vice ministerial level defence and foreign affairs dialogue in the "2+2" format; exchange of military officers through the National Defence College of India and the National Defence University of Korea for education; staff level talks between the two navies and regular exchanges of visits; and annual Track 1.5 dialogue between the Institute of Foreign Affairs and National Security (IFANS) of the Republic of Korea (ROK) and Indian Council of World Affairs (ICWA)

Vietnam	India-Vietnam Defence Cooperation agreement signed in 2009, which was elevated to 'Comprehensive Strategic Partnership' in 2016	2016	Joint Commission Meeting at the Foreign Ministers' level; Defence Secretary-level annual Defence Policy Dialogue; India-Vietnam Maritime Security Dialogue; Policy Planning Dialogue between the two Foreign Ministries at the level of Joint Secretary/Director General; Services Staff talks and High-level Meetings between the Coast Guards; India's training assistance for operating Russian made SU 30MKI jets and Kilo-class diesel-electric submarines; and New Delhi's $500 million lines of credit to Hanoi for defence procurement
The Philippines	Joint Declaration on a Framework of Bilateral Cooperation between the Government of Republic of India and the Government of Republic of the Philippines	2007	High level mutual visits on matters of security and defence, and port call of Indian naval ships
Indonesia	'Joint Declaration on Establishing Strategic Partnership' in 2005; and Comprehensive Strategic Partnership, and "Shared Vision on Maritime Cooperation in the Indo-Pacific between India and Indonesia"	2018	Ministerial level Joint Commission; Defence Ministers' Dialogue; Energy Forum at Ministerial level; Security Dialogue at NSA level; and regular bilateral dialogue and consultation on strategic defence and military issues of common interest
Malaysia	Joint Statement on enhanced Malaysia-India Strategic Partnership	2015	Joint Commission at the Ministers of Foreign Affairs level; Regular dialogue at the Defence Ministers level; Chiefs of the Armed Services and through Service-to-Service Staff Talks; India-Malaysia Defence

			Cooperation Meeting at Defence Secretary/Secretary General level; and SU-30 Forum for cooperation in training, maintenance, technical support and safety-related issues related to Russian made SU 30 MKM fighter jet
Australia	Elevated 'India-Australia Strategic Partnership' of 2009 to 'Comprehensive Strategic Partnership'	2020	2+2 Ministerial Dialogue; Mutual Logistics Support Arrangement; Defence Science and Technology Arrangement; and COVID-19 assistance for regional countries under the Quad framework
US	'New Framework for India-US Defence Relations' [Logistics Exchange Memorandum of Association (LEMOA)] signed in August 2016, Fuel Exchange Agreement signed in November 2015, Technical Agreement (TA) on information sharing on White (merchant) Shipping signed in May 2016, Information Exchange Annexe (IEA) on Aircraft Carrier Technologies signed in June 2016, Communications Compatibility and Security Agreement (COMCASA) signed in September 2018; and the Basic Exchange and Cooperation Agreement (BECA) signed in October 2020)	2005 & 2015	Quad Summit; 2+2 meeting; In 2016, the US declared India as a "Major Defence Partner"; Defence Policy Group (DPG), Defence Joint Working Group (DJWG), Defence Procurement and Production Group (DPPG), Senior Technology Security Group (STSG), Joint Technical Group (JTG), Military Cooperation Group (MCG), and Service-to-Service Executive Steering Groups (ESGs)

Source: Author's compilation from various sources.

Minilaterals

A minilateral is a group of three countries that share a common vision and work together to achieve a common purpose. It can be for trade and commercial interests, traditional and non-traditional security purposes, and can be formed for a specific purpose or a longer duration. It can be formed by geographically proximate countries targeting a specific area or distant countries focussing on specific strategic objectives. A successful minilateral formed in the region has been MALSIDO (Malaysia-Singapore-Indonesia), launched in 2004 by the navies of the three countries for patrolling in a coordinated fashion in their respective territorial waters to contain piracy and armed robbery in the Malacca Strait.[31] In recent times, the Indo-Pacific region has witnessed quite a few minilateral mechanisms such as Australia-India-Indonesia, Japan-US-India, Australia-India-Japan, Australia-United Kingdom-United States (AUKUS), and United States-Japan-Australia and the main objective of these formations is to foster security (maritime) cooperation in the Indo-Pacific region. India is active in such minilaterals to ensure the region is free from disruption. Among these groupings, the AUKUS is a military alliance to help Australia enhance its deterrent capability by acquiring nuclear powered attack submarines with the assistance of the US/UK.[32]

Quadrilateral

The quadrilateral is a major power mechanism to ensure freedom of navigation in the Indo-Pacific, and the members are India, Japan, Australia, and the US. It can also be seen as a regional balancing mechanism against the ambition of one state to become a regional hegemon. As Mearsheimer argues, threatened states come together and will be involved in a balancing effort against the powerful state because only their combined strength can challenge the might of the threatening state.[33] Similarly, Stephen Walt argues that strong neighbours of strong states prefer balancing rather than bandwagoning.[34] The regional countries, India, Japan, and Australia perceive China as their main security threat. They coordinate their policies to prevent China from getting a unipolar position in the Indo-Pacific region.

A modest beginning of coordinated rescue operations by the four countries during the tsunami rescue operations in 2005 in the Eastern Indian Ocean turned out to be a quadrilateral naval exercise, 'Malabar 07', held in the Bay of Bengal in September 2007. The quadrilateral concept was shelved for a while due to China's resistance, and the Malabar continued as an India-US bilateral naval exercise. Since 2009, it was decided to make it trilateral with Japan, when it was to be held in the Western Pacific, and bilateral in the Indian Ocean. When the Indian prime minister and the US president met in New Delhi in January 2015, both countries decided to upgrade the Malabar naval exercise.[35] As a result, Japan was formally inducted in the 2015 edition held in the Bay of Bengal, and Australia joined in 2020. The annual Malabar quadrilateral exercise is being held in the Indian Ocean and the Western Pacific in alternative years.

Besides the naval exercise, the four countries have formed a policy forum known as "Quadrilateral Security Dialogue', euphemistically called the 'Quad'. The Quad was proposed by former Japanese Prime Minister Shinzo Abe in 2017 to coordinate policy matters concerning the maritime security of the Indo-Pacific.[36] It started at the official level in Manila in November 2017 on the sidelines of the ASEAN Summit, followed by the foreign ministers meetings at various multilateral fora, and the first Quad Summit took place virtually on March 12, 2021, and the first in-person summit on September 24, 2021, in Washington. When the Quad was launched, it was expected that it could become a semi-military alliance in the future, however, with the AUKUS in place with which the US is focussing military alliances in the Indo-Pacific with its traditional allies, the Quad's focus is now on other areas such as "ending the COVID-19 pandemic, including by increasing production and access to safe and effective vaccines; promoting high-standards infrastructure; combatting the climate crisis; partnering on emerging technologies, space, and cyber security; and cultivating next-generation talent in all of our countries".[37] Even though countries from Southeast Asia are apprehensive about major power mechanisms because these would diminish ASEAN's centrality, the Quad is still relevant on security matters because, ultimately, it will become the responsibility of these powers to ensure peace and stability in the Indo-Pacific region, lest China becomes belligerent.

Defence Cooperation

The navy plays the role of both an expeditionary force and a benign one when it conducts 'far seas" operations.[38] From the Indian standpoint, the term 'far seas' denotes "a maritime space that either lies outside the known operating limits of a nation's maritime forces, or beyond the traditional sphere of influence of the state, where a maritime force faces a strong strategic imperative for operational presence."[39] In the Indo-Pacific, the Indian Ocean has always been the primary area of interest of the Indian Navy, beyond which are considered as far seas operations. The far seas operations can be seen to have both offensive and defensive purposes, the former projecting one's power beyond the traditional area of influence, while the latter provide protection of strategic interests allied with national security objectives. In both cases, a 'far seas' deployment of the navy shows a nation's maritime power and its capacity to influence events on land, albeit variably, in distant areas. A coercive operation could force littoral states to prevent taking a decision inimical to the home state or a harmful decision can be changed favourably. A benign operation is a signal indicating that the developments which are taking place in the region are not well received and may force the state to take a hard position to protect its interests. Although the Indian Ocean occupies the primary area of its interests, the developments in the South China Sea (SCS) could affect India's national security interests because it is an adjacent water body to the Indian Ocean and China looks to consolidate the SCS, hence, the SCS is increasingly becoming closer to the primary interests of the Indian Navy.

The navy can be deployed as a power projection force as well as a counter-containment force. When the US announced the 'pivot' strategy in 2010 to contain China, it had planned to divide its naval force in the 60:40 ratio between the Atlantic and Pacific, including its carrier strike groups, while the Chinese deployment in the Indian Ocean is more of a power projection one as its vital security interests are associated with the Western Pacific. India's naval expeditions to the Western Pacific can be seen as counter-measures to China's Indian Ocean operations and to safeguard vital commercial and security interests. These also extend the 'net security provider' role that the Indian Navy offers to the Indian Ocean littoral countries of the Southeast Asia region.[40] A 'net security provider' position in the far seas areas will naturally enhance India's power position across the region.

As part of the Look East policy, India began its naval cooperation activities with the Asia-Pacific countries with the 'Milan' multilateral exercise in 1995 in the Bay of Bengal in which the navies of Indonesia, Singapore, Sri Lanka, and Thailand participated, and which has now become a 46-member grouping. The first bilateral naval exercise was started with Singapore (SIMBEX) in 1995, followed by Indonesia (Ind-Indo CORPAT) in 2002, and with Thailand (Indo-Thai CORPAT) in 2005. Japan, for the first time, participated in a naval exercise with India in 2007 when the India-US bilateral Malabar excerise took place in the Western Pacific; a PASEX was organised between the Japanese Self-Defence Maritime Force and the Indian Navy post-Malabar. The bilateral India-Japan (JIMEX) naval exercise commenced in 2012 and takes place annually in the Indian Ocean and the Western Pacific post-Malabar. To demonstrate India's willingness for naval cooperation with the disputed South China Sea littoral countries, two Indian naval ships, INS *Ranvijay* and INS *Kora*, which were part of the naval contingent for the Western Pacific phase of the Malabar 2021, participated in a bilateral naval exercise with the Vietnamese Navy in the South China Sea and with the Philippines Navy in the West Philippines Sea in August 2021.[41] India's increasing naval presence in the Western Pacific indicates its resilience to deter threats, its confidence to project power in the backyard of its rivals, and its indigenisation capacity. The regional navies also show keen interest in cooperation with the Indian Navy, to project their strength too.

Cooperation between the air forces of India and the regional countries has been progressing well. In 2004, India and Singapore launched the bilateral air exercise SINDEX and five editions have been held so far. India conducted a bilateral air exercise with Japan, the 'India-Japan SHINYUU Maitri-18', in 2018;[42] with Indonesia and Malaysia in August 2018;[43] and with Thailand in 2017.[44] India also participates in multilateral air exercises such as 'Nellis', sponsored by the United States, and 'Pitch Black', sponsored by the Australian Air Force. Besides, India provides technical assistance to the air force personnel of Vietnam, Singapore and Malaysia.

Trade in defence systems is one of the important aspects in promoting defence cooperation. India's sale of the BrahMos missiles to the Philippines is not only to enhance the bilateral cooperation but as a strategic counterweight to China as Beijing and Manila are involved in territorial disputes in the East China Sea.[45] Vietnam could follow suit and other Southeast Asian countries may consider Indian systems to bolster their defence. India and Japan had agreed in 2010 for the sale of 12 Shinmaywa amphibious aircraft from Japan, but it is yet to be materialised.[46]

Conclusion

India is increasingly playing an active role in the security dynamics of the Western Pacific. This has been made possible through different levels of strategic partnerships signed with the regional countries and its growing strategic cooperation with the US. Even though India doesn't endorse the US' Indo-Pacific vision, it cooperates with it for protecting Indian interests. The US seeks hard military balancing against China; however, New Delhi's position is soft balancing, without a formal commitment to military contribution. New Delhi's effort is to expand its influence into the regions where India has strategic interests. A strategic influence in the Western Pacific also works as a counter-balancing mechanism against China's expansionism towards India's backyard.

However, India is also facing certain difficulties in expanding its influence beyond the Indian Ocean Region (IOR). Firstly, the Indian Navy has not fully achieved a blue water naval capability to project its power in distant waters—its main objective is to remain as an Indian Ocean naval power. Its ambitious three aircraft carrier plan is to deploy the carrier in the three seas—the Arabian Sea, Bay of Bengal and south of the peninsula. India operates only one nuclear-powered attack submarine, and all the other submarines in its fleets are conventional ones. Secondly, New Delhi has no plan to set up an overseas base in a distant location, nor a military alliance with a Western Pacific country: it operates independently and seeks only access facilities from them. Without any formal arrangements, use of their bases for military purposes by India is a difficult proposition. Thirdly, India is locked in a land border dispute with China in the Himalayas, which is unlikely to be resolved any time soon, so opening a second battlefield in the maritime domain would drain India's resources to counter the Chinese onslaught on land. And, finally, the regional countries depend on the US for their security against the Chinese threat; however, should that US guarantee fail, they might pursue a bandwagoning strategy with China rather than forming a counter-coalition under India's leadership. In such a situation, India would be isolated in the Western Pacific region, which would severely affect its security interests in South Asia.

Notes

1. Ulises Granados, "India's Approaches to the South China Sea: Priorities and Balances", *Asia & the Pacific Policy Studies*, Vol. 5, No. 1, 2018, pp. 122-137.
2. Rajesh Rajagopalan, "Evasive Balancing: India's Unviable Indo-Pacific Strategy", *International Affairs,* Vol. 96, No. 1, 2020, pp. 75-93.
3. Ibid. Also see Rajesh Basrur, "Modi's Foreign Policy Fundamentals: A Trajectory Unchanged", *International Affairs,* Vol. 93, No. 1, 2017, pp. 7-26; Darren J. Lim and Zack Cooper, "Reassessing Hedging: The Logic of Alignment in East Asia", *Security Studies*, Vol. 24, No. 4, 2015, pp. 696-727; Christophe Jaffrelot, "India's Look East Policy: An Asianist Strategy in Perspective", *India Review*, Vol. 2, No. 2, 2003, pp. 35-68; and Amitav Acharya, "India's Look East Policy," in David C. Malone, C. Raja Mohan, and Srinath Raghavan, eds., *The Oxford Handbook of India's Foreign Policy* (Oxford: Oxford University Press, 2015), pp. 452-65.
4. David R. Mares, "Middle Powers under Regional Hegemony: To Challenge or Acquiesce in Hegemonic Enforcement" , *International Studies Quarterly*, Vol. 32, No. 4, 1988, pp. 453-471.
5. Amitendu Palit, "India's Act East Policy and Implications For Southeast Asia", *Southeast Asian Affairs*, 2016, pp. 81-92.
6. David Scott, " India's 'Grand Strategy' for the Indian Ocean: Mahanian Visions", *Asia-Pacific Review*, Vol. 13, No. 2, 2006, pp. 97-129.
7. Indian Navy, "Indian Maritime Doctrine 2009". https://indiannavy.nic.in/sites/default/files/Indian-Maritime-Doctrine-2009-Updated-12Feb16.pdf
8. Christopher Colley, "A Future Chinese Indian Ocean Fleet?" *War On The Rocks*, April 2, 2021. https://warontherocks.com/2021/04/a-future-chinese-indian-ocean-fleet/
9. Michael Clarke, "Beijing's Pivot West: The Convergence of Innenpolitik and Aussenpolitik on China's 'Belt and Road'?" *Journal of Contemporary China*, Vol. 29, No. 123, 2020, pp. 336-353; Michael Clarke, "The Belt and Road Initiative:

China's New Grand Strategy?" *Asia Policy*, Vol. 24, July, 2017, pp. 71-79; *Nikkei Asia*, "China Looks to East Africa for Second Indian Ocean Foothold", June 30, 2021. https://asia.nikkei.com/Politics/International-relations/Indo-Pacific/China-looks-to-East-Africa-for-second-Indian-Ocean-foothold.

10. T.V. Paul, "Soft Balancing in the Age of US Primacy", *International Security*, Vol. 30, No. 1, 2005, pp. 46-71.
11. "China Potential Threat Number One: George Fernandes", *The Economic Times*, March 30, 2008. https://economictimes.indiatimes.com/news/politics-and-nation/china-potential-threat-number-one-george-fernandes/articleshow/2911194.cms?from=mdr
12. Export-Import Data Bank, Department of Commerce, Ministry of Commerce and Industry, Government of India. https://tradestat.commerce.gov.in/eidb/default.asp
13. Indian Navy, "Indian Maritime Doctrine 2009". https://www.indiannavy.nic.in/sites/default/files/Indian-Maritime-Doctrine-2009-Updated-12Feb16.pdf
14. Isabelle Saint-Mézard, "India's Act East Policy: Strategic Implications for the Indian Ocean," *Journal of the Indian Ocean Region*, Vol. 12, No. 2, 2016, pp. 177-190.
15. David Scott, "India's 'Extended Neighborhood' Concept: Power Projection for a Rising Power", *India Review*, Vol. 8, No. 2, 2009, pp. 107-143
16. Yashwant Sinha, "12th SAARC Summit and Beyond," February 3, 2004. https://www.mea.gov.in/Speeches-Statements.htm?dtl/3046/Seventh_Dinesh_Singh_Memorial_Lecture_by_Shri_Yashwant_Sinha_External_Affairs_Minister_on_12th_SAARC_Summit_and_Beyond
17. Ibid.
18. "China and India Cannot go to War: Lee Kuan Yew", *The Hindu*, January 24, 2011. https://www.thehindu.com/news/China-and-India-cannot-go-to-war-Lee-Kuan-Yew/article15534133.ece; Also see, Kishore Mahbubani, "The Not-So-Surprising Rise of China and India", *Journal of International Affairs* (Special Issue on Sino-Indian Relations), Vol. 64, No. 2, 2011, pp. 221-226.
19. Ulises Granados, "India's Approaches to the South China Sea: Priorities and Balances", *Asia & the Pacific Policy Studies*, Vol. 5, No. 1, 2018, pp. 122-137 .
20. "Sushma Swaraj Tells Indian Envoys to Act East and Not Just Look East", *The Economic Times*, August 28, 2014. https://economictimes.indiatimes.com/news/politics-and-nation/sushma-swaraj-tells-indian-envoys-to-act-east-and-not-just-look-east/articleshow/40907671.cms?from=mdr
21. "South China Sea Verdict: All Parties Must Abide by International Order of Seas and Oceans, Says India", *The Economic Times*, July 12, 2018. https://economictimes.indiatimes.com/news/defence/south-china-sea-verdict-

all-parties-must-abide-by-international-order-of-seas-oceans-says-india/articleshow/53177912.cms?from=mdr

22. "FDI Statistics", Ministry of Commerce and Industry, Government of India. https://dpiit.gov.in/publications/fdi-statistics.
23. Natalia Eremina, "Eurasian Economic Union as the Space of Security in the Context of English School of International Relations: Theoretical and Practical Aspects", in Maria Lagutina ed., *Regional Integration and Future Cooperation Initiatives in the Eurasian Economic Union* (St. Petersburg: IGI Global, 2019), pp. 56-74.
24. T.V. Paul, "Soft Balancing in the Age of US Primacy", *International Security,* Vol. 30, No. 1, Summer 2005, pp. 46-71.
25. Ministry of External Affairs, "India- ASEAN Relations", Government of India. https://mea.gov.in/aseanindia/20-years.htm.
26. Brad Glosserman, "A Path-Breaking Deal to Bolster Indo-Pacific Security", *The Japan Times*, September 21, 2021. https://www.japantimes.co.jp/opinion/2021/09/21/commentary/world-commentary/aukus-indo-pacific-security/
27. PHAM Quang Minh and PHAM Le Da Huong, "Vietnam-Japan Relations in the New Context of Regional and World Politics". https://core.ac.uk/download/pdf230778945.pdf
28. "Brief Note on India-Japan Bilateral Relations", Ministry of External Affairs, Government of India. https://www.mea.gov.in/Portal/ForeignRelation/India-Japan_Bilateral_Brief_feb_2020.pdf
29. Abhijnan Rej, "India and Japan Sign Military Logistics Agreement for All to See", *The Diplomat*, September 12, 2020. https://thediplomat.com/2020/09/india-and-japan-sign-military-logistics-agreement-for-all-to-see/
30. Joshy M. Paul, "India and Japan: Reluctant Idealism to Practical Realism", *South Asian Survey*, Vol. 15, No. 1, 2008, pp. 99-119.
31. Catherine Zara Raymond, "Piracy and Armed Robbery in the Malacca Strait," *Naval War College Review,* Vol. 62, No. 3, 2009, pp. 31-42.
32. "AUKUS: UK, US and Australia Launch Pact to Counter China", *Hindustan Times*, September 16, 2021. https://www.hindustantimes.com/world-news/us-uk-and-australia-launch-indo-pacific-pact-101631768286344.html
33. John J. Mearsheimer, "Better to Be Godzilla than Bambi", in Zbigniew Brzezinski and John J. Mearsheimer, "Clash of the Titans", *Foreign Policy,* Vol. 146, January/February 2005, pp. 46-50.
34. Stephen M. Walt, *The Origin of Alliances* (New York: Cornell University Press, 1987).

35. Ministry of External Affairs, "Joint Statement During the Visit of President of USA to India—'Shared Effort; Progress for All'," Government of India, January 25, 2015. https://mea.gov.in/bilateral-documents.htm?dtl/24726/Joint_Statement_during_the_visit_of_President_of_USA_to_India_Shared_Effort_Progress_for_All

36. Saki Hayashi and Yosuke Onchi, "Japan to Propose Dialogue with US, India, and Australia", *Nikkei Asian Review*, October 26, 2017. https://asia.nikkei.com/Politics/Japan-to-propose-dialogue-with-US-India-and-Australia2

37 The White House, "Fact Sheet: Quad Leaders' Summit", September 24, 2021. https://www.whitehouse.gov/briefing-room/statements-releases/2021/09/24/fact-sheet-quad-leaders-summit/

38. From the Indian standpoint, the term 'far seas' denotes "a maritime space that either lies outside the known operating limits of a nation's maritime forces, or beyond the traditional sphere of influence of the state, where a maritime force faces a strong strategic imperative for operational presence." See, Abhijit Singh, "In the Far Seas: Projecting India's Naval Power", in Anit Mukherjee and C Raja Mohan, eds., *India's Naval Strategy and Asian Security* (London: Routledge, 2017), p. 66.

39. Ibid., pp. 65-84.

40. Ibid.

41. "India and Vietnam Conduct Naval Exercise in the South China Sea, Ahead of the Quad's 'Malabar' off Guam", *The Times of India*, August 18, 2021. https://timesofindia.indiatimes.com/india/india-and-vietnam-conduct-naval-exercise-in-south-china-sea-ahead-of-the-quads-malabar-off-guam/articleshow/85429488.cms; "Indian Navy, "Maritime Partnership Exercise between Indian Navy and Philippine Navy—23 August 2021". https://www.indiannavy.nic.in/node/29629

42. Press Information Bureau, "EX SHINYUU Maitri-2018 With JASDF Commences", December 3, 2018. https://pib.gov.in/newsite/printrelease.aspx?relid-186087.

43. Press Information Bureau, "IAF Contingent Returns to India on Completion of Ex Pitch Black 2018", August 23, 2018. https://pib.gov.in/newsite/PrintRelease.aspx?relid=182029.

44. Press Trust of India,"IAF Participates in Joint Exercise with Thai Air Force", *Business Standard*, May 26, 2017. https://www.business-standard.com/article/pti-stories/iaf-participates-in-joint-exercise-with-thai-air-force-117052601523_1.html.

45. Dinaker Peri, "Philippines Inks Deal Worth $375 Million for BrahMos Missile", *The Hindu*, January 28, 2022. https://www.thehindu.com/news/

national/philippines-inks-deal-worth-375-million-for-brahmos-missiles/article38338340.ece.

46 Franz-Stefan Gady, "Are India and Japan About to Conclude a $1.3 Billion Military Aircraft Deal?", *The Diplomat*, April 17, 2018. https://thediplomat.com/2018/04/are-india-and-japan-about-to-conclude-a-1-3-billion-military-aircraft-deal/

3. Contest on the Waterfront: Limitations and Aspirations of India's Naval Strategy

Anil Jai Singh

> We cannot afford to be weak at sea. History has shown that whoever controls the Indian Ocean has, in the first instance, India's seaborne trade at its mercy and, in the second, India's very independence itself.
>
> Pandit Jawaharlal Nehru,
> India's first Prime Minister,
> on board INS *Mysore* in 1958

Introduction

The defining feature of the 21st century has been the shift in the global geopolitical and geoeconomic centres of gravity to the Indo-Pacific. This has been driven primarily by the rise of China and, to a lesser extent, India, the economic rise of the Pacific and Pacific Rim countries, the United States' (US') determination to continue as the status quo power in the region and the increasing relevance of the region in the emerging world order. This 'Confluence of Two Oceans' as described by Prime Minister Shinzo Abe of Japan when speaking of a 'broader Asia' in his address to the Indian Parliament in 2007,[1] has placed India in a pivotal position in the region as the preeminent Indian Ocean power, and has also coincided with India's foreign policy outreach in recent years. The Indo-Pacific, as its very name suggests, has a distinct maritime orientation that has highlighted the importance of the maritime domain and the numerous security challenges threatening its safety and security.

India's economic well-being and future sustenance are also inextricably linked to the sea, thus, requiring it to develop a commensurate maritime capability to project as well as protect its national interests. India's aspiration to play a larger role on the world stage and its focus on becoming an economic powerhouse will require it to mitigate its vulnerabilities and leverage its strengths in this region through its comprehensive national power, with the maritime dimension being perhaps the most significant.

The Importance of Maritime Power in the Indo-Pacific

History has established that maritime domination is the key to global power. The rise and fall of nations through the ages has been linked to their ability to dominate the oceans. In more recent history, 'the sun never set on the British Empire' because 'Britannia ruled the waves', and its subsequent decline after World War II was primarily due to its inability to sustain itself as a maritime power. The US took over the mantle and has retained its geopolitical primacy for almost eight decades,mainly with the overwhelming power of its navy. During the Cold War, which 'raged' for over four decades, Admiral Gorshkov, the commander-in-chief of the Soviet Navy, worked tirelessly towards building the Soviet Navy into a blue water force capable of challenging the US supremacy at sea, but the disintegration of the Soviet Union put a check to that. However, that legacy still drives President Putin's big power aspirations.

This century's global narrative is dominated by the phenomenal rise of China. It has focussed its attention on the maritime domain and has challenged the USA's primacy in the Western Pacific and the existing status quo of the rules-based order and the Free and Open Indo-Pacific. Its ambitious Belt and Road Initiative (BRI), formerly called the One Belt One Road (OBOR)connecting its mainland with Europe through a land (Belt) and maritime (Road) route is described by the Chinese government as "a bid to enhance regional connectivity and embrace a brighter future".[2] The BRI is ostensibly an economic initiative but is integral to China's strategic design of dominating the Indo-Pacific across its entire expanse. The Indian Ocean is not only its gateway to the West but is also critical for its trade and energy requirements, most of which transit through this region. Securing its interests in the Indian Ocean has provided it with the excuse to position a permanent naval presence with the intention of establishing its primacy in the region with a formidable naval presence by the end of this decade. The BRI has targeted strategic locations in the Indian Ocean littoral and the island territories and has offered to establish new infrastructure and augment the existing facilities with financial, material and manpower support in the form of loans at prohibitive rates of interest. Most recipient countries, finding themselves unable to repay these large amounts, are having to compromise their sovereign interests to the Chinese. This combination of its 'debt trap' diplomacy[3] and 'wolf warrior' diplomacy[4] has enabled China to establish a significant military and economic presence across the region in Myanmar, Bangladesh, Sri Lanka, Pakistan, Iran, Djibouti and it is actively wooing many other countries and the strategically located island states like Maldives, Seychelles and Madagascar. Its investments along the east coast of Africa,which borders the western extremity of the Indo-Pacific, have given it a stranglehold in the region.

In its 2015 White Paper, China had unambiguously stated its intent of becoming a leading military power by 2035 and the global numero uno by 2049 by achieving the "Chinese dream of the great rejuvenation of the Chinese people."[5] It has also made no secret of its intention to reorient the existing international rules-based order, particularly in the maritime domain, into one with Chinese characteristics. This has led to worldwide concern about China's hegemonistic ambitions in the maritime domain.

The Indo-Pacific is the economic hub of the future. Sixty-five per cent of the global population resides here; it generates more than 62 per cent of the global Gross Domestic Product (GDP), and 70 per cent of all global trade passes through this region.[6] It is home to three of the world's five largest economies and seven of the world's ten largest navies. Nine of the world's ten busiest ports are also located here. It is, therefore, not without reason that the USA wants to retain its primacy, and even major Euro-centric countries like Germany and the Netherlands have followed their European neighbours, France and the UK, in developing their Indo-Pacific strategy to ensure a free and open Indo-Pacific and a rules-based order, with other like-minded nations in the region, including India.

In its recent Integrated Review titled "Global Britain in a Competitive Age: The Integrated Review of Security, Defence, Development and Foreign Policy"[7] issued in July 2021, the UK has indicated a 'tilt' to the Indo-Pacific. France, which considers itself an Indo-Pacific power with over 90 per cent of its Exclusive Economic Zone (EEZ) in this region, has always maintained a robust naval presence in the region headed by a two-star admiral, and was the first country in the world to appoint an ambassador to the Indo-Pacific in October 2020.

India's Geostrategic Imperatives

India is the preeminent power in the Indian Ocean, with its future upward trajectory inextricably linked to the sea. Its peninsular geography notwithstanding, it is essentially a maritime nation. It has a coastline of 7,516 km which connects nine coastal states and four union territories to the sea. Over 200 million Indians live in the vicinity of this coastline and are directly or indirectly dependent on the sea for their livelihoods. Its resource rich EEZ,covering 2.37 million sq km, will become increasingly precious as humankind turns increasingly to the sea for its sustenance and economic development as land resources continue depleting at an alarming rate. Hence, this EEZ will need to be protected and exploited responsibly. If India's claim of its continental shelf extending beyond 200 nautical miles (nm) is accepted by the United Nations (UN),[8] the EEZ will extend to 350 miles, and its area will increase to more than 3 million sq km which will be only slightly less than the country's total landmass of 3.287 million sq km.

India was the first country to have been accorded a Pioneer Investor Status by the UN in 1987 and has been allocated 75,000 sq km in the Central Indian Ocean basin for poly-metallic nodule exploration. The resource potential of this is estimated at 380 million tonnes and will be an invaluable asset in the future technology intensive global environment.

More than 90 per cent of India's trade by volume and over 74 per cent by value travels over the sea and is serviced by 13 major ports and more than 200 non-major ports. As India aspires to increase its GDP to US$ 5 trillion by 2025 and US$ 10 trillion by 2032, from the current figure of less than US$ 3 trillion, the volume of seaborne trade will also grow exponentially. Therefore, ensuring the smooth and secure movement of this trade over the oceans will be critical to India's economic well-being.

India imports more than 80 per cent of its oil and gas requirements, all of which transit on tankers from different parts of the globe. Even a majority of the remainder (20 per cent) that is sourced indigenously is primarily from offshore oilfields. India's largest source of export revenue comes from its export of refined petroleum products, which are also transported to different parts of the globe by sea. Hence, ensuring India's energy security is a critical maritime security imperative.

India's mainland is flanked by two strategically located island territories: the Andaman and Nicobar (A&N) Islands on the country's eastern seaboard, and the Lakshadweep group of islands in the west. These are strategic assets and also a vulnerability. The archipelagic spread of the A&N group comprising 836 islands, of which only 38 are inhabited, is located more than 700 miles from the Indian mainland and offers a vital strategic outpost as well as a permanent Indian presence at the approaches to the Malacca Strait, one of the most strategic choke points in the world and critical to the future geopolitical outcomes in the region. It also enhances India's power projection and reach that much further eastwards The vulnerability of these islands lies in their proximity to politically volatile regions; their northern tip is only 22 miles from the shores of Myanmar,and the southernmost tip is about 95 miles from the Aceh region of Indonesia. The large number of uninhabited islands offer a safe haven for non-state disruptive actors fomenting trouble in the region, thus, requiring constant vigil. The Lakshadweep group, which is located about 200 miles from the west coast of the mainland, comprises 36 islands, of which only 10 are inhabited. The economic and strategic significance of these island chains is well understood, but their economic potential is yet to be tapped.

The Nature of the Maritime Threat in the Indo-Pacific

Traditional inter-state conflicts remain the *raison d'etre* of navies, and defending the country's territorial integrity and its maritime interests anywhere in the world, their primary focus. However, in recent years, the blurring of lines between competition and cooperation amongst states with economic imperatives often at odds with security considerations tempers provocation with restraint and has reduced the occurrence of inter-state conflict in the traditional sense. It is the rise of the non-traditional threats which may be lower on a scale of violence but are insidious and pose a more immediate threat to maritime security. These include maritime terrorism, piracy and armed robbery at sea, unregulated activities including Illegal, Unreported and Unregulated (IUU) fishing, climate change and natural and man-made disasters, amongst others. These require a different response strategy and have led to navies reorienting their force structure planning towards addressing this asymmetric challenge without compromising on their combat capability.

The wide expanse of the Indo-Pacific is a disaggregated region with inter-state and intra-regional tensions often simmering just below the surface. It is marked with political instability, civil insurgencies, low-intensity conflict, disaffected populations, trust deficit amongst states and existential crises due to global phenomena like climate change and natural and man-made disasters. Inimical elements prey on these vulnerabilities to destabilise the region, which leads to a wide spectrum of maritime security challenges ranging from the strategic to the hybrid and the sub-conventional.

This asymmetry was amply demonstrated in the scourge of piracy off the coast of Somalia between 2008 and 2012, where a bunch of gun-toting misguided youngsters from a failed state who embarked on small skiffs in a relatively less known part of the world could hold global trade to ransom. It took a coordinated response by over 20 leading navies more than four years to quell this menace.

The first incident of maritime terrorism that made international news was the attack by Al-Qaeda suicide bombers who exploded a small boat near the USS *Cole* while it was at anchorage off Aden. Many incidents have followed, including the audacious and well-coordinated attack on India's financial capital, Mumbai, on November 26, 2008, by a handful of men sent by Pakistan who landed from seawards in a small fishing boat and fanned out across the city to launch a series of well-coordinated attacks on carefully chosen targets. This exposed grave chinks in India's intelligence apparatus, security architecture and response capability and led to the complete overhauling of the national coastal security architecture with a robust, multi-agency framework and a well-defined command and control structure. While certain challenges in implementation still remain and ensuring impregnable security of such a long and porous coastline is a recurring challenge, constant vigil can mitigate the threat. The asymmetric challenges to maritime security will continue to plague this region. They will need to be effectively managed through a robust and proactive maritime security architecture backed by a robust regulatory mechanism, with adequate legal and punitive provisions to deter rather than react.

The China Factor

The multitude of maritime security challenges in the region notwithstanding, it is China that has emerged as the dragon in the room. It is a resident power in the Western Pacific, with global aspirations and intent on reducing the influence of the US, which has been the dominant power in the region for over seven decades and has no intention of relinquishing that position. There is a bipartisan consensus within the USA on this, which was reaffirmed by US Secretary of State Anthony Blinken during his recent visit to Indonesia. He expressed concern at China's increasing aggressiveness, reassured the USA's allies and partners of enhanced US commitment to the region, and highlighted that militarily, the USA would retain the competitive edge. Constructs like Australia United Kingdom, United States (AUKUS) and the military dimension of the Quadrilateral Security Dialogue (Quad) indicate that these waters are going to witness simmering tension and intense contestation, which are unlikely to remain bilateral issues and will further escalate in the coming years with the hardening of positions on both sides. Presently, this is restricted mainly to the east of the Malacca Strait, but its shift westwards into the Indian Ocean is inevitable, with China expanding its footprint west of the Malacca Strait and into the Indian Ocean. The US-China standoff is already being termed Cold War 2.0 and could force the other countries in the region to take sides. The Chinese Navy is already the largest navy in the world by numbers though it lags behind the US Navy in technology and capability. Presently, it has about 355 ships in commission and is expected to have a force level of about 460 technologically advanced and militarily powerful platforms by 2030.[9] Its third aircraft carrier has already been launched, and more are likely to follow. It has a robust shipbuilding programme with more than 20 ships and submarines getting commissioned year after year, which are catering not only for the replacement of old hulls with larger blue water capable ones but also a substantial increase in numbers and capability.

The PLA Navy (PLAN) also plans to double its nuclear submarine fleet with bigger and better armed strategic and attack submarine platforms under development. It has a robust sea-based deterrent with a force level of six SSBNs (nuclear powered ballistic missile submarines) armed with the JL-2 missile of about 7,500 km range. It can target New Delhi from its base in the South China Sea off Hainan and is in line with China's bastion strategy.

China also has an impressive force level of six Type 093 SSNs and modified Kilo class and Type 039 conventional diesel electric submarines (SSK). While SSBNs are in the strategic realm and require a different response strategy, the SSNs (submersible ship nuclear) and SSKs (diesel-electric submarine, specialised for anti-submarine duties) pose an operational threat. Its 'Civil-Military Fusion Development Strategy'[10] to develop cutting edge disruptive technologies simultaneously for civilian and military applications and the deployment of these as force multipliers in its Anti-Access/Area Denial (A2/AD) strategy is narrowing the technological asymmetry with the US Navy.

India's Maritime Threat Perception

The Chinese naval expansion has serious implications for India's present preeminence in the Indian Ocean region. It is no coincidence that despite a provocative standoff with India along the 3,800-km-long Line of Actual Control (LAC) since 2020 and repeated transgressions into Indian territory, which it refuses to vacate, China has remained relatively passive in the maritime domain and has avoided doing anything at sea that could provoke an Indian reaction. It is aware of its present limitations in the Indian Ocean and would not risk a loss of face in a possible confrontation with the Indian Navy. It is, therefore, biding its time in the Indian Ocean till it is ready. Domination of the Indian Ocean is fundamental to China's aspiration of being the leading global power by 2049. The PLA Navy already has a small but permanent presence in the Indian Ocean which is of concern to India and has been flagged by successive chiefs of the Indian Navy. While its naval expansion continues apace, it is consolidating its presence in the Indian Ocean in more ways than one.

China has established a base at Djibouti, located in the Horn of Africa at the western extremity of the Indo-Pacific where it is extending the length of the jetty to enable the berthing of aircraft carriers and other large naval vessels.[11] This base gives it access to the important choke point at Bab-el-Mandeb, connecting the Red Sea with the Indian Ocean. It is also expanding its presence and influence along the east coast of Africa[12] in its bid to dominate the Western Indian Ocean. It has a naval presence at the Pakistani deep water port at Gwadar from where the China-Pakistan Economic Corridor (CPEC) connecting the Arabian Sea to Xinjiang on the Chinese mainland originates. China is investing US$ 61 billion in the CPEC in the form of loans which Pakistan is already unable to repay[13] and for which, it will be forced to relinquish its sovereign interests in one form or another, ending up as a proxy state doing China's bidding. China is also arming Pakistan with four Type 054A/P frigates and eight Type 039 AIP fitted diesel-electric submarines. China has also been steadily increasing its influence in Iran and was quick to step in to fill the power vacuum created with the US abrogation of the Joint Comprehensive Plan Of Action (JCPOA) and imposition of sanctions on Iran. This also forced India to stop buying oil from its second largest supplier and cast a shadow on the historic relationship between the two countries. It also jeopardised India's involvement in the development of the Chabahar port and the North South Trade Corridor, linking the landlocked Central Asian Republics with the Arabian Sea, bypassing Pakistan. India's commitment to Chabahar continues, but the Chinese shadow looms large over it.

China's increasing influence in the Western Indian Ocean and a powerful naval presence resident there could seriously undermine India's unchallenged maritime presence in the region. Sixty per cent of India's oil and gas requirement is sourced from the Gulf on tankers transiting through the Strait of Hormuz, which is one of the most critical strategic choke points in the world. This then transits along the Arabian Sea to

India. A Chinese presence at the Strait of Hormuz and Gwadar, with proxy support by the Pakistan Navy with its formidable submarine capability has serious implications for India's energy security. Similarly, India's trade, a majority of which transits over the sea lanes to and from the Western Indian Ocean either around the Cape of Good Hope or through the Red Sea, could find itself being intimidated by a powerful PLA Navy presence off the Strait of Bab-el-Mandeb or in the southwestern Indian Ocean. To ensure the safe and secure passage of its trade and energy, the Indian Navy may, therefore, be required to deploy far more resources than at present.

China's vulnerability in the Indian Ocean originates primarily in the Eastern Indian Ocean; PLA Navy ships and submarines deploying to the Indian Ocean have to transit through narrow choke points and, therefore, cannot do so undetected. Most of China's trade and more than 80 per cent of its imported oil and gas transit across the Indian Ocean, passing south of Sri Lanka, close to India's peninsular tip and south of the Nicobar group of islands which almost straddle the approaches to the Malacca Strait. This offers India a significant strategic advantage over Chinese trade, energy and naval movements. Therefore, China views this as a critical vulnerability, that Hu Jintao, the Chinese president, in 2003, referred to as China's Malacca Dilemma.[14] In the event of a conflict, this passage could be blocked by its adversaries, leaving China with very limited alternatives, and degradation of its war-waging capability.

China has initiated various efforts to mitigate its Malacca Dilemma. The CPEC is linking its mainland directly with the Arabian Sea from the Pakistani port of Gwadar, located close to the Strait of Hormuz and in the Bay of Bengal, and the Kyaukpyu port in Myanmar is being linked to Kunming in China's Yunnan province.[15] The economic and strategic viability of these projects has been debated, but China remains convinced of their usefulness in obviating its Malacca Dilemma in a confrontational scenario.

A strong PLA Navy presence with a carrier battle group supported by nuclear attack submarines and an expeditionary capability permanently positioned in the Indian Ocean with base facilities and proxy support would provide the sustained reach and forward presence for China to effectively neutralise its vulnerability, and instead, bring pressure to bear on India in the Bay of Bengal and the Western Indian Ocean.

Pakistan, India's traditional adversary, is limited in its naval capability, and despite an appreciable increase in force levels over the next few years with ships and submarines being acquired from China and various other countries, will not be a significant maritime threat but could complicate India's maritime security matrix as a proxy for China. It has been sponsoring terrorism in India for over four decades and was behind both the maritime terror attacks on Mumbai, first in 1993, and again in 2008. India has a number of strategic industrial facilities, single buoy moorings and offshore facilities on its west coast not far from Pakistan, which are vulnerable to low intensity operations from that country. Its shrill rhetoric, sniping at India's heels, and threats to use its tactical nuclear weapons reflect on its instability within and, therefore, cannot be ignored.

Traditional threats develop over a period of time. Political and diplomatic efforts are made to diffuse them, and they are fairly predictable. Military force structures are designed to counter these, ensuring a degree of readiness to counter them. It is the non-traditional threats that are unpredictable and unexpected. Hence, the responses are often reactive. India has been a victim of maritime terrorism more than once; its trade was threatened by Somalian piracy, and as a provider of net security and the first responder in humanitarian disasters, it has to develop an effective domain and situational awareness mechanism to counter these.

India's Strategic Maritime Initiatives

The geostrategic significance of the maritime domain, its intrinsic link to India's security and economic stability and India's aspiration to play a larger role in the region, which is distinctly maritime in nature,has begun getting some traction in the last few years. The government has taken some significant initiatives to revitalise the maritime sector in India.

In 2011, it released the Maritime Agenda 2010-2020, a ten-year roadmap with ambitious targets.[16] Much of this was subsumed into Sagarmala, a twenty-year, multi-crore programme for the port-led development of India's maritime infrastructure focussing on port development, inland waterway network, coastal trade and navigation, efficient marine transportation, industrial clusters, development of coastal communities and maritime training and education.[17] This was initiated in 2015 and announced at the Global Maritime Summit held in Mumbai in April 2016, an event that showcased India's maritime potential to the world. Two months prior to this, in February 2016, the country hosted an International Fleet Review in Visakhapatnam on India's east coast, in which more than 50 navies participated and reinforced India's standing as a leading naval power. The second edition of the Global Maritime Summit was held in March 2021 with global participation, albeit virtually because of the pandemic. During this summit, the Prime Minister released the 'Maritime Vision 2030',[18] an ambitious ten-year plan for the country's development as a maritime power. This roadmap highlights the enhancement of India's shipbuilding capacity, creating a competitive maritime trade environment, enhancing India's port capacity and developing a world class maritime training infrastructure.

It is important to make a distinction between maritime power and naval power. Most of the contemporary narrative on India's maritime power is restricted to its military maritime capability. Maritime power is defined as the "ability of a nation to use the seas to safeguard and progress its national interests"[19] and is a function of the country's comprehensive national power. Naval power is without a doubt its most important constituent and its most powerful manifestation but is not the only one. India is undoubtedly a naval power of reckoning but is lagging in most other parameters that constitute maritime power.

Alfred Thayer Mahan, the doyen of maritime strategists, had listed six attributes for a maritime power in his seminal work, *The Influence of Sea Power Upon History*.[20] These included a country's geographical position, physical conformation, the extent of territory, size of the population, character of the people and character of the government. India has all these attributes except probably one. It is blessed with a favourable maritime geography with its peninsular landmass jutting almost 1,000 miles into the centre of the Indian Ocean; it has a long coastline and a large EEZ; it has the advantage of a young and aspirational population, with a large and vibrant coastal community; it has, however, lacked in transforming this potential due to inadequate government support. The recent initiatives and the 'Maritime Vision 2030' are steps in the right direction though the challenge will lie in their successful implementation.

India and the Indo-Pacific: Securing its Maritime Interests

The evolution of the Indo-Pacific as a strategic construct has coincided more or less with India's enhanced engagement with the Asia-Pacific region east of the Malacca Strait. Its 'Look East' and subsequent 'Act East policies' have made it an integral part of the Indo-Pacific construct. Its interpretation of the Indo-Pacific includes the entire Indian and Pacific Oceans, as was highlighted by Prime Minister Narendra Modi in his keynote address at the Shangrila Dialogue in Singapore in June 2018, where he said, "India's own engagement in the Indo-Pacific region—from the shores of Africa to that of the Americas—will be inclusive"[21] India's Foreign Secretary Harshvardhan Shringla while speaking at the Policy Exchange in London in November 2020 outlined India's vision of the Indo-Pacific and reiterated its importance, and India's commitment to the region. From a Pacific perspective, for the most part, however, the Indo-Pacific construct ends at India and does not necessarily include the rest of the wider Indian Ocean region. Other than the USA, no other prominent Pacific country in this construct has adequate capacity to influence the geopolitical outcomes in the Indian Ocean. Therefore, it becomes imperative for India to focus its attention on the 'Indo' of the Indo-Pacific, which remains its primary area of interest.

Capacity Building in the Indian Ocean

India has come a long way from its earlier stance in the 1970s when it distanced itself from the bipolar Cold War world order and created the Non-Aligned Movement (NAM). It resented any extra-regional presence in the Indian Ocean,believing that it would destabilise the region. It supported the Sri Lankan proposal (seconded by Tanzania), which led to the UN General Assembly Resolution 2832 (XXVI) on December 16, 1971, declaring the Indian Ocean as a Zone of Peace (IOZP) for all time.[22] The Cold War being largely centred in the Atlantic, the Indian Ocean was anyway peripheral to the global order of the time. The economic crisis of 1991 was the transformational moment for India,which began looking outwards, and as it opened up its economy, it also sought a greater engagement with the world.

Since then, India has embarked on a series of initiatives for capacity building in its maritime neighbourhood as well as in the wider Indian Ocean. Initiatives like the Indian Ocean Rim Association (IORA) to bring together various disaggregated regions of the Indian Ocean on a common platform and a common development agenda is one such. Similarly, India assumed a leadership role in BIMSTEC (Bay of Bengal Initiative for Multi-Sectoral Technical and Economic Cooperation) which began as a four-nation initiative and now comprises Bangladesh, Bhutan, India, Myanmar, Nepal, Sri Lanka, Thailand. This grouping is an important regional capacity building effort in the Bay of Bengal as it seeks to enhance connectivity between South Asia and Southeast Asia. It could become an effective mechanism to check the Chinese advance into the greater Bay of Bengal region. As an economic grouping too, it cannot be ignored as it is home to 21 per cent of the world's population and generates a Gross Domestic Product (GDP) in excess of US$ 3 trillion.

In 2015, during his visit to Mauritius, Prime Minister Modi made two very significant statements that highlighted the centrality of the maritime domain in India's future and its commitment to the region. Speaking at the commissioning ceremony of the CGS *Vigilant*, which was built in India for the Mauritius Coast Guard, he said, "To me, the blue chakra or wheel in India's national flag represents the potential of the 'blue revolution or the ocean economy'". He also enunciated his vision of SAGAR, an acronym for 'Security and Growth for All in the Region', which is also the Hindi word for sea, and further underscored the importance of the maritime dimension in India's regional security matrix.

SAGAR Doctrine: The SAGAR Doctrine highlights the importance of a cooperative and inclusive capacity building approach in the Indian Ocean region to enhance the collective security and economic progress of the countries in the region. In the six years since it was announced, several initiatives have been taken in the maritime domain led by the navy and the coast guard for enhancing regional security. It has supported maritime infrastructure development, training of naval personnel, joint exercises and building of defence industrial capability, etc. India has integrated

Bangladesh, Sri Lanka and the Maldives into its coastal radar network to provide seamless situational awareness across the region for enhancing coastal security. Search and rescue facilities have been established, with training and hardware being provided to the countries in the region. In 2020, India leased a Kilo class submarine to Myanmar in a bid to deepen its engagement with that country and strengthen the regional security framework on India's eastern seaboard. Military diplomacy has been given a boost, and the country is also exploring avenues to enhance the export of defence hardware to these countries.

The Quadrilateral Security Dialogue (Quad): At a politico-military level, the Quad amongst Australia, India, Japan and the USA is another significant development. After lying dormant for over a decade, this initiative gained momentum since 2017 with a focus on multisectoral activities and two Heads of Government Summits held in 2021 itself. With China becoming increasingly aggressive in the region, and its intention to reorient the Free and Open Indo-Pacific and the existing rules-based order into one with Chinese characteristics, this construct will be important in checking China's hegemonistic ambitions in the maritime domain.

Indo-Pacific Oceans Initiative: At the East Asia Summit held in Bangkok in November 2019, India launched the Indo-Pacific Oceans Initiative (IPOI). The Ministry of External Affairs described it as "an open global initiative. The IPOI draws on existing regional cooperation architecture and mechanisms to focus on seven central pillars conceived around Maritime Security; Maritime Ecology; Maritime Resources; Capacity Building and Resource Sharing; Disaster Risk Reduction and Management; Science, Technology and Academic Cooperation; and Trade Connectivity and Maritime Transport."[23]

NSA Trilateral on Maritime Security: In its immediate neighbourhood, the South Asian Association for Regional Cooperation (SAARC) has been less than successful due to a trust deficit generated by Pakistan. However, India has been far more successful in the maritime domain and has a robust relationship with its immediate maritime neighbourhood. Following the National Security Advisor (NSA) level trilateral meeting among India, Sri Lanka and the Maldives in November

2020, a secretariat for addressing maritime security issues was established in Colombo in March 2021.[24] The geographical proximity of these countries to each other highlights the significance of this mechanism in addressing mutual maritime security issues.

UNSC High Level Debate on Maritime Security: This focus on maritime security also found expression at the United Nations Security Council (UNSC) during India's presidency on August 8, 2021, which was chaired by Prime Minister Modi. In a debate on maritime security chaired by the Prime Minister, he highlighted five principles that reflect the Indian approach to maritime security. These included the removal of barriers to maritime trade, peaceful resolution of maritime disputes in accordance with international law, joint tackling of sub-conventional threats and natural disasters, conservation of the maritime environment and responsible maritime connectivity.[25]

Bilateral Engagement: India has established comprehensive strategic partnerships with most like-minded countries in the Indo-Pacific as well as the extra-regional powers operating here. Some of these have been elevated to the Defence and Foreign Ministers 2+2 level and more such arrangements are in the offing. These have a strong maritime security component but are not specific to the maritime domain. India has also engaged extensively with the strategically located island states in the Indian Ocean like Mauritius and Seychelles as part of the SAGAR framework despite these not being in India's immediate neighbourhood. India must leverage these relationships to extend its reach in the Indian Ocean towards enhancing the Maritime Domain Awareness (MDA) and information sharing mechanism.

Climate Change: Climate change has a profound effect on the oceans and is one of the gravest non-traditional threats facing the planet. In the Indo-Pacific region, many of the small island states and coastal territories, facing an existential threat of inundation from the rising sea levels, making them vulnerable to inducements that could have a direct impact on India's maritime security in more ways than one. As a leading global power with a deep commitment to combating climate change, India must support the concerns of these Small Island Developing States (SIDS) on global platforms. Many of these small states are strategically located, and their favourable disposition towards India can be an asset in ensuring the security of our maritime interests in the region. India is bringing these issues to global attention through less formal channels like the Indian Ocean Conference and the Indo-Pacific Regional Dialogue, amongst others.

Indian Navy in Support of Foreign Policy

As a major instrument of foreign policy and national power, the Indian Navy too has widened its engagement with foreign navies. Exercise Malabar, which began as a bilateral naval exercise between the USA and India in 1992, has grown into a quadrilateral exercise with Japan and Australia joining, in 2015 and 2020, respectively. The recent hardening of positions against China as a result of its belligerence with India, Australia and Japan has led to the shedding of the earlier hesitation and has almost come to symbolise the military dimension of the Quad. The scope and scale of the exercise has also expanded to include aircraft carriers,nuclear attack submarines and long range maritime patrol aircraft. Besides Malabar, India has bilateral exercises with more than 40 navies, including the British, French, Russian and Singaporean Navies, amongst many others. Ex MILAN, which began in 1995 with the presence of four navies assembling in Port Blair for a cultural and sports exchange, has, over the years, grown to an extent where 17 navies were scheduled to participate in 2020 off Visakhapatnam but had to be cancelled due to the pandemic. In 2001, the country hosted its first ever International Fleet Review with the theme 'Bridges of Friendship' in which 29 foreign navies participated. In the years since then, the Indian Navy's multilateral and bilateral engagements have increased manifold. The second International Fleet Review held in Visakhapatnam in February 2016 had 52 navies participating.

The navy's engagement with the region has also undergone an operational shift. Goodwill visits, as they were known in yesteryears, have given way to overseas deployments, with a focus on operations. The signing of four Foundational Agreements with the US Navy on the general security of information (GSOMIA), logistics exchange (LEMOA), communications (COMCASA) and sharing of geospatial information (BECA) has been followed by similar logistics arrangements that are in place with South Korea, Singapore, France, Australia, and are being negotiated with other countries such as the UK and Russia.[26] Several countries in the Indian Ocean littoral have given basing rights to visiting Indian naval ships, which facilitate its multi-mission deployment strategy with 12 to 15 major surface combatants deployed across the length and breadth of the Indo-Pacific, including the choke points for better situational awareness, enhanced MDA and a larger operational footprint in the region.

These initiatives notwithstanding, tackling the numerous security challenges in the oceanic space of the Indian Ocean and the larger Indo-Pacific requires a cooperative and well coordinated approach from like-minded navies in the region.

India's Maritime Security Strategy

In 2015, the Indian Navy issued a Maritime Security Strategy document titled "Ensuring Secure Seas,"[27] which superseded the previous document issued in 2007 titled "Freedom to Use the Seas". The change in the title itself reflected the evolving nature of the regional maritime security dynamics and the Indian Navy's approach towards ensuring the security of India's maritime interests. It was driven by the following three major developments impacting the nation's maritime security:

(a) The shift in the geostrategic focus from the Euro-Atlantic to the Indo-Pacific and its impact on the Indian Ocean region.
(b) The change in India's threat security calculus with the rise of non-traditional threats.
(c) A national outlook towards the seas and the maritime domain and increasing recognition of maritime security are vital to the country's economic progress and international engagement.

Contemporary maritime security is centred on certain critical requirements. These have been listed in the strategy document and include Maritime Domain Awareness, Force Structure and Capabilities, Preparedness and Presence, Networked Operations, Jointness and Coordination and Strategic Communication.[28]

Maritime Domain Awareness: The nature of the maritime threat has highlighted the importance of deterring or preempting a developing situation. This requires a robust and effective MDA framework across the Indo-Pacific. In the Indian Ocean, the navy has taken several steps towards enhancing this through a multi-dimensional approach incorporating the space, air, surface, sub-surface and cyber domains. As the mandated provider of net security in the region, India has taken the lead in establishing the Indian Ocean Region-Information Fusion Centre (IOR-IFC) in Gurugram, a suburb of the national capital. India has signed white shipping agreements with more than 25 countries for sharing and disseminating information, and a few more are in the offing. A number of countries have appointed observers at the IOR-IFC to ensure seamless dissemination of this information. Coordination and information sharing between the IOR-IFC and similar IFCs located in Singapore and Madagascar will provide a comprehensive coverage of the entire Indo-Pacific.

Force Structuring in the Indian Navy

In the 75 years since independence, the Indian Navy has grown from a modest 37-ship brown water force into a balanced multi-dimensional blue water force, with full spectrum capability. It has about 130 ships in commission and intends to be a 170-ship navy by 2027[29] with commensurate air and sub-surface elements, and dedicated space and cyber capability.

Force level development in the Indian Navy is based on a 15-year Maritime Capability Perspective Plan, which is revised periodically and runs concurrent with the country's fiscal Five-Year Plans to facilitate better financial planning. It is understood that this will be aligned with a 10-year Integrated Capability Development Plan (ICDP) for the integrated force development of the three services.[30] From the time India became independent, naval planners envisioned a major role for the Indian Navy in consonance with India's aspirations to become a leading global power. Hence, the very first plan's paper approved in 1948 envisaged the Indian Navy as a balanced aircraft carrier-centric blue water force and included three aircraft carriers and four submarines. Since then, the navy has been on a steady upward trajectory and, despite a few setbacks in its force level aspirations due to a range of factors, not the least being the country's socioeconomic development imperatives, has been able to balance its requirements of becoming a multi-mission capable force across the strategic, operational and tactical domains.

Power Projection and Sea Control: In 2022, with the commissioning of the *Vikrant*, the first indigenously built aircraft carrier and named after its illustrious predecessor, the Indian Navy will be able to deploy two Carrier Battle Groups (CBGs) with power projection capabilities. Its induction will greatly enhance India's maritime strength with the navy's ability to deploy two CBGs, which will greatly enhance the country's ability to project power far beyond its shores in pursuit of its national objectives. From an operational perspective, the enhanced reach and sustainability will enable it to exercise sea control, which is one of the strategic roles of the Indian Navy. Plans for a third aircraft carrier, larger and more powerful than these two, have been on the anvil for many years and are awaiting clearance at the highest level.[31]

A force level of three aircraft carriers is an inescapable requirement to ensure that two CBGs are operational at all times. Aircraft carriers have a long build time, so if India wants to retain its maritime primacy, and be able to project power and adequately protect its maritime interests in the Indian Ocean in the next decade, the government has to act now.

Strategic Deterrence: The proliferation of nuclear weapon states in the region and the presence of two adversarial nuclear powers on either side with a deep strategic relationship between them underlines the importance of a robust nuclear deterrence and retaliatory capability. The successful deterrence patrol by India's first nuclear powered ballistic missile submarine (SSBN) INS *Arihant* in 2018 validated India's nuclear triad. SSBNs are very complex platforms, and their indigenous construction is a testimony to India's technological skills and industrial prowess. Since the cornerstones of India's nuclear doctrine are 'no first use' and 'credible minimum deterrence', an invulnerable second strike capability is essential for the doctrine to be credible. An SSBN, with its inherent advantages of stealth and concealment, is the ideal platform. Reports indicate that India's second SSBN is expected to get commissioned soon, and two larger, and more capable SSBNs are under construction. A force level of four will enable at least one to be on patrol at any given time, thus, ensuring continuous deterrence at sea and making the country's strategic posture truly credible.

Undersea Warfare: India's tryst with nuclear submarine propulsion began in 1988 with the leasing of a Charlie 1 class SSN for three years from the erstwhile Soviet Union. In 2012, India leased an Akula-2 class SSN from Russia for ten years which was returned in 2021. It is understood that the lease of another Akula-2 class submarine for ten years from 2025 is being progressed, and depending on the operational circumstances, more might follow. This has given the Indian Navy a valuable insight into the complexities of operating, supporting and maintaining these sophisticated platforms. An indigenous programme for the indigenous construction of six SSNs is awaiting the approval of the Cabinet Committee on Security (CCS). SSNs are integral to a navy's blue water force structure and, in India's context, even more so. They are extremely versatile platforms and can do high speeds with unlimited endurance. Armed with a lethal mix of torpedo tube-launched cruise missiles with land attack capability and heavyweight torpedoes, they can shape not only the maritime battle space but also influence the outcome of the war on land.

Modern SSKs, while lacking the versatility of SSNs in terms of speed and endurance, can be deployed more effectively in a littoral battlespace. With the advent of Air Independent Propulsion (AIP) systems, anti-ship cruise missiles and smart heavyweight torpedoes, they are equally effective in attack and defence, and constitute the cutting edge of the navy's offensive frontline element. India's SSK fleet, though ageing, has been kept in fine operational fettle with regular modernisation and life extension cycles. However, they need to be replaced sooner rather than later. Four new indigenously built submarines of the Kalvari class have been commissioned between 2017 and 2021, with two more to follow within the next two years; the next programme, called Project 75(I), is still at the discussion stage, and it will take more than a decade for the first of these six submarines to come online. Hence, there will be a capability gap in India's undersea warfare readiness if the SSK induction programme is not given the priority it deserves.

Surface Forces: The navy has a versatile mix of major surface combatants with destroyers, frigates, missile and Anti-Sea Warfare (ASW) corvettes and replenishment ships. With an increase in numbers within the next few years, this capability is set to improve further with sophisticated, technologically advanced and networked platforms. Presently, four Project 15B destroyers, seven Project 17A and four Type 1135.6 stealth frigates are under construction besides numerous other smaller combatants. These will provide a formidable surface warfare capability.

Naval Aviation: The Indian Navy's aviation arm, equipped with a balanced mix of fixed and rotary wing aircraft and unmanned Unmanned Aerial Vehicles (UAVs), is a vital asset in India's maritime security matrix. It provides the Indian Navy critical long and medium range maritime reconnaissance, carrierborne fighter strikes at targets afloat and ashore, airborne early warning, airborne anti-surface and anti-submarine warfare capability, combat air patrol, close air support, vertical replenishment at sea, expeditionary and special forces operations, vertical replenishment, and search and rescue, amongst others. There is presently a capacity deficit in certain areas, which is being addressed through various acquisition programmes that are being simultaneously progressed.

Logistic Support: There is also a focus on improving and streamlining the logistic supply chain commensurate with the deployment pattern and maintenance cycles with an aim to reduce the turn-around time of platforms and optimise their operational availability at sea.

Indigenisation and Self-Reliance

Indigenisation and self-reliance have been key strategic parameters in the development of the Indian Navy. Recognising that import dependence is a critical vulnerability for an aspiring power, the focus from independence was on becoming a 'builder' Navy and not remain a 'buyer' Navy. The Indian Navy commissioned its first indigenously built ship, INS *Ajay*, in1960, and there has been no looking back since. Presently 37 of the Navy's 39 ships and submarines are being built in Indian shipyards. These include an aircraft carrier, strategic and conventional submarines, destroyers, frigates and corvettes. The indigenous content in these is increasing with every platform as the country's defence-industrial complex grows and matures. The Indian Navy has promulgated a 15-year Indigenisation Plan (INIP 2015-30) in which it has identified the technologies it expects from the industry. However, there are capacity limitations, coupled with budgetary constraints and procedural delays in decision-making, that have stymied the growth of the Indian Navy. The government must, therefore, create an enabling environment to address these and also support the Indian industry's attempts at developing cutting edge technologies to ensure that the Navy's quantitative and qualitative requirements are met indigenously in the envisaged timeframe to meet the country's growing security challenges in the maritime domain.

Future Trajectory

The Indian Navy is poised for a technologically intensive future growth trajectory. In addition to enhancing its traditional three-dimensional capabilities in the air, surface and undersea domains, with a focus on advanced platforms, smart weapons, precision weapon technologies and advanced propulsion and stealth technologies, the navy is focussing on harnessing the space and cyber domains. Satellite technologies for surveillance, navigation and network-centric operations, quantum communications and navigation, deployment of electro-magnetic and laser technologies for directed energy weapons, unmanned air, surface and underwater vehicles with modular applications, cyber security, nano-technologies and green initiatives are some of the areas that the Indian Navy is focussing on.

Conclusion

India is poised on a transformational cusp in the maritime domain. The government appears to have recognised the country's sound maritime credentials and the economic benefit that can be derived from India's favourable maritime geography. However, India still has to travel some distance to become a maritime power; this will depend on the course the government charts to ensure a smooth and time-bound passage.

As the leading Indian Ocean power, India has a significant stake in the emerging geopolitical and geoeconomic contours in the Indo-Pacific.

As a maritime nation with its future firmly anchored in the oceans,it has to develop a national strategy to shape the future outcomes in the region and not allow itself to be shaped by them. In the next two decades, the Indo-Pacific is going to be the scene of intense competition and fierce contestation, with confrontation an inevitability, and conflict a distinct possibility. India will, therefore, have to develop a suitable maritime security strategy across the political, diplomatic, economic and military domains to ensure the security of its maritime interests across the globe. In addition to ensuring its territorial integrity and protection of its EEZ, it will have to focus on the safety of its trade and energy flows, specifically in the Indian Ocean, the importance of ensuring freedom of navigation and overflight in a free and open Indo-Pacific, and building regional capacity through an inclusive and cooperative framework. The Indian Navy, as the principal element of India's maritime power, will have to contend with a widening range of traditional and non-traditional threats which could seriously undermine India's preeminence in the Indian Ocean, both for securing its own maritime interests and also as a provider of net security in the Indian Ocean region. The Indian Navy, which is structured as a balanced multi-dimensional blue water force having full spectrum capability with a focus on indigenisation and self-reliance, will have to be agile and flexible in adapting to the rapidly evolving regional security dynamic and an increasingly technology driven networked battlespace of the future.

Notes

1. www.mofa.po.jp/region/asia-pac/pmv0708/speech2.html. Accessed on December 11, 2021.
2. www.gov.cn/news/top_news/2015/03/28/content_281475079055789.htm. Accessed on November 27, 2021.
3. Debt trap diplomacy is defined in www.tradefinanceglobal.com/posts/debt-trap-diplomacy-how-financial-hegemony-hinders-trade-and-development/. Accessed on December 4, 2021.
4. Definition of China's wolf warrior diplomacy in www.nbr.org/publication/understanding-chinese-wolf-warrior-diplomacy. Accessed on December 4, 2021.
5. Chinese White Paper 2015. www.gov/cn/archive/white_paper/2015/05/27/content_281475115610833.htm

6. Prabir De, March 11, 2019. www.economic times.india times.com/blogs/et_commentary/navigating-the-indo-pacific-cooperation/. Accessed on November 26, 2021.
7. UK's Integrated Review. www.gov.uk/government/publications. Accessed on November 27, 2021.
8. https://www.un.org/depts/los/clcs_new/submissions_files/submission_ind_48_2009.htm
9. US Department of Defence Annual Report to Congress, "Military and Security Developments Involving the People's Republic of China 2021". https://media.defence.gov/2021/Nov/03/2002885874/-1/1/0/2021-CMPR-FINAL.PDF. Accessed on November 26, 2021.
10. Ibid., p. 24.
11. https://news.usni.org/2021/04/20/africom-chinese-naval-base-in-africa-set-to-support-aircraft-carriers. Accessed on December 10, 2021.
12. Ibid.
13. https://www.livemint.com/news/world/cashstrapped-pakistan-requests-another-year-to-pay-back-chinese-loans-11623679847639.html. Accessed on December 10, 2021.
14. Abdullah Khan, "The Malacca Dilemma: A Hindrance to Chinese Ambitions in the 21st Century". https://bpr.berkeley.edu/2019/08/26/the-malacca-dilemma-a-hindrance-to-chinese-ambitions-in-the-21st-century/. Accessed on December 10, 2021.
15. Dipanjan Roy Chaudhury, "Myanmar Junta Expedites Work on China Funded Kyaukphyu Port," Updated on November 9, 2021. https://economictimes.indiatimes.com/news/international/world-news/myanmar-junta-expedites-work-on-china-funded-kyaukphyu-port/articleshow/85167272.cms. Accessed on December 12, 2021.
16. Press Information Bureau, Government of India, Ministry of Shipping, Maritime Agenda 2010-2020. Launched January 13, 2011. https://pib.gov.in/newsite/PrintRelease.aspx?relid=69044. Accessed on December 12, 2021.
17. http://sagarmala.gov.in/. Accessed on December 12, 2021.
18 Ministry of Ports, Shipping and Waterways Government of India, Maritime India Vision 2030, February 22, 2021. https://sagarmala.gov.in/sites/default/files/MIV%202030%20Report.pdf.
19. Indian Maritime Doctrine 2009, Indian Navy Strategic Publication 1.1, p. 11.
20. A. T. Mahan, "Contents," in *The Influence of Sea Power upon History, 1660–1783*. Cambridge Library Collection—Naval and Military History (Cambridge: Cambridge University Press, 2010), pp. vii-xxii.

21. https://www.mea.gov.in/Speeches-Statements.htm?dtl/29943/Prime+Ministers+Keynote+Address+at+Shangri+La+Dialogue+June+01+2018. Accessed on December 11, 2021.
22. https://www.un-ilibrary.org/content/books/9789210579872s005-c003. Accessed on December 11, 2021.
23. Ministry of External Affairs, Indo-Pacific Briefs. https://mea.gov.in/Portal/ForeignRelation/Indo_Feb_07_2020.pdf. Accessed on December 10, 2021.
24. https://www.financialexpress.com/defence/inauguration-of-nsa-trilateral-secretariat-a-step-forward-for-maritime-security-cooperation-with-sri-lanka-and-the-maldives/2206173/. Accessed on December 6, 2021.
25. https://www.thehindu.com/news/national/prime-minister-narendra-modi-chairs-high-level-open-debate-at-united-nations-security-council/article35817763.ece. Accessed on December 12, 2021.
26. Dinakar Peri, "Logistics Agreement with Russia Shortly, in Final Stages with U.K.," *The Hindu* September 5, 2021. https://www.thehindu.com/news/national/logistics-agreement-with-russia-shortly-in-final-stages-with-uk/article36303672.ece. Accessed on December 12, 2021.
27. "Ensuring Secure Seas: Indian Maritime Security Strategy," Indian Navy Naval Strategic Publication (NSP), October 12, 2015.
28. Ibid., p. 43.
29. Vice Admiral SN Ghormade, vice chief of the Naval Staff, at a media interaction on November 16, 2021. Reported by Huma Siddiqui in the *Financial Express* dated November 17, 2021. "Boost to Indian Navy's Capabilities! "Indigenous Aircraft Carrier on Track, Navy to get 170 Ships by 2027". https://www.financialexpress.com/defence/boost-to-indian-navys-capabilities-indigenous-aircraft-carrier-on-track-navy-to-get-170-ships-by-2027/2370958/. Accessed on December 12, 2021.
30. Ibid.
31. Krishn Kaushik, "Navy has Catered for 3rd Aircraft Carrier in its Planning, says Vice Chief", *Indian Express*, November 17, 20. https://indianexpress.com/article/india/indian-navy-aircraft-carrier-7626202/. Accessed on December 12, 2021.

4. Changing Balance of Air Power in the Indo-Pacific

Savinder Pal Singh

Introduction

The first quarter of the 21st century marks the emergence of a New World Order of geopolitical alliances for dominance in critical areas of the economy, technology, and natural resources, with the aspirations of a regional power like China surging ahead towards becoming a global power. Such aspirations are not without the modernisation and expansion of military might, especially in the maritime and air domains. China has steadily increased its politicoeconomic influence beyond the South China Sea (SCS), across the Indian and Pacific Oceans, through well crafted plans like the Belt and Road Initiative (BRI), coercive diplomacy and copious use of military prowess. The expansionist moves of China, with large scale deployment of its maritime and air military assets has led to a steep rise in traditional and non-traditional challenges in the Indo-Pacific region. The Indo-Pacific has, thus, emerged as the new geographical construct for the strategically integrated space of cooperation and arena of fierce competition for power.

The expansion plans of the People's Republic of China (PRC), beyond the SCS, across the Indian and Pacific Oceans, not only pose a threat to the well-established, rule-based free trade regulations over the Sea Lines of Communication (SLOCs) but also infringe on the sovereignty of small island countries in the region.[1] The proliferation of weapons of mass destruction and missile technologies, cyber and space threats, and security threats jeopardising the extraction and maritime transportation of valuable raw materials as well as energy resources represent grave challenges to the global community in the Indo-Pacific region. Geostrategic competition and rivalry among regional and global powers can often create sub-regional, regional and trans-regional instability. The rise of China as a global economic, political, and military power during this period has raised concerns for the strategists and policy-makers across the world—concerns that might provide a new perspective on global security for years to come. At the centre of this concern is China's expanding maritime and air power capability and its impact on the Indo-Pacific region, causing countries to reevaluate their own military modernisation needs.[2]

Strategic Landscape in Indo-Pacific Region

The dependence of members of the international community on raw materials and energy resources emanating from the littoral countries of the Indian Ocean basin and Western Pacific alone makes it imperative to ensure the security of maritime transit through the international waters of the Indian Ocean and the Western Pacific. The vision paper of the PRC on "China's National Defence in the New Era", published in July 2019, clearly indicates China's intent in establishing its supremacy in the SCS. In the vision document, China has, without any ambiguity, defined its objective that would safeguard its maritime rights overseas interests, as well as oppose and contain "Taiwan independence".[3] China, over the last decade, has clearly demonstrated strong and growing strategic interests beyond the near waters of the South and East China Seas and well into the Indian Ocean Region (IOR). In particular, the Eastern Indian Ocean is of increasingly diversified significance to Beijing. This includes securing the SLOCs through the Indian Ocean and to South Asia, Europe, Africa, and the Middle East; increasing economic ties with these regions (as well as with Southeast Asia); and legitimising its own global security role (while also limiting or diluting the US' influence).[4] China is determined to increase its fleet strength of aircraft carriers, nuclear-powered submarines, surface combat ships, Medium-Range Ballistic Missiles (MRBMs), Intercontinental Ballistic Missiles (ICBMs), ballistic missile launch submarines and multi-role combat aircraft to strengthen its comprehensive military power in the Indo-Pacific Maritime Zone (IPMZ).[5]

China's expansionist moves in the region with large force deployment, leading to imbalance of forces in an otherwise peaceful oceanic zone, are now being viewed with serious concern. On March 12, 2021, the leaders of the Quadrilateral Security Dialogue (Quad), the United States, India, Japan and Australia, held a virtual meeting to discuss regional and global issues of shared interest, and exchange views on practical areas of cooperation towards maintaining a stable Indo-Pacific region. In a joint statement released at the end of the virtual meeting, the Quad leaders reaffirmed their commitment to "a region that is free, open, inclusive, healthy, anchored by democratic values, and unconstrained by coercion."[6] The Quad joint statement also stated that they would "launch a critical- and emerging-technology working group to facilitate cooperation on international standards and innovative technologies of the future."[7]

This change in the focus of the Quad towards creating a rule-based zone of cooperation in the Indo-Pacific region was observed as the initiation of a check on a belligerent China that was muscle flexing its way to becoming the sole Asian superpower. Within the same year, a large number of alliances and lateral agreements in the form of bilateral, trilaterals and multilaterals emerged on the world map. Some notable alliances that soon followed the Quad were the Quad plus (with South Korea, Vietnam, and New Zealand), Australia, Japan and India (AJI), Japan-America-India (JAI), Russia-India-China (RIC) trilaterals and Regional Comprehensive Economic Partnership (RCEP) of six Association of Southeast Asian Nations (ASEAN) and five non-ASEAN nations. Though most of these alliances are for preserving the autonomy and cooperation of trade and economy in the Indo-Pacific, the military focus has not yet been observed except for Australia, United Kingdom, United States (AUKUS), that was formally announced on September 15, 2021, as a trilateral security pact for the Indo-Pacific region among Australia, the UK and the US.

Militarisation Dynamics and Deployment

China: China's continued ascendance in extending its maritime influence in the Indo-Pacific region raised the alarm for the various nations affected, directly or indirectly, by the turn of events in this otherwise peaceful maritime zone. A large number of factors in various domains covering diplomatic ties, economic interests, political ambitions and security and sociocultural issues that are in focus, have led to intense rivalry between the competing powers in the Indo-Pacific. Such a development in the region is leading to large scale military build-up, that could soon be the *raison-d'etre* for destabilising the regional equilibrium. In the recent past, China has escalated its efforts to reclaim its control over islands in the SCS. As reported by the study group report of US Department of Defence China, Anti-Access/Area Denial (A2/AD) capabilities build-up is one of the top priorities for the PRC.[8]

The People's Liberation Army (PLA) is the world's largest standing ground force, with approximately 900,000 active-duty personnel in combat units. It is developing capabilities to provide options for the PRC to dissuade, deter and, if called upon, militarily challenge such threats, during a large-scale theatre campaign such as a Taiwan contingency referred to under the A2/AD capabilities. The PLA has focussed on building operational potential and strategic concepts towards conducting effects-based operations within the SCS to gain control over the second island chain, as well as in the Indo-Pacific zone. China, while developing information, cyber, and space and counter-space operations, including Anti-Satellite (ASAT) capability, is continuing to enhance its conventional strike, air and missile defence, anti-surface and anti-submarine capabilities also.[9]

The PRC also has one of the largest navies in the world with an overall potential of approximately 360 ships and submarines. The People's Liberation Army Navy (PLAN) is a composite force with modern advanced anti-ship, anti-air, and anti-submarine sensors and weapons. Over the last decade and a half, the PLAN has built twelve nuclear submarines, that include 2 Shang I class and 4 Shang II class SSNs (submissile ship nuclear) respectively with 6 Jin class Submersible Ship Ballistic Missile Nuclear (SSBN). Each Jin class SSBN, the PRC's credible sea-based nuclear deterrent, can carry up to 12 JL-2 Submarine Launched Ballistic Missiles (SLBMs). The PRC commissioned its first domestically built aircraft carrier in late 2019. China expects its second domestically built aircraft carrier to enter service by 2023.[10] To further add punch to its might, China launched the stealth guided Type-055 missile destroyers in the Indo-Pacific region, to demonstrate its oceanic superiority. The T-055 is the largest surface combat vessel in Beijing's inventory, that is designed for multi-mission roles, including anti-submarine warfare and area air defence. Presently, there are four such destroyers operating in the area of the SCS. These destroyers have vertical launch, cannister-based, missile carriage systems that can destroy targets up to a range of more than 1,500 km. These destroyers have a combination of different missiles, with ranges varying from 500 km to almost 2,000 km. The weapons onboard the destroyers include Anti-Ship Cruise Missiles (ASCMs) HHQ-9 Surface-to-Air Missiles (SAMs) and Land Attack Cruise Missiles (LACMs).[11]

China, like the US and Russia, realised very early that air power would play a decisive role in any armed conflict, be it over land or sea. The PLA Air Force (PLAAF), as an instrument of the global ambition of the PRC, has grown exponentially in terms of both technology and numbers. The PLAAF and PLAN Aviation have a majority of their aerial combat potential comprising the fourth generation aircraft, more than half of about 1,500 fighters on the inventory. The PLAAF, in all likelihood, would become a major fourth generation aircraft force within the next few years. The PLAAF has also focussed on operationally fielding limited numbers of its new J-20 fifth generation fighters. The development on the smaller FC-31/J-31 is continuing at an accelerated pace for induction as a future naval fighter for future aircraft carriers of the PLAN. The newer fifth generation fighter aircraft, the J-20, and other fourth generation-plus aircraft are fast replacing the ageing J-7s. As far as the stealth fighters are considered, the J-20 and J-131 programme seems to be forging ahead as per schedule. The J-20 aircraft, once operational, would meet the PLAAF's requirements of a high speed stealth interceptor against Airborne Warning and Control Systems (AWACS) and other High Value Air Assets (HVAAs) of the US Air Force (USAF). Though the J-31 is not likely to be in service before 2035, the PLAAF appears to be focussed on the early roll out of this highly capable platform, that may prove to be a game-changer.

During the PRC's 70th anniversary parade in October 2019, the PLAAF showcased its high-profile advanced fighters, the J-20, J-10C and J-16. All these fighters were armed with the latest Air-to-Air Missiles (AAMs). The PRC, with the completion of delivery of all 24 SU-35 advanced fourth generation fighters from Russia, has now reached a formidable strength in its fighter fleet. With the plan of increasing the number of AAMs that the fighter can carry, the PLAAF is progressing well in the upgrade programme for the J-20. The upgrade is likely to include the addition of thrust-vectoring engine nozzles, advanced super cruise capability, with higher-thrust producing indigenous WS-15 engines.[12] The H-6 Badger strategic bombers with the H-6N variant modified to externally carry either a drone or an Air-Launched Ballistic Missile (ALBM) constitute the long range bomber force of the PRC. These are likely to be nuclear capable. The PLAAF's advanced Airborne Early Warning and Control (AEW&C) aircraft KJ-500, IL-78 Flight Refuelling Aircraft (FRA) and Y-20 strategic heavy lift aircraft form the backbone of the PLAAF's operational strength.

China has also built its fleet of Unmanned Aerial Vehicles/Unmanned Combat Aerial Vehicles (UAVs/UCAVs) along with armed capable Yunying, Caihong CH-4 and CH-5, Yilong (Wing Loong). The low-observable flying-wing aircraft such as the CH-7, Tianying, and Yaoying III that are capable of long range missions, with very high endurance with multiple payloads, will soon become the mainstay of the force. China, while deploying its resources, has remained focussed on the development of the Shendiao along with the upgrade programme for the BZK-005 Changying as an aerial platform with larger endurance. The rocket-powered, high-speed Wuzhen-8 advanced unmanned aerial systems as well as the Gongji11 stealth UCAVs were also displayed during the PRC's 70th anniversary parade.[13] The PLAAF, with such large deployment of air assets, continues to be the largest single national air force in the Indo-Pacific Maritime Zone (IPMZ).

USA: The United States Indo-Pacific Command (USINDOPACOM) is a unified combatant command of the United States Armed Forces responsible for the Indo-Pacific region, with the Pacific Air Forces (PACAF) being the air component command. The PACAF has more than 300 aircraft and works closely with the Japanese forces operating from Kadena (F-15C/D Eagle, E-3B/C Sentry and KC-135R), Misawa

(F-16CJ/DJ) and Yokota (C-12J, C-130J Hercules). The PACAF has also deployed the E-8C Joint-Surveillance and Target Attack Radar System (J-STARS) at Kadena. As far as the marine force deployment is concerned, the United States Pacific Fleet (USPACFLT) has about 200 ships and at least two Carrier Battle Groups (CBGs) in the oceanic zone around Taiwan. These are large nuclear-powered aircraft carriers of the Nimitz class that can operate about 90 fixed wing aircraft, including F-35 and helicopters. The US also has more than ten similar large carriers that can be tasked to move in the Indo-Pacific zone at short notice. The US Navy also has about 75 submarines that include more than 10 SSBNs. These SSBNs are deployed at vital locations to ensure effective nuclear deterrence. Most of the ships of the US Navy are designed as multi-mission capable vessels that can undertake simultaneous operations of different types except that of strategic nuclear deterrence. The different types of ships on the inventory include attack submarines, destroyers, frigates with support craft like minesweepers and amphibious ships. The US Navy also has state-of-the-art logistics supply ships that undertake continuous replenishment operations to ensure unhindered operation by ships of different types.[14]

The PACAF also has a large reserve component stationed at air bases in the mainland USA and at Hawaii and Guam operating the F-22A Raptor, F-35, C-17 Globemaster III, C-130 Hercules, among many others. Additionally, F-16C/D, A-10C Thunderbolt II of the Seventh Air Force operate from US bases in South Korea. Thus, with a significant number of around 2,000 aircraft, the US has a clear edge in air power in the region. The PACAF, with a large number of UAVs and UCAVs on its inventory, that include the RQ-4 Global Hawk, MQ4-C Triton, RQ-170 Sentinal would be a dominant force in the region. Air operations of the PACAF including long-range strike, strategic lift, stealth operations will be enabled by fifth generation aircraft, net-centric operations, hypersonic weapons, hyperglide vehicles, space control—all controlled through the state-of-the-art Air Battle Management System (ABMS) along with Joint All Domain Command and Control (JADC2).

India: The Indian Navy presently has a single aircraft carrier with a range exceeding 7,000 nautical miles (nm) along with 137 ships and submarines, and 291 aircraft. The aircraft carrier is capable of undertaking simultaneous operations by a large number of fighters of the MiG 29K/ Sea Harrier class as well as many helicopters like the Chetak, Sea King, Kamov 31. The Indian Navy has a reasonable strength of about 20 submarines with only one of them being nuclear-powered. A strong fleet of destroyers and frigates is also being maintained by the Indian Navy. The BrahMos and Klub class anti-ship cruise missiles are the mainstay of the land-attack capability of offensive operations by the Indian Navy. The induction of P-8I multi-mission maritime patrol aircraft and carrier based MiG 29-K fighter jets has enhanced the capabilities of the Indian Navy many times. Both the Heron and Searcher class UAVs have also boosted the search and strike capabilities.[15]

The Indian Air Force (IAF) is a formidable and highly capable force with more than 1,800 aircraft. It has state-of-the-art technology weapons, and on-board systems supported by a secure robust Air Defence (AD) network. The IAF has a large inventory of fighters, including the fourth generation Rafale and SU-30 MKI ASFs, MiG-29 UPG, Mirage 2000, indigenous Light Combat Aircraft (LCA), Jaguar and MiG-21 Bison. HVAAs like Airborne Warring and Control Systems (AWACs), Airborne Early Waving and Control (AEW&C) aircraft, IL-78 Flight Refuelling Aircraft (FRA) with heavy airlift aircraft including the C-17 Globemaster, IL-76 and Chinook helicopters that give an enviable capability to the IAF in the IOR. The C-130Js for special operations with Apache attack helicopters can prove to be the most lethal combination in the region. A large variety of helicopters like the Mi-17, Mi-17 1V, Mi-17V 5, LCH and Rudra are in service with not only the IAF but with the Indian Navy and Indian Army as well. The Heron, Searcher UAVs with Harpy UCAVs give an edge to the IAF for search and strike capability.

Japan: The JMSDF, even though a smaller force as compared to China and the US, has a reasonable size marine force that includes more than 150 ships and about 300 plus aircraft. The Japan Air Self-Defence Force (JASDF), has around 750 aircraft, including approximately 350 fighters with about more than 200 of them being of the fourth generation. Japan has 20 active air bases, 11 marine operation bases and more than 10 naval aviation bases, distributed across the geographic stretch of the country.

The US has stationed a large portion of its forces in Japan. The major resources deployed by the US include the USS aircraft carrier *Ronald Reagan*, that is one of the most potent carriers. The US has also forward deployed approximately 40,000 military personnel along with its Seventh Fleet, US Marine commandos, USAF assets, including F-35 and certain special operations units in Japan.[16] An area covering approximately 300 miles stretching north to south, between mainland Japan and Taiwan has been planned to be covered by formidable missile launchers, spread across the zone. The defended area includes the Senkaku Islands, and the defence shield so created would be able to target any naval or air threat developing in the zone. In a joint surveillance network operation to detect, locate and track Chinese ships and submarines as they leave port, Japan has not only deployed its submarines along with the US, but is also fast expanding its fleet to about 22 submarines. This integrated undersea surveillance grid has a vast network of sensors that maintain a close watch on all activities across the Yellow and East China Seas. Approximately 80 fixed-wing aircraft and about a similar number of helicopters, operating from fixed bases on the Ryukyus or through deck operations from surface ships, pose a serious threat to the PLAN submarines. Japan has robust mine warfare capabilities and can deploy in a short span of time a large number of mines that can target specific vessels in the sea.[17] The JASDF operates the F-15J (155), Mitsubishi F-2 (62) and F-35 (42) fighter aircraft. It has 10 FRAs and a significant number of AEW&C aircraft. Japan has created a very potent A2/AD capability by the skilful deployment of Air Defence (AD) fighters, KC-46 FRAs and HVAAs like the Advanced Hawkeye and E-767 AWACS.[18]

Australia: The Royal Australian Navy has a fleet of 46 ships comprising mostly patrol boats with a limited number of destroyers and frigates.[19] The Royal Australian Air Force (RAAF) operates the majority of the military fixed wing aircraft, although both the Australian Army and Royal Australian Navy also operate aircraft in various roles. The RAAF has 259 aircraft, of which 110 are combat aircraft. The main combat aircraft are 69 Boeing F/A-18, 24 F/A-18E/F (multi-role), and 37 F-35 Lightning II. It has 18 dedicated Electronic Warfare (EW) aircraft, 14 Boeing P-8 maritime patrol aircraft, and seven Airbus A330 MRTT air refuellers.

Other Nations: A large number of nations other than the four Quad members have, as brought out earlier, engaged with each other either in bilateral or trilateral or multilateral alliances to further their own interest, as well as protect their sovereign rights and freedom of trade in the Indo-Pacific area. Even though most of these alliances are based on diplomatic ties, a few of the nations either already have military alliances or are moving a certain amount of their military forces in the region mostly in the shadow of 'friendly exercises' over the oceanic front.

The Republic of Korea Navy (ROKN) has about 150 ships and 70 aircraft. It has about 16 submarines, with no SSBN. The ROKN is likely to have its own aircraft carrier by 2033. The ROK Air Force has the F-5. F-15, F-16 and F-16 along with AEW&C and Air-to-Air Refuelling (AAR) aircraft. It also has about 30 transport aircraft and about 60 helicopters. The ROK has acquired a large number of US aircraft, missiles and other combat equipment from the USA. F-16s, F-35A Joint Strike Fighters (JSFs) and Apache attack helicopters form the mainstay of the ROK's air strike capability. The ROK also hosts about 28,000 personnel from various operational units of the US Marines, US Army and a contingent of the USAF. Sufficient numbers of technologically advanced weapons with support equipment have also been pre-positioned by the US forces. The ROK is in the process of procuring P-8, advanced munitions, upgraded PAC-3 missiles with additional F-16s. These systems are compatible with the existing ones and, thus, would enhance the interoperability with the US forces.[20] Other nations like France, the UK, Germany, Taiwan and Singapore have also committed some of their naval and air force elements in the region.

Joint Training Exercises: Realising the criticality of enhancing the interoperability amongst the naval and air force elements of Quad partners as well the other friendly nations of the IPMZ, a large number of training exercise were conducted in the region in the recent past. The major objectives of most of these exercises were to undertake drills like live weapon firing, advanced naval warfare manoeuvres, anti-submarine, anti-air, and anti-surface warfare drills along with large scale air operations from both carrier-based forces as well as land-based aerial platforms. The first of the series of such exercises was "Ex-Passex"; a bilateral exercise between the Indian Navy and the United States Navy. This was the first time that IAF fighters (SU-30 MKI and Jaguar) along with AWACS, FRA and AEW&C aircraft operated together with carrier-based aircraft from the USS *Ronald Reagan* Carrier Strike Group (CSG). This exercise was soon followed by the multilateral "Ex-Malabar-2021" amongst the forces of the Quad countries. This exercise was aimed at enhancing synergy and mutual understanding among the four navies in undertaking joint maritime security operations with large scale air operations from carrier and shore-based aircraft, under the high density air defence coverage. During the bilateral Exercise "Simbex" between Singapore and India, Fokker-50 maritime patrol aircraft, and F-16 fighters of the Singapore Navy undertook air operations along with the P-8I and MiG 29-K of the Indian Navy, besides the participation of a large number of naval warships. Subsequently, "Ex Konkan Shakti 2021" was conducted between the tri-service forces of India and the UK. The major highlight of all such training exercises was the substantial increase in the numbers and types of air operations; especially the carrier-based air operations, that unambiguously highlighted the criticality and war-winning capability of air power.

Air Power as the Balancing Force in the Region

Air power is primarily a flexible instrument of national policy that can efficiently be applied simultaneously in a wide variety of operational challenges comprising multiple traditional and non-traditional threats. Air power is especially useful in conducting intelligence, surveillance, and reconnaissance operations. It contributes to deterrence and, if required, can enable a "show of force"; engage in aerial denial operations (no-fly zones); and assist in facilitating economic sanctions via quarantine. In addition, if necessary, after seizing local or general air superiority, air power can conduct raids against specific targets; facilitate forced entry; and coerce adversaries. Finally, during periods of general armed hostilities, especially following the establishment of air superiority, air power can, alone or in combination with other elements of military power, perform such operational functions as theatre and point air defence, strategic bombing operations in order to degrade/destroy the adversary's critical infrastructure, war-waging potential, logistical capabilities, disrupt the adversary's ability to concentrate and deploy military and naval force,; conduct deep interdiction operations, provide close air support for friendly forces as they engage and, optimally destroy the enemy's field forces while ensuring uninterrupted support to sustain friendly forces in theatre.

Though the present combined lethal air power of the PLAAF and PLAN could be sufficient to retain its dominance in the Indo-Pacific over the joint might of India, Japan, the ROK, Taiwan and any other smaller country of Asian region, it would, however, fall short of its objectives, when faced with the combined might of the US and its alliance partners. This tilt of balance of power is primarily due to the large differential of air power in terms of strength, technology, weapon capability, precision, HVAA and AD capability that exists between the USAF combined forces and the PLAAF's capability. The large number of air operational missions that can be generated from the Carrier Battle Groups (CBGs) of USINDOPACOM will outnumber the combined effort of the single CBG of the PLAN and land-based air operations of the PLAAF. Such differential would not only limit the operational reach of the PLAAF but also that of the PLAN. The most crucial role in the air battle over the oceanic zones would be played by air operations launched from CBGs, specially the air operations like anti-submarine reconnaissance, air patrol, search and strike, Combat Search and Rescue (CSAR) and long range strike missions over enemy naval surface ships. A large number of CBGs of the USINDOPACOM, afloat the zone of contest, would be a force to reckon with, as round the clock fighter/UCAV air strike and air defence missions that can be launched to gain a Favourable Air Situation (FAS) over a specified zone would not only enable freedom of operation to friendly naval elements, but also would severely hamper the operations of the PLAN.

As observed in the recent past, the PLAAF has restricted itself to incursion over the skies of Taiwan only, while it continues to extend its naval reach into the Indian Ocean and part of the Western Pacific. Such outreach of the PLAN also had to be gradually restricted due to the large number of naval forces of the US, UK, France, Japan and Australia gradually moving into the zone of interest in the Indo-Pacific. Even within these naval elements, the aircraft carriers play the critical balancing role due to the reach and lethality of the aircraft and weapons on board these aircraft carriers, that severely restrict the movement of surface as well as sub-surface elements of naval power.

The airlift capability, aerial reconnaissance, Precision Guided Munitions (PGMs), extent and strength of AD systems with networks, extent of accessibility to satellite-based war-fighting capability, UCAV capability and technology advancement would all be the critical factors for achieving and retaining the edge for dominance over the IPMZ.

Conclusion

Air power would continue to play the pivotal role in any military engagement and the Indo-Pacific is no different. The balance of air power in numbers and quality is significantly in favour of the Quad countries and alliance partners vis-à-vis China. Future technology investments will be required by all four nations, coupled with the imperative to demonstrate seamless integration through new battle management systems. India and the US have already signed the four defence security cooperation enabling agreements, and with the ROK, Japan and Taiwan being the defence allies of the US, very potent air power exists over the IPMZ. The recent trilateral military alliance AUKUS raises this level of differential of military balance further in favour of the Quad forces.

Beijing is continuing to invest more in defence modernisation. It is focussed on securing regional dominance through building a networked, precision-strike capability. This would have to be countered. Space battle management is an area of key priority. Retaining space superiority is important. India's role in space development will provide the IOR connectivity and situational awareness. The need of speed would mean accelerated development of hypersonic weapons, especially for anti-shipping and high-value targets. The BrahMos would be the critical weapon of air superiority. The United States would need to have a larger bomber fleet to out-match China's projected 120 H-6s and 30 H-20s by 2030. More joint naval-air exercises in the Indo-Pacific region are required to bolster interoperability and synergy amongst the alliance member nations, be it Quad, AUKUS, JAI or AJI.

In addition to the large air and naval bases in Guam, joint-use basing in Papua New Guinea and the Andaman and Nicobar Islands could be considered. The latter is just west of the Malacca Strait, and can increase Quad air and naval presence in the IOR, and also serve as a strategic blunting option to deter aggression near the key trade corridor. The islands now have four air bases that can operate SU-30 MKI and take the P-8I. The US' exit from Afghanistan should allow a shift of resources and attention to the Indo-Pacific. Whether the Quad formally declares an alliance or not, the member nations must increase integration and expand basing options. These four nations are best positioned to ensure balance and freedom across the Indo-Pacific and air power would be the key balancing factor in any military engagement in the zone.

The rapid modernisation with cutting edge technology like hypersonic weapons at one end and UCAVs at the other; the reach, lethality, swift response firepower and net-centric operations make air power the dominant force, even over the vast expanse of the oceanic zone of the IPMZ.

Notes

1. Sheila A. Smith, "The Quad in the Indo-Pacific: What to Know", Council on Foreign Affairs, May 27, 2021. https://www.cfr.org/in-brief/quad-indo-pacific-what-know. Accessed on November 20, 2021.
2. Daisuke Atimoto, "China's Grand Strategy and the Emergence of Indo-Pacific Alignments", ISDP, April 14, 2021. https://isdp.eu/chinas-grand-strategy-and-the-emergence-of-indo-pacific-alignments/. Accessed on November 22, 2021.
3. "China's National Defence in the New Era", State Council Information Office of the People's Republic of China, July 2019, pp. 6-7. http://www.xinhuanet.com/english/2019-07/24/c_138253389.htm. Accessed on November 25, 2021.
4. Mordechai Chaziza, "China's Military Base in Djibouti", 2018. https://besacenter.org/wp-content/uploads/2018/08/153-Chaziza-Chinas-Military-Base-in-Djibouti-web.pdf. Accessed on November 24, 2021.
5. Thangavel K Balasubramanian and Ashok Kumar Murugesan, "China's Rising Missile and Naval Capability in Indo-Pacific", p. 2. https://media.defence.gov/2020/Jun/08/2002312001/-1/-1/1/DO_BALASUBRAMANIAM.PDF. Accessed on November 25, 2021.

6. The White House, "Statements and Releases", March 12, 2021. https://www.whitehouse.gov/briefing-room/statements-releases/2021/03/12/quad-leaders-joint-statement-the-spirit-of-the-quad/. Accessed on November 27, 2021.
7. Ibid.
8. Annual Report to Congress: Military and Security Developments Involving the People's Republic of China 2020. https://media.defence.gov/2020/Sep/01/2002488689/-1/-1/1/2020-DOD-CHINA-MILITARY-POWER-REPORT-FINAL.PDF. Accessed on December 4, 2021.
9. Ibid.
10. Ibid.
11. Balasubramanian and Murugesan, n. 5.
12. n. 8.
13. *The Military Balance 2021*, February 24, 2021. https://www.tandfonline.com/doi/full/10.1080/04597222.2021.1868790. Accessed on December 9, 2021.
14. *Defence Primer: Naval Forces*, In Focus, Congressional Research Service https://sgp.fas.org/crs/natsec/IF10486.pdf. Accessed on December 11, 2021.
15. Hemanth Kumar, "India vs China: A Comparison of the Indian and Chinese (PLA) Navies", *Naval Technology*, September 9, 2020. https://www.naval-technology.com/features/india-vs-china-indian-and-chinese-pla-navies compared/?utm_source=Army%20Technology&utm_medium=website&utm_campaign=Must%20Read&utm_content=Image. Accessed on December 18, 2021.
16. Indo-Pacific Strategy Report, Department of Defence, June 1, 2019. https://media.defence.gov/2019/Jul/01/2002152311/-1/-1/1/DEPARTMENT-OF-DEFENSE-INDO-PACIFIC-STRATEGY-REPORT-2019.PDF. Accessed on December 19, 2021.
17. Michael Beckley, "The Emerging Military Balance in East Asia: How China's Neighbors Can Check Chinese Naval Expansion", November 1, 2017. https://direct.mit.edu/isec/article/42/2/78/12177/The-Emerging-Military-Balance-in-East-Asia-How. Accessed on December 19, 2021.
18. n. 16.
19. "Australian Navy". https://www.navy.gov.au/fleet/ships-boats-craft/current-ships. Accessed on December 23, 2021.
20. PTI, Washington, August 27, 2020. https://www.business-standard.com/article/current-affairs/indo-pacific-epicentre-of-great-power-competition-with-china-esper-120082700534_1.html. Accessed on December 24, 2021.

PART II

India: A Critical Link in the Quad Diamond

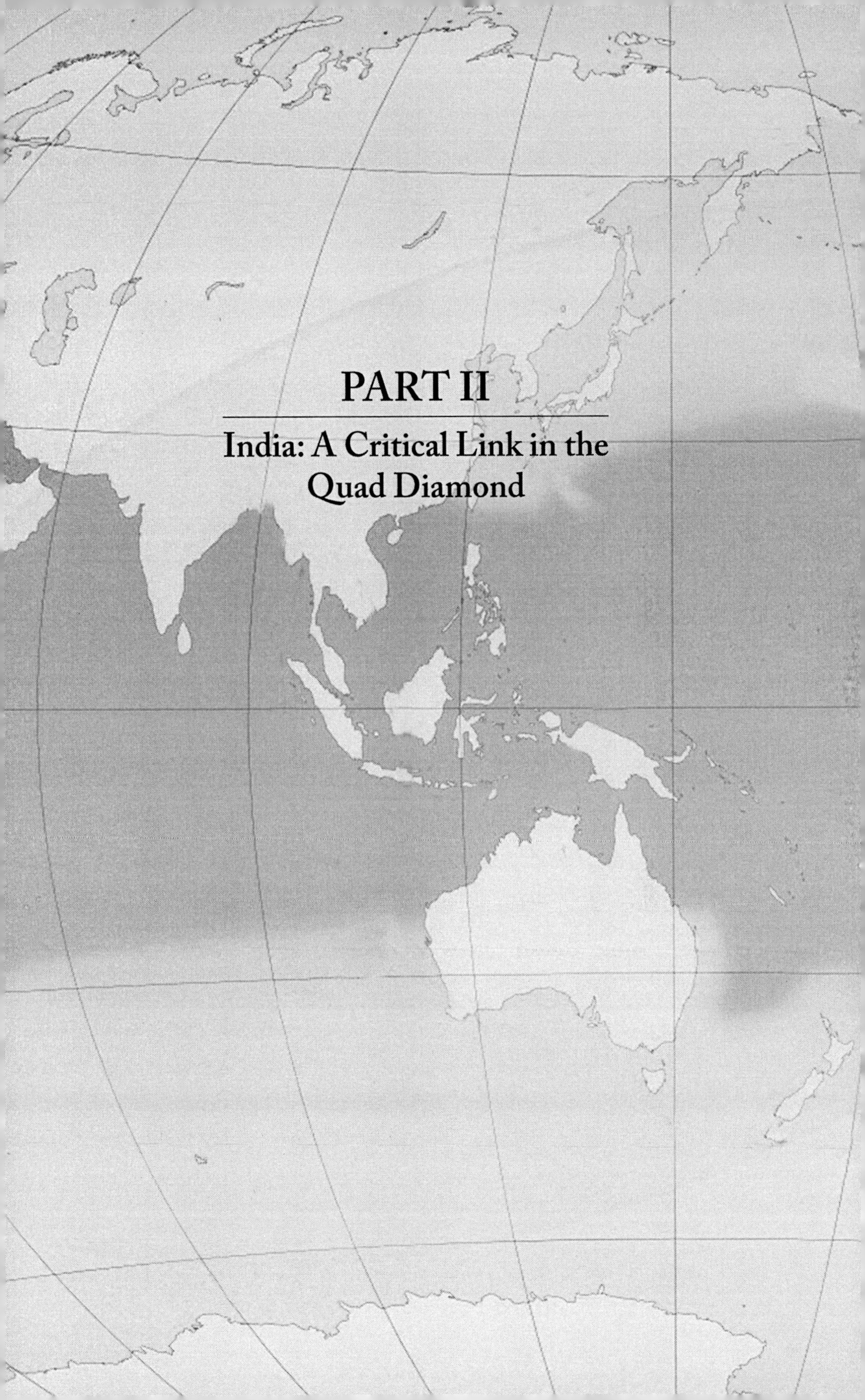

5. India-Japan Security Partnership: Convergence of Ideas, Interests and Strategies

Shamshad A. Khan

For Japan, the US was the "first, second and third"[1] most important partner country in the world. India did not fit into its strategic priorities. This remained so till a decade ago. Following the relative decline of the US; with the rise of China, the Japanese strategic thinking vis-à-vis India has changed drastically. Now, Japan considers India among the "primary drivers" of change in the "global balance of power." After acknowledging India's ascendance among the countries driving change in the global balance of power, Tokyo has shown keenness to "strengthen its relationship" with New Delhi in a "broad range of fields," including in "maritime security." It is worthy to note here that Shinzo Abe, in his much-talked book, *Towards a Beautiful Country*, had identified India as a country with which Japan should advance its "national interests". He predicted that "it will not be a surprise if in another decade, Japan-India relations overtake Japan-US and Japan-China ties."[2] He prophesied this in 2006 when he was the Chief Cabinet Secretary of Japan and was yet to assume the prime minister's post. After becoming prime minister and achieving the record of being the longest serving Japanese prime minister, Abe made utmost efforts to nurture the bilateral relations. However, almost one-and-half- decades after his speculation, India is yet to overtake the US as Japan's number one partner. Nonetheless, it occupies a central place in Japan's security and foreign policy priorities. This is evident from the number of agreements that the two countries have signed at both bilateral and multilateral levels. At the bilateral level, the strategic partnership agreement signed in 2006 was elevated to a "special strategic partnership" in 2014. The bilateral cooperation between the two countries has progressed in a broad range of fields including maritime security, trade, civil nuclear energy, space, human resource training and in the infrastructure sector.

At the minilateral level, Japan is partnering with India in at least two trilaterals: the Japan-India-America trilateral and Japan-India-Australia trilateral. Moreover, India is part of almost all the grand designs or ideas that the Japanese leaders have mooted at the multilateral level, especially after the end of the Cold War period. This includes Confluences of the Two Seas, which has transformed into an Indo-Pacific construct as well as the Democratic Security Diamond which has evolved into the Quadrilateral Security Initiative or Quad.

This raises the question: what led to this shift in the Japanese thinking towards India? Why did Japan, which, according to an Indian diplomat, "perceived India as a chaotic, dysfunctional, desperately poor country and not as a potential partner,"[3] start to consider India as worthy for partnership and a country with which its leadership was keen to advance Japan's "national interests"? To find the possible answers, two important events, one each taking place at the international and regional levels can guide us to understand the factors that led to India gaining prominence in the Japanese strategic thinking and policy priorities.

Starting with the international factor: with the collapse of the United Soviet Socialist Republics (USSR) and the end of the Cold War, the US achieved its primary purpose—containing the USSR—for stationing its forces in Japan. The American Administration's decision to scale down the presence of its troops in Europe brought the debate of a possible withdrawal of US forces in Japan to the fore, with Japan fearing a possible "abandonment" by its sole security ally: the US. Shintaro Ishihara, a maverick Liberal Democratic Party (LDP) leader, who later became governor of Tokyo and also formed his own political party, quotes a US Congressman in his book, *The Japan That Can Say No*, telling him, "US-Soviet ties have dramatically improved, and it is quite possible that the partnership between Washington and Tokyo might be dissolved... The United States may even abandon Japan."[4] Japan not meeting the US' expectation by not sending Japanese troops in the US led 1990 Iraq

War to liberate Kuwait had created a fissure and unease in the US-Japan security alliance. Though the Japanese leadership at that time did not pronounce it openly, it was probably looking for partners to complement the weakening US-Japan partnership. Around that time, Japanese Prime Minister Toshiki Kaifu announced a policy to make Japan a bridge between Asia and the West. Kaifu's pronouncement was a departure from the previous Japanese leaders' views who considered Japan a 'member of the West' although geographically located in Asia. Amid the rapidly changing political situation following the end of the Cold War, the collapse of the USSR and the Gulf War, which coincided with India's decision to liberalise its market, Toshiki Kaifu made a visit to New Delhi in 1990, becoming the fourth Japanese prime minister to visit India. During the visit, he announced a South Asia Initiative. Promotion of political and economic relations with India and other South Asian countries was an important pillar of this initiative. Kaifu also expressed Japan's commitment to support "the economic redevelopment and stability of South Asia by engaging in dialogue and cooperation."[5]

Among the regional factors, two events—India's decision to open its market, and the Indian Coast Guards' rescue operation of a Japanese flagged ship hijacked by pirates in the Indian Ocean—can be cited as events that drew Japan closer to India. As various analysts have pointed out, Japan viewed India as tilting towards the USSR during the Cold War period, even though New Delhi was spearheading the Non-Aligned Movement (NAM), a group of Afro-Asian nations neither siding with the US-led bloc nor joining the USSR-led world. Japan, on the other hand, was a US ally and firmly aligned with the West, politically and economically. During the Cold War set-up, and the perception about India in Japan, the political and economic interaction between India and Japan remained minimal. However, with the end of the Cold War, the political barrier that separated the two countries was over. Japanese investors and traders also saw opportunities in the newly liberalised Indian market and pushed their government for a fresh beginning with India. India also saw Japan as a potential partner for "both investment and technology"[6] required by India in the 1990s soon after liberalisation of the market. A series of political interactions between India and Japan took place at the time and both were looking to benefit from each other economically. A few years after India's economic liberalisation, both countries were on the path of forging a "complementary" economic relationship. India, however, remained low in Japan's strategic and security priorities.

Meanwhile, in the "Japan-US Joint Declaration on Security Alliance for the 21st Century," issued in 1996, the American leadership renewed its "commitment to the defence of Japan as well as peace and stability in the Asia-Pacific."[7] The joint declaration noted that "there has been some adjustment of US forces in the Asia-Pacific region since the end of the Cold War,"[8] but the US assured Japan of continued US military presence in Japan. In the joint declaration, it was also noted that the US will maintain its "current force structure" in East Asia "including about the current level in Japan."[9] This allayed Japan's concern of the US abandoning it, which was doing the rounds in strategic circles and, thus, Japan's quest for a new security partner following a possible US drawdown from the region was put to rest. However, policy planners in Tokyo decided to continue political and economic engagement with India which it had built up amid the possibility of an American abandonment of Japan.

The event that triggered Japan to think about security cooperation with India was the hijacking incident of the *Alondra Rainbow* by pirates in the Indian Ocean in 1999. The *Alondra Rainbow*, a Japanese flagged merchant vassal, was hijacked by pirates and was subsequently rescued by the Indian Coast Guard. The growing cases of piracy in the Indian Ocean and beyond and interruption of its trade threatened Japan's economic security. For Japan, a trading island nation which depends on the sea lanes for 98 per cent of its in-bound and out-bound trade, India became an indispensable partner, especially after this incident. The rescue mission of the *Alondra Rainbow* by the Indian Coast Guard, "opened a new chapter in Indo-Japan relations."[10] The next year, India and Japan agreed to conduct "joint training in tackling piracy"[11] by the Japanese and Indian Coast Guards. The maritime cooperation that started with cooperation between the Coast Guards has been elevated to the navies level.

After deepening its economic as well as security cooperation, especially maritime security cooperation, with India, Japan turned its focus towards forging a "global partnership" between the two countries. During

Japanese Prime Minister Yoshiro Mori's visit to New Delhi in 2000, India and Japan agreed that "relations between the two nations, which offer great possibilities for both parties, would be further strengthened, not just bilaterally but also by playing a role together regionally and internationally."[12]

The relationship got further impetus in 2006 during Japanese Prime Minister Junichiro Koizumi's visit to New Delhi when Japan signed a global and strategic partnership agreement with India. The two countries in their joint statement agreed that they "view each other as partners that have responsibilities for, and are capable of, responding to global and regional challenges in their global partnership."[13] Moreover, the joint statement asserted that "a strong prosperous and dynamic India is ... in the interest of Japan and vice versa." This set the tone and tenor of the India-Japan future partnership. Both countries announced the "eight-fold initiative" to advance their partnership. This included almost all possible areas of bilateral cooperation from the fields of culture, economy, trade, science and technology to security. In the same year, India-Japan agreed to "institutionalise" an annual prime ministerial level meeting which would take place alternating between the two capitals, New Delhi and Tokyo. Ever since the institutionalisation of summit level talks, the prime ministers of the two countries have met almost each year (except during the pandemic period when in-person interaction could not take place) and have reviewed the bilateral agenda; they have assessed the progress on the commitments they took during the previous years; and have identified further areas of bilateral cooperation. Before the institutionalisation of summit level talks, the relationship between India and Japan was a bilateral one and largely ad-hoc. It was personality driven and lacked consistency.[14] The annual summit meetings have helped it make an interest-driven and agenda-driven bilateral partnership. This is evident from the fact that the change of leadership and government in both countries has not hampered the ongoing bilateral relationship. For example, in India both the United Progressive Alliance (UPA) and National Democratic Alliance (NDA) governments have accorded it the same priority when to deepening the relationship with Japan. Similarly, in Japan, the change from the Liberal Democratic Party (LDP) to the Democratic Party of Japan (DPJ) in

2009, the foreign policy priorities of the Tokyo regime remained the same. On the issue of promoting the security, economic and people-to-people relationship between India and Japan, there is a bipartisan consensus in Japan as well as in India. In short, because of the institutionalisation of the prime ministerial level summit talks, the bilateral relationship between the two countries remains immune to a political change in both countries.

India-Japan Relations: Convergence of Ideas

This section explains why there is bipartisan support in both New Delhi and Tokyo, briefly discussed above, for the India-Japan relationship and why the bilateral relationship is likely to remain immune from political changes in both countries. To understand the present and future course of any country's foreign policy priorities and national interests towards another country or region, its strategic doctrines give clear clues. As regards Japan, its National Security Strategy (NSS), unveiled for the first time in 2014 by the country and various National Defence Guidelines which the East Asian country releases at intervals of ten years, or a bit early if a drastic overhaul of the security priorities is needed, give definite clues about its strategic priorities' vis-à-vis a country and region. The first noticeable change in Japan's strategic thinking vis-à-vis India in its defence policy doctrine was witnessed in the 2011 Defence Guidelines. While the Defence Guidelines issued during the DPJ government considered the US "indispensable" for Japan's security with which it will continue to deepen its security relationship, it added that Japan will "strengthen the network of security cooperation through bilateral and multilateral frameworks in the Asia-Pacific region." It identified India among countries with which Japan will "enhance security cooperation."[15] India also figured prominently in securing Japan's maritime security from the Horn of Africa to Japan. Japan's 2011 Defence Guidelines noted that Japan shares "common interests" with India in "ensuring the security of maritime navigation from Africa and the Middle East to East Asia."[16]

Considering that Japan treated the US as its sole security ally and other countries did not even figure remotely in its security policy, this was a perceptible shift in Japan's defence policy. When Japan unveiled its first National Security Strategy (NSS) document in 2014, clubbing the country's defence and diplomatic policies to enhance Japanese security, India yet again figured prominently. First, it identified India as among the countries that are "primary drivers" of change in the global "balance of power."[17] Second, it acknowledged that India remains "important for Japan" because of its "geographic location." For these two main reasons, Japan stated that it will strengthen cooperation with India to secure its maritime interests.[18] The NSS doctrine articulated that Tokyo will strengthen cooperation in maritime security through joint training and exercises as well as joint implementation of international peace cooperation activities.[19] Most importantly, it noted that "India is becoming increasingly influential" in the international community and Japan "shares universal values and strategic interests with it."[20]

In the successive National Defence Programme Guidelines (NDPG) issued in 2014 and 2019, India was mentioned among the countries with which Japan wants to enhance its security partnership. The 2014 NDPG, issued by the LDP government noted that there has been a "relative change of influence of the United States" because of the rise of China and India.[21] The document reiterated that "Japan will strengthen its relationship with India in a broad range of fields, including maritime security, through joint training and exercises as well as joint implementation of international peacekeeping activities."[22] Continuing on the commitment to deepen bilateral security cooperation, the 2019 Defence Guidelines, expressed the willingness to "promote joint training and exercises and defence equipment and technology cooperation"[23] with India. It also hinted at the revival of the quadrilateral partnership which had been shelved in 2007, following China's objections. The Defence Guidelines noted that "Japan will also strengthen cooperation among Japan, India and the United States."[24]

The Japanese strategic thinking vis-à-vis India in the official documents also finds resonance in the opinion papers written by Japanese experts and foreign policy analysts. A few examples representing the Japanese strategic thinking are cited here. Yuriko Koike, a former Defense Minister of Japan, present Tokyo Governor, had written a number of opinion pieces advocating greater cooperation between India and Japan. In one of the opinion pieces contributed to the *Japan Times*, she argued for the need to construct a security architecture without China. She opined that "America alone cannot construct a viable security structure for the region. From India to Japan, every Asian country must play its part."[25] Koike added that "fear of provoking China should not stop Asia's leaders from seeking a regional security consensus …".[26] Similarly, academician Takashi Shiraishi, who in the past has held various to positions in institutions in Tokyo, and is currently vice chancellor of Kumamoto Prefectural University, considers India as one of the important elements in forging a regional balance of power. He opines that "Japan's relations with India should remain grounded in the Japan-US alliance. Engaging with India within the framework of the Japan-US alliance is a balancing act in some aspects."[27]

A greater convergence is found in the Indian view about partnership with Japan. Even though India does not officially release strategic documents, the priority it accords to Japan is evident from the statements of Indian leaders. In the context of India-Japan relations, the then Indian Prime Minister Manmohan Singh, voiced his support for creating a stable regional order in Asia[28] and his willingness to partner with Japan. Manmohan Singh said, "India's relations with Japan are important not only for our economic development, but also because we see Japan as a natural and indispensable partner in our quest for stability and peace in the vast region in Asia…."[29] He further emphasised that "there are strong synergies between our economies, which need an open, rule-based international trading system to prosper."[30] Similarly, Prime Minister Modi on various occasions, has termed Japan as India's most trusted partner.[31]

This thinking has percolated down to the level of analysts, academicians, and strategic experts. A few representative views of Indian strategic experts are being cited here because of the paucity of space. Indian strategic thinker and analyst, Brahma Chellaney views the deepening India-Japan bilateral relationship as a significant milestone in building the "Asian power equilibrium."[32] Similarly, K.S. Bajpai also sees India-Japan relations from the prism of "power-politics and balance of power calculations" terming these as "facts of life" and strongly advocates increasing defence cooperation with Japan amid the growing Chinese hostility against India.[33] C. Rajamohan believes that "a genuine strategic partnership between India and Japan will be a game-changer for Asian geopolitics."[34] Another leading Indian strategic thinker, Harsh V. Pant, writing about the bilateral strategic partnership opines that "India seems most willing to acknowledge Japan's centrality in shaping the evolving Asia-Pacific security architecture."[35]

Given how India viewed Japan, especially during the Cold War period, it becomes amply clear how drastically the perceptions of both countries about each other have changed. Lalit Mansingh, a retired Indian diplomat, reminiscing about the bilateral relationship during the Cold War period said that India had at that time dismissed Japan as a "camp follower of the US," and Japan viewed India as "a chaotic, dysfunctional, desperately poor country and not as a potential partner."[36] Quite contrary to this, their present strategic thinking reflects a profound change in their attitude towards each other. Rather than looking at each other through the old Cold War prism, they have added pragmatism to their strategic thinking and see each other as indispensable partners.[37] As a result of continuous interactions between the Indian and Japanese leaders, various grand ideas have emerged from such strategic thinking. This has been discussed in the next section.

The Convergence of Ideas and Strategic Thinking: Assessing the Impact

The India-Japan strategic partnership has paved the way for greater engagement between the two countries at the global and bilateral levels. Let me examine the impact of strategic convergence at the global level first. As mentioned earlier, India has been part of Japan's grand ideas and designs mooted and formulated after the Cold War. When Japan mooted the idea of an Arc of Freedom and Prosperity, consisting of existing and budding democracies in 2006, India was considered an indispensable partner in creating this arc. Then came the idea of the Confluence of the Two Seas in 2007, mooted by Abe during his address to the Indian Parliament, which gradually transformed into an Indo-Pacific construct in 2016. Japan's idea of the Indo-Pacific is based on the "two continents" and "two oceans" strategy. Its Diplomatic Bluebook elaborates that "two continents", Asia and Africa, and the "two oceans", the free and open Pacific and Indian Oceans, hold the key to stability and prosperity in the international community.[38] Soon after Japan's Indo-Pacific strategy, the US also announced its own Indo-Pacific strategy. In both versions of the Indo-Pacific strategies, India figures prominently. Both powers want to engage and partner with India in all the three dimensions—military, economic and infrastructure—of the Indo-Pacific strategy. The Quad, revived in 2017, is anchored towards achieving military objectives. At the consultative level, it serves as a mechanism to discuss various security issues, and at the operational level, the navies of the four countries have revived the Malabar naval exercise. An apparent aim of the naval exercise is to keep the sea lines of communication free and open so that flow of trade and goods takes place without interventions from both non-state and state actors.

Another emerging strand of the Indo-Pacific strategy is focussed on geoeconomics. This strategy aims to counter China's growing economic clout in Asia and beyond, and seeks China's economic isolation. It stems from the assumption that China has financially benefited from the post-war liberal economic order created by the West after joining the World Trade Organisation (WTO) in 2001 but has not democratised itself as per the Western expectations. As the economic interdependence between the US and China has not yielded the expected results, Washington and its Asian allies are mulling on various strategies, from easing their economic interdependence to "decoupling of China."[39] The Japanese administration's policy to provide subsidies to its companies to move out their production bases from China to other countries, including ASEAN, India and Bangladesh, is aimed in that direction. In addition to this, India, Japan, and Australia have launched a new Supply Chain Resilience Initiative (SCRI) with apparent American backing. The new supply chain initiative aims at easing the three countries' economic dependence on China, especially after the COVID-19 crisis which impacted the flow of supply of critical goods and resources. Efforts are also on to not let China dominate the telecommunication sector with its 5G technology. Most of these mechanisms and strategies are aimed at China's economic and technological isolation, the way the United Socialist Soviet Republics

(USSR) was isolated from the West-led liberal order during the Cold War period, leading to its political demise.

Infrastructure is another area where India and Japan are trying to match China strength to strength, especially following China's Belt and Road Initiative (BRI), which has given Beijing enough political and diplomatic clout in the recipient countries. The democratic countries have various plans, including Japan's Partnership in Quality Infrastructure and India's and Japan's bilateral cooperation in the Asia-Africa Growth Corridor.

All the three dimensions of the Indo-Pacific strategy, mentioned above, are aimed at achieving one strategic objective: balancing China.

As regards the impact of convergence of strategies between India and Japan at the bilateral level, the impact can be seen on security and defence cooperation, economic cooperation, technology transfer and infrastructure cooperation. The most visible impact can be witnessed on security cooperation at both consultative and operational levels. At the consultative level, India and Japan have elevated the 2 plus 2 dialogue to a ministerial level. Till 2018, the 2 plus 2 talks between the two countries used to take place between India's defence and foreign secretaries and their Japanese counterparts. It must be noted here that other powers such as the US, Japan, Australia, etc. had been conducting 2 plus 2 dialogues at the defence and foreign ministers level to discuss security and defence issues. India kept the 2 plus 2 dialogue with Japan at the bureaucratic level, apparently, not to offend China, as experts in the Chinese strategic circles viewed the growing ties with Japan as a China containment strategy. However, following the Chinese hostility growing towards India, New Delhi has shed its inhibitions and has agreed for elevating this dialogue to the ministerial level since 2019. A 2 plus 2 dialogue led by ministers will help the two countries discuss emerging security challenges and develop strategies to address those challenges.

As a result of the enhanced consultative mechanism between the two countries at the leadership level, bilateral engagement between the defence forces has increased at the operational level. The impact is most visible in the field of maritime security. Maritime cooperation between the Indian Navy and its Japanese counterpart, the Maritime Self-Defence Force, has increased. The bilateral naval exercises between the two navies, including port calls have become a routine event. Moreover, the two countries are institutionalising an annual maritime dialogue. In this forum, India and Japan discuss a plethora of issues pertaining to traditional and non-traditional security, including maritime security, cooperation in shipping, marine science, and technology and marine biodiversity.

In the security realm, signing of the Acquisition of Cross Services Agreement (ACSA) in September 2020 is another noteworthy development. The ACSA ensures "reciprocal provision of supply and services" between the two countries' armed forces.[40] The ACSA will help enhance interoperability and logistics support between the Japanese and Indian armed forces during international peace and security cooperation as well as in disaster relief operations. The implementation of the provisions of the ACSA will promote closer cooperation between the two strategic partners that are keen to play an active role in the promotion of peace and security of the international community.

Economy and trade comprises another area where cooperation between the two countries has deepened. As India signed the strategic partnership with Japan, it realised that the volume of bilateral trade between the two countries remains low. The Indian leadership was of the view that it is important to forge a complementary economic relationship to give a fillip to the strategic partnership. After rounds of negotiations, a Comprehensive Economic Partnership Agreement (CEPA) was signed in 2011. As part of CEPA, India and Japan agreed to bring down the tariff on almost 90,000 goods traded between the two countries in a phased manner.[41] The CEPA increased the volume of bilateral trade within years of coming into effect. The bilateral trade between India and Japan jumped to US$ 18 billion in 2010-11, from US$ 13 billion a year before the implementation of CEPA. However, it also increased the trade imbalance between the two countries, putting this in Japan's favour.[42]

Cooperation in the field of technology is another area where the bilateral partnership has made substantial progress. Notable in this technological cooperation is the signing of a civil nuclear cooperation agreement between India and Japan in 2016. The Japanese government had hesitated because of opposition from some of its domestic constituencies.[43]

However, because of India's consistent nudging, and considering the economic benefits for its nuclear companies, the Japanese government gave its consent to sign nuclear deal. Even though the Japanese technology is yet to be used in the proposed nuclear plants in India, the deal will pave the way for increasing the percentage of renewable energy in India's overall energy mix. As India has committed during the Conference of the Parties-26 (COP-26) to achieve net zero carbon emission by 2070, Japanese nuclear technology will help the country achieve this target.

Notable progress has also been made in India-Japan cooperation in the infrastructure sector. India has already improved its mass transit system by building the metro network in Indian cities with the help of Japan. Japan has also helped upgrade the capacity of various ports in the Indian coastal cities. India has launched two mega projects, the Delhi Mumbai Industrial Corridor and Mumbai-Ahmedabad High Speed Railway with the help of Japan. Both projects have the potential to transform India's economic and infrastructural landscape.

Conclusion

The short analysis of India-Japan relations presented above, suggests that both countries have made substantial progress in their bilateral relationship, especially after the end of the Cold War. There is greater convergence in the ideas and strategies of Japan and India at the bilateral and global levels. However, there are areas where the partnership still has to cover some ground. One such area is cooperation in defence technologies and their transfer to India. India had shown interest in procuring Japan's US-2 amphibious aircraft as well as the diesel propelled Soryu class submarine. Despite the government-to-government understanding between India and Japan over the US-2 amphibious aircraft, actual procurement has been delayed. There are reports in the media that the US-2 Shinmeiwa will jointly be produced with Mahindra. However, when the first aircraft will be handed over to the Indian Navy to be used for search and rescue operations remains unclear. As regards sharing of other Japanese defence technology with India, there remains some hesitancy among a section of Japanese companies. Despite the Indian defence market having a huge potential for Japanese companies, some remain cautious and concerned about a possible leakage of their defence technologies.[44] They believe that leakage of their technology will undermine their competitive edge in the global market.

Lastly, while India and Japan have a greater understanding about the emerging security threat in the Asian region and beyond, it will, according to a Japanese security expert, be difficult for Japan to undertake a "joint operation" with India in a "real battle" should a situation arise in the future. This is largely because India uses "Russian military equipment." While Japan has already entered the US network, "the United States will not allow the Russian or Chinese equipment to enter the network." The actual battle, nowadays, is based on network-centric operations. In a real battle situation, India and Japan would have to use common assets or equipment.[45] Given the "network" bottleneck, the India-Japan cooperation would have a limited option in the wake of a real crisis or conflict situation. In the other fields, it will continue to deepen further.

Notes

1. Shinzo Abe, "Two Democracies Meet at Seas: For a Better and Safer Asia," remarks made at the Indian Council of World Affairs (ICWA), New Delhi, during the ICWA-Japan Institute for National Fundamentals joint seminar, September 20, 2011. https://en.jinf.jp/wp-content/uploads/2011/09/HP-E%E3%82%A4%E3%83%B3%E3%83%89%E6%BC%94%E8%AA%AC%E4%BC%9A%E5%A0%B4%E9%85%8D%E5%B8%83%E7%94%A8916.pdf
2. Shinzo Abe quoted by Yasushi Watanabe in Shamshad A. Khan, *Changing Dynamics of India-Japan Relations: Buddhism to Special Strategic Partnership* (New Delhi: Pentagon Press), p. xi.
3. Lalit Mansingh, "India-Japan Relations", IPCS Issue Brief No. 43, Institute of Peace and Conflict Studies, New Delhi, January 2007. https://www.files.ethz.ch/isn/44657/IPCS-IssueBrief-No43.pdf
4. Shintaro Ishihara, *The Japan that Can Say No* (New York 1991: Simon and Schuster), pp. 77-78.
5. Toshiki Kaifu, "Japan and South Asia: In Pursuit of Dialogue and Cooperation," April 30, 1990, Text of Prime Minister Kishis' address available in PA Narsimha Murthy, *India and Japan: Dimensions of their Relations* (New Delhi: Lancer Book, 1992), pp. 434-448.
6. J.N. Dixit, *My South Block Years: Memoirs of a Foreign Secretary* (New Delhi: Publishers and Distributors, 1996), pp. 262-263.

7. Ministry of Defence (Japan), "Japan-US Joint Declaration on Security Alliance for the 21st century," April 17, 1996. https://www.mod.go.jp/en/j-us-alliance/joint-declaration/21century/index.html#:~:text=Major%20Exercises-,Japan%2DUS%20Joint%20Declaration%20on%20Security%2C%20Alliance%20for%20the%2021st,1.&text=The%20strong%20Alliance%20between%20Japan,economic%20growth%20in%20this%20region.
8. Ibid.
9. Ibid.
10. Prabhakaran Paleri, "The Pirates and Indo-Japan Relations", *Ship and Ocean News Letter*, No. 198, No. 5, 2206, pp. 7-8.
11. Nayan Chandra, "After the Bomb, India is Forging Ties with Japan and Vietnam as it Seeks to Establish Itself as a Player in Regional Security," *Far Eastern Review*, April 13, 2000.
12. Ministry of Foreign Affairs (Japan), "Japan-India Summit Meeting (Summary)," August 23, 2000. https://www.mofa.go.jp/region/asia-paci/pmv0008/india_s.html
13. Ministry of External Affairs (India), "India-Japan Relations". https://www.mea.gov.in/Portal/ForeignRelation/Japan_Relations_-_Jan_2013.pdf
14. Shamshad A. Khan, "Role of Forums and Institutional Mechanisms in the India-Japan Partnership of Prosperity," in Jagannath P. Panda, ed., *Scaling India-Japan Cooperation in Indo-Pacific and Beyond 2025: Corridors, Connectivity and Contours*, (New Delhi: KW Publishers, 2019).
15. Shamshad A. Khan, "Japan's New Defence Guidelines: An Analysis," *Strategic Analysis*, Vol. 35, No. 3, 2011, pp. 391-395.
16. Ministry of Foreign Affairs (Japan), National Defence Program Guidelines, 2011, p. 9. https://www.mofa.go.jp/policy/security/pdfs/h23_ndpg_en.pdf
17. Ministry of Foreign Affairs (Japan), *National Security Strategy,* Government of Japan, 2013, p. 6.
18. Ibid., p. 24.
19. Ministry of Defence (Japan), "National Defence Programmes Guidelines for 2014 and Beyond" (Summary), p. 24.
20. n. 17, p. 23.
21. n. 19.
22. Ibid., p. 11.
23. Ministry of Defence (Japan), "National Defence Programme Guidelines for FY 2019 and Beyond," p. 16.
24. Ibid.
25. Yuriko Koike, "To Kowtow or Cooperate in Asia," *The Japan Times*, September 18, 2014.
26. Ibid.

27. Takashi Shiraishi, "Crafting Japan's Asia Policy in a Multipolar World," *Japan Echo*, August 2008, p. 29.
28. Also see, Shamshad A. Khan, "India-Japan Cooperation Towards a Rule Based Order in the Asia-Pacific: Mapping Indian and Japanese Strategic Thinking," Japan Institute for International Affairs, Tokyo, December 15, 2018. https://www2.jiia.or.jp/pdf/fellow_report/151218_Shamshad_Khan_JIIA_paper_Final.pdf. Accessed on May 30, 2019.
29. Ministry of External Affairs (India), "Prime Minister's Address to Japan-India Association, Japan-India Parliamentary Friendship League and International Friendship Exchange Council;" full text of Manmohan Singh's speech is available at http://www.mea.gov.in/Speeches-Statements.htm?dtl/21754/Prime+Ministers+address+to+JapanIndia+Association+JapanIndia+Parliamentary+Friendship+League+and+International+Friendship+Exchange+Council
30. Ibid.
31. "Japan is One of India's Most Trusted Partners, says Modi Ahead of Visit", *Xinhua*, October 27, 2018. http://www.xinhuanet.com/english/2018-10/27/c_137562206.htm
32. Brahma Chellaney, "Japan, India: Natural Allies," *The Japan Times*, August 16, 2017.
33. K.Shankar Bakpai, "Japan, India and the Balance of Power," *The Hindu*, January 27, 2014.
34. C. Rajamohan, "Talking Tokyo," *The Indian Express*, May 27, 2013.
35. Harsh V. Pant, "Turning Towards Tokyo," *Business Standard*, January 1, 2012.
36. Mansingh, n. 3.
37. n. 14.
38. Ministry of Foreign Affairs (Japan), "Japan's Diplomatic Blue Book 2017, p. 30.
39. Jason Morgan, " Japan Decoupling from China the Best Thing That Could Happen to East Asia," *Japan Forward*, June 24, 2020. https://japan-forward.com/japan-decoupling-from-china-the-best-thing-that-could-happen-to-east-asia/
40. Ministry of Foreign Affairs (Japan), The text of ACSA can be accessed at https://www.mofa.go.jp/files/100091751.pdf
41. Shamshad A. Khan, "India-Japan Politico-Economic Engagement, Institute for Developing Economy-*JETRO*, VRF Series No. 482, 2013.
42. Shamshad A. Khan, "India-Japan Economic Partnership: Potentials, Promises and Prospect," Policy Research Institute, Ministry of Finance, Government of Japan, Tokyo, 2019. https://www.mof.go.jp/pri/international_exchange/visiting_scholar_program/Shamshad2.pdf
43. Shamshad A. Khan, "Indo-Japan Memorandum on Civil Nuclear Cooperation Concerns and Challenges," *Economic and Political Weekly*, Vol. 51, Issue No. 14, April 2, 2016.

44. Shamshad A. Khan, *Changing Dynamics of India-Japan Relations: Buddhism to Special Strategic Partnership* (New Delhi: Pentagon Press 2017), p. 180.
45. Author's interview with a Japanese security expert who previously served in the Japanese Maritime Self-Defence Force, in New Delhi, on September 16, 2015.

6. Accelerating India-Australia Cooperation for a Secure and Prosperous Indo-Pacific

Peter Layton

Australia and India are both continental-sized nations within the Indo-Pacific region and on whose shores the Indian Ocean washes up. Even so, for some decades, it seemed that the relationship between the two was limited to simply the Commonwealth, cricket and curry. The times have changed. Geostrategic forces, globalisation and the rush of technology are now overcoming geographic separation and pushing the two nations into an ever closer political, economic, diplomatic and military embrace.

This shift has not happened slowly. Instead, the last five years have seen an accelerating flurry of activity both between the two nations, and between them and other regional and extra-regional states. The most important of these for both Australia and India has arguably been the formation of the Quadrilateral Security Dialogue (Quad), a formal but rather loose arrangement that brings the US, Japan, India and Australia together.

The Quad remains work-in-progress but has quickly become a dynamic grouping with considerable ambitions. Prime Minister Narendra Modi, speaking recently, declared that the Quad is now a "force for global good", with a positive and practical agenda that will advance prosperity and security in the Indo-Pacific and beyond.[1]

This chapter focusses on the evolving relationship between Australia and India in this time of Indo-Pacific dynamism. This immense area, where more than half the people of the world live, is moving towards adopting a new regional order but what that will be is not yet decided. In this, Australia and India intend to use their agencies to shape a favourable future for themselves. This chapter accordingly takes a forward leaning stance, looking out across the forthcoming decade.

The first section of this chapter reviews the current Australia-India relationship with its newly created institutions and rapidly developing interactions. The second section considers some key contemporary issues concerning prosperity where cooperation might deepen the relationship: cyber, hydrogen energy, rare earths, and critical and emerging technology. The third section deliberates on security collaboration through discussing the two nations' strategic foci, the possibilities for increased defence interaction and a potential defence technology cooperation approach. The final section considers the different longer-term aspirations of both nations and concludes that Australia may need to be as pragmatic as India now is, that future progress will require effort, and given both nations' limited resources, some tough prioritisation may be necessary.

A Suddenly Deepening Bond

In June 2020, Australia and India upgraded their relationship to the level of a Comprehensive Strategic Partnership (CSP). This strategic-level agreement is built on a vision of an open, free, rules-based Indo-Pacific, common national interests and their shared values of democracy and the rule of law. The CSP is remarkably wide-ranging and covers many diverse areas for cooperation, including science, technology, maritime security, defence, economics, agriculture, education, culture and tourism.[2] At the same time, Australia and India decided to upgrade their secretaries 2+2 dialogue (defence and foreign affairs) to the ministerial level. Their first meeting was held in New Delhi in September 2021.[3]

The two countries are also members of several regional and global institutions and sometimes coordinate their positions on specific issues. These include the Indian Ocean Rim Association (IORA), the G20 intergovernmental forum, and three Association of Southeast Asian Nations (ASEAN)-led groups: the ASEAN Regional Forum (ARF), ASEAN Defence Ministers' Meeting Plus and East Asia Summit (EAS). There are further connections through two minilateral groupings: the Australia-India-Japan dialogue, with the most recent involving trade ministers; and the Australia-India-Indonesia dialogue, recently promoted to foreign and defence ministers level.[4] At times, these various institutions may overlap, but nonetheless in combination, considerably thicken the web of regional cooperation and trust building.

Given this increasing contact, a number of specialised arrangements have been agreed between Australia and India, with three particularly pertinent to this chapter. First, in June 2020, the Mutual Logistic Support Arrangement and the Defence Science and Technology Implementing Arrangement were both concluded. The logistics arrangement aims to improve military interoperability through enhanced cross-servicing, enabling more complex military-to-military engagement and faster responsiveness to regional humanitarian disasters. The science and technology arrangement provides a solid framework for Australian and Indian defence research collaboration supporting the maintenance of a technological edge and the development of new defence capabilities.[5]

Second, in April 2021, the Supply Chain Resilience Initiative was launched by the Australian, Indian and Japanese trade ministers. The initiative aims to create resilient supply chains through risk management, continuity plans, trade and investment diversification, enhanced utilisation of digital technology and sharing of best practices.[6] Third, in November 2021, the establishment of an Australia-India Centre of Excellence for Critical and Emerging Technologies was announced. This centre will provide a practical platform for Australia and India to work together to shape technology governance that aligns with their shared values and advances an open, inclusive, rules-based Indo-Pacific. The centre will also work to reduce delays in policy and regulatory changes needed for emerging technologies, promote emerging technologies and serve as a prototype for an envisioned Indo-Pacific critical technology network.[7]

In the defence domain, there is also an increasing pace of activity. The principal bilateral Australia-India Exercise (AUSINDEX) has been held every two years since 2015. AUSINDEX 2019 was the largest ever Australian defence deployment to India and involved four warships, P-8 maritime patrol aircraft and more than 1,000 navy, army and air force personnel. A Collins class submarine also participated.[8] The 2021 exercise, while impacted by the pandemic, saw two Indian warships, the INS

Shivalik and *Kadmatt*, operate from Darwin and exercise with Australian warships, P-8s and fighter aircraft.[9]

Australian warships also participated in the large multilateral Exercise Malabar in 2020 and 2021, working with Indian, American and Japanese naval vessels.[10] India agreed at the inaugural Foreign and Defence Ministers 2+2 meeting to Australia's ongoing participation in this major exercise.

In 2018, the Indian Air Force first participated in Exercise Pitch Black, a major multinational air defence exercise in Darwin. India deployed four Sukhoi SU-30MKI fighters, a C-17 strategic transport, and a C-130 tactical transport aircraft. The exercise also included the first mid-air refuelling of an Indian fighter aircraft by an Australian air-to-air refuelling aircraft, a KC-30A.[11] These exercises highlighted that the Australian and Indian militaries are becoming increasingly interoperable in operating C-17, C-130 and P-8 aircraft, as well as Chinook heavy-lift helicopters. Less apparent are the ongoing personnel and training exchanges, for example, both nations send senior officers to their respective staff and defence colleges.

Against this backdrop of an accelerating bilateral relationship has been the sudden revitalisation of the Quad. The Quad's origins date back to the December 2004 tsunami, the associated humanitarian crisis and the cooperation it engendered. After some membership turmoil, the Quad was reconfigured and recommenced in 2017 as a senior officials meeting. By 2021, it had grown into a significant international meeting at the national leadership level and was hosted by the US at the White House. The Quad has become a diplomatic network where Australia, India, Japan and the United States engage through four principal channels: leaders, foreign ministers, senior officials, and experts.

From initially lacking purpose, through unease about possibly being a quasi-military pact, the Quad now has a declared galvanising "spirit." Drawing on this, the four leaders have defined the Quad as being committed "to promoting a free, open rules-based order, rooted in international law to advance security and prosperity and counter threats both in the Indo-Pacific and beyond."[12] Such a broad vision means that today's Quad is not narrowly focussed but instead covers an expansive set of issues including vaccines, critical and emerging technology, cyber security, climate change, infrastructure, maritime security, countering disinformation, counter-terrorism, and humanitarian assistance and disaster relief.[13]

Such diversity of interests reflects that in the contemporary international system, issues cannot be easily separated from one another. Instead, the complex relationships and dynamic interaction between issues cannot be addressed by a narrow focus. Recognising this, the Quad offers a forum where each partner can share assessments of the region's emerging challenges and discuss possible initiatives that might be implemented individually, collectively or even in conjunction with other states outside the group.[14]

In this, the Quad is by design highly flexible. It is not being institutionalised and there will be no permanent secretariat. Nor are there plans to expand the Quad's membership, although some other countries have apparently displayed interest. Instead, the intention is to allow the four countries to develop patterns of cooperation as they seek to advance prosperity and security, regionally and beyond.[15]

Fast-Tracking Prosperity

In the Australia-India relationship and the wider Quad association, there is an increasing emphasis on both defending prosperity and building it. In today's globalised world, there are non-traditional threats that can potentially adversely impact prosperity at the individual, national and global levels. These threats include cyber issues, global warming and politically instigated supply chain disruptions. On the other hand, building future prosperity is now seen as requiring being involved in technological innovation, not being left behind technologically and being able to access trusted and resilient global supply chains.

Cyber is deeply embedded across the modern world in all societies and economies. However, cyber's rapid development and spread has meant that the laws, regulations and norms governing its use and future development have been left behind.[16] India has so far been non-committal in the major contemporary debates on international cyber norms and accordingly less influential than it could be in the elaboration of new laws and regulations.[17] India has the global heft to swing the debate away from the adoption of the norms that some authoritarian states would prefer, and become a rule maker rather than a rule taker. Cyber norms is an area where Australian and India could collaborate in the 'spirit of the Quad'.

Beyond norms, cyber security remains a significant problem impacting all information technology developers and users. Keeping ahead of cyber threats is greatly helped by information sharing. Australia and the US can share through the Five Eyes network, but India and Japan are outside this. A framework for effective cyber security information sharing between the Quad partners could be usefully established.[18]

Another non-traditional threat is that of global warming. Accordingly, a Quad Climate Working Group has been recently established to act as a platform for cooperation on climate mitigation, adaptation, resilience, technology, capacity-building, and climate finance.[19] A particular focus area is hydrogen energy, a technology of direct interest to Australia and India. Hydrogen can be converted into a storable and high-efficiency fuel that can be used in fuel cells to generate electricity and heat. Cooperation is envisaged across the hydrogen value chain including in its production, transportation and use.

Australia and India are both undertaking high quality research into hydrogen energy, with India more advanced than Australia in related policy development. Beyond the government, Australian and Indian companies are both actively exploring production possibilities along similar timelines, about 5-10 years, to reach initial hydrogen production.[20]

Collaboration opportunities concerning hydrogen energy and related to prosperity are readily apparent, with some useful overlaps with the security objective. Moreover, this would link into other research within Quad working groups concerning supply chains including a Quad Shipping Task Force examining the major ports of Los Angeles, Mumbai Port Trust, Sydney (Botany), and Yokohama forming a decarbonised shipping network.[21]

Trusted, resilient supply chains are a prominent issue in the importation of rare earths which are increasingly being used in advanced technology manufacturing. Australia and India both have significant reserves of rare earths but have only limited processing capabilities. There may be value in collaborative research partnerships that devise more cost-effective and environmentally sound methods of rare earth extraction and processing.[22] For that, Australia's long established Australia-India Strategic Research Fund could provide the seed funding.[23]

Beyond rare earths, in June 2020 Australia and India signed a Memorandum of Understanding (MoU) on cooperation in the field of mining and processing of critical and strategic minerals that supports not just research but also building trusted and resilient supply chains.[24] For many critical minerals, India largely relies on imports. These include cobalt, lithium, germanium, rhenium, beryllium, niobium, tantalum, vanadium, strontium, nickel, and rare earths.

In contrast, Australia has significant reserves of many of these minerals that are available to be developed to form part of an integrated mining and mineral processing supply chain. Australia, for example, has the world's largest concentration of battery minerals, including lithium, cobalt, nickel, and manganese reserves.[25] The Supply Chain Resilience Initiative,noted earlier, could further contribute to, and combine with, the 2020 MoU in the development of a reliable supply chain for critical minerals involving Australia and India.

With stress on building prosperity, and less connected to non-traditional threats, is the new Quad Critical and Emerging Technology Working Group. Strategically important technology areas are termed 'critical' technologies, defined by Australia's foreign minister as "technology that can significantly enhance or pose risks to … national interests, including … prosperity, social cohesion and national security."[26]

The Critical and Emerging Technology Working Group's early tasks include: facilitating coordination on technology standards development; encouraging cooperation on telecommunications deployment, equipment supplier diversification and when developing future telecommunications technology; monitoring trends and opportunities concerning critical and emerging technology developments, including biotechnology; and convening dialogues on critical technology supply chains.[27]

An initial focus for collaboration is the 5G wireless network which, with high data throughput and very low latency, is essential for fully implementing the fourth industrial revolution and Internet-of-

Things devices and systems. However, the centrality of 5G in a modern networked society has raised concerns about its vulnerability to cyber-attack, intrusion and spying. The initial solution appeared to be using only trusted suppliers but, in the last two years, the option of open radio access networks (open-RAN) has taken hold. With this, many of a network's functions done using vendor-specific hardware are undertaken by vendor-agnostic software, a process called network virtualisation. Advantages include better interoperability, supply chain resiliency, improved security, and probable cost savings.[28]

The Quad countries are well-placed to collaborate in actively assisting 5G open-RAN development, acquisition, rollout and use across the Indo-Pacific and globally. Open-RAN supporters see the technology as meeting the 'spirit of the Quad', attuned to democratic values and norms, and countering so-called techno-authoritarianism and foreign state surveillance.[29] Further downstream, 6G is now being actively developed in several countries; early design involvement by Australia, India and the Quad could avoid the cyber security problems that 5G brought.[30]

Terrestrial 5G networks connect to other critical global communications infrastructure, in particular seabed cables across which 95 per cent of intercontinental global data transmissions flow. There are concerns about possible espionage or sabotage but there appear to be no easy technological solutions. Some advocate that Quad members adopt a multifaceted approach involving public diplomacy to warn of the dangers, targeted industry collaboration incentives, government financing, cable monitoring and strengthened legal frameworks.[31] Seabed cables appear to be another area where Australia and India can use the Quad Critical and Emerging Technology Working Group to advance their common national interests and protect against shared worries.

Hastening Security

There has been a flurry of recent activity between Australia and India concerning prosperity, arguably accelerated and strengthened by the increasing importance of the long-term security interests of both nations. These interests only partly overlap,although they are significant enough to closely engage the two countries.

India's upgrade of its 1992 Look East policy in late 2014 to the more activist Act East policy has noticeably repositioned India's geostrategic focus. While the Look East policy focussed more on the South Asia region, the Act East policy places ASEAN at the centre of the Indo-Pacific, takes in the Pacific Islands and Australia, and "incorporates the entire region from the east coast of Africa to the Western Pacific up to the US."[32] This is an expansive vision.

In the Pacific Ocean,practicalities associated with India's relatively limited economic and military power, constrain India's attention mainly to the geographically closer ASEAN region. Importantly, this includes the strategically important waters between the Strait of Malacca and the Taiwan Strait, and crucially, the South China Sea.[33]

In contrast, it is in the Indian Ocean in which India has the greatest capabilities and capacities to act. Across the Western and Eastern Indian Ocean littorals, India has fostered valuable diplomatic, economic and military links with many nations. In so doing, the Indian Ocean has steadily become a part of modern India's national identity, how it sees itself relative to others. Taking a more utilitarian perspective, the Indian Ocean is the only practical way India can undertake merchandise trade with the wider world, given its geographic position. For India, the Indian Ocean in its entirety will always take geostrategic precedence over the Pacific.[34]

On the other hand, Australia's strategic gaze is different: Southeast Asia will always be the nation's key geostrategic area, with the Southwest Pacific effectively considered in strategic terms, perhaps with some hubris, as an extension of Australia. The rise of the Indo-Pacific terminology has however, served to promote the Indian Ocean in Australia's strategic consciousness. In matters of security, Australia historically perceived the Indian Ocean as being stabilised by the British and then, after the UK forces withdrew in the 1970s, by the US. In recent years, with America's focus shifting to the Pacific, Indian Ocean security is now becoming more a matter for its littoral states, with India prominent as the region's most powerful state.

Australia's Indian Ocean gaze is mainly limited to the eastern half, although that reaches south to the MacDonald and Heard Islands, and

Antarctica. Most attention is given along the Indonesian archipelago, Christmas and Cocos Islands and then into the Bay of Bengal. The maritime security of this area and freedom of passage across it is an abiding Australian interest. It is in this portion of the Indian Ocean that some feel that the most powerful security alignment between the two nations lies.[35]

Advancing Defence Interaction

The overarching framework for Australia-India defence interoperability is mostly in place and proven in large maritime exercises like AUSINDEX and Malabar. The time seems favourable to be more ambitious, particularly in the air domain.

The Indian Air Force has deployed to Australia's Pitch Black Exercise with expectations that this will become a regular event. India and the US Air Force (USAF) have held several Cope India air exercises, the last in West Bengal.[36] The Royal Australian Air Force (RAAF) could perhaps join and deploy Super Hornets and a KC-30A tanker, mirroring Indian participation in Pitch Black. The involvement of an E-7A Wedgetail Airforce Early Warning and Control (AEW&C) aircraft might also be useful.

More operationally, Australia is upgrading the Cocos Islands airfield for P-8 deployments while India is upgrading the runways at the Indian Naval Station (INS) *Kohassa* and *Baaz* on North Andaman and Great Nicobar Islands respectively.[37] Consequently, the two countries could consider undertaking reciprocal P-8 maritime surveillance patrols through the other's airfields. Such patrols would deepen interoperability and significantly increase maritime domain awareness across the strategically important Malacca, Lombok and Sunda Straits. Until the INS *Kohassa* or *Baaz* are ready, Australian P-8s could operate from the Veer Savarkar International Airport at Port Blair on the South Andaman Island, as Indian P-8s occasionally do now.

Further maritime surveillance opportunities are unfolding with Australia buying 12 MQ-9 Sea Guardian uncrewed air vehicles and the Indian Navy on the cusp of also acquiring 10.[38] The Indian Navy already has experience, having recently operated two leased MQ-9B Sea

Guardians from the INS *Rajali* in Tamil Nadu. The relatively small, turbo-prop powered Sea Guardians are slow to fly to an operating area but can then be on-station for some 24 hours or more conducting long duration maritime surveillance. In contrast, a P-8's typical on-task endurance is about 8 hours or so. Both Australia and India could gain from exchanging experiences and lessons learned as these advanced uncrewed aircraft enter service, and when in service, there are also attractive possibilities of operating them from Cocos and Andaman and Great Nicobar Islands, as noted earlier about P-8 aircraft.

In a similar manner, the Royal Australian Navy (RAN) could usefully develop a deeper relationship with the Indian Coast Guard. The RAN is in the early stages of bringing 12 PV80 Arafura Offshore Patrol Vessels (OPVs) into service. These 1,640-tonne vessels built by Leurssen-Australia, will undertake constabulary missions, maritime patrol and response duties replacing the much smaller 300-tonne Armidale and Cape class patrol boats. The Indian Coast Guard has considerable OPV experience with some 26 OPVs in service, some quite large, being twice the Arafura class' tonnage. Both services could gain through cooperating in this potential new field for collaboration.

Another new area with potential for collaboration could be joint warfare. The Indian Army, Navy and Air Force have considerable individual expertise and experience, however, some consider there is less jointness than there could be.[39] Australia, having much smaller individual services, embraced jointness several decades ago. For example, Australia's chief of defence force was first appointed 1984, whereas India's comparable position was established in 2020.[40] India could leverage off Australia's considerable experience in joint organisational structures, staff processes and doctrinal matters to avoid repeating Australia's earlier missteps and to gain possibly useful insights from Australia's perceived successes.

At the recent 2+2 Ministers' meeting, Australia invited India to fully participate in the Talisman Sabre Exercise in 2023.[41] This is Australia's largest combined and joint, multilateral military training exercise and is held biennially in Queensland. Talisman Sabre 21 included amphibious forces, brigade-sized land forces and considerable air assets from Australia, the US, Canada, Japan, South Korea, the UK and New Zealand.[42] Being part of Talisman Sabre would enhance the joint warfare capabilities of the Quad partners overall. Some consider this crucial as joint warfare seems a potential key area of military strength relative to regional competitors.[43]

Finally, the above possibilities would be more achievable and effective if an agreement on secure communications could be formalised. This would appear a sensible next step in the overall building of formal Australia-India defence cooperation agreements given the collaboration engendered in signing the mutual logistics supply arrangement in 2020. India already has a Communications Compatibility and Security Agreement with the US and this might form a useful model for an Australia-India bilateral secure communications agreement.[44]

Defence Technology Cooperation

Defence industrial cooperation is a problematic issue for many countries that instinctively default to supporting their own defence companies, fret over the reliability of the implicit multinational supply chains and worry about other nations' equipment security measures. Such cooperation can also be fraught with bureaucratic complexities that dramatically delay programmes. A recent examination of critical technology collaborations amongst Quad partners proposed purposefully avoiding such problems through designing the defence technology cooperation approach quite differently. This framework envisaged:[45]

1. basing the cooperation on innovation rather than on developing and then mass producing new major military equipment;
2. placing the focus on start-ups rather than on large defence companies that, given their scale, always concern public policy-makers as they are too big to fail and employ many people; and
3. avoiding an accidental coupling of the advocacy of cooperation with implementing protective trade measures to stop innovations being shared as this reduces development possibilities and constrains local manufacturers' thinking.

The fourth industrial revolution (4IR) has made this framework a practical option as it allows research organisations, start-ups and small companies to quickly innovate and produce small numbers of items. Under 4IR, small organisations can directly design one-of-a-kind items over the internet; pass these to an advanced manufacturing facility; negotiate schedules; be part of the testing regime; and arrange delivery. With techniques such as additive manufacturing, production batch sizes can now be small or on-demand without significant impact on production efficiency.4IR's key drivers are: "big data" analysed using artificial intelligence; high capacity connectivity; new human-machine interaction modes such as touch interfaces and virtual reality systems; and improvements in transferring digital instructions to the physical world including robotics and 3D printing.

Such processes allow implementing a two-phase prototype warfare concept. In the first phase, a wide array of diverse prototypes are developed and then evaluated in short experimentation programmes. In the second phase, prototypes that have proved successful in the trials are produced in limited numbers and quickly introduced into service. The intent would be to rapidly field a variety of low-cost, less complex systems and then replace these with improved variants or something totally new on a regular basis. In some respects, these could be called 'short-life cycle capabilities' but the 'prototype warfare' phrase captures that these limited production items are rather immature and less than fully developed.[46]

Importantly, a crucial factor is that these would be best suited for operations other than war. Nations always wish to keep their best capabilities concealed in case a major war erupts. Operations other than war cover a large field with both nations deeply involved in humanitarian and disaster relief activities, maritime security, counter-terrorism and the countering of grey zone activities.[47]The Australian Defence Force already has a range of organisations and processes in place to find such new technology applications including the Defence Innovation Hub, Army Innovation Days, Navy Warfare Innovation Workshops and Air Force Plan Jericho.

As an example, future Australia and India defence technology innovation could use the Jericho process that accords with the framework earlier noted. In this, the Jericho Edge team initially engages with partners to identify and understand opportunities. The Jericho Edge team,together with Jericho Labs, then convenes communities across organisations, start-ups, small companies and universities to discover, test, and prototype opportunities and explore problem areas. The separate Jericho Analytics team tests the new ideas using net assessment, war-gaming and red teaming.[48] Recent examples include balloon-borne sensors to quickly give wide-area situational awareness useful to finding and tracking bushfires, using artificial intelligence to locate life rafts in disaster at sea situations, and command and control using augmented reality.[49]

Embracing the prototype warfare concept and using the Jericho processes could allow Australia and India to readily collaborate in the near term to create innovative capabilities. This would seem to be a better and much faster way to develop patterns of cooperation rather than considering together developing and then mass producing some very complicated, leading-edge military hardware optimised for major conflict war-fighting. That approach could easily take decades, as European defence cooperation has illustrated on many occasions.

Same Bed, Different Dreams

Over the last five years, Australia and India have considerably deepened their cooperation in their pursuit of national prosperity and security. This cooperation could wax or wane in the future as circumstances change. The two nations do not necessarily always share aspirations although they currently share several significant interests.

Under Prime Minister Modi, India is aiming to become a 'leading power' able to shape international order, in contrast to a great power that might determine international order by using force, if necessary.[50] The grand strategy to become a leading power includes *atmanirbharta*, considered by the Indian foreign secretary to translate as 'strategic autonomy' and as the first pillar of Indian diplomacy.[51]

Strategic autonomy is the ability of a state to pursue its national interests and adopt its preferred foreign policy without being unduly or disproportionately constrained by other states. Such autonomy is most achievable in a multipolar international system where the several great powers can be purposefully manoeuvred between, that is played off, against each other.[52] Unsurprisingly then, the second pillar of Indian diplomacy "is its multipolar focus."[53]

The objective of strategic autonomy in a multipolar world has shaped India's current approach to international diplomacy. India's foreign policy and strategic orientation has shifted from the last century's idealism to this century's pragmatism.[54] Great strategic flexibility is required to purposefully manoeuvre in the international system, and for this, taking a pragmatic issue-by-issue approach, rather than deciding all matters based on fixed values is necessary. In turn, the need for strategic flexibility means that India prefers strategic partnerships rather than formal alliances, and managing multiple alignments rather than committing to particular allies.[55] Indian foreign policy may then at times appear unpredictable and sometimes perplexing to its major partners. Harsh V. Pant and Chirayu Thakkar write:

> The frequency at which India votes in line with the United States at the United Nations remains dismal compared to most US allies. This chasm has been a source of both frustration and anxiety for US policy-makers. Given India's frequent multilateral alignment with Russia and China, some believe India is part of a counter hegemonic bloc that can jeopardize many Western interests.[56]

Australia has some definite differences. Australia is a middle power whose ambition is mostly limited to remaining a prosperous, secure country rather than influencing the international system; it is generally a rule taker not a rule maker. In this, Australia commonly sees a sharp distinction between prosperity and security.

Concerning prosperity, Australia in its relationship with India, often places much weight on trade and economic issues. In contrast, over the last several years, for India, security engagements have taken precedence with both Australia and the wider Indo–Pacific.[57] Indeed, unlike Australia, India is not part of any regional economic architecture in the Asia-Pacific. India's recent rejection of the ASEAN-led Regional Comprehensive Economic Partnership (RCEP) was "disappointing" to Australia and other Indo-Pacific nations, although efforts to finalise a bilateral Australia-India Free Trade Agreement continue.[58]

In terms of security, Australia has long placed great store on its close alliance with the US and built this around a strong expectation of reciprocity.[59] Australia assiduously promotes the concept of mutual obligation; each party should support the other because they have previously. The latest Defence White Paper sees Australia developing its relationship with the North Atlantic Treaty Organisation (NATO) similarly: it will "grow on the basis of reciprocity."[60] This notion of building locked-in, reliable support over time is rather different from India's pragmatic approach that uses nimble diplomatic shifts and strategic agility to achieve *atmanirbharta.*

Australia's strategy approach to security translates down to the military operational level. Over the 70 years of the alliance, Australians have internalised the high level of integration of the Australian Defence Force (ADF) with the US, extending to integrated signals intelligence, embedded personnel in command structures, operational intelligence sharing and US officers serving in ADF units, ships and squadrons—and vice versa. India's very different approach means there is at times little appreciation of the habits of cooperation developed within long standing alliance structures. Australians can, accordingly, be surprised by both the inability and the unwillingness of the Indian armed forces to seamlessly integrate with US alliance-led operational protocols and procedures as they can and instinctively wish to.[61]

There are two important implications from these differences between Australia and India.

First, Australia needs to accept India's pragmatic approach to its international relationships and similarly embrace pragmatism in its relationship with India, notwithstanding any lingering nostalgia for the Commonwealth, cricket and curry. India's use of strategic flexibility to achieve its sought after leading power status can be expected to drive it towards making particular strategic decisions that may occasionally disappoint Australia. Constancy is not a characteristic of the relationship that Australia should seek, nor feel aggrieved by if it is not met. Influential international relations scholar Michael Wesley writes: "Great powers, whatever their politics, are selfish, solipsistic and capricious. Other states must learn to live with them on these terms."[62]

Implicit in this, is that Australia needs to carefully build its relationship with India in a manner independent from the US or the Quad. American perspectives will change over time just as the Quad will evolve. Care should be taken in designing the future Australia-India relationship so that such changes will not upend it. Neither should Australia expect that India being a democracy automatically means perpetual alignment with other democracies such as Australia.

The second implication is that the relationship between Australia and India is not evenly balanced. It has been deliberately deepened in recent years but driven forward more by Australia than India, despite the Modi government's energy and pledges of commitment.[63]

In some respects, this reflects that outside the security domain, the Indian government has only a limited bureaucratic capacity, which restricts its ability to engage diplomatically, particularly with middle and smaller powers.[64] Other Indian writers are much more critical, complaining that the institutional capacity problem is actually a combination of confusion, non-responsiveness, and lack of delivery. They warn, "The lack of tangible engagement, steady institutional capacity, and slow delivery together create a perception of Indian deficiency in actualising the Act East policy."[65]

The result is that Australia needs to put efforts into advancing the relationship. Left untended, like any relationship, it may wither. Australia cannot rely on India, the US, the Quad or both nations being democracies to drive the relationship further.

In that regard, Australia like India is also short of resources and so for both countries, the areas for cooperation need to be prioritised. Not all things can be done at once and so specific collaborative areas need to be sought out and given precedence. The Australia-India Comprehensive Strategic Partnership takes a broad gaze but perhaps the actions taken under it need to be prudently focussed into particular areas.

Conclusion

The Australian-India relationship has deepened considerably in recent years. This chapter suggests that numerous further enhancements are possible. In terms of building prosperity, possible cooperative areas include: cyber norms and security, hydrogen energy, and creating trusted critical mineral and rare earth supply chains. In addition, critical and emerging technology is an area of specific long-term future importance, in particular 5G wireless networks, open radio access networks (open-RAN) and seabed communication cables.

In terms of security, both nations' strategic interests most closely overlap in the Eastern Indian Ocean and in maritime Southeast Asia. Defence forces' interaction could be enhanced through reciprocal maritime patrol aircraft patrols from each other's airfields, both countries exchanging experiences as their new MQ-9 Sea Guardian uncrewed air vehicles enter service, OPV interactions, Australia joining with India and the US in Exercise Cope India, joint warfare exercise participation, exchange of information on joint warfare processes and doctrine, and evolving a secure communications agreement.

There also appear further possibilities in cooperating on defence technology if this is initially focussed on small scale innovation rather than major equipment acquisitions. Embracing the prototype warfare concept and using the Jericho processes could allow Australia and India to readily collaborate in the near term to create innovative capabilities.

The Australia-India relationship may in some aspects be unevenly balanced but that does not mean it should be unproductive. With both nations taking a pragmatic approach informed by their individual national goals and shared strategic interests, much can be accomplished. The relationship now has the momentum to keep accelerating towards improved security and prosperity for Australia and India, and the wider Indo-Pacific region. Australia and India individually have the agency needed, now it's up to them to work together to achieve this.

The views expressed in this chapter are the author's and do not reflect the official position of the RAAF, the Department of Defence nor the Australian government.

Notes

1. Press Trust of India, "Quad to Act as a Force for Global Good: PM Modi," *The Hindu*, September 25, 2021. https://www.thehindu.com/news/international/

quad-to-act-as-a-force-for-global-good-modi/article36660779.ece. Accessed on December 2, 2021.

2. Department of Foreign Affairs and Trade, "Joint Statement on a Comprehensive Strategic Partnership between Republic of India and Australia," June 4, 2020. https://www.dfat.gov.au/geo/india/joint-statement-comprehensive-strategic-partnership-between-republic-india-and-australia. Accessed on December 5, 2021.
3. M. Payne, "Joint Statement on Inaugural India-Australia 2+2 Ministerial Dialogue,"*Media Release*, September 11, 2021. https://www.foreignminister.gov.au/minister/marise-payne/media-release/joint-statement-inaugural-india-australia-22-ministerial-dialogue. Accessed on December 1, 2021.
4. D. Jaishankar, *The Australia–India Strategic Partnership: Accelerating Security Cooperation In The Indo–Pacific* (Sydney: Lowy Institute, 2020), pp. 18-19.
5. L. Reynolds, "Australia and India Sign Defence Arrangement," Minister for Defence, June 4, 2020. https://www.minister.defence.gov.au/minister/lreynolds/media-releases/australia-and-india-sign-defence-arrangement. Accessed on December 2, 2021.
6. Department of Foreign Affairs and Trade,"Joint Statement on the Supply Chain Resilience Initiative by Australian, Indian and Japanese Trade Ministers," April 27, 2021. https://www.dfat.gov.au/news/media-release/joint-statement-supply-chain-resilience-initiative-australian-indian-and-japanese-trade-ministers. Accessed on November 29, 2021.
7. Critical Technologies Policy Coordination Office, *The Action Plan for Critical Technologies* (Canberra: Australian Government, 2021), pp. 32-33. https://www.pmc.gov.au/sites/default/files/publications/ctpco-action-plan-for-critical-technology-amalgamated.pdf. Accessed on December 1, 2021.
8. C. Pyne, "AUSINDEX 2019 Commences in India," Minister for Defence, April 9, 2019. https://www.minister.defence.gov.au/minister/cpyne/media-releases/ausindex-2019-commences-india. Accessed on December 2, 2021.
9. Department of Defence, "NT Hosts India for Maritime Exercise," September 5, 2021. https://news.defence.gov.au/media/media-releases/nt-hosts-india-maritime-exercise#:~:text=This%20week%20the%20Northern%20Territory,and%20secure%20Indo%2DPacific%20region. Accessed on December 4, 2021.
10. Department of Defence, "Australia Back for Indo-Pacific Maritime Exercise MALABAR," August 23, 2021. https://news.defence.gov.au/media/media-releases/australia-back-indo-pacific-maritime-exercise-malabar. Accessed on November 30, 2021.
11. Jaishankar, n. 4, p. 21.
12. The White House, "Quad Leaders' Joint Statement: 'The Spirit of the Quad'," March 12, 2021. https://www.whitehouse.gov/briefing-room/statements-

releases/2021/03/12/quad-leaders-joint-statement-the-spirit-of-the-quad/. Accessed on November 27, 2021.

13. Department of Foreign Affairs and Trade, “Quad,”. https://www.dfat.gov.au/international-relations/regional-architecture/quad. Accessed on December 4, 2021.
14. I. Hall, “Australia and the Quad”, forthcoming.
15. I. Bagchi, “Japan Will Host the Next Quad Summit in 2022, Announced Kurt Campbell, US President Joe Biden's Indo-Pacific Coordinator,” *The Times of India*. https://timesofindia.indiatimes.com/world/us/japan-will-host-the-next-quad-summit-in-2022-announced-kurt-campbell-us-president-joe-bidens-indo-pacific-coordinator/articleshow/87843099.cms. Accessed December 7, 2021.
16. A. Basu, I. Poetranto, and J. Lau, “The UN Struggles to Make Progress on Securing Cyberspace”, Carnegie Endowment for International Peace, May 19, 2021. https://carnegieendowment.org/2021/05/19/un-struggles-to-make-progress-on-securing-cyberspace-pub-8449. Accessed on November 26, 2021.
17. Ibid.
18. K. Takahashi, et al., *Building Cooperation: Cyber, Critical Technology And National Security*, Quad Tech Network Series (Canberra: Australian National University, 2021), p. 20.
19. Australian Government, “Quad Summit Fact Sheet,” March 12, 2021. https://www.pm.gov.au/sites/default/files/files/quad-summit-fact%20Sheet.pdf. Accessed on December 1, 2021.
20. K. Liao, et al., *Benchmarking Critical Technologies: Building an Evidence Base for an Informed Critical Technologies Strategy* (Canberra: Australian Strategic Policy Institute, 2021), p. 14.
21. The White House, “Fact Sheet: Quad Leaders' Summit”, September 24, 2021. https://www.whitehouse.gov/briefing-room/statements-releases/2021/09/24/fact-sheet-quad-leaders-summit/. Accessed on December 4, 2021.
22. T. Ray, et al., *The Digital Indo-Pacific: Regional Connectivity And Resilience*, Quad Tech Network Series (Canberra: Australian National University, 2021), p. 23.
23. AUSTRADE, *Unlocking Australia-India Critical Minerals Partnership Potential: India Critical Minerals Demand Report* (Canberra: Commonwealth of Australia, 2021), p. 18.
24. Department of Industry, Science, Energy and Resources, “Working with India on Critical Minerals,” June 4, 2020. https://www.industry.gov.au/news/working-with-india-on-critical-minerals. Accessed on December 4, 2021.
25. n. 23, pp. 23-27.
26. M. Payne, “Launch of the International Cyber and Critical Technology Engagement Strategy”, April 21, 2021. https://www.foreignminister.gov.au/minister/marise-payne/speech/launch-international-cyber-and-critical-technology-engagement-strategy. Accessed on December 7, 2021.

27. Australian Government, "Quad Summit Fact Sheet," March 12, 2021. https://www.pm.gov.au/sites/default/files/files/quad-summit-fact%20Sheet.pdf. Accessed on December 1, 2021.
28. M. Rasser, and A. Riikonen, "Open Future: The Way Forward on 5G," Centre for a New American Security, July 28, 2020. https://www.cnas.org/publications/reports/open-future. Accessed on December 1, 2021.
29. L. Curtis, and M. Rasser, *A Techno-Diplomacy Strategy For Telecommunications In The Indo-Pacific*, Quad Tech Network Series (Canberra: Australian National University, 2021), pp. 2-4.
30. M. Rasser, A. Riikonen, and H. Wu, *Edge Networks, Core Policy Securing America's 6G Future* (Washington: Centre for a New American Security, 2021), pp. 11-16.
31. Curtis and Rasser, n. 29, pp. 5-7.
32. U.B. Singh, "The Geopolitics of Acting East: Past, Present and Future,"in *Five Years of India's Act East Policy*, Special Report #207 (Delhi: Institute of Peace and Conflict Studies, 2020), p. 5.
33. A. Nagda, "Act East in Practice: Gains, Hurdles, and Competition,"in *Five Years of India's Act East Policy*, Special Report #207 (Delhi: Institute of Peace and Conflict Studies, 2020), pp. 7-9.
34. P. Basu, "Maritime India: The Quest for a Steadfast Identity," *ORF Occasional Paper* No. 339 (Delhi: Observer Research Foundation, 2021).
35. M. Wesley, "Modi Operandi: Why India is Vital to Our Regional Strategy,"*The Australian*, November 12, 2021. https://www.theaustralian.com.au/inquirer/modi-operandi-why-india-is-vital-to-our-regional-strategy/news-story/cbce79121ea80b3843ec7c028683baae. Accessed on November 14, 2021.
36. Press Trust of India, "Indian, US Air Force Learn From Each Other at COPE India 2018,"*Economic Times of India*, December 11, 2018. https://economictimes.indiatimes.com/news/defence/indian-us-air-force-learn-from-each-other-at-cope-india-2018/articleshow/67037763.cms. Accessed on December 4, 2021.
37. M. Price, "Contract Awarded for Cocos (Keeling) Islands Runway Upgrade," January 31, 2020. https://www.minister.defence.gov.au/minister/melissa-price/media-releases/contract-awarded-cocos-keeling-islands-runway-upgrade. Accessed on November 25, 2021; Abhijit Singh, "Militarising Andamans: The Costs and the Benefits: Analysis,"*Hindustan Times*, July 29, 2020. https://www.hindustantimes.com/analysis/militarising-andamans-the-costs-and-the-benefits/story-J3mGWFQS3NgLUiPYwIVb2N.html. Accessed on December 5, 2021.
38. V. Insinna, "US State Department Clears Australia to buy MQ-9B Drones,"*DefenceNews*, April 27, 2021. https://www.defencenews.com/global/asia-pacific/2021/04/26/state-department-clears-australia-to-buy-mq-9b-drones/. Accessed on November 28, 2021; S.A. Philip, "US Offers India Discount on Guardian Drones, Proposes to set up Maintenance Facility too,"*The Print*, November 16, 2021. https://theprint.in/defence/us-offers-india-discount-on-guardian-drones-proposes-to-set-up-maintenance-facility-too/766946/. Accessed on December 4, 2021.

39. A.S. Hashim, "Can Asians Fight? Organisational-Cultural Impediments to the Conduct of Asian High-Tech Conventional Warfare,"*Australian Journal of Defence and Strategic Studies,* Vol. 3, No. 2, 2021, pp. 225-227.
40. S.A. Philip, and A.N. Dutta, "Gen. Bipin Rawat is First CDS—In Charge of Jointness, Defence Diplomacy, Reforms," *The Print*, December 30, 2019. https://theprint.in/defence/gen-bipin-rawat-is-first-cds-in-charge-of-jointness-defence-diplomacy-reforms/339959/. Accessed on December 4, 2021.
41. D. Peri, "Australia Keen India Joins Exercise Talisman Sabre,"*The Hindu*, August 3, 2021. https://www.thehindu.com/news/national/australia-keen-india-joins-exercise-talisman-sabre/article35708489.ece. Accessed on December 4, 2021.
42. Department of Defence, "Talisman Sabre 21 Participants."https://www.defence.gov.au/exercises/talisman-sabre-21/participants. Accessed on December 4, 2021.
43. Hashim, n. 39, p. 233.
44. Jaishankar, n. 4, p. 21.
45. Takahashi, n. 18, p. 22.
46. P. Layton, *Prototype Warfare, Innovation and the Fourth Industrial Age* (Canberra: Air Power Development Centre, 2018), p. 24.
47. P. Layton, *China's Enduring Grey Zone Challenge* (Canberra: Air Power Development Centre, 2021).
48. Royal Australian Air Force, "Jericho Implementation Model." https://www.airforce.gov.au/our-mission/plan-jericho/jericho-implementation-model. Accessed on December 4, 2021.
49. S. Kitchener, "Balloons give RAAF Cutting Edge in Aerospace,"*Defence News*, June 9, 2020. https://news.defence.gov.au/technology/balloons-give-raaf-cutting-edge-aerospace. Accessed on December 4, 2021; Royal Australian Air Force "AI-Search To Transform Search & Rescue", *Air Force News*, May 2019. https://www.airforce.gov.au/news-and-events/news/ai-search-transform-search-rescue. Accessed on December 4, 2021; S. Kitchener, "A New Way of Looking at Battlespaces,"*Defence News*, June 9, 2020. https://news.defence.gov.au/capability/new-way-looking-battlespaces. Accessed on December 4, 2021.
50. A.J. Tellis, *India As A Leading Power* (Washington: Carnegie Endowment for International Peace, 2016), pp. 3-6.
51. Ministry of External Affairs, "Foreign Secretary's Remarks on 'India's Foreign Policy and Its Strategic Imperative: The Way Forward' at the 6th JP Morgan "India Investor Summit" (September 20, 2021)." https://mea.gov.in/Speeches-Statements.htm?dtl/34287/Foreign_Secret. Accessed on December 3, 2021.
52. S. Kalyanaraman, "Aravind Devanathan Asked: What is 'Strategic Autonomy'? How Does it Help India's Security?," Manohar Parrikar Institute for Defence Studies and Analyses, January 20, 2015. https://idsa.in/askanexpert/strategicautonomy_indiasecurity. Accessed on December 1, 2021.
53. Ministry of External Affairs, "Foreign Secretary's Remarks on 'India's Foreign Policy and Its Strategic Imperative: The Way Forward'" at the 6th JP Morgan

"India Investor Summit", September 20, 2021. https://mea.gov.in/Speeches-Statements.htm?dtl/34287/Foreign_Secret. Accessed on December 3, 2021.

54. V. Kukreja, "India in the Emergent Multipolar World Order: Dynamics and Strategic Challenges,"*India Quarterly*, Vol. 76, No. 1, 2020, p. 10.
55. F. O'Donnel, and M. Papa, "India's Multi-Alignment Management and the Russia–India–China (RIC) Triangle," *International Affairs*, Vol. 97, No. 3, 2021, p. 821.
56. H.V. Pant, and C. Thakkar, "The United States and India: Multilaterally Abridged Allies," Observer Research Foundation, August 24, 2021. https://www.orfonline.org/research/the-united-states-and-india-multilaterally-abridged-allies/. Accessed on December 5, 2021.
57. Jaishankar, n. 4, pp. 25-26.
58. K.V. Prasad and S. Dixit, "India's RCEP Stand Disappointing," *The Tribune*, February 5, 2020. https://www.tribuneindia.com/news/nation/%E2%80%98india%E2%80%99s-rcep-stand-disappointing%E2%80%99-35844. Accessed on December 1 2021. Shiro Armstrong and Evgeniia Shannon, "Can an Australia–India FTA Succeed Where RCEP Failed?,"*East Asia Forum*, March 8, 2021. <https://www.eastasiaforum.org/2021/03/08/can-an-australia-india-fta-succeed-where-rcep-failed/. Accessed on November 28, 2021.
59. J. Howard, "Australian Foreign Policy," *Sydney Papers*, Vol. 15, No. 2, 2003, p. 63.
60. *2016 Defence White Paper* (Canberra: Commonwealth of Australia, 2016), p. 136, para 5.77.
61. Jaishankar, n. 4, p. 26.
62. Wesley, n. 35.
63. I. Hall, "Australia and India in the Modi Era: An Unequal Strategic Partnership?,"*International Politics*, February 2, 2021. https://link.springer.com/article/10.1057/s41311-020-00278-w. Accessed December 7, 2021.
64. Jaishankar, n. 4, p. 25.
65. Nagda, n. 33, p. 8.

7. The US' Indo-Pacific Strategy and the Role of India

Stuti Banerjee

Introduction

The maritime domain has gained ascendancy in the past few years, especially as countries recognise the emerging challenges to security, both traditional and non-traditional, and also due to the competition and convergences for trade and connectivity. If one were to look at history, it would be evident that the maritime domain has been critical for nations that want to establish themselves as powers that shape the emerging security architecture of the region. This is true in the current contestations that one is witnessing in the Indo-Pacific region. The region has witnessed the rapid rise of China, and with its rise, there is a reimagination of the maritime space. China has challenged the established security architectures dominated by the United States since the end of World War II. There are growing concerns within the region that is economically tied to China and dependent on the United States for security, that the outcomes of this competition will shape the regional dynamics and/or shape the larger security architecture in the region. Apart from these two, the other central actors are Australia, India, Japan and the Association of Southeast Asian Nations (ASEAN).

The importance of the region can be gauged from the fact that the Indian Ocean is the world's busiest and most strategically significant corridor for trade and commerce, with close to one-third of the world's trade and energy resources traversing these waters. The region can rightly be called the highways of the seas. It is a multipolar region, contributing more than half of the world's Gross Domestic Product (GDP) and population.

"In recent decades, the Indo-Pacific has undergone a remarkable transformation. The people of the region have climbed out of poverty, the region has become the headquarters to world-class companies and an important engine of global economic growth."[1] It is also a region that has visible asymmetric powers—developing and developed economies with differing military capabilities, threat perceptions, and security needs—working in cooperation with each other.

The importance of the Indo-Pacific for the United States can be gauged from the fact that some of its most important trading partners are in the region and it is also the destination for nearly one-third of US exports. The region is the source of US$ 900 billion in foreign direct investment which has led to the creation of millions of jobs across in the United States. The Indo-Pacific is also important militarily for the United States. A number of its allies and strategic partners are in this region. It has bases across the region with more US military personnel stationed in the region than anywhere else outside the continental US. The US is also tied by the people as there are more than 24 million Asian Americans living in the United States.[2]

This paper presents a brief overview of the United States' Indo-Pacific strategy. As the United States, under President Joe Biden, explores building an economic framework along with the security architecture in the Indo-Pacific, India plays a critical role in the United States' vision for the region. The paper highlights the role of India within the United States' Indo-Pacific strategy, both in the areas of shared interests and some divergences within this shared vision.

From Obama to Biden: Evolving Indo-Pacific Strategy

The term "Indo-Pacific" emerged under the Obama Administration's pivot to Asia, or rebalancing to Asia strategy. However, there was no clear and coherent geographical definition of the "Indo-Pacific" under the Administration. The then Secretary of State Hillary Clinton defined the region as "stretching from the Indian subcontinent to the western shores of the Americas", and "[spanning] two oceans—the Pacific and the Indian."[3] Expanding on the idea, the then Secretary of State John Kerry in 2013, while highlighting India's economic growth and investments, spoke about the need for regional connectivity. He stated, "India and the United States are cooperating to realise the potential of the 'Indo-Pacific Economic Corridor' which can spur development and investment as well as trade and transit between the dynamic economies of South and Southeast Asia."[4] In April 2014, the then assistant secretary of the US State Department's Bureau of South and Central Asian Affairs described the "Indo-Pacific" as "the vast littoral arc stretching from South Africa to Australia."[5]

It was under the Trump Administration that the term 'Indo-Pacific' and its geographical outlines were defined and became a part of the official discourse. During the Asia-Pacific Economic Cooperation (APEC) Summit in Vietnam in 2017, President Trump spoke about "our [the US'] vision for a free and open Indo-Pacific—a place where sovereign and independent nations, with diverse cultures and many different dreams, can all prosper side-by-side, and thrive in freedom and in peace."[6] He also identified the United States as a member of the region by stating, "America stands as a proud member of the community of nations who make a home on the Pacific. We have been an active partner in this region since we first won independence ourselves."[7] Former Secretary of State Rex Tillerson also pointed to the Indo-Pacific as "... including the entire Indian Ocean, the Western Pacific and the nations that surround them, will be the most consequential part of the globe in the 21st century."[8]

The Trump Administration laid out the United States' Indo-Pacific strategy in four documents. The first was the *2017 National Security Strategy* (NSS 2017) document that defined the region as one "... which stretches from the west coast of India to the western shores of the United States, represents the most populous and economically dynamic part of the world." The document officially defined the Indo-Pacific for the United States. The area defined was within the purview of the then US Pacific Command. The document also identified China and Russia as revisionist powers that were challenging "American power, influence, and interests, attempting to erode American security and prosperity." It added that "China seeks to displace the United States in the Indo-Pacific region, expand the reaches of its state-driven economic model, and reorder the region in its favour."[9]

The second key document was the *Indo-Pacific Strategy Report: Preparedness, Partnerships and Promoting a Networked Region* (2019) published by the Department of Defence. The document identified the United States as a Pacific nation through its five Pacific states: Hawaii, California, Washington, Oregon, and Alaska, as well as through America's Pacific territories on both sides of the International Date Line such as Guam and American Samoa. The document also highlighted that the region has become a priority for the Department of Defence and is now the single most consequential region for the United States' future. In May 2018, the United States renamed its Pacific Command, USPACOM, to US Indo-Pacific Command (USINDOPACOM). This command name change implied that the United States had come to regard the Indo-Pacific strategy within its long-term future regional security policy framework. In continuation from the 2017 NSS, the 2019 Defence Department document also recognised China's economic and military ascendance, as China seeks Indo-Pacific regional hegemony in the near-term and, ultimately global preeminence in the long-term. The document identified a range of transnational challenges that could destabilise the region and affect the security of the United States. These include terrorism; illicit arms; drugs, human, and wildlife trafficking; and piracy, as well as dangerous pathogens, weapons proliferation, and natural disasters. It also pointed to multiple terrorist organisations that have established bases here, including the Islamic State of Iraq and Syria (ISIS), which has cells in countries throughout the region.[10]

The third document that laid the foundation of the United States' Indo-Pacific strategy is the Department of State's *Free and Open Indo-Pacific: Advancing a Shared Vision*. It emphasised the need to have a strong partnership and, notably, highlighted the importance of India to the future of the region. It further spoke of enhancing economic prosperity by building business-to-business ties, cooperation on high quality infrastructure, enhancing energy security, including support for renewable energy, and cooperation on high technology, among others. Addressing the security aspect, the document highlighted that the United States will work with the regional countries, including India, to build a flexible, resilient network of like-minded security partners to address common challenges. "To protect the maritime domain, we cooperate with Indo-Pacific partners to maintain freedom of navigation and other lawful uses of the sea so that all nations can access and benefit from the maritime commons."[11]

Lastly, the National Security Council's document titled *US Strategic Framework for the Indo-Pacific*, which was declassified in January 2021, begins by raising the question of how to maintain the US' strategic primacy in the Indo-Pacific. A desired end result is to maintain diplomatic, economic and military preeminence in the region. One of the core objectives is to counter-balance the Chinese model of government and to prevent Chinese acquisition of military and strategic capabilities.[12]

The Biden Administration has continued the focus on the Indo-Pacific, introducing new initiatives and emphasising the importance of working with allies and partners. President Biden's first official multilateral meeting, held virtually, was with the other leaders of the Quad. The Joint Statement, "The Spirit of the Quad" reaffirmed the commitment of the four nations to "promoting a free, open rules-based order, rooted in international law to advance security and prosperity and counter threats to both in the Indo-Pacific and beyond."[13] It also reaffirmed the support for ASEAN and its centrality to the Indo-Pacific. Going beyond just the security realm, the joint statement outlined the common challenges which include climate change, addressing the economic and health impact of the COVID-19 pandemic, strengthening cyber security, developing critical technologies, cooperation on counter terrorism, investment in quality and sustainable infrastructure projects and humanitarian assistance and disaster relief.

President Biden also hosted the Quad Heads of State in Washington in September 2021, identifying the need to work together on fighting the global health crisis. They emphasised the need to take forward the Quad COVID-19 vaccine partnership to help enhance equitable access to safe and effective vaccines in the Indo-Pacific and the world. Apart from the cooperation between the Quad members, the United States also entered into a military partnership with Australia and the United Kingdom. The AUKUS (Australia, United Kingdom and United States) "is a trilateral military partnership where technology, scientists, industry and defence forces will work together to 'deliver a safer and more secure region'". The partnership aims to bolster the existing American alliances in the Indo-Pacific region and contribute to helping it strengthen its network of partnerships in the Indo-Pacific region. Apart from AUKUS, the United States has close relations with the ASEAN nations, bilateral strategic partnerships and the Quad and Five Eyes countries. It has been reported that the first major initiative of AUKUS will be to deliver a nuclear-powered submarine fleet for Australia.

Between March and September 2021, Secretary of State Antony Blinken, Deputy Secretary of State Wendy Sherman, Defence Secretary Lloyd Austin, and US Special Presidential Envoy on Climate Change John Kerry made multiple visits to the region, with stops in Bangladesh, China, Mongolia, India, the Philippines, Singapore and Vietnam, apart from Japan and South Korea. An unofficial delegation of former US Senator Chris Dodd and former Deputy Secretaries of State Richard Armitage and James Steinberg also visited Taiwan to mark the 42nd anniversary of the Taiwan Relations Act, for which President Biden had voted as a senator. Taiwan was also invited to participate in the Summit of Democracy—a virtual summit that looked at corruption, authoritarianism and protection of human rights. The Biden Administration has also reiterated the United States' commitment to Taiwan's security. Vice President Kamala Harris' trip to Singapore and Vietnam further added to the Biden Administration's efforts to reengage with key partners in Southeast Asia. During the visit, Vice President Harris spoke of America's commitment to the international rules-based order and the pursuit of a free and open Indo-Pacific that promotes the shared interests of the United States and its partners and allies.[14] She added that the United States will support its allies in the region against Beijing's intimidation and claim of territories in the region. Apart from these in-person visits, the officials of the Biden Administration have been holding virtual meetings with their counterparts in the region on a regular basis.

Apart from visits to the region by the officials, President Biden, in October 2021, during his participation in the annual East Asia Summit, announced that the United States will explore the possibility of developing the Indo-Pacific economic framework with its partners in the region. The framework will work to help trade, build digital economies, cooperation in the technology sector, build supply chain resilience, decarbonisation and clean energy development, sustainable infrastructure development, implementation of worker standards and labour laws. With this, President Biden outlined the broad spectrum of the United States' economic strategy towards the region. Taking the strategy forward, President Biden, along with the other leaders of the G-7, also launched the Build Back Better World (B3W) initiative. The Biden Administration describes "it as a values-driven, high-standard, and transparent infrastructure partnership led by major democracies to help narrow the $40+ trillion infrastructure need in the developing world."[15] The initiative competes with China's tremendous infrastructure development programme for low and middle income countries. The White House has stated that infrastructure under the programme will be developed in consultation with the local communities, keeping in mind their needs and requirements. It further stated that the projects would be developed in an environmentally sustainable manner, with financing that would be transparent. The points highlight the contrast with China's development initiatives which are viewed as financially unsustainable for most countries.

While there is a view that President Biden and his Administration's engagement with the international community is different in manner and tenor from that of his predecessor, one finds that there is continuity in the United States' policy towards the Indo-Pacific and commitment to counter the growing influence of China in the region and across the world. The United States' Indo-Pacific policy and within it, its relations with India, are examples of the bipartisan consensus in Washington. And while the approach and language of American foreign policy may have changed under the Biden Administration, evidence suggests continuity and stability.

Challenges for the United States in the Region

As mentioned earlier, the region is economically important for the United States as it trades more with the countries of the region than anywhere else. Some of its most important allies are located there, and the region is home to more than half of the world's population. As a result, the Indo-Pacific has become, and will continue to be, linked to the security and prosperity of the United States. Nonetheless, strategic thinkers and military planners have identified the challenges that will confront the United States in the region. This section mentions four challenges that need to be addressed.

China

All the strategic documents have highlighted the challenges posed by a rising, revisionist China that is increasingly in competition with the United States. China is gradually emerging as the dominant military power in the region after the United States. Its military budget has grown over the years to roughly equal the military budgets of nearly all nations in the region. The Stockholm International Peace Research Institute (SIPRI) has estimated that "China's military spending far exceeds that of its neighbors and was greater than the combined expenditure of India, Russia, Japan, South Korea, and Taiwan in 2019."[16] Although high defence spending may not necessarily translate into actual military power, it remains an indicator of the effort that China has put into the development and enhancement of its military capabilities. It also indicates the long-term planning that China has with respect to its future military strength. China has over time taken steps to expand its military influence. Building on the experiences of its anti-piracy missions, it has slowly emerged as a partner for small island and littoral states in the Indian Ocean. Along with this, China has also been promoting the Maritime Silk Road, under Beijing's larger Belt and Road Initiative (BRI). The Maritime Silk Road provides China with an additional platform to engage with the regional nations on economic and security issues. A affirmation of its growing influence and the position that it seeks for itself can be gauged from the fact that in 2017, Beijing set up its first overseas military facility in Djibouti on the Indian Ocean coast.[17] The opening of such bases is an indicator of its maritime ambitions. It also symbolises that China has the capabilities to engage like other maritime nations such as France, Japan, and the United States which already have facilities in Djibouti. The growing presence of China and its behaviour in the region has become a source of shared anxiety for France, India, the United States, and others. As a major power that is part of the region, most countries would like the United States to continue to be politically and militarily engaged in the Indo-Pacific to counter China's domination. The challenge also arises in the economic sphere as China expands its engagements with the countries of the region through development projects and enhanced trade mechanisms.

Russia

While Russia has not yet accepted the concept of the Indo-Pacific, it has reservations about the United States' policies in the region. Russia has stated that the policies are non-inclusive and could undermine the universal framework of cooperation. With the growing differences between the 'West' and Russia, on Afghanistan, Ukraine, the Arctic, etc, Moscow has increasingly turned to strengthening ties with its Indo-Pacific partners such as China and India. It is also now actively engaging with the ASEAN nations. Russia is engaged in talks to bring stability to Afghanistan, and is also expanding its regional diplomatic profile by highlighting the importance of inter-state cooperation on security matters. Moscow and Beijing have both been identified as national security threats by the US and a combined challenge for the North Atlantic Treaty Organisation (NATO). In response, both Russia and China have increased military cooperation. In 2020, Russia announced that it has entered into a pact with Sudan to create a naval base in Sudan.[18] The base would provide Russia with strategic access to the Red Sea and, by extension, to Bab-el-Mandeb, one of the key choke points in the Indian Ocean. Russia's increased engagement in the region will pose a challenge for the United States, even as they try to diffuse tensions in other sectors. Apart from this, Saudi Arabia and Turkey are also strengthening their economic and diplomatic ties with the islands of the Indian Ocean, highlighting that regional players are now charting their policy independent of outside influence.

Non-Traditional Security Challenges

Non-traditional security issues such as illegal fishing, drugs smuggling, and human trafficking are the prevailing security concerns. Climate change has further added to the security challenges in the region as the frequency of, and devastation caused by, natural disasters like hurricanes and typhoons has led to the loss of human lives. Humanitarian assistance cooperation through a disaster management exercise is a part of the maritime strategy of the countries in the region. For smaller nations, these non-traditional issues are the primary security challenges. While these issues may not be given much priority, they remain deeply relevant to the island nations. For the island nations of the region, these issues are intrinsically linked to their security and carry strategic implications. They are linked to livelihood issues as fishery is a major industry, and to coastal erosion, loss of human life due to natural phenomena. Hence, they will significantly impact the region's ongoing geopolitical competition. The United States, along with its partners and allies in the region, would have to address these concerns as they try to maintain their influence in the region and address their own security interests.

The Challenge Posed by Geography and the Asymmetry of Powers

The Indo-Pacific as described by the United States is a vast theatre, which includes the Strait of Malacca, the coast of Australia, the Indian Ocean and the Pacific Ocean, smaller Pacific island nations and larger states like India and Australia, ranging from developed economies to developing ones, from militarily powerful nations to those that are dependent on the security provided by the regional powers, varied government systems and also diversity of religious followings. The region's size and diversity are of geoeconomic importance, however, this can also lead to the emergence of new power dynamics. It is a vital trading hub, connecting the Middle East to Southeast and East Asia, as well as Europe and the Americas. Thus, the stability of the Indian Ocean is crucial to the global economy.[19]

India in the United States' Indo-Pacific Strategy

The shift from the Asia-Pacific to the Indo-Pacific in the United States' terminology is important to note. It is a recognition of the current geopolitical reality of the region in which India plays a significant role in East Asia, Southeast Asia and the Indian Ocean. It is also indicative of the fact that the United States would like India to play a more prominent role in the region. The United States is increasingly revaluating its overseas deployments, and as it tries to focus on the region, it would like to share the burden with like-minded nations. In this, India as a democracy that is invested in a free, open and inclusive Indo-Pacific, is an ideal partner to anchor the free and open Indo-Pacific order. The United States has publicly called India-US cooperation the lynchpin of its strategy in the region.

India's vision of the Indo-Pacific finds a common cause with the United States, allowing for the growth of a seamless partnership. India wants a free, open, prosperous, and inclusive Indo-Pacific region that serves the long-term interests of all the countries in the region and the world at large. India's focus is on cooperation with regional and extra-regional partners based on their converging visions and values for the promotion of peace, stability, and prosperity in an increasingly inter-connected region. In this vast and complex region, India wants to build a rules-based regional security architecture. India is also increasing its profile in the region. Sharing data on threats to commercial shipping is an important component of enhancing maritime security. The physical manifestations of India's rising profile are showcased through its joint exercises in the region. Apart from bilateral naval exercises with the US Navy and working with the Japanese Maritime Defence Forces, India is conducting multilateral exercises with partner nations such as the Malabar Milan, and RIMPAC Exercises, and engagements with the French and UK Navies which are increasingly engaging in patrolling and freedom of navigation exercises in the region. The development is significant given the increased Chinese presence in the Indian Ocean.

Areas of Shared Interests

For the United States, India is pivotal to maintain strategic balance in the Indo-Pacific. Over the years, through various joint statements, the two sides have expressed common concern on maintaining freedom of navigation and in air spaces in the region, promoting liberal norms and structures such as free markets, rule of law, open access to commons, respect for the United Nations Convention on the Law of the Seas (UNCLOS) and an international rules-based order. Officials from the

Obama and Trump Administrations to now the Biden Administration, along with military officials, have repeatedly pointed to the "Indo-Pacific" interests in their analysis of US relations with India. This is evident from the four documents that have been mentioned above. The NSS 2017 states that the US will "welcome India's emergence as a leading global power and stronger strategic and defence partner ... deepen our strategic partnership with India and support its leadership role in Indian Ocean security...."[20] The Department of Defence 2019 strategy report, in its section on India, highlights, "... the United States and India continue to use their deepening relationship to build new partnerships within and beyond the Indo-Pacific....The establishment of the US-India 2+2 Ministerial Dialogue ... (is) a tangible demonstration of our commitment to promoting the shared principles of a free and open Indo-Pacific."[21] Similarly, the Department of State 2019 vision report on the Indo-Pacific, states that the US vision and approach for the region closely align with India's Act East policy and "a strong US-India partnership is vital to the US' Indo-Pacific vision."[22] The declassified National Security Council document highlights that one of the key goals of the US Indo-Pacific strategy includes "strengthening India, ensuring unimpeded commerce in the Indian Ocean, and the creation of a free and open order in the Indo-Pacific." It calls for "building regional support for US-India Common Principles in the Indian Ocean, including peaceful resolution of territorial disputes".[23]

The New Framework for Defence Cooperation (NFDC) established in 2005 and strengthened further in 2015, along with the Joint Principles of Defence Cooperation 2013, has led to significant exchanges between the armed forces of the two nations, especially the naval and air force bilateral exercises in both the Indian and Pacific Oceans. India has also signed the foundational documents that would facilitate the Indian aircraft and ships to communicate with each other seamlessly. In defence trade, the political-military affairs is committed to further streamlining US-India defence sales through both the Foreign Military Sales (FMS) and Direct Commercial Sales (DCS) processes. "Total defence trade with India from has grown from negligible in 2008 to over $20 billion in 2020. Recent and significant sales include: Apache helicopters, MH-60R

Seahawk helicopters and the Large Aircraft Infrared Countermeasure. India was the first non-treaty partner to be offered a Missile Technology Control Regime Category-1 Unmanned Aerial System—the Sea Guardian—by the USA."[24] The revival of the Quadrilateral Framework in 2017 was with an aim for a shared vision for a free and open Indo-Pacific. The joint statement by Prime Minister Modi and President Trump in 2017 defined their two countries as "democratic stalwarts of the Indo-Pacific" that "agreed that a close partnership between the United States and India is central to peace and stability in the region."[25]

India's close historical relations with the countries of the region, reinforced by cultural ties, people-to-people contacts, economic and political engagements, make it an ideal partner for the United States in the region. The shared concern that the two nations have over the rise of an assertive China also brings them together. India has had skirmishes with China on its land borders. The presence of the Chinese Navy in the Indian Ocean, which is a part of its hinterland and linked to the security of the country, is a worrying factor. China's outreach and growing influence within South Asia had led India and the United States to counter China's assertive and aggressive behaviour through sustained cooperation at both bilateral and multilateral levels.

Looking at the partnership beyond the hard security requirement, the United States, under the Biden Administration, is also looking to capitalise on opportunities to collaborate with India on capacity building and infrastructure development within the Indo-Pacific, especially in the health care sector in view of the global pandemic. The United States, with its Quad partners, has launched an initiative to supply COVID-19 vaccines to the nations in the region; in this, India is the lead partner as the nation that supplies the vaccines, with Japan taking the lead in logistics management. Even in recent meetings, President Biden and Prime Minister Modi have discussed the Indo-Pacific with the focus on building partnerships to fight the global health crisis.

Another area of cooperation within the Indo-Pacific is climate change. This aspect was not in prominence under President Trump, but President Biden has revived the United States' role in global climate change and it has also become a part of its Indo-Pacific strategy. The Indo-Pacific is a maritime space that faces unique threats from climate change, such as rising sea levels threatening the very existence of some of the region's island nations; coastal erosion that would lead to internal and external migration; and rising ocean acidification accelerating competition over food resources such as fish stocks, threatening food and nutritional security. In this aspect, India plays a prominent role in the US' strategy, which has called for close cooperation between the two nations and to lead the development of a sustainable blue economy.

Perhaps the weakest link in the India-United States partnership for the region has been in their efforts to deepen their economic cooperation with countries in the region. Both countries are not part of the two new emerging economic agreements. India chose to not sign the Regional Comprehensive Economic Partnership (RCEP) and the United States under the Trump Administration withdrew from the Trans-Pacific Partnership (TPP). The United States is also not part of the Comprehensive and Progressive Agreement for Trans-Pacific Partnership, the new version of the TPP. While both countries have argued that their decisions have been promoted by domestic economic considerations, the fact that they remain outside the two economic integration platforms has not gone unnoticed by countries in the region.[26] Improving bilateral trade is also a priority for both nations. Under the Biden Administration, US Trade Representative Katherine Tai visited India in November 2021 to hold discussion on means to enhance economic cooperation. The two nations are taking steps to expand the bilateral trade relationship and ensure the future success of the US-India Trade Policy Forum.

Divergences Within the Shared Vision

While the two nations have found a role for the other in their larger Indo-Pacific strategies, it is not to say that they do not have differences. The most important being the differences in the geographical extent of the region. While for the US, it stretches from "the west coast of India to the western shores of the United States", India has a much larger maritime space that stretches from the east coast of Africa to the west coast of the Americas. This includes the Western Indian Ocean region, which is critical to India. India would like the United States to look beyond the Eastern Pacific with a focus on Southeast and Northeast Asia and to also take into consideration the Western Indian Ocean which includes Pakistan, Afghanistan, the Gulf region and small islands of the Indian Ocean and the east coast of Africa. For India, this geographical space is critical for its security. India shares significant concerns with its partner in this Western Indian Ocean region such as counter-terrorism, privacy, etc. India would like the United States to engage with it to strengthen maritime security to the west, which would contribute to towards creating an Indo-Pacific strategy that aligns with both US and Indian interests.[27]

The United States, on the other hand, has desired a larger military role for India in the Pacific Ocean, whereas India, mindful of the regional geostrategic interest and its military capabilities, has acted with restraint. India has always supported dialogue and cooperation as the preferred manner of engaging with the region. Considering that India is a central partner for the United States' Indo-Pacific strategy, the United States would have to take into account the aims and objectives of both parties. This means that the United States would have to look beyond the area of responsibility of the US Indo-Pacific Command. As pointed out above, the Western Indian Ocean is a primary region of strategic and economic importance to India, nonetheless, China's growing presence in this area necessitates an integrated approach to the sub-region.[28] India's defence attaché in Bahrain is also attached to the US Naval Forces Central Command—this was a significant first step. It is perhaps time for the United States to consider if its US Central Command and US Africa Command could be a part of at the Indo-Pacific strategy, which is coordinated through the US Indo-Pacific Command.

Nonetheless, it needs to be pointed out that differences are not necessarily a negative aspect in a strategic relationship, especially the kind that is shared between India and the United States. It is an indication of the robustness of the relations and the fact that channels of communication remain frank and open.

Conclusion

With the continued shift in the balance of power from the Atlantic to the Pacific region and from the trans-Atlantic to Asia, the Indo-Pacific is the emerging theatre of global power competition with the possible risk of conflicts. It is in the interest of the United States and other powers in the region to maintain the peace and stability in the Indo-Pacific region for harnessing economic opportunities that it already provides and the security challenges it is likely to witness. Any major conflict would have flow-on effects on peace and security beyond the region.

The United States' strategy builds on the previous strategies that were advanced by President Bush and President Obama, which focussed on Asia. President Trump defined the scope of the strategy by terming it as Indo-Pacific in the official discourse. The United States has accepted the challenge posed by China in the economic, military and technology spheres. It has recognised that it will have to find a collective response to the challenge. President Biden, played a central role in the Obama Administration's "pivot," and later "rebalance," policies towards Asia. His first year in office is an indication that he will continue to pursue these goals. However, in doing so, his Administration also inherits the gaps in the Indian and US approach to the Indo-Pacific. It is hoped that given his experience in the US Congress, as part of the Senate Foreign Relations Committee, and his deep understanding of India, these gaps would be bridged. The United States will need to be sensitive to Indian concerns, and understand India's objectives in the region, given that the latter is located at the heart of the region. The Biden Administration will have to take these into consideration as it takes forward the strategy by incorporating democratic values and human rights, which could open gaps for the United States in the region. The Indo-Pacific region is a mix of developing and developed economies, following diverse political systems and diverse security perspectives and developmental choices.

Despite these divergences of ideas, there is no doubt that the Indo-Pacific region will continue to be the driving force of global prosperity for decades to come. Therefore, it is in the interest of all the partners to work together to maintain peace and stability in the Indo-Pacific region. For the United States, the Indo-Pacific remains a region of importance; its future is inextricably intertwined with the stability in the region.

Notes

1. "A Free And Open Indo-Pacific Advancing a Shared Vision," Department of States, November 4, 2019. https://www.state.gov/wp-content/uploads/2019/11/Free-and-Open-Indo-Pacific-4Nov2019.pdf. Accessed on December 18, 2021.
2. Figures have been taken from the speech by Secretary of State Blinken, which is available at US Department of State. https://www.state.gov/a-free-and-open-indo-pacific/. Accessed on December 29, 2021.
3. Hillary Clinton, "America's Pacific Century", *Foreign Policy*, 189, November 2011, pp. 56-63.
4. US Department of State, "Remarks on the US-India Strategic Partnership," June 23, 2013. https://2009-2017.state.gov/secretary/remarks/2013/06/211013.htm. Accessed on January 28, 2022.
5. Wada Haruko, "The 'Indo-Pacific' Concept Geographical Adjustments and Their Implications," March 16, 2020, p. 2. https://www.rsis.edu.sg/wp-content/uploads/2020/03/WP326.pdf. Accessed on December 16, 2021.
6. US Embassy of Vietnam, "Remarks by President Trump at APEC CEO Summit, November 10, 2017." https://vn.usembassy.gov/20171110-remarks-president-trump-apec-ceo-summit/. Accessed on December 16, 2021.
7. Ibid.
8. Centre for Strategic and International Studies, "Defining Our Relationship with India for the Next Century: An Address by US Secretary of State Rex Tillerson", p. 5. https://csis-website-prod.s3.amazonaws.com/s3fs-public/event/171018_An_Address_by_US_Secretary_of_State_Rex_Tillerson.pdf?O0nMCCRjXZiUa5V2cF8_NDiZ14LYRX3m. Accessed on December 20, 2021.
9. The White House, "National Security Strategy, 2017." pp. 25, 45-46. https://trumpwhitehouse.archives.gov/wp-content/uploads/2017/12/NSS-Final-12-18-2017-0905.pdf. Accessed on December 16, 2021.
10. US Department of Defence, "Indo-Pacific Strategy Report Preparedness, Partnerships, and Promoting a Networked Region" June 1, 2019. https://media.defence.gov/2019/Jul/01/2002152311/-1/-1/1/DEPARTMENT-OF-DEFENSE-INDO-PACIFIC-STRATEGY-REPORT-2019.PDF. Accessed on December 16, 2021.
11. US Department of State, "A Free And Open Indo-Pacific Advancing a Shared Vision", November 4, 2019." https://www.state.gov/wp-content/uploads/2019/11/Free-and-Open-Indo-Pacific-4Nov2019.pdf. Accessed on December 16, 2021.
12. The White House, "US Strategic Framework For the Indo-Pacific." https://trumpwhitehouse.archives.gov/wp-content/uploads/2021/01/IPS-Final-Declass.pdf. Accessed on December 17, 2021.
13. The White House, "Quad Leaders' Joint Statement: The Spirit of the Quad" March 12, 2021." https://www.whitehouse.gov/briefing-room/statements-

releases/2021/03/12/quad-leaders-joint-statement-the-spirit-of-the-quad/. Accessed on January 28, 2022.

14. The White House, "Remarks by Vice President Harris on the Indo-Pacific Region." https://www.whitehouse.gov/briefing-room/speeches-remarks/2021/08/24/remarks-by-vice-president-harris-on-the-indo-pacific-region/. Accessed on September 3, 2021.
15. The White House, "FACT SHEET: President Biden and G7 Leaders Launch Build Back Better World (B3W) Partnership." https://www.whitehouse.gov/briefing-room/statements-releases/2021/06/12/fact-sheet-president-biden-and-g7-leaders-launch-build-back-better-world-b3w-partnership/. Accessed on January 31, 2022.
16. Centre for Strategic and International Studies, "Understanding China's 2021 Defence Budget", March 5, 2021." https://www.csis.org/analysis/understanding-chinas-2021-defence-budget. Accessed on January 28, 2022.
17. Reuters, "China Formally Opens First Overseas Military Base in Djibouti." https://www.reuters.com/article/us-china-djibouti-idUSKBN1AH3E3. Accessed on January 28, 2022.
18. Dipanjan Roy Chaudhury, "Russia Naval Base in Sudan Could Expand its Partnership with India in Indo-Pacific Region". https://economictimes.indiatimes.com/news/defence/russia-naval-base-in-sudan-could-expand-its-partnership-with-india-in-indo-pacific-region/articleshow/79571684.cms?from=mdr. Accessed on January 28, 2022.
19. Darshana M. Baruah, "What Is Happening in the Indian Ocean?," March 3, 2021. https://carnegieendowment.org/2021/03/03/what-is-happening-in-indian-ocean-pub-83948. Accessed on December 24, 2021.
20. n. 9, pp. 46, 49.
21. n. 10, pp. 33-34.
22. n. 11, pp. 8-9.
23. https://trumpwhitehouse.archives.gov/wp-content/uploads/2021/01/IPS-Final-Declass.pdf
24. US Department of State, "US Security Cooperation With India," January 20, 2022. https://www.state.gov/u-s-security-cooperation-with-india/. Accessed on January 28, 2022.
25. Ministry of External Affairs, Government of India, "Joint Statement—United States and India: Prosperity Through Partnership," June 27, 2017. https://www.mea.gov.in/bilateral-documents.htm?dtl/28560/Joint+Statement++United+States+and+India+Prosperity+Through+Partnership. Accessed on December 22, 2021.
26. Aman Thakker, "US-India Cooperation in the Indo-Pacific," February 11, 2021. https://www.csis.org/blogs/adapt-advance-refreshed-agenda-us-india-relations/us-india-cooperation-indo-pacific. Accessed on January 1, 2022.

27. Alyssa Ayres, "The US Indo-Pacific Strategy Needs More Indian Ocean," January 22, 2019. https://www.cfr.org/expert-brief/us-indo-pacific-strategy-needs-more-indian-ocean. Accessed on December 26, 2021.
28. Walter C. Ladwig III and Anit Mukherjee, "The United States, India, and the Future of the Indo-Pacific Strategy," June 20, 2019. https://www.nbr.org/publication/the-united-states-india-and-the-future-of-the-indo-pacific-strategy/. Accessed on December 26, 2021.

8. The Strategic Imperatives of the Quad: Prospects for the Future

Hina Pandey

On September 24, 2021, the leaders from the Quad countries met for the first in-person summit amidst the global pandemic in Washington DC to further align and take forward their shared and long-term strategic goals vis-à-vis the Indo-Pacific—a fast-evolving geopolitical space driven by global politics. The first summit holds relevance for various reasons, primarily being a renewed call for action in issue areas of global importance that were set in the previous Quad Summit meeting that was held virtually. This paper draws upon the agendas of the last two of Quad meetings held on March 12, 2021, and September 24, 2021, to discusses the potential that Quad holds in future and how the broad contours of strategic visions and prospective deliverables shared in both meetings can be expanded to further broaden the Indo-Pacific strategic construct while contributing to the growth of the Quad itself. The objective of this chapter is to look at three areas of growth-security and prosperity, wherein the Quad can significantly benefit the shared vision of the Indo-Pacific: (a) the Quad as an instrument of regional security stabiliser; (b) the Quad as assuming the role of being one of the platforms to address longstanding protracted proliferation challenges such as North Korea, and, finally; (c) the Quad being able to deliver on its recently set and long-term goal of 'high standard infrastructure development' in the region by promoting the civilian use of nuclear energy.

The Indo-Pacific Strategic Construct and Quad

The Indo-Pacific strategic construct is increasingly expanding as an accepted geostrategic and geopolitical construct which finds immense significance in the security policies of countries such as India, Japan, US, Australia, France; further extending to regions as well as regional-international organisations such as the Association of Southeast Asian Nations (ASEAN) and European Union (EU) in the most recent time. The Indo-Pacific today is no longer only a geographical region (albeit contested) but also a grand strategy agreed among several countries, including India, aimed at securing stability not only in the current state of international affairs but also within the region. It is a renewed approach towards influencing inter-state diplomacy, expanding economic interests and also shaping security drivers; and in this manner, it also provides for a foundation for long-term policy decisions.

Indeed, the Indo-Pacific is neither a new nor an exotic idea; if not explicitly aimed at containing China, it does dilute its influence, and much of its context largely gets defined as a response to the growing Chinese power. Whether or not the Indo-Pacific countries remain in full agreement on this particular aspect, the Indo-Pacific is being hailed as an idea whose time has come and it is today being taken seriously as a viable regional definition and a basis for policy in capitals from Tokyo to New Delhi, Washington to Jakarta, and Canberra to Paris. It is 'the answer to one of the great international dilemmas, mainly, how to respond to an assertive and coercive China without resorting to capitulation or conflict. It is a region whose foremost strategic challenge remains China; while some countries may have explicitly acknowledged this, others have done so rather implicitly.[1]

The Quad momentum (officially the Quadrilateral Security Dialogue, initially a grouping of four—the United States, Australia, India, and Japan) also referred to as the Quad 2.0 has become an evident dynamic shared by several other countries that remain outside of the initial security dialogue. Not only have the Quad leaders from these four countries that have carried forward the strategic construct of the Quad narrative have become more aligned in terms of their shared expectations vis-à-vis China's assertive behaviour but the Quad agenda itself has evolved into becoming more constructed. Amidst the unprecedented pandemic, in March 2021, following the virtual Quad Summit, working groups on COVID vaccines, climate change, critical and emerging technology were created. Subsequently, on September 24, 2021, during the first ever in-person summit, the leaders from the four countries set an ambitious agenda encompassing a spectrum of issues such as the pandemic, climate change, education, critical and emerging technologies, 5G diversification, cyber security and space. The most immediate of these being the pledge to *vaccinate the world* by offering to donate more than 1.2 billion[2] vaccine doses globally in the quest to put an end to the pandemic. The agenda of the Indo-Pacific's fight against the pandemic also included a COVID-19 Crisis Response Emergency Support Loan programme of $3.3 billion and the relevant coordinated support required, with international organisations as well as national governments to deliver on this goal.

Previously, the first ever virtual summit of the Quad also pledged strengthening of cooperation towards several pressing issues in the Indo-Pacific, including "prioritising the role of international law in the maritime domain as reflected in the United Nations Convention on the Law of the Sea (UNCLOS) … to meet challenges to the rules-based maritime order in the East and South China Seas"[3] and hinted at the possibility of the pursuit of the goal of complete denuclearisation of North Korea in accordance with the United Nations Security Council (UNSC) Resolutions. It also initiated the process of annual meetings of foreign ministers.

Clearly what began as a response to the humanitarian crisis in the aftermath of the tsunami in 2004, metamorphosed into one of the most important geopolitical grouping of issue areas and shared synergies among various countries. While each Quad member followed its own path, a decade later, it is being identified as the common pursuit of a rules-based international order, freedom of navigation, and peaceful settlement of territorial disputes. One may argue that the expectations from the Quad in terms of long, short and mid-term deliverables might mean different things to each country, in addition to these common pursuits. For instance, for India, it might mean addressing a part of the China challenge in the long term, responding to immediate foreign and security policy issues such as the pandemic in the short term, but securing India's emerging clout in the international arena. For the US, it implies securing and sustaining of its overall global prominence in international affairs and counter-balancing the assertive Chinese foreign and security policies that directly threaten American global interests. For Japan, it is one way to achieve the value-based shaping of a 'free and open Indo-Pacific', and for Australia, it might mean an inevitable response to Chinese coercion. In any case, as Australian Prime Minister Scott Morrison stated in the first virtual Quad Summit, it is an engagement and partnership of "strategic trust, of common hope and shared values.[4]" Additionally, each country also brings in its own unique expertise and advantages in shaping and expanding not only the Quad agenda but also the Indo-Pacific construct as a whole, thereby adding to the economic growth, security and stability of the region. For instance, with regard to the target of manufacturing COVID-19 vaccines for the Indo-Pacific region, "India's manufacturing capacity, Japan's soft loans to expand that production and Australia's last mile delivery support, all are being leveraged to produce at least 1 billion doses of COVID-19 vaccines by the end of 2022."[5] The statement titled *Spirit of Quad* captured this essence as striving for a region that is "free, open, inclusive, healthy, anchored by democratic values, and unconstrained by coercion."[6]

The Quad as a Regional Security Stabiliser

In understanding the strategic imperative of the Quad, it remains important to focus not only on what it can bring to the table in terms of ensuring stability in the region, in the current times and also in the future. Both the landmark meetings of the Quad held in March and September 2021 indicated a commitment toward increased cooperation on issues such as North Korean denuclearisation, and Afghanistan, that have led some analysts to suggest that the "Quad is poised to evolve into a much collaborative multilateral framework with specified domain and programs ... however, dedicated focus on certain critical areas (especially from the US and India) is crucial to establishing a stronger foundation for the Quad."[7] Considering the current issue basket of the Quad, this remains a reasonable assertion. However it is also to be reiterated that the Quad is not an Asian North Atlantic Treaty Organisation (NATO), rather, "it reflects globalisation and compulsion of countries to work together ... and a platform for countries to cooperate for their benefit and for the benefit of the world."[8] This clarification by Indian External Affairs Minister Jaishankar tacitly sets the tone for the Quad's possible transition into a platform for the regional security architecture without being explicitly framed as solely a military-alliance. This is not impossible to imagine especially when trilateral security cooperation among Japan-US-Australia and Japan-US-India has already taken place; while quadruple military cooperation among all four has not yet kicked off.

Additionally, the recent embracing of the issue area of counter-terrorism into the Quad discussions post the US withdrawal from Afghanistan has also expanded the Quad's policy areas. In their recent joint statement, the Quad leaders offered to closely coordinate their "diplomatic, economic and human rights policies towards Afghanistan and deepen their counter-terrorism and humanitarian cooperation there in accordance with United Nations Security Council Resolution 2593."[9] Additionally, the recent counter-terrorism table-top exercise (CT-TTX) for Quad members by India's National Investigation Agency (NIA), hosted for the first time, indicates opportunities for collaboration in areas that promote regional security. While it remains to be seen if these discussions eventually get institutionalised into a continued working model, the recent exercise is the right step in that direction and a broad arrangement on countering terrorism in the region does add to the overall stability in the region; even this goal is certainly achievable especially when terrorism remains a recognised issue in the growing Quad momentum.

Furthermore, the Quad's strength lies in the fact that while it might be on its way to becoming institutionalised in a manner that is acceptable to all four member states, even in the interim period, it can cater to strengthening security concerns emanating from within the region, especially in the face of the rising Chinese military and political coercion. "China's reclamation and militarisation of reefs and islets in the South China Sea, the stand-off between India and China in Doklam, and other issues such as the denuclearisation of the Korean peninsula are just some of the key strategic issues that regional states are concerned with and the Quad can serve as a convenient platform for the four members to come together."

While there is no such official indication and the lack of a desire for this in the current dynamic, hypothetically, the Quad's (albeit) limited military focus on maritime security has the potential to respond to any regional contingency collectively. It would not be completely out of place to expect collective deterrence at the tactical level from the member states in the future, at least in the maritime domain. The growing assertiveness in the Chinese foreign and security policies in the past decade has increased the Quad countries' awareness of the threat it poses. It is important to reiterate that the Chinese military spending is more than that of all its Indo-Pacific neighbours combined. If the Indo-Pacific has evolved into a "geography of strategies… then Quad is concretizing them through policies and actions and now is the time to think and invest in *vertical and horizontal* development of Quad" to further a shared regional security agenda.

In fact, since the understanding of security today is not limited only to traditional notions such as the military, the Quad countries' cooperation in the economic sphere can also facilitate growth and stability in the post pandemic world order. Currently, the combined Gross Domestic Product (GDP) among the Quad countries is around "$34 trillion, with the US having the maximum share; in terms of trade, the total share within the grouping stands at 41 per cent for the US, 34 per cent for Japan, 14 per cent for India, and 11 per cent for Australia"; while there remains resistance to establishing free trade agreements among the Quad nations, they could pave the way for enhanced trade cooperation and commercial activity and also balance each other's respective economic weaknesses. If ever a Quad trade agreement were to become a reality, a reduction in trade costs would go a long way towards fulfilling the economic potential of the alliance.[10]

The Quad and Nuclear Challenges in the Indo-Pacific

It is evident that one of the essential organising values in the Indo-Pacific construct that is shared by almost all the countries is that of a free, open, inclusive, rules-based region. Expanding further, this implies, "freedom of navigation, the rule of law, freedom from coercion, respect for sovereignty, private enterprise, and open markets, and the freedom and independence of all nations".[11] Notwithstanding the definitional contestations, the security and stability of the region remains an implicit and stated goal for all the countries supporting the Indo-Pacific strategic construct. The nuclear conundrum posed by North Korea that is situated within the region does not align well with the broader objective of peace and security for the region. While the North Korean proliferation problem exists in the Indo-Pacific region, it has not been able to become a part of the conversation since some time. Indeed, though the issue has been recognised as a global proliferation challenge for many years and has invited condemnation by countries individually, especially the North Korean nuclear test of 2017, that initiated a nuclear crisis, it was only in the recent Quad meeting that the proliferation challenge posed by the country received a mention.

Unfortunately, in January 2022, North Korea had conducted a number of missile tests that carrier with it potential to disturb the stability of the Korean peninsula: not only does this set dangerous nuclear brinkmanship precedents, it also fuels the security dilemmas of South Korea which recently tested a ballistic missile from a submarine, becoming the only non-nuclear weapon state to do so. There is no denying that the North Korean nuclear conundrum poses a security threat in the region and is also well acknowledged by the countries. North Korea has been a nuclear proliferation challenge for more than a decade and till today it is the only nuclear Non-Proliferation Treaty (NPT) country that has challenged the non-proliferation regime in a manner as to have pursued its weapons capability, to further transcend into becoming a nuclear deterrent capability.

Post the nuclear crisis in 2017, a landmark summit between President Trump and the supreme leader, Kim Jong Un took place in Singapore in 2018. However, the promise of denuclearisation was lost after the second summit at Hanoi in 2019 failed to make any progress. Subsequently, in 2020, amidst the unprecedented pandemic, North Korea, with the revelation of its newest Intercontinental Ballistic Missile (ICBM) during the October Parade, once again conveyed its nuclear resolve, that it has been able to withstand the most stringent sanctions in the UN's history.[12]

If one takes a long view of the Indo-Pacific, one may argue that with time, the leading state actors in the region may have to take cognisance of the fact that an innovative approach may be required to resolve the nuclear conundrum.

The North Korean nuclear issue challenges the NPT from the outside, especially Articles I, II and IV and X of the treaty;[13] as mentioned earlier, its brinkmanship further sets unhealthy precedents for the security of the region. Furthermore, a longtime sanctions approach has failed to reverse the country's nuclear ambitions. Pyongyang has been able to manoeuvre the sanctions' pressure in a manner that only strengthens its nuclear commitment. It is evident that despite the most stringent sanctions, the country has shown an almost relentless resolve to strengthen its nuclear capability in scope and size. Finally, there exists no multilateral approach that addresses the issue. Ever since the failure of the Six-Party talks, the multilateral approach to negotiation in this context seems to have been abandoned. In fact, the goal of denuclearisation is viewed by countries such as China and Russia as a bilateral issue between the US and North Korea. In the recent past, even this approach has not manifested any result. In this context, the adoption of a multilateral approach might promise some progress like it had been able to break the longstanding Iranian nuclear impasse with the signing of the Joint Comprehensive Plan of Action (JCPOA) in 2014.

Within the strategic construct of the Indo-Pacific, currently, there exists no formal arrangement of countries that aims at taking up the North Korean nuclear issue, however, there is an implicit recognition of proliferation concerns vis-à-vis North Korea in almost every Indo-Pacific country's long-term view of regional stability. Unfortunately, mere recognition of the issue cannot facilitate a collective containment of the nuclear challenge that North Korea poses. In this context, a case for the Quad to take up the matter can be made based on one; crucial assumption. The Quad is an informal grouping that brings together like-minded countries, vibrant and pluralistic democracies, with shared values for a rules-based international order. The containment of nuclear proliferation in the region through the 'Quad-Squad' may not be entirely impossible to imagine; especially, if it aspires "to emerge as a major grouping in the world".[14] Additionally, if taken forward, this might be able to counter the narrative of an 'Asian NATO' as the main thrust of the endeavour would be upon enhancing the security of the region.

The Promise of Nuclear Power: An Asset for the Quad?

The recent (2021) Quad leaders summit took on three interrelated (green) goals to be delivered in the long run through the Quad Infrastructure Coordination Group, the prospective Green Shipping Network and the establishment of Clean Hydrogen Partnership Building. The infrastructure coordination group would lead the development of high standard infrastructure in the Indo-Pacific region through projects supporting "rural development, health infrastructure, water supply and sanitation, renewable power generation (e.g., wind, solar, and hydro), telecommunications, road transportation, and more"; alongside it will also focus on addressing the issue of climate change with urgency. Similarly, the Green Shipping Network and Clean Hydrogen Partnership Building would deliver on deployment of "green-port infrastructure and clean-bunkering fuels at scale" and also form a network dedicated to greening and decarbonising the shipping value chain. The Quad Shipping Task Force is to shape its work around several lines of efforts and aims to establish "two to three Quad low-emission or zero-emission shipping corridors by 2030." Additionally, the call for a clean hydrogen partnership would cater to the development of technology to scale up the production of clean hydrogen including "hydrogen produced from renewable energy, fossil fuels with carbon capture and sequestration, and *nuclear* for those who choose to deploy it." The stated goal also includes "delivery, store, distribute and safe transport of clean hydrogen for end-use applications."[15]

The same fact sheet has also highlighted shared concerns with the findings of the report of the August Intergovernmental Panel on Climate Change. This recent setting of the agenda is to be viewed as a follow-up from the first Quad meeting held in March 2021, where the countries declared the formation of a Climate Working Group (CWG) towards implementation of the Paris Agreement on Climate Change. Indeed, the Quad countries form a formidable region, including the Pacific, South Asia, East Asia and Australia that not only share, but also bear, the consequences of climate change. These countries are also home to a significant percentage of the world's GDP and thriving economic activity. Delivering on the Quad climate goals would not only have an overall stabilising effect but also have the potential to provide a global impetus to the climate change agenda. Nuclear energy being a low emission electrical source of energy, is often considered for clean hydrogen production. Additionally, "switching to less carbon intensive fuels such as nuclear is often seen as part of strategies addressing mitigation for stabilization of atmospheric greenhouse gas concentrations."[16]

Nuclear energy promotion by the Quad countries in the region as a part of the mix of strategies towards delivering on the goal of carbon reduction is worthy for long-term consideration. What is most crucial is that the market for such an endeavour does exist. In the year 2017, the ASEAN pre-feasibility study on the establishment of nuclear power plan in the ASEAN indicated the prospects of civilian nuclear power. It identified member states such as Indonesia, Malaysia, Vietnam, Thailand and the Philippines as frontrunners to establish civilian nuclear power programmes in the region. It further highlighted the possibility that the region may have its "first operational civilian nuclear power plant by 2030"[17] with Indonesia taking the lead. Media reports[18] have further suggested that two years later, the countries' interest in nuclear power persists. Malaysia, on the other hand, has taken the view to postpone the development of nation's first two nuclear power plants to 2030,[19] partly owing to public perceptions. In 2017, China and Thailand signed an agreement to cooperate in the peaceful use of nuclear energy,[20] Vietnam already has peaceful nuclear cooperation agreements with Japan and Russia. Recently, in June 2020, the Philippines took a giant step towards the possibility of incorporating nuclear power by creating an inter-agency panel to study the adoption of a national nuclear energy policy.[21] Considering the exceedingly low risk of states in the Southeast Asian region acquiring nuclear weapons,[22] it is plausible to suggest that exploration of the promise of nuclear power by the Quad countries with a view to accelerate engagement in the Indo-Pacific region could be a promising option. It is to be noted that the Southeast Asian region represents a strong commitment to the norm of nuclear non-proliferation and is one of the regions in Asia that is also a Nuclear Weapon Free Zone (NWFZ). Furthermore, the ASEAN states have adhered to their commitment to the 1968 nuclear Non-Proliferation Treaty (NPT) and the comprehensive Safeguards Agreements with the International Atomic Energy Agency (IAEA). The region is in good standing with the IAEA, the only organisation that oversees the monitoring of all the civilian nuclear cooperation agreements. Looking at the Indo-Pacific region through a nuclear lens is a relatively new idea, and it is unclear if the Quad countries have an appetite for it, as the official statements released in the past two summits have not explicitly cited this goal, nonetheless, the promise of nuclear energy is a long-term investment and has the potential to benefit the region in terms of economic security. However, this particular aspect, if it materialises may carry with it risk of getting labelled as a response to China's Belt and Road Initiative (BRI). Last year, in September (2021), India's Foreign Secretary Harsh, Shringla indicated that infrastructure partnerships between the Quad nations were independent of any other parameter, indirectly denying that the Quad infrastructure initiative was a counter to China's ambitious BRI.[23] This line of argument needs to have more resonance in the public policy spaces in case the Quad countries choose to take a lead on nuclear energy partnerships in the future.

The Quad and Internationalisation of the Taiwan Issue: A Dilemma Rather than a Challenge

While the Quad's first in-person summit statement did propose many deliverables, what it did not produce was a joint statement mentioning Taiwan. Even today, the four countries do not have a consensus on how to deal with the question of internationalisation of the Taiwan issue. While this reflects the reality that the four countries' interests and calculations remain individualistic on a matter that is directly related to China, the issue will remain a dilemma among the Quad countries for some time to come.

China seems to be developing a routine of escalation of tensions vis-à-vis Taiwan through its consistent and regular military posturing across the strait. In the recent past, Taiwan's Air Defence Identification

Zones (ADIZ) has reported some of the largest Chinese air incursions.[24] In fact, since mid-September of 2020, Beijing seemed to have stepped up its grey-zone tactics by regularly sending planes into Taiwan's ADIZ."[25]

The message is clear: to reiterate the 'one-China policy' in the year of the Chinese Communist Party's (CPC's) centenary celebrations to bolster the nationalist rhetoric. These incursions have become more pronounced, almost becoming a part of the strategic signalling between China on one side, and the US and its allies, on the other. Responding to this, the US too "conducted several rounds of naval patrols transiting the Taiwan Strait and signed a coast guard agreement with the country."[26]

Responding to this growing Chinese aggressive posture, the calls for supporting and defending Taiwan have become a part of the security conversations of significant Indo-Pacific players. This is being reflected in the recent joint statements from the US-Japan, Japan-Australia 2+2 Foreign-Defence Ministerial Consultation, European Union (EU)-Japan Summit and US-Republic of Korea (ROK), all of which have "underscored the importance of maintaining peace and stability in the Taiwan Strait".[27] Additionally, the reference to the bolstering of Taiwan's defence, even adding to such a power projection, is increasingly gaining acceptance. In a recent Australian National University (ANU) podcast, US diplomat Michael Goldman mentioned that "Taiwan figures as part of one of the contingencies in the US-Australia strategic planning".[28] The recent statement by Japan's deputy prime minister reiterating "the country's need to defend Taiwan with the United States in case the island was invaded"[29] resonates the same sentiment.

In a *Foreign Affairs* article titled, "American Support for Taiwan Must Be Unambiguous (2020)", the author, Richard Hass, made a convincing case for a shift in the US policy towards Taiwan: to adopt a policy of "strategic clarity" to replace the four-decade old policy of "strategic ambiguity". He further explained why now is the time for the US to explicitly declare the certainty of its response in the case of any contingency that directly or indirectly threatens the security of Taiwan.

This implies that the question of whether the US would come to the aid of Taiwan in the case of a Chinese attack should no longer be left as a guessing game. Haas argued that the US should not only declare its intention of preventing a misadventure in the Taiwan Strait, signalling a departure from the previous policy of ambiguity, but also dedicate and direct the American efforts towards the defence of Taiwan as a top priority, involving consultations with allies such as Japan and South Korea. For the US, the policy shift can be initiated in the form of a pledge, "in a manner that is consistent with the US' one-China policy, at the same time, laying down a clear indication that, in no way, this should be interpreted as US support to Taiwan's independence. It is noteworthy that the rationale for suggesting such a shift emanates mainly from two factors: one, the rising military gap between Taiwan and China; and, two, the growing assumption that China might attempt to gain control of Taiwan with the use of force.

It now appears that the long standing debate pertaining to supporting Taiwan's security is gaining currency within the strategic visions of the Indo-Pacific countries and gradually, the Taiwan issue is being 'internationalised' in the official conversations of Indo-Pacific players including important global platforms such as the G-7. The recent G-7 communique has come down heavily on China's pervasive practices that are not aligned with the global rules-based order and values. This includes human rights issues as well as economic practices. It has further reiterated the importance of "peace and stability across the Taiwan Strait, and … the peaceful resolution of cross-Strait issues."[30]

In the above context, the Quad is often talked about as an available and evolving framework to incorporate Taiwan. While some scholars have even argued in favour of taking forward the Taiwan agenda via the Quad plus framework as an attempt to "aid the … regional goals of balancing China and ensuring a free and open Indo-Pacific", [31] there are others who favour the Quad being supported as " a crucial part of the India-Australia-Japan proposed Supply Chain Resilience Initiative (SCRI)".[32] Some have even argued that "… the Quad countries should build up Taiwan's defensive capabilities … (and) the best option would be for Taiwan to produce its own weapons, and the Quad countries should support this ..."[33]

Viewed in the light of the recent Chinese behaviour that includes, isolation of Taiwan in international agencies such as the World Health Organisation (WHO), its increased military assertiveness surrounding the island which includes, "conducting 380 incursions into the island's air defence identification zone in 2020 alone"[34] and the recent public opinion polls in the state-run *Global Times* that are suggestive that "70 percent of mainlanders strongly support using force to unify Taiwan with the mainland"[35], there may be merit in considering with seriousness the internationalisation of the Taiwan issue within the Indo-Pacific Quad-Plus framework. Indeed, the evolving Chinese military and diplomatic postures have certainly created the space for such a policy execution; however, it is also true that internationalising the Taiwan issue within the evolving security contours of the Indo-Pacific will take its own course and will be largely governed by the countries' individual security priorities and their view on the future of their bilateral relations with China.

Additionally, if this happens, it would also come with a complex set of challenges of predicting the Chinese response towards the same. Will China interpret it as an infringement upon its sovereignty? Or a dilution of other countries' one-China policy? There are no clear answers. Amidst all this, what is becoming more pronounced, albeit faintly, is the idea of the Quad's strategic counterweight to be exploited to counter China, not only diplomatically but also militarily, especially for changing the military balance in the geography of the Indo-Pacific region, such as in the context of China Taiwan.

Furthermore, the idea of the inclusion of Taiwan as a part of any institutionalised mechanism in the Indo-Pacific, such as the Quad Plus, is possible for two reasons: (1) The Quad remains an issue-based alignment that is open to countries willing to cooperate on areas of mutual interests. If viewed in this context, the space for such inclusion exists; and (2) Taiwan itself has indicated its willingness[36] to participate in the Quad Plus framework. Yet, it is important to note here with caution that the Taiwan issue does not seem to be a strategic priority among the Quad countries for now. Thus, it remains to be seen how the Taiwan issue will be adopted as a part of any evolving mechanism in the Indo-Pacific, keeping intact the One China policy.

However, it is possible that in a situation of escalating tensions directly and imminently threatening peace across the Taiwan Strait, the internationalisation of the Taiwan issue within the Indo-Pacific strategic construct may take place. If that happens, it would largely be in response to the immediate Chinese security posture.

In this regard, the views from India, an important actor from the Indo-Pacific, definitely deserve mention. While the current joint statements from various players point in one direction, it is important to note that India has refrained from directly addressing the issue as yet. While India benefits from a prosperous and conflict-free Indo-Pacific, 'strategic ambiguity' may be the best course of action for now. The current interactions between the Governments of India and Taiwan are limited to unofficial, non-governmental ties, including "trade, investment, tourism, culture, education and other such people-to-people exchanges"[37] and would likely remain so in the immediate future. Yes, a possibility of India getting roped into the debate because of the expectations from the Indo-Pacific allies exists. However, in this case, the Indian equation with China as well as Taiwan, in relation to Taiwan's position on the India-China conflict, would likely determine the Indian response. One may argue that the possibility of India responding to the issue like the US may not be an immediate reality and would come with New Delhi's own reevaluation of its equation with Taiwan. Finally, the question of America's strategic clarity on Taiwan is to be addressed with caution. While the narrative suggests a policy shift, it would only be revealed later. Indeed, the passing of the "Taiwan Allies International Protection and Enhancement Initiative (TAIPEI) Act of 2019"[38] is significant; however, it has only "broadened the foundation of the (US') Taiwan policy and reinforced key commitments of the existing policy".[39] It doesn't reflect a significant shift; it is a call for mobilising diplomatic support for Taiwan. In the long run, it would be the most effective "in persuading ... some of Taiwan's 15 remaining diplomatic partners and other non-diplomatic partners to not switch ties from Taiwan, switching to Beijing or [encouraging them in] strengthening their ties with Taiwan ..."[40] For now, the Taiwan issue would only continue to figure in the strategic signalling of not the only US and its allies but also China.

Conclusion

The Quad was initially viewed as an aspirational development, but it has moved effectively in the past two years by expansion of its issue basket through the addition of newer working groups. In India's External Affairs Minister Jaishankar's words, "Quad being a contemporary arrangement, that is loose, creative, open minded ... has been able to take a sensible view of the problems to find effective solutions."[41] Not only has the Quad in Indo-Pacific survived, contrary to the Chinese view of it being a headline-grabbing idea(s) "...that may get some attention, but soon will dissipate,"[42] it has grown organically and shown progress. In fact, it is increasingly becoming a critical instrument to manage the China challenge not only vis-à-vis what China brings to the bilateral dyads but also with regard to responding to the repercussions of the assertive Chinese rise. Soon, on February 11, 2022, the fourth meeting of the Quad is to take place in Australia. The ministerial meeting is likely to further discussion on issues raised in the previous summits and discuss a range of bilateral and global priorities. Clearly, the future of the Quad holds immense significance not only for the region but also for the state of international affairs as its 'to-do list' ranges from rebuilding the post-pandemic economy, addressing non-traditional security threats such as climate change and maritime security in addition to emerging threats emanating from cyber, space, etc. The Quad has the potential to stabilise the global order and can be a remarkable strategic construct that is able to address the synergies between nations to be able to deliver on goals of 'common good' at the same time, while preserving and sustaining long-term peace in the region. It can be an answer to resolving and approaching conflicts, and a tool of politics to shape the direction of world politic; and therein lies its strategic imperative.

Notes

1. Rory Medcalf, "Indo-Pacific Visions: Giving Solidarity a Chance", *Asia Policy*, Vol. 14, No. 3, July 2019, pp. 79-95, at https://nsc.crawford.anu.edu.au/sites/default/files/publication/nsc_crawford_anu_edu_au/2019-08/ap14-3-medcalf-july2019.pdf. Accessed on October 18, 2021.
2. Statement and Releases, Fact Sheet: Quad Leaders' Summit, The White House Briefing Room, at https://www.whitehouse.gov/briefing-room/statements-

releases/2021/09/24/fact-sheet-Quad-leaders-summit/. Accessed on January 15, 2022.

3. Statements and Releases, "Quad Leaders' Joint Statement: The Spirit of the Quad", The White House Press Briefing, March 12, 2021, at https://www.whitehouse.gov/briefing-room/statements-releases/2021/03/12/Quad-leaders-joint-statement-the-spirit-of-the-Quad/
4. Prime Minister Scott Morrison, Media Release, March 13, 2021, at https://www.pm.gov.au/media/opening-remarks-virtual-Quad-leaders-meeting. Accessed on January 18, 2022.
5. Harsh V Pant and Shashank Mattoo, eds., "The Rise and Rise of the 'Quad': Setting an Agenda for India," ORF Special Report No. 161, September 2021, Observer Research Foundation, at https://www.orfonline.org/research/the-rise-and-rise-of-the-Quad-setting-an-agenda-for-india/. Accessed on January 10, 2022.
6. "Quad Leaders' Joint Statement: The Spirit of the Quad", March 12, 2021, Ministry of External Affairs (MEA), India, at https://mea.gov.in/bilateral-documents.htm?dtl/33620/Quad+Leaders+Joint+Statement+The+Spirit+of+the+Quad#:~:text=We%20support%20the%20rule%20of,democratic%20values%2C%20and%20territorial%20integrity.&text=Full%20of%20potential%2C%20the%20Quad,resilience%2C%20based%20on%20universal%20values. Accessed on January 18, 2022.
7. Jagannath Panda, "The Quad's Survival Depends on Managing Security and Trade Troubles", *National Interest,* October 3, 2021, at https://nationalinterest.org/feature/Quad%E2%80%99s-survival-depends-managing-security-and-trade-troubles-194772. Accessed on January 15, 2022.
8. " NATO is Cold War Term, Quad Looks into Future: EAM Jaishankar", *Business Standard,* September 11, 2021, at https://www.business-standard.com/article/international/nato-is-cold-war-term-Quad-looks-into-future-eam-jaishankar-121091100702_1.html.
9 Mark S Cogan, Vivek Mishra, "Quad and Indo-Pacific: The Counterterrorism Strategy", *Deccan Herald,* November 16, 2021, at https://www.deccanherald.com/opinion/main-article/Quad-and-indo-pacific-the-counterterrorism-strategy-1051514.html. Accessed on January 19, 2022.
10. Mukesh Aghi, "Why the Quad Needs to Improve Its Economic Game", *The Diplomat,* August 30,2021, at August 30,2021, https://thediplomat.com/2021/08/why-the-Quad-needs-to-improve-its-economic-game/#:~:text=With%20a%20trade%20partnership%2C%20the,the%20dynamic%20Indo%2DPacific%20region.&text=In%20March%2C%20the%20Quad%20made,the%20ASEAN%20nations%20by%202022. Accessed on January 10, 2022; Shijith Kunhitty, "Reimagining the Quad as Trade Alliance", *Mint,* November 9, 2020, at https://www.livemint.com/news/world/reimagining-the-Quad-as-a-trade-alliance-11604896433148.html. Accessed on January 11, 2022; "A Free Trade

Agreement Between Quad Nations: Vision or Reality?", *Financial Express,* August 26, 2020, at https://www.financialexpress.com/economy/a-free-trade-agreement-between-Quad-nations-vision-or-reality/2066170/

11. Mark J. Valencia, "What Does a 'Free and Open Indo-Pacific' Actually Mean?", *The Diplomat,* March 30, 2018, at https://thediplomat.com/2018/03/what-does-a-free-and-open-indo-pacific-actually-mean/. Accessed on October 20, 2021.
12. For details, see Hina Pandey, "Why Sanctions on North Korea Remain Ineffective", *Defence and Diplomacy Journal,* Vol. 9 No. 2, January-March 2020, pp. 83-92; and Hina Pandey "Assessing North Korea's Nuclear Resolve in the Times of COVID-19", *Japan Forward,* October 12, 2020, at https://japan-forward.com/assessing-north-koreas-nuclear-resolve-in-the-times-of-covid-19/. Accessed on November 20, 2021.
13. See the Non-Proliferation Treaty Text, UN Office of Disarmament Affairs, at https://www.un.org/disarmament/wmd/nuclear/npt/text, Accessed on November 18, 2021.
14. Ram Madhav, "Quad Must be Built on Agendas, not Emotions. Can't Afford to Become Another NATO", *Print,* October 16, 2020, at https://theprint.in/opinion/Quad-must-be-built-on-agendas-not-emotions-cant-afford-to-become-nato/524749/. Accessed on November 19, 2021.
15. Fact Sheet: Quad Leaders' Summit, MEA India, September 24, 2021, at https://www.mea.gov.in/bilateral-documents.htm?dtl/34319/Fact+Sheet+Quad+Leaders+Summit. Accessed on January 19, 2022; and ("Quad Infrastructure Coordination Group Launched during Summit in US", September 25, 2021. Available at https://sg.news.yahoo.com/Quad-infrastructure-coordination-group-launched-082234865.html. Accessed on January 12, 2022
16. "Carbon Dioxide Capture and Storage", IPCC Report, at https://www.ipcc.ch/site/assets/uploads/2018/03/srccs_wholereport-1.pdf. Accessed on January 28, 2022.
17. Nur Azha Putra and Philip Andrews-Speed, "Prospects for Nuclear Power in ASEAN", *The Diplomat,* December 28, 2021.
18. Yogi Sugiawan and Shunsuke Managi, "Taking the Nuclear Option", *Inside Indonesia,* at https://www.insideindonesia.org/taking-the-nuclear-option. Accessed on November 22, 2021.
19. Martin Carvalho, "Malaysia Will Only Have Nuclear Plants after 2030, *Nation,* November 3, 2016, at https://www.thestar.com.my/news/nation/2016/11/03/malaysia-to-have-nuclear-power-after-2030. Accessed on November 22, 2021.
20. "China, Thailand Agree to Nuclear Energy Cooperation", April 5, 2017, *World Nuclear News,* at https://www.world-nuclear-news.org/NP-China-Thailand-agree-to-nuclear-energy-cooperation-0504174.html. Accessed on November 21, 2021.
21. Enrico Dela Cruz, "Philippines Takes 'Major Step' Toward Using Nuclear Power, at https://www.reuters.com/article/us-philippines-energy-nuclear-idUSKCN24U14E. Accessed on November 21, 2021.

22. Trever Findlay, "The Asia–Pacific Nuclear Governance Architecture Part I: Assessing the Need", Asia Pacific Leadership Network (APLN) & Centre for Nuclear Non-proliferation and Disarmament CNND, Policy Brief, 40, December 21, 2021, at http://www.apln.network/briefings/briefings_view/Policy_Brief_No_40_-_The_Asia-Pacific_Nuclear_Governance_Architecture_Part_I:_Assessing_the_Need. Accessed on November 21, 2021.
23. "Quad Infra Partnership Independent of BRI, Indian Foreign Secretary Tells Wion", https://www.wionews.com/india-news/Quad-infra-partnership-independent-of-bri-indian-foreign-secretary-tells-wion-415770. Accessed on January 28, 2022.
24. "Taiwan Reports Largest Daily Incursion yet by Chinese Air Force", June 16, 2021, https://edition.cnn.com/2021/06/15/asia/taiwan-china-warplanes-largest-adiz-incursion-intl-hnk-ml/index.html. Accessed on December 18, 2021
25. "Chinese Warplane Enters Taiwan's Air Defence Zone, 4th Incursion This Month", *Business Standard*, July 8, 2021, at https://www.business-standard.com/article/international/chinese-warplane-enters-taiwan-s-air-defence-zone-4th-incursion-this-month-121070800154_1.html. Accessed on December 21, 2021.
26. Melissa Conley Tyler, "Biden Wins over Taiwan", *East Asia Forum*, June 29, 2021, at https://www.eastasiaforum.org/2021/06/29/biden-wins-over-taiwan/. Accessed on December 22, 2021.
27. "US- Japan Joint Leaders' Statement: "US– Japan Global Partnership For A New Era", White House Briefing, April 16, 2021, at https://www.whitehouse.gov/briefing-room/statements-releases/2021/04/16/u-s-japan-joint-leaders-statement-u-s-japan-global-partnership-for-a-new-era/. Accessed on June 13, 2021; and "US-ROK Leaders' Joint Statement", White House, May 21, 2021, at https://www.whitehouse.gov/briefing-room/statements-releases/2021/05/21/u-s-rok-leaders-joint-statement/. Accessed on June 13, 2021, and Joint Statement, "EU-Japan Summit 2021. Taking Forward a Flourishing Partnership". Available at https://www.consilium.europa.eu/media/49922/eu-japan-summit-may-2021-statement.pdf and Ninth Japan-Australia 2+2 Foreign and Defence Ministerial Consultations, June 9, 2021, at https://www.foreignminister.gov.au/minister/marise-payne/media-release/ninth-japan-australia-22-foreign-and-defence-ministerial-consultations
28. National Security Podcast, "Charge d'Affaires Mike Goldman on US-Australia Relations and Regional Security", Australian National University, at https://play.acast.com/s/the-national-security-podcast/charged-affairesmikegoldmanonus-australiarelationsandregionalsecurity. Accessed on December 14, 2021.
29. "Japan Deputy PM Comment on Defending Taiwan if Invaded Angers China", *Reuters*, July 6, 2021, at https://www.reuters.com/world/asia-pacific/japans-aso-peaceful-solution-desirable-any-taiwan-contingency-2021-07-06/. Accessed on December 22, 2021.

30. G-7 Statement, "Carbis Bay G7 Summit Communiqué", June 13, 2021, at https://www.whitehouse.gov/briefing-room/statements-releases/2021/06/13/carbis-bay-g7-summit-communique/. Accessed on December 15, 2021.
31. Jagannath Panda, "Will the Quad Evolve and Embrace Taiwan?", *National Interest,* February 17, 2021, at https://nationalinterest.org/blog/buzz/will-Quad-evolve-and-embrace-taiwan-178351. Accessed on December 14, 2021.
32. Ibid.
33. Satoru Nagao, "The Quad Must Strengthen and Support Taiwan," August 2, 2020, at https://www.sundayguardianlive.com/news/Quad-must-strengthen-support-taiwan. Accessed on December 14, 2021.
34. Oriana Skylar Mastro, "The Taiwan Temptation: Why Beijing Might Resort to Force," July/August 2021, at https://www.foreignaffairs.com/articles/china/2021-06-03/china-taiwan-war-temptation. Accessed on December 13, 2021.
35. Ibid.
36. Martin Greene, "DPP Legislator Suggests Taiwan Join Quad", *Taiwan News,* December 30, 2020, at https://www.taiwannews.com.tw/en/news/4090313. Accessed on December 18, 2021.
37. "Rajya Sabha: Unstarred Question No. 1205, to Be Answered on 11.02.2021", at https://mea.gov.in/rajya-sabha.htm?dtl/33511/question+no1205+peopletopeople+contact+with+taiwan. Accessed on December 15, 2021.
38. 116th Congress Public Law 135, US Government Publishing Office, Taiwan Allies International Protection And Enhancement Initiative, (Taipei) Act Of 2019, at https://www.govinfo.gov/content/pkg/PLAW-116publ135/html/PLAW-116publ135.htm. Accessed on December 23, 2021.
39. Mercy A. Kuo, "Trump and the TAIPEI Act", *The Diplomat,* April 21, 2021, at https://thediplomat.com/2020/04/trump-and-the-taipei-act/. Accessed on December 23, 2021.
40. Ibid.
41. Transcript of Interview of External Affairs at the Global Technology Summit 2021, *MEA,* December 14, 2022, at https://mea.gov.in/interviews.htm?dtl/34656/Transcript_of_Interview_of_External_Affairs_Minister_at_the_Global_Technology_Summit_2021_14_December_2021, Accessed on February 5, 2022.
42. "Quad Move will Dissipate like Sea Foam: China" *The Times of India,* March 8, 2018, at https://timesofindia.indiatimes.com/world/china/quad-move-will-dissipate-like-sea-foam-china/articleshow/63221055.cms. Accessed on February 5, 2022.

PART III

Moving Beyond the Quad

9. India-ASEAN Geoeconomic Engagement in the Indo-Pacific: Potential Role of Rare Earth Elements

Neha Mishra

Introduction

The geoeconomic goals of India began to take shape with the Raisina Dialogue in 2016, a joint strategic initiative by the Ministry of External Affairs (MEA) and the Observer Research Foundation (ORF). The dialogue emphasised the theme of 'Asian Connectivity' as the key to the energy security as well as economic growth of India. As part of her inaugural address to the Raisina Dialogue Conference, the then External Affair Minister Sushma Swaraj said, "Connectivity is the key not just to India's development ambition but also its vision for international cooperation ... this is in our DNA, after all, we are the inheritors of two powerful connectivity legacies: the message of the Buddha and the Spice Route."[1]

In his address to the conference, organised by the Gateway House Mumbai and MEA on the theme, "Where Geopolitics Meets Business", S. Jaishankar, the former foreign secretary and current minister of external affairs, said, "There is a sharper realization that the real strengths of any nation are primarily economic, that, in turn, has led to a growing recognition that business provides the ballast for many of our important international relationships: ASEAN, the Gulf, the US and China are examples."[2] However, India, as a geoeconomic country is yet to develop, considering its limited capacity to deploy economic instruments to achieve geopolitical objectives as famously stated, "To practise geoeconomics, a country needs not just the economic cards valuable to others but must be prepared to play them well".[3]

The Indo-Pacific is one such area, having significant geopolitical and geostrategic importance for India. The significance of the 'Indo-Pacific' has been analysed from three faces or International Relations (IR) perspectives: the 'Realist Face' perceives balancing against China as a preferable strategy; the 'Liberal Face' perceives cooperation by forming new 'institutional settings' as ideal for the Indo-Pacific states; and the 'Constructivist Face' emphasises the ideational construct along with value-oriented and norm-based diplomacy to alter the power relations in the region. However, these three faces follow a limited perspective based on asymmetric power division—that is, all regional nations vs China reflect more a Western perspective.[4]

The Indian approach to the Indo-Pacific needs to go beyond the three faces or perspectives and shift to enhancement of regional geoeconomic interaction. The Indian engagement with the Indo-Pacific is to counter China and secure its geopolitical access to resources in the Indo-Pacific littorals. The need for a changed economic strategy and diplomacy was also stressed by the former Foreign Secretary of India Shivshankar Menon (2006-09) when he said, "India's deepening integration into the global economy required changes in India's external behaviour, a thorough revamping of the Government of India's machinery, and moving the focus of much of our diplomatic work to economic diplomacy".[5] India's engagement with the Indo-Pacific and Southeast Asian regions developed due to multiple factors like China's expanding southward orientation, the renewing interest of Japan in the Asian sub-regions, and the rebalancing by the United States (US) vis-à-vis Asia and the Indo-Pacific region.[6] The partnership with multilateral forums like Association of Southeast Asian Nations (ASEAN), Quadrilateral Security Dialogue (Quad), Indian Ocean Rim Association (IORA), ASEAN Regional Forum (ARF), and so on, has been enhancing India's engagement with the region.

India-ASEAN Geoeconomic Engagement in the Indo-Pacific

ASEAN is the most successful example of regional multilateralism, whose combined Gross Domestic Product (GDP) rose from US$ 95 billion in the 1970s to US$ 2.55 trillion in 2016 and is even predicted to reach US$ 6.4 trillion in 2027. Besides sharing geographical proximities and cultural roots, bilateral diplomacy has enhanced the India-ASEAN partnership from a sectoral dialogue (1992) to a full dialogue (1996), and then to a strategic partnership since 2016.[7]

The India-ASEAN economic relations began to take a good shape with India's 'Look East' policy, which is believed to have gone through two implementation phases. The first phase (1990-2003) strengthened the economic and trade relations, and the second phase (2004-2014) enhanced the diplomatic, security and political linkages between India and ASEAN. In 2014, the shift from Look East to Act East was adopted under Prime Minister Narendra Modi to counter the increasing Chinese expansion in the South China and East China Seas.[8] The India-ASEAN Free Trade Agreement (IAFTA) that was signed in 2009 enhanced their trade volume as well as trade deficit.[9] The interaction was further enhanced by the "Indo-Pacific Treaty of Friendship and Cooperation" (2013) that Marty Natalegawa, the foreign minister of Indonesia, proposed to contain the increasing dominance of China in the Indo-Pacific region.[10] Besides multilateral association with ASEAN, India has also built individual security and strategic ties with the ASEAN countries. Besides IAFTA, India has separate FTAs with Singapore and Malaysia, making India's first and third-largest trading partners among ASEAN members (see Table 9.2). On a bilateral level, India has a joint declaration on a strategic partnership with Vietnam; defence cooperation with Singapore; Artificial Intelligence (AI) sharing with Myanmar, and massive Foreign Direct Investment (FDI) inflows from Thailand, Malaysia and Indonesia.[11] At the same time, India's economic integration with the ASEAN in services trade, despite not joining the Regional Comprehensive Economic Partnership (RCEP), shows how India's trade interests are taken into consideration by the ASEAN members.

Table 9.1: India-ASEAN Bilateral Trade Statistics

India's trade with ASEAN	2014-15	2015-16	2016-17	2017-18	2018-19	2019-20	2020-21
Export (Billion US$)	31.81	25.13	30.96	34.20	37.47	31.55	31.49
% Growth	-3.99	-21.00	23.19	10.47	9.56	-15.82	-0.19
Import (Billion US$)	44.71	39.91	40.62	47.13	59.32	55.37	47.42
% Growth	8.33	-10.75	1.77	16.04	25.86	-6.66	–14.36
Total (Billion US$)	76.53	65.04	71.58	81.34	96.80	86.92	78.90
Trade Balance (Billion US$)	-12.90	-14.78	-9.66	-12.93	-21.85	-23.82	-15.93

Source: Ministry of Commerce and Industry, Department of Commerce https://commerce.gov.in/about-us/divisions/foreign-trade-territorial-division/foreign-trade-asean/

ASEAN's policies acknowledge the Asia-Pacific and Indian Ocean region as closely integrated and interconnected regions and the Indo-Pacific for dialogue and cooperation rather than rivalry.[12] It has been an inclusive institution that has maintained cordial relations with the Indo-Pacific littorals, including India and China, inviting them to be observer members. In addition, initiatives like ASEAN-plus three (China, Japan and Korea) and ASEAN-plus six (Australia, China, Japan, India, Korea and New Zealand) reflect its attempt at inclusive institutionalisation of the Indo-Pacific.[13] However, the Chinese regional activities impacting ASEAN's trade and commercial priorities invoked ASEAN to reshape its geostrategies towards China and the Indo-Pacific region. In an interview, Chinese Foreign Minister Wang Yi stated that the "Indo-Pacific concept is like the sea foam in the Pacific or the Indian Ocean-that may get some attention but soon will dissipate". It has been observed that the US' acknowledgement of the 'Indo-Pacific' term and emphasis on a free and open Indo-Pacific strategy while abandoning the Trans-Pacific Partnership (TPP) alarmed China to enhance its dominance in the Indo-Pacific.[14] As a result of increased Chinese dominance, the regional polarisation and marginalisation began to expand in the Indo-Pacific and, thereby, affected ASEAN's policies.[15] It should be noted that

India-ASEAN interaction in the Indo-Pacific has developed due to their common needs to both balance the reassurance with China individually and counter-balance Chinese preeminence in the Indo-Pacific region at the same time.[16]

Table 9.2: Country-wise India-ASEAN Trade Figures

Asean	Trade (in billion US$)			
Country	2017-18	2018-19	2019-20	2020-21
Singapore	17.67	27.85	23.67	21.98
Malaysia	14.71	17.25	16.15	14.43
Vietnam SOC Rep	12.83	13.7	12.34	11.12
Thailand	10.79	11.88	11.09	9.92
Indonesia	20.4	21.13	19.19	17.50
Philippines	2.46	2.32	2.05	2.02
Myanmar	1.61	1.73	1.52	1.30
Cambodia	0.18	0.24	0.23	0.21
Brunei	0.5	0.65	0.64	0.39
Lao Pd Rp	0.19	0.04	0.03	0.03
Asean	81.34	96.8	86.92	78.92
World	769.11	844.16	788.07	686.24
% Share	10.58	11.47	11.03	11.50

Source: Ministry of Commerce and Industry, Department of Commerce https://commerce.gov.in/about-us/divisions/foreign-trade-territorial-division/foreign-trade-asean/

Like ASEAN, India is also concerned about China's strategic encirclement, its navigation politics in the South China Sea, naval forays, and anti-piracy patrols in the Indian Ocean. But, unlike ASEAN, India has been unwilling to explicitly admit China as the primary determining element of its Indo-Pacific policies. India's approach towards the Indo-Pacific region may be explained as neither hedging and balancing, but as an 'evasive balancing strategy' that includes elements of both balancing and reassurance.[17] The ASEAN countries want India to play a more significant counter-balancing role to a rising China. However, they continue to see India as an unreliable security partner due to New Delhi's non-confrontational nature.[18]

It is believed that India can utilise its services sector exports to the ASEAN countries to get a hold on its relationship with them.[19] In terms of geoeconomic engagement, India and the ASEAN countries have been interdependent in trading essential metals and minerals (Table 9.3). For example, India exports a large amount of refined petroleum and raw aluminium to the ASEAN member countries. The ASEAN countries export copper and iron wire, structures and pipes to India.

Table 9.3: India-ASEAN Geoeconomic Trading

ASEAN Country	Major Metals Import from India	Major Metals Export to India	Major Minerals Import from India	Major Minerals Export to India
Singapore	Raw Aluminium, Iron and Steels Bars	Scrap Iron and Aluminium, and Ferro alloys	Refined Petroleum	Refined Petroleum
Malaysia	Raw Aluminium	Copper Wire, Raw Aluminium and Copper Pipes	Refined Petroleum	Crude Petroleum
Myanmar	Stranded Aluminium Wire and Metal Mountings	Raw Zinc, Lead, Iron Structures and Scrap Aluminum	Refined Petroleum	Cement and Ores
Laos	Iron Fasteners	Zinc Powder	-	-
Brunei	Other Copper and Iron products	Small Iron Pipes	Barium Sulphate	Crude Petroleum
Cambodia	Metal Fasteners	Iron structures and Metal Office Supplies	-	Refined Petroleum, Salt and Clays
Thailand	Semi-finished Iron, Raw Aluminium and Ferro alloys	Copper Wire, Scrap Iron and Iron Fasteners	Refined Petroleum, Salt, Soapstone and Clays	Molybdenum ores, Refined Petroleum and Coal Tar Oil
Vietnam	Hot Rolled Iron and Raw Lead	Copper and Small Iron Pipes, Copper Wire and Raw Lead	Feldspar, Salt, Granite, Quartz, Iron and Clays	Crude Petroleum, Gravel Stone and Limestone

Philippines	Semi-Finished Iron, Iron Structures, Stranded Aluminium Wire and Iron Products	Scrap Iron, Raw Lead and Scrap Aluminium	Refined Petroleum	Copper and Iron ore, Coal Briquettes and Iron ore
Indonesia	Semi-Finished Iron, Stainless Steel, and Raw Zinc	Copper Wire, Raw tin, Semi-Finished Iron	Refined Petroleum, Iron Ore and Coke	Coal Briquettes, Copper ore and Petroleum Coke

Source: The table has been prepared by the author using the data sourced from the Observatory of Economic Complexity (OEC).

India and Myanmar-Malaysia: Case Studies for Geoeconomic Engagement

Singapore is the largest trade partner of India among all the ASEAN members and even matches the rule of economic-resource dependence as part of the geoeconomic engagement. Moreover, their economic-resource linkage has been increasing, with India exporting US$ 552 million worth of petroleum to Singapore, and Singapore exporting integrated circuits and semiconductors worth US$ 163 million.[20] Singapore is also strategically as well as geopolitically significant, being located at the connecting point of the Indian Ocean and Pacific Ocean.[21] It is noteworthy that Singapore has already been established as India's geoeconomic gateway to ASEAN.

However, the focus of this chapter is 'Rare Earth Elements' (REEs) to suggest the enhancement of geoeconomic engagement between India and ASEAN. Out of all the ASEAN members, Myanmar and Malaysia have rare earth reserve-production capacity that can be a new frontier for cooperation.

India-Myanmar

Myanmar's geostrategic importance, being located at the centre of the Indo-Pacific region, developed with (a) China's strategic presence and engagement with the Myanmar mining industry; (b) the security concerns arising in the northeast region due to border sharing with Myanmar. Rajiv Bhatia, a former ambassador to Myanmar, explained how India's approach towards Myanmar changed following the "two-track policy". Through the twin-track policy, India deals with both the military and democratic forces of Myanmar simultaneously, putting itself in an advantageous position.[22]

Myanmar is a crucial part of India's Act East policy towards the Southeast Asian region. Although the India-Myanmar bilateral/ trade relations go back to their Treaty of Friendship (1951) and Trade Agreement (1994), China managed to have a more effective engagement with Myanmar than India. The location of Myanmar as a bridge between South Asia and Southeast Asia and its membership of organisations like ASEAN, Bay of Bengal Initiative for Multi-Sectoral and Economic Cooperation (BIMSTEC), and Greater Mekong Sub-region (GMS), or other sub-regional blocks, further its geopolitical and geostrategic significance for India. India already has multiple connectivity projects running in Myanmar, of which the India-Myanmar-Thailand Trilateral Highway is the most important that will further India's connectivity with the ASEAN countries. Besides the geopolitical significance, Myanmar has great geoeconomic importance, being rich in natural resources, non-metallic minerals and other precious stones.[23]

India-Malaysia

The countries established their diplomatic relations long ago in the 1960s after the independence of Malaysia, which grew further under the governments of Prime Minister (PM) Nehru and PM Tunku Abdul Rahman Putra. Later, Malaysian PM Abdullah Badawi and his successor PM Dato' Seri Mohd. Najib Tun Abdul Razak worked to enhance the cordial relationship with India. In 2015, during the visit of Indian PM Narendra Modi to Malaysia, a joint statement was issued to strengthen the strategic partnership between India and Malaysia. In 2017, the visit of PM Najib Razak to India marked the 60th anniversary of India-Malaysia diplomatic relations. The bilateral Comprehensive Economic Cooperation Agreement (CECA) signed in 2011 has been guiding the economic and commercial relationship between the two countries. As per MEA data (2019), the US$ 17.24 billion trade figure was reported between the two, as part of which India majorly imported mineral fuels, electrical machinery and equipment from Malaysia. Malaysia also ranked as the 24th largest investor in India with a total FDI inflow of US$ 932.19 million and the infrastructure/construction sector is the key area of investment.[24]

Besides economic and diplomatic relations, India and Malaysia share robust maritime connectivity considering the geographical proximity of Malaysia for India. The Malay peninsula is a very significant stopover for Indian vessels sailing between the Middle and the Far East.[25] Peninsular Malaysia serves as a strategic stopover or rest/repairing stations for Indian vessels to trade through the Indian Ocean region. In addition, India shares maritime boundaries with Malaysia through the Andaman and Nicobar Islands.[26] The global status of Malaysia as an independent and non-aligned country, and its regional status as a trade power, with a critical role in regional associations like ASEAN, reflects its idea of foreign policy. In addition, the strategic proximity of Malaysia to the Malacca Strait, Sunda Strait, and South China Sea amplifies its maritime importance.[27]

What are Rare Earth Elements?

According to the International Union of Pure and Applied Chemistry (IUPAC) definition, "rare earth metals comprise a family of 15 elements in the periodic table, starting with lanthanum and ending with lutetium, together known as the 'lanthanides group".[28] Because of their unique electronic configuration with "$4f^0$ to $4f^{14}$" orbital electrons cells ($[Xe]4f^0$ to $[Xe]4f^{14}$), their physical and chemical properties are comparable and occur in nature under similar physical-chemical conditions. Two more elements from Group 3A, Yttrium (Atomic# 39) and Sc (Atomic# 21), are also often included as Rare Earth Elements (REEs) because of their similarity in physical and chemical properties and geochemical affinity with REEs.[29]

These elements have been subdivided into Heavy (HREE, At# 65 to 71) and Light REEs (LREE; At# 57 to 64) based on their atomic weights; however, the exact boundary between heavy and light is often not well defined. It has been observed that light rare earth elements are much more abundant in the earth's crust than the heavy ones, which makes

Table 9.4: The Seventeen Rare Earth Elements

Rare Earth Name	Discovery Year	Atomic Name & Number	The Chemist who Named it	Light/ Heavy REE	Critical/ Uncritical	Abundance in the Earth Crust (Parts per million)	Usage
Yttrium	1788	Y-39	Sweden-Johan Gadolin	Heavy	Critical	-	Metal Alloys and Night Vision Goggles
Cerium	1803	Ce-58	Europe- John Jacob Berzelius	Light	Excessive	60.0	Automobiles
Lanthanum	1839	La-57	Sweden- Carl Gustaf Mosander	Light	Uncritical	30.0	Optical Glasses, Night Vision Goggles
Erbium	1842	Er-68	"	Heavy	Critical	2.1	Fibre and Optic Cables Machine
Terbium	1843	Tb-65	"	Heavy	Critical	0.7	Visual Display and Fuel Cells
Ytterbium	1878	Yb-70	Sweden- Jean-Charles Galissard	Heavy	Excessive	2.0	Stainless Steels
Holmium	1878	Ho-67	Sweden- Per Teodor Cleve	Heavy	Excessive	0.8	High Strength Magnets and Glass Colouring
Scandium	1879	Sc-21	Scandinavia- Lars Fredrik Nilson	Heavy	Critical	16.0	Defence Equipment
Samarium	1879	Sm-62	France- Paul-Émile Lecoq de	Light	Uncritical	5.3	Nuclear Reactors
Thulium	1879	Tm-69	Sweden- Per Teodor Cleve	Heavy	Excessive	0.3	Lasers, Portable X-ray Machines

Praseodymium	1885	Pr-59	Germany- Carl Auer von Welsbach	Light	Uncritical	6.7	Lasers
Neodymium	1885	Nd-60	-	Light	Critical	27.0	Laser Ranger Finders Communication
Dysprosium	1886	Dy-66	France- Paul-Émile Lecoq de	Heavy	Critical	3.8	Permanent Magnets
Europium	1886	Eu-63	Europe- Eugène-Anatole Demarçay	Heavy	Critical	1.3	Optical Fibres
Gadolinium	1886	Gd-64	Sweden- Johan Gadolin	Heavy	Uncritical	4.0	X-ray and Scanning
Lutetium	1907	Lu-71	Austria- Carl Auer von Welsbach and Georges Urbain	Heavy	Excessive	0.4	Petroleum Refining
Promethium	1947	Pm-61	America- Jacob A. Marinsky, Lawrence E. Glendenin, and Charles D. Coryell	-	-	10^{-18}	Doesn't exist on earth, but its isotopes are available in the radioactive elements.

Source: Rose Ragsdale, "Rare Earth Metals See New Medical Uses", *Metal Tech News*, June 27, 2020. https://www.metaltechnews.com/story/2020/04/29/tech-metals/rare-earth-metals-see-new-medicaluses/217.html#:~:text=Holmium%20lasers%20emit%20at%202.1,problems%20with%20a%20thulium%20laser. Accessed on July 16, 2021.

HREEs critical. Among LREEs, neodymium is the most critical one as it is extensively used in all mobile phones, medical equipment and electric vehicles. In addition, the permanent magnets used in wind turbines and data storage systems use neodymium as an essential ingredient. Heavy elements like dysprosium, yttrium, and cerium are critical for clean energy technologies; however, they have a small market due to their limited supply[30] (see Table 9.4 for the use of other elements). It has been challenging to balance the abundance of rare earth ores and their products as per their demand in the market.

Table 9.5: Application of Rare Earth Elements

Rare Earth Use	Sector
Magnesium alloys involve REE elements for strengthening steels, weld ability and ductility of iron.	Aerospace Engineering
A mixture of La, Nd and Pr	Petroleum Catalyst
Cerium for self-cleaning ovens	Polymerisation Catalyst
La-oxide for memory elements of video displays, storage system	Ceramics
Cerium used as mixed compounds and separated high-purity materials for polishing, optics, decolouring, colouring, radiation control, fluorescence, glass coatings.	Glass
Samarium-cobalt magnets to reduce the size and weight of magnets in television, microwaves, watches, radar missile guidance systems, and computer communications	Permanent Magnets
Neodymium-iron-boron-magnets are used in brushless motors, computer devices, and automobiles.	Permanent Magnets
REE used for cathode-ray tubes, X-ray screens, lamps and lasers.	Phosphors

Chinese Monopoly on Rare Earth Value Supply Chain

The nuclear arms race started among countries like the Soviet Union, the US, Germany, China, and other countries shaped the politics around rare earth elements until the 1960s. The US was established as a primary producer in the 1960s and continued to remain so until the 2000s. When China conducted its first nuclear weapon test in 1964, the realisation developed for the need to develop research programmes for rare earth and other non-ferrous metals. Professor Guangxian worked on isolating uranium as a part of his discovery of the 'cascade theory of counter current extraction', which revolutionised rare earth production and marked the beginning of China's technological superiority in the rare earth sector—and the veritable end of US dominance in the early 21st century.

During the atomic period, the stance of the US government on rare earth was different as reflected in the statement, "If rare-earth were to become unavailable, the effect on our present standard of living would not be catastrophic because in most applications the rare earth is merely replacing materials that are less effective for the particular purpose".[31] However, the expanding Chinese rare earth industry changed the stance of the US. In the 1980s, a regulation was imposed by the Nuclear Regulatory Commission and International Atomic Energy Agency that eliminated extraction of rare earth minerals bearing uranium and thorium. The US rare earth market depended on the phosphate ores (Th-U-REE-P) or monazite minerals, and the regulation affected its dominance on the supply chain. This brought the Mountain Pass Era to an end with increased Rare Earth Element Oxide (REO) production in China (particularly in Baotou in Inner Mongolia) in the 1990s.[32]

The declining US supply chain in the rare earth market was ideally used by China to enhance its REE leadership and gain geopolitical influence. To achieve the same, China launched two high-tech innovation Programs 863 and 973, to implement a third modernisation process to develop high-tech for space, information, laser, automation, energy. Professor Xu Guangxian, father of the Chinese rare earth industry, with his research enabled extracting isotopes of uranium in rare earth extraction and development of REEs cutting-edge technologies, which contributed to enhancing the REE exporting capabilities of China.[33] In 1997, Magnequench, the world's leading American REE manufacturing facility, shut down and was later sold to two Chinese companies, whose ownership helped China to dominate in the rare earth value chain, eliminating its Western competitors. In 2005, the Chinese government implemented the 'Rare Earth Industry Development Plan (2009-2015)' to have a long-lasting transformation of the REE industry.[34]

China began to dominate in all aspects of REE supply chains: production, processing, consumption, and research and development. It has developed 13 rare earth deposits over the years, out of which the Inner Mongolia deposit has become the largest in the world. The Bayon Obo rare earth iron ore in Inner Mongolia has the minerals bastnaesite and monazite, enabling China to deal with the regulatory constraints and fill the breach or gap.[35] The growing extraction of rare earth elements and their environmental impacts made the Chinese government work on cleaner production of these and shift towards greener hydrometallurgy of the bastnaesite. In 2012, the 'Rare Earth Industry Accession Requirements' was released by the Raw Materials Office of China's Ministry of Industry and Information Technology (MIIT) to uplift production and stop illegal mining.[36] To improve the extraction and separation process, China initiated new leaching processes using roasting-acid oxidation, bake-water sulfuric acid, and NH_4CI roasting. These efforts enabled China to reduce the environmental impacts by taking initiatives like eliminating the waste water discharge having thorium-radioactive solid, fluorine, ammonium nitrogen or high salinity.[37] The 'Implementation Proposal of Cleaner Production Technologies in Rare Earth Industry' issued by the MIIT in 2014 led to the publication of the 'Plan for the Development of Rare Earth Industry (2016-2020)', which generalised the rare earth engineering and reform for cleaner production.[38] These initiatives furthered Chinese dominance in the rare earth supply chain and market.

Chinese resource trade diplomacy enhanced with its joining the World Trade Organisation (WTO) in 2001 as an official member, bringing China into the global market as a potential trading power.[39] For China, resource security is both a national strategic priority and an economic 'soft rib', and its potential for geostrategic use of REEs reflects in its 95-97 per cent of critical elements production capacity. In the opinion of several experts, China has an opportunity to get economic leverage over other great powers if their demand for rare earth continues.[40]

First Geopolitical Employment of REE: China-Japan Senkaku Island Conflict

China imposed export restrictions on critical REE minerals to Japan in response to the detention of a Chinese fishing trawler captain which affected Japan's auto industry, being the largest importer of REEs.[41]

The same export restriction was used during the China-Japan Senkaku/ Diaoyu Island dispute (2012), but China didn't issue any official statement considering the diverse REEs sources accessed by Japan after the 2010 event.[42] China's resource geostrategy was taken as a severe threat by the United States, European Union and Japan, which led them to file a suit in WTO, which ruled that China could not put limits on REE exports. But, the ruling of the WTO came four years later, and then China denied the accusation, claiming that it restricted the export because it needed more REEs for its own industries.[43]

With the rise of digital economies, satellite communication significance to the International Political Economy (IPE), security and science, the US stance changed as reflected in its 2013 House of Representatives passing HR 761 that declared the availability of rare earth to be essential for economic growth, national security, technological innovation, and manufacturing and agricultural supply chains. In this phase, the REEs had a different significance for different countries: Germany; spice metals; China; MSG (monosodium glutamate) of industry; Japan: vitamins of modern industry.[44]

Second REE Trade Embargo: US-China Trade War

In 2018, the actions and decisions of US President Donald Trump, such as withdrawal from the Trans-Pacific Partnership, renaming of the North American Free Trade Agreement (NAFTA) as the US-Mexico Canada Agreement (USMCA) and allegation on China for disrespecting the intellectual property rights of US companies. As a result, the US Administration first imposed tariffs on China in July 2018, and added the Huawei technologies to the entity list in May 2019. The tariffs reached more than US$ 250 million by June 2019. In retaliation, China also imposed tariffs and restricted market access for American products. However, the most important retaliation was the embargo on rare earth metals and their compounds exports.[45] The official newspaper of the Chinese Communist Party's Central Committee, *Renmin Ribao*, wrote, "We advise the US side not to underestimate the Chinese side's ability to safeguard the development rights and interests. So don't say we didn't warn you."[46] This reflected China's confidence in its monopoly over the

REE supply chain that can affect the importing countries in very serious terms, and how China can use the rare earth metal as a potential bait to negotiate its demands.[47]

Table 9.6: World Mine Production and Reserves (in metric tonnes)

Country	Mine Production		Reserves
	2019	2020	
United States	28,000	38,000	1,500,000
Australia	20,000	17,000	4,100,000
Brazil	710	1,000	21,000,000
Burma (Myanmar)	25,000	30,000	NA
Burundi	200	500	NA
Canada	-	-	830,000
China	132,000	140,000	44,000,000
Greenland	-	-	1,50,000
India	2,900	3,000	6,900,000
Madagascar	4,000	8,000	NA
Russia	2,700	2,700	12,000,000
South Africa	-	-	7,90,000
Tanzania	-	-	8,90,000
Thailand	1,900	2,000	NA
Vietnam	1,300	1,000	22,000,000
Other Countries	66	100	310,000
Total	220,000	240,000	120,000,000

Source: United States Geological Survey 2021 (https://pubs.usgs.gov/periodicals/mcs2021/mcs2021-rare-earths.pdf)

Geoeconomic Engagement in Rare Earth Industry

India has increasingly prioritised energy-rich countries to ensure its energy security and economic expansion, and determining its geo-economic strategies. The rare earth industry is one such area increasingly receiving attention.

The Department of Atomic Energy (DAE) estimated the total reserves of rare earth in India at 10.21 million tonnes. India has been engaged in mining and extraction for more than five decades. The main element of the rare earth source found in India is monazite, which is located in the heavy minerals, inland placer deposits, and beach sands.

Monazite contains both elements of thorium and uranium, but its mining is allowed only to the government body—the DAE—due to the presence of radioactive elements. Under the DAE, Indian Rare Earth Limited (IREL) has been a responsible, autonomous body as the sole producer of rare earth oxides since 1949. IREL derives most of its income from developing and selling minerals obtained from the beach sands such as ilmenite, rutile, sillimanite, and zircon.

India has 6 per cent of the world's rare earth reserves but produces only 2 per cent of the total rare earth oxides globally. In India, certain REEs are present in large quantities, such as lanthanum, cerium, praseodymium, neodymium, samarium, gadolinium, yttrium, dysprosium. However, these elements become useful only with the valorisation and the eco-system. The growth of the Indian rare earth industry has been noticeable since the 1950s, from engaging in purely mining efforts to the set-up of the separation plants PRINCE and HERO by IREL. The production of carbonate and oxalates that further get converted to oxides are the preliminary separation products from the Indian rare earth industry.[48]

Despite being one of the first countries to enter into the mining and processing of rare earth, India did not put much effort to go up in the value supply chain like China. According to some records, India and Brazil remained the only source of rare earth for more than a decade, then China entered the industry in 1959, followed by the USA in 1968.[49]

The net potential of the Indian rare earth industry is around Rs 90,000 crore that has been lying waste and underused. The experts of the Beach Minerals Producers Association have estimated that the Indian rare earth mineral downstream industry could net capital employment of about Rs 121,000 crore, including Rs 50,000 crore worth of foreign exchange. The significant rare earth minerals found in India include ilmenite, sillimanite, garnet, zircon, monazite, rutile, collectively called beach sand minerals.[50]

India has 35 per cent of the world's total beach sand minerals deposits. The large monazite deposits in India are primarily found in the coastal tracts of Orissa on the east coast, and Kerala on the west coast. Bastnaesite—a source of cerium—is found in the state of West Bengal. Monazite in carbonatites is found in Meghalaya, Tamil Nadu and Assam. Xenomite containing REE dysprosium is found in the states of Chhattisgarh and Jharkhand.[51] IREL handles the upstream sector of the Indian rare earth industry, which produces high-quality rare earth oxides from its 10,000 tonnes per annum monazite processing plant in Odisha. With the advancement in the upstream sector, India exports rare earth oxides while importing intermediate products required for various applications due to the less advanced downstream industry.

REE Industry of Myanmar

According to the US Geological Survey (USGS) data[52], Myanmar is the third-largest source of mined rare earth, mostly rich deposits of dysprosium and terbium. As per the 2020 USGS survey, Myanmar mined 30,000 tonnes of rare earth oxides that is equivalent to 12.5 per cent of global production.[53] Myanmar has the most diverse and rich collection of natural resources in the whole of Southeast Asia, containing substantial deposits of tin, tungsten, copper, gold, gemstones, zinc, lead, nickel and silver. However, this geological jurisdiction of Myanmar had remained unacknowledged and poorly examined, but is now increasingly receiving the attention of the international mineral investment community. Myanmar has been divided into several metallogenic provinces: the Wuntho-Popa Arc, the MMM Belt and the Shan Plateau.[54] The geographical belt of Myanmar is divided into four highlands, from east to west: the eastern highlands, the central lowlands, the western ranges, and the Arakan coastal belt. In the Union of Myanmar, the most known and investigated rare earth mineral deposits are xenotine (in southern Myanmar), monazite (in the mountain ranges extending from Myanmar through western Thailand), and columbite and tantalite (in Dawei and Myeik areas of southern Myanmar).[55]

The more than 100 rare earth mines in Kachin state have close ties to the Tatmadaw, Myanmar's armed forces. As a result, even the leading global REE supplier China, is now heavily dependent on Myanmar for raw materials.[56] However, China has been illegally exporting the raw elements from the Kachin mines through the highly porous Kachin-China border.[57] To eliminate the Chinese miners' unregulated or illegal presence and the resulting environmental crisis, the Myanmar government banned rare earth export to China in 2018. According to Chinese customs data

(2020), despite the restriction, China's rare earth import from Myanmar increased by 23 per cent going up to around 35,000 tonnes. The recent political turmoil in Myanmar and the pandemic caused crisis increased the presence of Chinese miners and their illegal export, instead of restricting it.[58]

REE Industry of Malaysia

In the east coast of the peninsular Malaysia region, sediments are transported by several rivers into east Malaysia's South China Sea estuary. The concentration of rare earth elements from La to Yb was measured in five dated sediment cores from the east coast of peninsular Malaysia. The sediments were reported to contain higher concentrations of LREEs, such as La.[59] The study suggests higher enrichment of HREE than LREEs in the core marine sediments of coastal east Malaysia.[60] Malaysia is located in the west of the South China Sea, and is divided into two significant landmasses, i.e., peninsular Malaysia and east Malaysia, on the island of Borneo. The coastal marine ecosystem of the South China Sea off the east coast of peninsular Malaysia involves the REE abundance whose order follows Ce>La>Sm>Eu for the LREEs, and Dy>Yb>Tb>Lu for the HREEs.[61] Based on the residual tin deposits findings, Malaysia has an abundant amount of monazite that contains more LREEs than HREEs.[62] Malaysia has been blessed with a significant amount of non-radioactive rare earth deposits. The USGS estimates that some 30,000 metric tonnes of rare earth ores can be found in peninsular Malaysia. Although this represents less than one per cent of the world's total deposits, it is more than enough for the country to become a significant regional player in rare earth mineral supply. As a result, the rare earth mines of Malaysia are predicted to attract investments of up to $33 billion in the coming years.[63] Malaysia's leading rare earth processing plant, the Lynas Advanced Materials Plant (LAMP), imports Lanthanide Concentrate (LC) from the Mount Weld mine in Australia and processes it. Considering Malaysia's lower labour and construction costs, the Mount Weld mine follows a series of thermal, chemical, and physical processes to extract the LC, then transfers it to LAMP for processing.[64]

LAMP follows three stages for the processing: (a) Stage I: Cracking and leaching that mixes LC with concentrated sulphuric acid, then cracks it at high temperature (350-450 degree Celsius) to convert it into rare earth sulphate; (b) Stage II: Solvent extraction mixes the converted rare earth sulphate solution with hydrochloric acid (HCl), then follows organic and aqueous liquid phases to separate the rare earth into groups and individual elements; (c) Stage III: Finished products that are mainly light rare earth elements such as praseodymium/neodymium, which are precipitated as solid carbonates or oxalates such as neodymium oxide or cerium carbonate.[65]

Potential of Geoeconomic Engagement

To limit the monopoly of China in the rare earth supply chain, the world requires to enhance both the upstream and downstream sectors of rare earth production. With its high reserves, India needs specific reforms and adjustments in its rare earth industry. Indian REE industries can only mine and extract the rare earth ores but cannot convert the REOs into pure metal for manufacturing. Thus, it needs to scale up the upstream and downstream processes in the rare earth value chain, move from just low-cost rare earth ores production to high-cost manufacturing products.[66] Myanmar, with its third-largest rare earth producing capacity but no recorded reserves, has the potential to fill the gap for India as well as itself. The two-track approach of India towards Myanmar currently keeps it in an advantageous position to build the rare earth reserve production interdependence. However, this interdependent connectivity will still lack processing capacity, which again supports the dependence of India, Myanmar and other countries on China. The processing capacity of Myanmar's LAMP, the second largest after China, can brim over the geoeconomic interdependence. Like Myanmar, Malaysia also lacks rare earth reserves, and its production capacity is also in the developing process, which makes the engagement with India a beneficial deal. The geoeconomic engagement in the rare earth sector will strengthen the rare earth industry of India, Malaysia and Myanmar and contribute to their economic and clean energy goals.

Myanmar and Malaysia are the emerging players in the rare earth geopolitics, considering the increasing presence of the leading major players like China, the USA and Australia in their mining. India's initiative in this direction has been comparatively low but can potentially enhance its geoeconomic partnership, both inter and intra-regionally. However, it is noteworthy that the rare earth sites of both Malaysia and Myanmar are generating rising environmental concerns due to the increased presence of major powers like China, the USA and Australia. The environmental concerns have been causing public objections to the rare earth mining in both Malaysia and Myanmar, considering its impact on health and lifestyle.[67, 68] In this context, India's perspective geoeconomic engagement with both countries, with its sixth-largest rare earth reserves (see Table 9.5), carries a beneficial deal for all the parties.

Conclusion

India-ASEAN geoeconomic engagement has all the potential and possibilities to progress. The high trade interdependence of minerals and metals, continuous increase in trade figures, and common need to balance China have set the tone for geoeconomic engagement between India ASEAN. The interdependence in the rare earth industry with Myanmar and Malaysia will further strengthen India-ASEAN geoeconomic engagement. ASEAN members are increasingly emphasising sustainable green and smart cities projects,[69] clean energy transition, and ambitious climate change targets, require access to the and a secure supply of rare earth elements.

Taking inspiration from China's geoeconomic ingenuity with countries in South Asia and Africa, India can also develop engagement with Southeast Asia. China is increasing its presence in African countries like Madagascar to ensure its monopoly in the rare earth supply chain. However, while Chinese geoeconomic engagement aims at exploiting the resources with promising economic benefits in exchange, India's geoeconomic engagement carries a different character with the availability of both high economic growth and large unexploited rare earth reserves. The geoeconomic elements were first shaped in India's foreign policy after the economic reforms and liberalisation of the Indian economy in 1991 but evolved as defining foreign policy characteristics in the aftermath of the global financial crisis of 2008-09. Factors like business, trade, multilateralism and regional trade integration have been altering Indian statecraft and its goal of sustained economic growth.[70] In May 2014, Prime Minister Narendra Modi set the goal of international engagement and a more significant place for India in the world. His speeches at the Paris Summit in 2015 emphasised the comprehensive approach of India towards climate change.[71] In the national conference (2016) jointly organised by Gateway House, Mumbai, and the MEA on the theme, "Where Geopolitics meets Business', S. Jaishankar, the former foreign secretary and current minister of external affairs, said, "There is a sharper realisation that the real strengths of any nation are primarily economic, that, in turn, has led to a growing recognition that business provides the ballast for many of our important international relationships; ASEAN, the Gulf, the US and China are examples."Touching on resource dependence, he said that "the area most worthy of strategising for is energy, which has also seen the greatest activism in India's recent diplomatic interactions."[72]

The Indian geoeconomics was defined by the Raisina Dialogue in 2016, a joint strategic initiative by the MEA and the Observer Research Foundation (ORF) that emphasised the theme of 'Asian Connectivity' as a key to energy security as well as the economic growth of India. As part of her inaugural address to the Raisina Dialogue Conference (2016), the then External Affairs Minister (late) Mrs. Sushma Swaraj said, "Connectivity is the key not just to India's development ambition but also its vision for international cooperation ... this is in our DNA, after all, we are the inheritors of two powerful connectivity legacies: the message of the Buddha and the Spice Route."[73] In India, the shift from 'economic autarky' and import-substitution-industrialisation to economic reforms, liberalisation, and capital-intensive-industrialisation was not an easy development.[74] Underlining the importance of economic diplomacy, the former Foreign Secretary of India, Shivshankar Menon (2006-09) also said, "India's deepening integration into the global economy required changes in India's external behaviour, a thorough revamping of the Government of India's machinery, and moving the focus of much of our diplomatic work to economic diplomacy".[75]

Blackwill and Harris have identified seven instruments to practise geoeconomics in the contemporary world: trade, investment policy, economic sanctions, cyber, economic assistance, financial and monetary policy, and national policies governing energy and commodities.[76] India has shown leverage in five principal geoeconomic instruments:

(a) Leverage in the trade regime but terms of import share instead of export.
(b) The increasing outward Foreign Direct Investment (FDI) from India.
(c) India as largest emigration country.
(d) The economic sanctions have increasingly become part of Indian geostrategy against Pakistan or other neighbouring countries.
(e) India's defensive financial lending mechanism.[77]

The security dilemma of India-ASEAN has resulted from the twin challenges of maritime trade security and Chinese preeminence playing an important role in shaping their geoeconomic ties. The requirement of economic and resource security in the Indo-Pacific region is leading India-ASEAN to enhance their geoeconomic ties. India-ASEAN collaboration would ensure a stable and peaceful Indo-Pacific regional order and can transform the anarchical regional order based on relative gains into a liberal cooperative order based on absolute gains. The geoeconomic engagement between India and the ASEAN countries is being perceived as a counter to Chinese dominance in the Indo-Pacific region and increasingly shifting from inclusive to exclusive institutionalisation.

The future will obviously unfold new developments in the India-ASEAN relationship, but interdependence in the rare earth industry will be the most feasible area.

Notes

1 Raisina Dialogue 2016, Observer Research Foundation, January 4, 2021. https://www.orfonline.org/raisina-dialogue/raisina-dialogue-2016/. Accessed on November 2, 2021.

2 "The Business of Indian Diplomacy", *The Hindu*, June 14 2016. https://www.thehindu.com/news/cities/mumbai/news/The-business-of-Indian-diplomacy-is business/article14421126.ece. Accessed on November 4, 2021.

3. Ibid.

4. K. He, "Three Faces of the Indo-Pacific: Understanding the Indo-Pacific From an IR Theory Perspective", *East Asia,* 35(2), 2018, pp. 149-161.
5. Shivshankar Menon, "Foreign Policy in the Wake of Economic Reforms", in Rakesh Mohan, ed., *India Transformed: Twenty-Five Years of Economic Reforms* (Gurgaon: Penguin Random House, 2018), pp. 165-174.
6. K. Yhome, "Book Review: Rajiv Bhatia: India–Myanmar Relations—Changing Contours", *Journal of Current Southeast Asian Affairs*, Vol. 35(3), 2018, pp. 195-197.
7. Srihari Avuthu, "ASEAN's Success has Transformed the Geopolitics and Geoeconomics of Southeast Asia", *The Sunday Guardian*, January 22, 2018. https://www.sundayguardianlive.com/news/12489-asean-s-success-has-transformed-geopolitics-and-geo-economics-southeast-asia. Accessed on December 22, 2021.
8. Nilanjan Banik and Misu Kim, "India–ASEAN Trade Relations: Examining the Trends and Identifying the Potential", *Global Business Review*, 2020, pp. 1-19.
9. Loitongbam Bishwanjit Singh, "Impact of India-ASEAN Free Trade Agreement: An Assessment from the Trade Creation and Trade Diversion Effects", *Foreign Trade Review*, 2021, pp. 1-15.
10. D.F. Anwar, "Indonesia and the ASEAN Outlook on the Indo-Pacific", *International Affairs,* 96(1), 2020, pp. 111-129.
11. N. Kipgen, "India-ASEAN Relations: The Initiatives, Successes, and Challenges". *Indian Review,* 19(3), 2020, pp. 207-222.
12. Ibid.
13. K. H. A. H. Feng, "The Institutionalisation of the Indo-Pacific: Problems and Prospects", *International Affairs*, 2020, pp. 149-168.
14. Ibid.
15. Ibid.
16. F. Liu, "The Recalibration of Chinese Assertiveness: China's Responses to the Indo-Pacific Challenge", *International Affairs,* 96(1), 2020, pp. 9-27.
17. Ibid.
18. R. Rajagopalan, "Evasive Balancing: India's Unviable Indo-Pacific Strategy". *International Affairs,* 96(1), 2020, pp. 75-93.
19. Stefania Massari, Marcello Ruberti, "Rare Earth Elements as Critical Raw Materials: Focus on International Markets and Future Strategies," *Resource Policy* 38, 2013, pp. 36-43.

20 The Observatory of Economic Complexity, "India-Singapore". https://oec.world/en/profile/bilateral-country/ind/partner/sgp#:~:text=The%20main%20products%20that%20India,to%20%249.53B%20in%202019.

21. Pilar de Alvear, "Singapore, a Great Teacher of the Geopolitical Game", *Atalaya*, September 20 2021. https://atalayar.com/en/content/singapore-great-teacher-geopolitical-game.

22. Ibid.
23. Pratnashree Basu, "Employing Proximity: Boosting Bilateral Ties Between India and Myanmar", in Pahi Saikia and Anasua Basu Ray Chaudhury, eds., *India and Myanmar Borderlands: Ethnicity, Security and Connectivity* (New York: Routledge, 2020), pp. 129-140.
24. Ministry of External Affairs, "Brief on India-Malaysia Bilateral Relations", https://www.mea.gov.in/Portal/ForeignRelation/India-Malaysia_bilateral_brief-_February_2020.pdf.
25. Tharishini Krishnan, "Indian Ocean: The Maritime Links of India-Malaysia", *The Hindustan Times*, August 18, 2021. https://www.hindustantimes.com/ht-insight/international-affairs/indian-ocean-the-maritime-links-of-indiamalaysia-101629273230463.html. Accessed on December 22, 2021.
26. Manoj Joshi, "India and the Malacca Conundrum", Observer Research Foundation (ORF), August 14 2020. https://www.orfonline.org/research/india-and-the-malacca-conundrum/. Accessed on December 20, 2021.
27. Sharifah Munirah Alatas, "A Malaysian Perspective on Foreign Policy and Geopolitics: Rethinking West-Centric International Relations Theory", *Global Studies Quarterly* Vol. 1, 2021, pp. 1-11.
28. Shiv Padhy, "Rare Earth Metals: Heavy vs Light," *Rare Earth Investing News*, 2017. https://investingnews.com/daily/resource-investing/critical-metals-investing/rare-earth-investing/investing-in-rare-earth-heavy-vs-light/. Accessed on September 30, 2021.
29. Patrick H. Brown, Anne H. Rathjen, Robin D. Graham, and Derek E. Tribe. "Rare Earth Elements in the Biological Systems," in K.A. Gchneidner Jr. and E. Eyring, eds., *Handbook on the Physics and Chemistry of Rare Earths*, (Elsevier Science Publisher, 1990), pp. 243-449.
30. C. Morteani, and G. Preinfalk, "Industrial Applications of Rare Earth Elements," *Lanthanides, Tantalum and Niobium* (1998), pp. 359-370.
31. Julie Michelle Klinger, "A Historical Geography of Rare Earth Elements: From Discovery to the Atomic Age", *The Extractive Industries and Society* 2(3), 2015, pp. 572-580.
32. James C. Kennedy, "Rare Earth Production, Regulatory USA/International Constraints and Chinese Dominance: The Economic Viability is Bounded by Geochemistry and Value Chain Integration," in *Rare Earth Industry* (Edinburgh: Elsevier Inc., 2016), pp. 37-55.
33. Jost Wübbeke, "Rare Earth Elements in China: Policies and Narratives of Reinventing an Industry," *Resource Policy* 38 (3), 2013, pp. 384-394.
34. June Teufel. Dreyer, "China's Monopoly on Rare Earth Elements," Asia Program Analysis, Foreign Policy Research Institute, October 7, 2020.
35. Wang Liangshi, et al., "Towards Cleaner Production of Rare Earth Elements from Bastnaesite in China," *Journal of Cleaner Production* 165 (2), 2017, pp. 231-242.

36. Wübbeke, n. 33, pp. 384-394.
37. Liangshi, et al., n. 35, pp. 231-242.
38. Ibid.
39. Xiaojun Li, "China's Geo-Economic Strategy: China as a Trading Superpower", The London School of Economics and Political Science, 2013.
40. Shane, Bilsborough, "The Strategic Implications of China's Rare Earths Policy." *Journal of Strategic Security* 5 (3), 2012, pp. 1-12.
41. Keith Bradsher, "Amid Tension, China Blocks Vital Exports to Japan," *The New York Times*, September 22, 2010.
41. Ibid.
42. Klinger, n. 31, pp. 572-580.
43. Ibid.
44. Erdey Laszlo, Fenyes Veronika, Adam Markus and Tibor Tokes, "China Does Not Want a Trade War—The Case for Rare Earth Elements." *Polgári Szemle*, 15, 2019, pp. 281-295.
45. Ibid.
46. Dreyer, n. 34.
47. Ibid.
48. Angela Saini, "India to Reopen Mining for Rare Earth Elements", *MRS Bulletin*, 37(9), 2012. https://www.cambridge.org/core/journals/mrs-bulletin/article/India-to-reopen-mining-for-rare earth-elements/15E7B5AF75BCC8EC592D406C5ECAC5AC. Accessed on December 20, 2021.
49. K. Akshay, "India not Realizing Potential of Rare Earth Industry", *The Economic Times*, October 19, 2016. https://economictimes.indiatimes.com/industry/indl-goods/svs/metals-mining/india-not-realising-potential-of-rare-earth-industry/articleshow/54940321.cms. Accessed on December 22, 2021.
50. Anirudh Kanisetti, "Here's How India can end Chinese Dominance in Rare Earth", *Business Insider India*, February 13, 2021. https://www.businessinsider.in/policy/economy/news/heres-how-india-can-end-chinese-dominance-in-rare-earths/articleshow/80883001.cms. Accessed on November 30, 2021.
51. Ibid.
52. "USGS Rare Earth Data 2021". https://pubs.usgs.gov/periodicals/mcs2021/mcs2021-rare-earths.pdf.
53. Dominic Oo, "China's Rare Earth Supplies Disrupted by Myanmar Tumult", *Asia Times*, March 22, 2021. https://asiatimes.com/2021/03/chinas-rare-earth-supplies-disrupted-by-myanmar-tumult/. Accessed on December 21, 2021.
54. N.J. Gardinger, L.J. Robb and M.P. Searle. "The Metallogenic Provinces of Myanmar", *Applied Earth Sciences*, No. 1, 2014, pp. 25-38.
55. U Kyaw Thein, "Rare Earth Minerals in the Union of Myanmar", *Materials Science Forum*, No. 70-72, 1991, pp. 149-150.
56. Sribala Subramanian, "Rare Earths in Myanmar: Unobtanium?", *The Diplomat*, June 14, 2021. https://thediplomat.com/2021/06/rare-earths-in-myanmar-unobtanium/. Accessed on December 16, 2021.

57. Jauman Naw, Emily Fishbein and Ronja Pilgaard, "'Weapons, Power and Money: How Rare-Earth Mining in Kachin Enriches a Tatmadaw Ally," *The Frontier*, August 3, 2021. https://www.frontiermyanmar.net/en/weapons-power-and-money-how-rare-earth-mining-in-kachin-enriches-a-tatmadaw-ally/. Accessed on December 20, 2021.
58. Oo, n. 53.
59. Khadijeh Rezaee Ebrahim Saraee, Saion B. Elias, Abdul Khalik Wood and Abdi Mohammad Reza, "Rare Earth Elements Distribution in Marine Sediments of Malaysia Coasts", *Journal of Rare Earths*, No. 27(6), 2009, pp. 1066-1071.
60. Ashraf Ahmadreza, et al., "Rare Earth Elements in Core Marine Sediments of Coastal East Malaysia by Instrumental Neutron Activation Analysis", *Applied Radiation and Isotopes*, No. 107, 2016, pp. 17-23.
61. Khadijeh Rezaee, E. B. Saion, A. Khalik Wood and M. R. Abdi. "Rare Earth Elements Determination and Distribution Patterns in Surface Marine Sediments of the South China Sea by INAA, Malaysia", *Journal of Radioanal Nucl Chem*, No. 283, 2010, pp. 823-829.
62. Che Bahri, Nor Aniza, Che Zainul, et al., "Production of Rare Earth Elements from Malaysian Monazite by Selective Precipitation", *Malaysian Journal of Analytical Sciences*, Vol. 20, No. 1, 2016, pp. 44-50.
63. Noorhana Yahya, "Rare Earth Could be Music for Malaysians", *New Strait Times*, May 31, 2021. https://www.nst.com.my/opinion/columnists/2021/06/694807/rare-earth-could-be-music-malaysians#:~:text=Malaysia%20has%20been%20blessed%20with,be%20found%20in%20Peninsular%20Malaysia. Accessed on December 17, 2021.
64. Seng How Kuan, Lip Huat Saw and Yousef Ghorbani, "A Review of Rare Earth Processing in Malaysia", Universiti Malaysia Terengganu International Annual Symposium on Sustainability Science and Management, 2016.
65. Ibid.
66. Ibid.
67. Subramanian, n. 56.
68. Austin Bodetti, "Malaysia's Rare Earth Debate", *The Diplomat*, January 10, 2019. https://thediplomat.com/2019/01/malaysias-rare-earth-debate/. Accessed on December 30, 2021.
69. Association of Southeast Asian Nations, "Smart Green ASEAN Cities: New Initiative to Promote Sustainable and Smart Cities in ASEAN", ASEAN News, November 22, 2021. https://asean.org/smart-green-asean-cities-new-initiative-to-promote-sustainable-and-smart-cities-in-asean/. Accessed on January 2, 2022.
70. Sanjaya Baru, "India and the World: Essays on Geoeconomics and Foreign Policy", Academic Foundation, India.
71. Ministry of External Affairs, 2017, "Prime Minister Narendra Modi- Select Speeches on Foreign Policy 2014-2015," February 3. https://mea.gov.in/in-focus-topic.htm?260. Accessed on February 10, 2021.

72. "The Business of Indian Diplomacy", *The Hindu* June 14, 2016. https://www.thehindu.com/news/cities/mumbai/news/The-business-of-Indian-diplomacy-is-business/article14421126.ece. Accessed on December 14, 2021.
73. Observer Research Foundation, "ORF Raisina Diaologue", March 1-3, 2016. https://www.orfonline.org/raisina-dialogue/raisina-dialogue-2016/. Accessed January 4, 2021.
74. Amit Ahuja and Devesh Kapur, "India's Geoeconomic Strategy", *India Review* 17 (1), 2018, pp. 76-99.
75. Shivshankar Menon, "Foreign Policy in the Wake of Economic Reforms", in Rakesh Mohan, ed., *India Transformed: Twenty Five Years of Economic Reforms*, (Gurgaon: India: Penguin Random House, 2018), pp. 165-174.
76. Robert D. Blackwill and Jeniffer M. Harris, "Today's Leading Geoeconomic Instruments", in *War by Other Means: Geoeconomics and Statecraft*, (Cambridge, UK: Harvard University Press, 2018), pp. 49-92.
77. Ibid.

10. Tracing the Connection: Indo-Pacific and Persian Gulf in India's Maritime Strategy

Anu Sharma

Setting the Stage

The maritime domain is growing in significance, with the Sea Lines of Communication (SLOC) becoming an important feature of the foreign policies of various nations. In the historical times, the sea was a significant mode, responsible for economic prosperity. So, the seaways were the medium through which trade was facilitated, further resulting in the growth of the maritime diplomacy of nations. Since then, the dependence of nations on waterways for commercial purposes and as a competent means of transport has increased considerably. However, with this, there have also emerged various threats which are raising concerns about the safety of these SLOCs. In turn, any act of any nation state which can be inimical to the safety of the SLOCs, almost by definition, challenges security.[1] In this lies the context of this paper, wherein it tries to trace the connection between the Persian Gulf and Indo-Pacific regions. It further tries to place India's maritime diplomacy in terms of its "Act East" and "Look West" policy and the emerging debates related to the Indo-Pacific region.

The narrative amongst the scholars of international relations is related to the limitations or the delimitations of the sea/ocean boundaries with respect to the concerned regions. The way nations are visualising and underlining the maritime domain has changed drastically in the past few decades. This is despite the fact that there are maritime boundary disputes on all continents.[2] This highlights the issues of limiting or delimiting the boundary in terms of oceans and seas. Ocean/sea limitations are primarily man-made paradigms owing to various commercial aspects such as oil and gas production, fisheries and environmental protection. However, the greater interdependence results in probable vulnerabilities. Vital SLOCs also highlight the possible bottlenecks. Developing these maritime transit routes can threaten the natural environment. These lead to new kinds of security hazards that emerge due to climate change, asymmetric threats e.g., sea piracy, drugs trade, terrorism, etc. To pedal through this complex maritime domain of the Indo-Pacific region, there is a need for the policy-makers to formulate the strategies which can discuss various interrelated strategic, socioeconomic and environmental factors that will continue to affect this region in the near future.[3]

The significance of the Indo-Pacific region is visible with it occupying the centre-stage in global strategic discussions owing to the security, economic, technological and environmental challenges that are emerging there. However, the peripheries of the seas and oceans are also being debated in international politics. In this context, there are several questions that need to be answered, such as: what are the peripheral limitations of the Indo-Pacific region? Various scholars, analysts and practitioners of international relations feel that the answer to this question is filled with consequences. The inherent core area of the 'Indo-Pacific' is from India to the Southeast Asian countries and the waters of the Eastern Indian Ocean to the South China Sea. However, the geographical definitions of this region have in a way conveyed various diplomatic messages from a number of nations. For the US, it stretches from the "...US West Coast through the Bay of Bengal" clearly highlighting the significance of this region for the US in its 2019 Indo-Pacific Strategy Report. Similarly, for Australia, the 'Indo-Pacific' region extends from "...India through South-East Asia to North-East Asia, including the Sea Lines of Communication." So, it can be said that the Australian geographical perception of the Indo-Pacific was limited to the Eastern Indian Ocean and the Western Pacific Ocean. On the contrary, both India and Japan have mentioned that the geographical expanse of the Indo-Pacific is extending from "...US West Coast to Africa's East Coast." In fact, for Japan the definition of

'Indo-Pacific' changed in 2018 extending "... from the eastern shore of the African continent, through the Indian Ocean, through the ASEAN countries, through the Pacific Ocean, to the western coast of the North and South American continents."[4]

This region is also marked by polarisation and rising tensions. There has been a visible enhancement of China's strategic influence and its territorial claims in the Indo-Pacific region through its 21st century Maritime Silk Road (MSR)—part of its Belt and Road Initiative (BRI). This has further led to the rising competition between China and the United States and the latter's "Pivot to Asia" strategy. Through this, the United States aims to counter the growing Chinese influence. Further, the aspirations of the regional nations, as well as external actors, to play a significant role in the Indo-Pacific region, are responsible for the altering regional balances of power, thereby making strategic calculations more complex. The significance of the Indo-Pacific region is due to its maritime dimension, which is responsible for more than 90 per cent of the global trade flows.

In a similar context, the Persian Gulf region, the Arabian Sea and the Red Sea around the Arabian peninsula are also amongst the most congested and contested maritime transit routes globally. Through these routes, nations strive to secure energy resources. In fact, in the case of China, most of its energy supplies pass through these waterways to help sustain its economy as well as support it in its quest to become a maritime power, apparently as in the Pacific and Indian Oceans.

However, in the past few years, these maritime routes have witnessed a rise in military incidents owing to persisting rivalries between Iran and the United States or Iran and Saudi Arabia. The security situation prevalent in the West Asian region is also influenced by this region's maritime characteristics, wherein the Persian Gulf provides both opportunities and threats for strategic planners in all the nations surrounding this region. Furthermore, there are major shifts in the alliances that are happening in this region. This has been due to diminishing American influence in the region or the rapprochement between Israel and the Arab states (namely the United Arab Emirates or UAE and Bahrain).[5]

Fig 10.1 depicts the SLOCs, choke points, and maritime transit routes in the Indian neighbourhood, providing a fair idea of the significance of both the Persian Gulf and Indo-Pacific regions. It is fairly obvious that the economic growth through trade and transit will rely on these SLOCs. The sections ahead will discuss the linkage between the Persian Gulf and Indo-Pacific regions and India's maritime diplomacy in these regions.

Fig 10.1: The SLOCs, Choke Points and Maritime Transit Routes

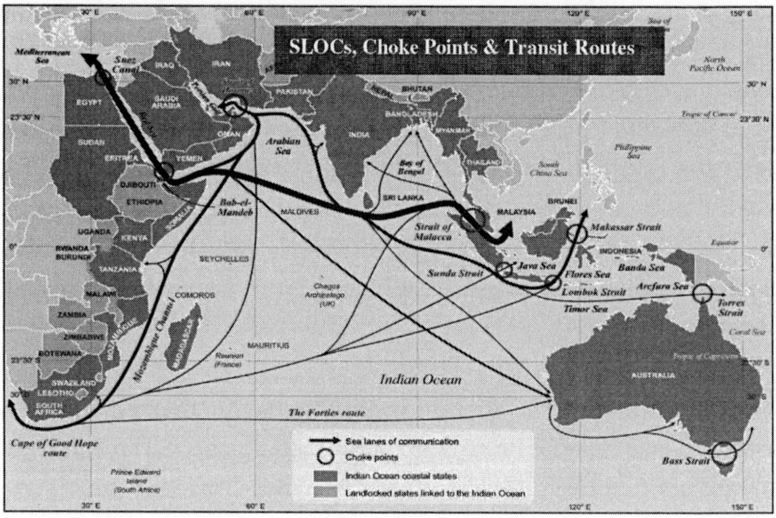

Source: https://books.openedition.org/cei/469. Accessed on January 5, 2022.

Connecting the Dots: Indo-Pacific and the Persian Gulf

It is difficult to geographically connect the Persian Gulf and Indo-Pacific regions. Both are strategically significant regions that are connected through the SLOCs through which nations conduct their trade. In this context, they hold significance for Indian strategic maritime thinking vis-à-vis the growing Chinese influence in the Indian neighbourhood to enhance its presence in both the Indo-Pacific and the Persian Gulf maritime spheres. The positioning of an Indo-Pacific perspective in Indian strategic thinking is a recognition of the rapidly changing geopolitics in the entire region stretching from the western coast of the United States to the eastern coast of Africa, where India's vital interests also rest.[6]

This is an unconventional way to understand the linkage between the Indo-Pacific and Persian Gulf regions. In this context, there also arises the question, as to whether the external actors consider the Persian Gulf an extension of the Indo-Pacific? It is still difficult to assess who will be the beneficiaries of this inclusion of the Persian Gulf in the Indo-Pacific region; and whether major regional or world powers stand to lose in case the Indo-Pacific region's peripheries extend to include the Persian Gulf. Furthermore, another question is whether the geostrategic competition in the Indo-Pacific region will also affect the West Asian region's political, economic and security environment. In this context, it is important to understand the crucial factors of this variation, but it cannot be ignored that, since historical times, the maritime domain has been a vital space in shaping regional dynamics and the larger security architecture by the existing or emerging powers.[7]

On the face of it, the Persian Gulf region does not feature significantly in the Indo-Pacific. The West Asian nations situated around the Persian Gulf region have had ancient maritime legacies which linked them to other Indian Ocean nations. However, they seldom leaned eastward in their approach towards the Southeast Asian nations in the ancient times. During modern times also, they were more focussed on the larger Arab region or the Western nations in their foreign policymaking criteria. Geopolitically, the most crucial choke point of the Persian Gulf region is the Strait of Hormuz, which eventually links the West Asian region to the Indian Ocean's maritime transit routes.[8]

In this context, the discussions about the linkages between the Strait of Hormuz and the Strait of Malacca (Fig 10.2) have been established to deliberate on the issues related to the significance of the SLOCs. It is noteworthy that both the Strait of Hormuz and the Strait of Malacca figure in the list of six major oil transit choke points around the world, as identified by the United States Energy Information Administration (EIA) (Fig 10.2). These maritime choke points are critically important due to oil and other kinds of trade; they are also extremely vulnerable to acts of piracy and shipping catastrophes. Nearly 50,000 shipping vessels pass through the Strait of Malacca every year. This is because it is the shortest possible transit route between the Southeast Asian nations such as China, Japan and South Korea, connecting them with the West Asian oil and gas resources.[9] Stemming from the above discussion, the Indian Defence Ministry described the Indian maritime security environment as ranging from the Persian Gulf in the Western Indian Ocean to the Strait of Malacca.[10] In fact, the cooperative approach adopted by the Indian Navy in developing security relationships around the wider Indian Ocean region has been relatively successful. This has also been responsible for connecting the Indian maritime efforts in both the Persian Gulf and the Indo-Pacific region.

Fig 10.2: Strait of Hormuz and Strait of Malacca

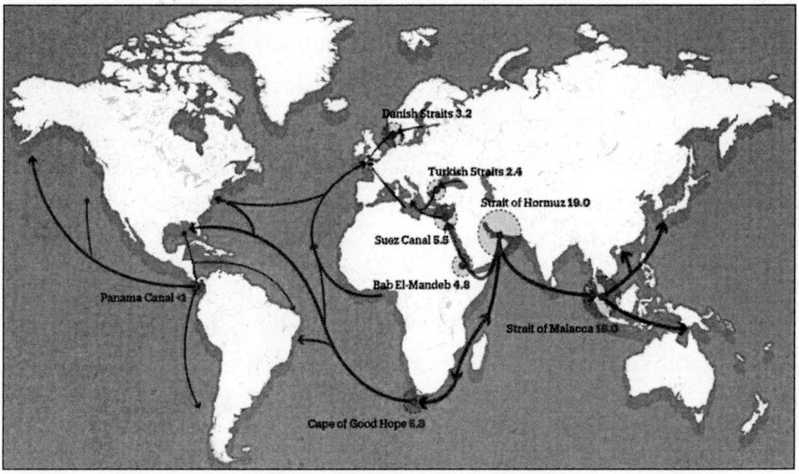

Source: https://www.trtworld.com/business/what-makes-strait-of-hormuz-a-maritime-flashpoint-27876. Accessed on January 8, 2022.

Maritime Geopolitics of the 'Indo-Pacific'

The Indo-Pacific region emerged as the new and contested geographic space in the past decade. Connecting the Indian and Pacific Oceans, it characterises the strategic reality in the maritime domain of contemporary times. Several nations, including Japan, Australia, China, the United States, France, India, etc. visualise the "Indo-Pacific" as a new geographical and strategic reference point, somewhat replacing the "Asia-Pacific" construct. The term has found parlance in national security strategies, Defence White Papers of various nations, including the deliberations by academicians, analysts, political elites and leaders. In fact, it would not be wrong to say that it has gradually become the "geopolitical terminology."[11]

The Indo-Pacific has become the theatre of growing strategic tensions between the United States and China, gaining geopolitical and geoeconomic significance in the past two decades. Divergent deliberations about the delineation of the geographical limitations of this region have led to the debate about its accurate geographic boundaries. Still, the common factor binding all the Indo-Pacific littorals has been their sea trade dependent economies. Despite the increasing significance of the oceans, issues related to governance, including the formation of an integrated stratagem to deal with a myriad maritime threats and challenges, remain unreciprocated. With the SLOCs becoming the "oceanic highways" for transit and movement, the issue of security has become the foremost concern for most nations.[12] However, there is another emerging reiteration that describes the Indo-Pacific as a geographical construct and an alternative to the Chinese BRI.[13] The Indo-Pacific plays a significant role in Beijing's grand BRI plans, which comprise both a land route known as the Silk Road Economic Belt and a maritime route known as the MSR Initiative. Through the BRI, China is striving to enhance its influence substantially through various BRI-related projects. In all of this, the rising Chinese presence due to its MSR projects across the Indo-Pacific region provides the context for the increased diplomatic synergy in this region as a response to Chinese actions.[14] So, it can be said that the deep desire of the Asian nations and external actors to play a more prominent role has resulted in a struggle for power in this region. This has further accentuated over the period, with the diminishing American influence and the emergence of new nodes of power throughout the Indo-Pacific region.[15]

Another aspect to consider is that while some issues appear explicitly connected to either the Indian Ocean or Western Pacific Ocean, there has been a constant connection between the two regions. This linkage between the two regions is one of the major reasons that enhanced the geopolitical significance of the Indo-Pacific region. The sea-based nuclear and missile proliferation concerning nations such as China, Pakistan, North Korea, etc. is one of the serious concerns, another being the regional security aspect. Extra-regional powers are becoming the major stakeholders in the region, leading them to play a dominant role in the security paradigm of the Indo-Pacific region. However, there lies the paradox, as this enhanced role of the extra-regional players also leads to concomitant insecurities and instabilities due to increased rivalries, which has made this regional security environment more complex.[16] In this context, the role of India becomes more enhanced, being one of the littoral states and a significant stakeholder in the Indo-Pacific region. The section ahead discusses India's maritime diplomacy in both the Indo-Pacific and Persian Gulf regions.

India's Maritime Diplomacy

In the maritime domain, national security aims and aspirations have scope beyond the state's boundaries and its littoral. In the past decade or so, there have been dynamic security situations and geopolitical imperatives that broadened India's diplomatic quest in its maritime domain. As India has a unique peninsular character and geographic position, the Indian policy-makers have been forming strategies considering it as a maritime power arising due to the geographical features.[17] In the past few years, India has adopted an active maritime strategy in which issues related to trade, security and connectivity form part of its maritime diplomatic goals. India's maritime strategy has been in response to a myriad geopolitical quandaries, including its ambitions in the emerging global order. Through this, India aims to acquire this maritime space by developing a unified maritime security architecture—capacity building through suitable military and naval acquisitions and ramping up indigenous production, as well as increasing investments in these sectors have been significant aspects.[18]

India has a large population, a developing economy and an expansive coastline. This includes the Andaman and Nicobar Islands, which straddle the Strait of Malacca, and the Arabian Sea connecting the West Asian region. This further makes India a vital stakeholder in the maritime commons adjacent to the Indian and Pacific Oceans. Keeping in mind its national interest, India has been trying to preserve and promote its major maritime advances. These include protection of the territorial integrity from various maritime threats, evolving aspects of a blue economy in order to protect the SLOCs and maritime resources within and beyond its maritime zones.[19]

India's major maritime concerns, based on its maritime security strategy, stretch through the adjacent Indo-Pacific and Persian Gulf regions. These include geoeconomic interests, secure maritime transit routes, freedom of navigation, etc. In order to achieve these, India is developing maritime partnerships with the littoral nations in the Indian Ocean Region (IOR) to illustrate its robust outreach. With the aim to develop a congenial and holistic maritime domain, India's maritime strategic blueprints or naval doctrines can be considered a manifestation of its maritime ambitions.[20]

"Diplomatic manoeuvring" is another significant aspect of India's maritime strategy to counter the emerging challenges due to growing friction between China and the United States in the adjacent Indo-Pacific region. Stemming from this, Prime Minister Narendra Modi's 2018 Shangri-La speech charted India's maritime vision in the direction of greater connectivity and equal access to the IOR.[21] India's maritime vision also discussed the need for a comprehensive status quo in the maritime domain, which can be delineated through its "Act East" and "Look West" policies and rule-based maritime order. This also included removing barriers in the ways of enhancing cooperation, and uninterrupted quests for the optimal utilisation of economic benefits offered by these regions. In this context, India has also been engaging in the strategic spaces e.g., the Bay of Bengal, to ensure the security of its external trade volume, primarily the oil imports along the crucial transit routes in the Bay of Bengal, and utilising these aspects for its benefit in the broader Indo-Pacific region.[22] In the following sub-sections, India's maritime aspirations and quests in the Indo-Pacific and Persian Gulf regions are discussed in detail.

The China Challenge

In the past few years, China has been pursuing its maritime diplomacy through its Maritime Silk Road. This has continued all through the past two years of the COVID-19 pandemic, which resulted in staggered economic growth and struggling health sectors in almost all the nations around the world. By aggressively pursuing its Health Silk Road, it is trying to reinforce itself as a major regional player in both the Indo-Pacific and Persian Gulf regions. However, in the past few years, most of the Southeast Asian nations have been facing Chinese expansionist policies. In this context, India has always voiced the need for declaring various oceanic regions as "global commons." In more contemporary times, India has been emphasising the need for maritime security initiatives in the Indo-Pacific region, extending up to the Western Pacific region. So, through engagements with other like-minded nations in the Indo-Pacific littoral region in various minilateral and multilateral fora, India is trying to promote a peaceful global maritime order. This is also being witnessed through an increase in various middle power coalitions like India, Indonesia and Australia or India, France and Australia.[23]

The Quad

India has been participating in various 2+2 discourses such as the 'Quadrilateral Security Dialogue' (Quad) among India, Australia, Japan and the United States or the newly formed Quad II among India, Israel, the United States and the UAE. Through Quad, it is being relayed that the nations are coming together regarding mutual security concerns, extending issues related to supply chains and a free and open Indo-Pacific region. Various multilateral organisations essentially discuss matters related to Chinese expansionism in the South China Sea and East China Sea regions. In this context, the Quad can also discuss issues besides the hard security realm, such as connectivity, blue economy and capacity building in the maritime sphere, etc. India, through the Quad fora, can organise maritime security and law related workshops, further collaborating on developing port infrastructure. This can be done to promote enhanced connectivity amongst the Indian Ocean littoral nations involving various infrastructure development initiatives, including the Sagarmala projects, Blue Dot, the Expanded Partnership for Quality Infrastructure and Asia-Africa Growth Corridor.[24] In all of this, France has become the most prominent European nation to be involved in the maritime security facets of the Western Indian Ocean. This has led to capacity building measures amongst all the littorals in the Indo-Pacific region. Through this, France and, to some extent, the United Kingdom have welcomed greater Indian participation in this region.[25]

India and its 'Indo-Pacific' Calculus

As the strategic significance of the Indo-Pacific region rises, nations are developing strategies to reinforce their influence in this region. For India, it is crucial to maintain the strategic balance in the Indo-Pacific region by actively reinforcing its interests and aspirations. The Indo-Pacific paradigm has distinct meanings for different nations. For the United States, it ranges from the western coast of India, which also forms the part of geographic boundary of the United States' Indo-Pacific Command; while for India it comprises of the entire IOR, including the Western Pacific region. The Indo-Pacific has refashioned India's foreign policy engagements and predilections. In turn, it also sets the basis for India's role in the emerging global security architecture. In this quest, India's position in the Indo-Pacific region is considered significant by various nations i.e., Australia, Japan, and the United States. This eventually provided India with opportunities to promote its strategic interests while acknowledging changes in the security architecture.

Based on this, it can be said that India's Indo-Pacific strategy, first, highlights the Indo-Pacific region as an opportunity to enhance its influence across the region, even though with limited capacity and capital limitations. Second, it places bilateral and multilateral partnerships at the centre of India's Indo-Pacific aspirations. As part of this, India has been extending partnerships with nations such as Australia, France, Japan, and the United States in the form of the Quad as a platform for New Delhi to expand its diplomatic footprint. These relationships, along with partnerships with the littoral nations, help in shaping India's role in the Indo-Pacific region.

The emerging scenario in the Indo-Pacific region provides India with a significant opportunity to partner with littoral nations and other major stakeholders in this region among whom the interests converge. This is further facilitated by the geographic proximity of various island nations such as Maldives, Sri Lanka, Mauritius, Seychelles, etc. with India; and their relations with India, including their foreign policy choices, will have a consequence on the Indian security milieu. Third, Indo-Pacific initiatives can help in fulfilling India's great power aspirations as well as becoming a major security provider in the larger Indian Ocean region.

To achieve the above-mentioned goals, India has been an enthusiastic participant in various multilateral platforms such as the East Asia Summit (EAS), Indian Ocean Rim Association (IORA), ASEAN Defence Ministers Meeting, etc. This indicates India's rising concerns in the Indo-Pacific region. Furthermore, India has also been conducting the Free and Open Indo-Pacific (FOIP) approach[26] and the Indo-Pacific Oceans Initiative (IPOI)[27] besides holding various multilateral naval exercises in the Andaman and Nicobar Islands such as "Milan", "Malabar" and "Tiger Triumph" military exercises. Furthermore, India is also enhancing its coastal surveillance network which includes the wide-ranging live monitoring of ship movements in the IOR and links Indian radars to other systems in Mauritius, Sri Lanka, Maldives and Seychelles.[28] In similar instances, India has also initiated the concept of SAGAR (Security and Growth for All in the Region),[29] and emphasises that the Indo-Pacific region is open, free and inclusive; it is only established through a cooperative and shared rules-based system.[30] So, through its substantiated efforts, India has been promoting the aim of a free and secure Indo-Pacific region with other "like-minded" nations and middle powers in this region to uphold a feasible global order. Therefore, it can be said that multilateral diplomacy, robust naval capabilities, and economic integration with the regional nations are vital for India to counter the challenges stemming from this region.

India's Maritime Quest in the Persian Gulf Region

For Indian regional maritime aspirations to be realised, it is necessary for New Delhi to project itself as a reliable and supportive partner of regional maritime forces in the Western Indian Ocean. In fact, to realise the above-mentioned goal, it is necessary for New Delhi to establish long-lasting relationships and deter challenges to achieve strategic pre-eminence in the maritime domain. So, India's political leadership must realise the significance of having balanced relationships with the West Asian nations. This is visible from the increased high-level visits between

India and various West Asian nations, which include the growth of bilateral maritime security cooperation, mainly through the Indian Navy. In the past few years, the Indian Navy has established itself as "a robust and professional force" with which the Arab Gulf navies are keen to engage in terms of training and technical assistance.[31] These engagements between the Indian Navy and the navies of various West Asian nations, through joint exercises, port calls and training programmes, have led to the creation of durable maritime relations in the Western Indian Ocean region. Through these efforts, there are chances that India will persist and emerge as a reliable maritime partner in the context of the rising Chinese influence in the West Asian region through its BRI plans. In all of this, India's West Asian diplomacy as well as crucial rebalancing strategies and the strategic hedging narratives further New Delhi's interests in the regional and maritime domains. It should be noted that these naval exercises, in due course, serve as diplomatic means, through which military-to-military relations are consolidated. In this scenario, these military/naval exercises can also become the means of potential defence equipment and military hardware sales.[32]

It is noteworthy that India stands for the protection of the SLOCs traversing through the Persian Gulf and Red Sea in the Horn of Africa region, which are fraught with piracy threats. In this context, the Indian Navy has positioned its warships in the Gulf of Oman and the Persian Gulf region to make it a safe passage for Indian sea vessels traversing through these regions.[33] So, through its consistent presence and conducting operations as well as providing various training and hydrographic support, India has established close and friendly relations with the maritime nations of the Gulf region.[34] India's maritime strategy has mainly two aspects: (1) The SLOCs in the Northern Indian Ocean are critical globally, thus, facilitating the trade and transit of goods and commodities, oil and natural gas. And (2) India is the major beneficiary of the goods and energy trade transits through the West Asian littorals. However, in order to achieve this, India must continue with political and maritime engagements to add force to its diplomatic efforts.

As mentioned above, the Indian Navy conducts various joint naval exercises with two major Gulf Cooperation Council (GCC) nations, i.e., Oman and the UAE. In view of the successful conduct of military exercises with these two nations, India can recommend expanding such engagements with other GCC nations too. Furthermore, India should dynamically elevate the level of engagement with Oman and the UAE to establish a stable training facility, along with options for defence trade and assistance with other navies in the region. In this regard, India can look forward to the swift operationalisation of maritime cooperation with Saudi Arabia, further exploring the options of joint defence production. As, for example, Saudi Arabia is considering the induction of submarines as part of its defence modernisation process.[35] Furthermore, demonstrating its presence in the Persian Gulf region also signifies the Indian defence forces' power projection across the IORA region, leading to enhanced engagement. Through these maritime exercises, various issues related to search and rescue, electronic warfare, tactical manoeuvres, and over the horizon targeting can help in strengthening the interoperability and synergy among the navies of other nations also.[36]

To serve the above-mentioned aims, India could make the proposition of basic submarine training and technical assistance to the Saudi Navy. So, it can be said that there are numerous realms in which strategic maritime cooperation can occur. These could be explored by the Indian Navy; however, the responsibility lies with India to grab the opportunity to enhance its security ties with the West Asian nations.

Conclusion

The waterways around the world are becoming theatres of geopolitical struggles, especially in the IOR. At the same time, it cannot be ignored that stretching the concept of the Indo-Pacific to extend it to the Persian Gulf region can further agitate the Indo-Pacific region. As, in the contemporary scenario, the Persian Gulf region is fragmented by territorial disputes, inter-state rivalries, inchoate regional organisations and the formation of new alliances between old rivals, which can further complicate the Indo-Pacific construct. However, there are chances that the extension of the Indo-Pacific region to the Persian Gulf region could happen in the foreseeable future. This is due to the fact that many West Asian nations with stable maritime structures are considering a connect with the Indo-

Pacific region due to their SLOCs or transit routes traversing through their maritime territories. This is further complicated by the strenuous relations between extra-regional powers such as China and the United States, which have their own individual interests to connect the Persian Gulf with the Indo-Pacific region. But it remains to be seen how these ideas and interests materialise in the future.

The Indian maritime approach is visible through its stakes in the prevailing balance-of-power scenario where the altering equations between major regional and global powers have been linked to their own national interests. Contemporary geopolitical quests in the Indo-Pacific region can affect the other connected maritime transit routes. Therefore, it necessitates the formation of a capable institutional infrastructure which can address the challenges emanating from both the Persian Gulf and Indo-Pacific regions. The challenges range from strategic and institutional insufficiencies, destabilising non-traditional security threats of climate change, drugs trade, piracy and state fragility. So, Indian maritime diplomacy has to navigate through these challenges by cautious collaborations with other extra-regional powers along with calibrating its own capacities and the soft power it enjoys in both regions.

In this context, India has started leveraging on the idea of it being a 'net security provider' and a capable regional power in both the Indo-Pacific and Persian Gulf regions, promoting regional security and stability. New Delhi remains one of the actors that can manoeuvre along with other international actors in the Indo-Pacific and Persian Gulf regions owing to its good relations with them. In this context, India can act as bridge between the two significant maritime regions. Along with the FOIP, various agreements and associations have also culminated in the creation of sustainable multilateral platforms for India with other like-minded partners in both regions. As, for instance, the ideas of creating the Quad (the United States, Japan, Australia and India) or Quad II (the United States, Israel, the UAE and India) partnerships, strengthening bilateral naval exercises, etc. Through these efforts, there are chances that India can act as a bridge between the Indo-Pacific and Persian Gulf regions. It is only through such a renewed geopolitical vision that India would be able to position itself in the global maritime outlook.

Notes

1. Vijay Sakhuja, "Indian Ocean and the Safety of Sea Lines of Communication", *Strategic Analysis*, Vol. XXV, No. 5, August 2001. https://ciaotest.cc.columbia.edu/olj/sa/sa_aug01sav01.html. Accessed on January 7, 2022.
2. Andreas Osthagen, "Troubled Seas? The Changing Politics of Maritime Boundary Disputes", *Ocean and Coastal Management*, Vol. 205, May 2021. https://www.sciencedirect.com/science/article/pii/S096456912100020X?dgcid=raven_sd_search_email. Accessed on January 7, 2022.
3. Diane French, David Michel, and Ricky Passarelli, eds,, *Sea Change: Evolving Maritime Geopolitics in The Indo-Pacific Region* (Stimson Centre, 2014), pp. 11-17. https://www.stimson.org/wp-content/files/file-attachments/SEA-CHANGE-WEB.pdf. Accessed on January 9, 2022.
4. Wada Haruko, "The 'Indo-Pacific' Concept: Geographical Adjustments And Their Implications", *RSIS Working Paper*, No. 326, March 16, 2020, pp. 1-27. https://www.rsis.edu.sg/rsis-publication/rsis/the-indo-pacific-concept/?doing_wp_cron=1643985503.6898028850555419921875#.Yf06YepN02w. Accessed on February 4, 2022.
5. Cornelius Adebahr, "Collective Security in the Persian Gulf: Preparing for an Opening", *Carnegie Europe*, July 20, 2021. https://carnegieeurope.eu/2021/07/20/collective-security-in-persian-gulf-preparing-for-opening-pub-84959. Accessed on January 8, 2022.
6. Yogendra Kumar, "India's Maritime Diplomacy in the Indo-Pacific in Pursuit of its National Objectives", MEA-Distinguished Lecture Series, October 18, 2019. https://www.mea.gov.in/distinguished-lectures-detail.htm?852. Accessed on January 5, 2022.
7. Ernest Gunasekara-Rockwell, et al., "The Persian Gulf and the Indo-Pacific", *Indo-Pacific Perspective Series-JIPA*, December 2021, pp. 1-35. https://media.defence.gov/2021/Dec/28/2002915336/-1/-1/1/IPP%20-%20DECEMBER%20 2021%20-%20JIPA.PDF/IPP%20-%20DECEMBER%202021%20-%20JIPA.PDF. Accessed on January 8, 2021.
8. Jonathan Fulton, "The Gulf Between the Indo-Pacific and the Belt and Road Initiative", *Rising Powers Quarterly*, Vol. 3, Issue 2, 2018, pp. 175-193. https://risingpowersproject.com/files/wp-content/uploads/2018/10/vol3.2-fulton.pdf. Accessed on January 10, 2019.
9. "Strait of Hormuz: Assessing the Threat to Oil Flows Through the Strait", Robert Strauss Centre for International Security and Law, May 2008. https://www.strausscenter.org/wp-content/uploads/Strait_of_Hormuz.pdf. Accessed on January 10, 2021.

10. David Brewster, "An Indian Sphere of Influence in the Indian Ocean?" *Security Challenges*, Vol. 6, No. 3, Spring 2010, pp. 1-20. https://www.jstor.org/stable/pdf/26459796.pdf?refreqid=excelsior%3A3a60d39fda19245615adad4a2ea44116&ab_segments=&origin=. Accessed on January 9, 2022.
11. Felix Heiduk and Gudrun Wacker, "From Asia-Pacific to Indo-Pacific", SWP Research Paper, July 1, 2020. https://www.swp-berlin.org/en/publication/from-asia-pacific-to-indo-pacific/#hd-d24373e339. Accessed on January 8, 2022.
12. P. K. Ghosh, "The Indo-Pacific Region and the Rise of Transnational Maritime Threats and Challenges", in David Michel and Ricky Passarelli, eds., *Sea Change: Evolving Maritime Geopolitics in The Indo-Pacific Region* (Stimson Centre, 2014), pp. 19-29. https://www.stimson.org/wp-content/files/file-attachments/SEA-CHANGE-WEB.pdf. Accessed on January 9, 2022.
13. Daisuke Akimoto, "China's Grand Strategy and the Emergence of Indo-Pacific Alignments", Institute of Security and Development Policy, April 14, 2021, https://isdp.eu/chinas-grand-strategy-and-the-emergence-of-indo-pacific-alignments/; Liu Zongyi, "The Belt and Road Initiative and the US Indo-Pacific Strategy", *Turkish Policy Quarterly*, September 8, 2019. http://turkishpolicy.com/article/969/the-belt-and-road-initiative-and-the-us-indo-pacific-strategy; Weixing Hu and Weizhan Meng, "The US Indo-Pacific Strategy and China's Repsonse", *The China Review*, Vol. 20, No. 03, August 2020, pp. 143-176. https://www.jstor.org/stable/26928115; Shoji Tomotaka, "Belt and Road" vs. "Free and Open Indo-Pacific": Competition over Regional Order and ASEAN's Responses", *Boei Kenkyusho Kiyo (NIDS Journal of Defence and Security)*, Vol. 22, No. 2, January 2020, pp. 3-24. http://www.nids.mod.go.jp/english/publication/security/pdf/2021/01/04.pdf. Accessed on January 8, 2022.
14. Fulton, n. 8.
15. Ghosh, n. 12, pp. 19-29.
16. Gurpreet Singh Khurana, "Maritime Security and Geopolitics in the Indo-Pacific Region", *Artha journal of Social Sciences*, Vol. 18, No. 4, 2019, pp. 71-86. https://journals.christuniversity.in/index.php/artha/article/view/2181/1741. Accessed on January 10, 2022.
17. Ibid.
18. Vivek Mishra, "Emerging Dynamics of India's Maritime Strategy", STS Forum, March 1, 2018. http://stsfor.org/content/emerging-dynamics-indias-maritime-strategy. Accessed on January 11, 2022.
19. Pradeep Chauhan, "India's Proposed Maritime Strategy", National Maritime Foundation, February 3, 2020. https://maritimeindia.org/indias-proposed-maritime-strategy/. Accessed on January 11, 2022.
20. Ibid.
21. "Prime Minister's Keynote Address at Shangri La Dialogue", Ministry of External Affairs—Speeches and Statements, June 1, 2018. https://

www.mea.gov.in/Speeches-Statements.htm?dtl/29943/Prime+Ministers+Keynote+Address+at+Shangri+La+Dialogue+June+01+2018. Accessed on January 5, 2022.

22. Anasua Basu Ray Chaudhury, Pratnashree Basu and Sohini Bose, "Exploring India's Maritime Connectivity in the Extended Bay of Bengal", Observer Research Foundation, November 2019. https://www.orfonline.org/wp-content/uploads/2019/11/ORF_Report_India-ExtendedBOB.pdf. Accessed on January 11, 2022.
23. The AII Trilateral Initiative is also known as the Australia-India-Indonesia Trilateral Initiative. This was initiated in 2017. Jagannath Panda, "The Australia-India-Indonesia Trilateral: Fostering Maritime Cooperation between Middle Powers", The National Bureau of Asian Research, April 23, 2021. https://www.nbr.org/publication/the-australia-india-indonesia-trilateral-fostering-maritime-cooperation-between-middle-powers/; "India-France-Australia Joint Statement on the Occasion of the Trilateral Ministerial Dialogue", Ministry of External Affairs, May 4, 2021. https://mea.gov.in/bilateral-documents.htm?dtl/33845/IndiaFranceAustralia+Joint+Statement+on+the+occasion+of+the+Trilateral+Ministerial+Dialogue+May+04+2021. Accessed on January 14, 2022.
24. Jagannath Panda, "India, the Blue Dot Network, and the 'Quad Plus' Calculus", *Journal of Indo-Pacific Affairs*, Fall 2020, pp. 1-21. https://media.defence.gov/2020/Aug/21/2002482235/-1/-1/1/PANDA.PDF. Accessed on January 14, 2022.
25. Premesha Saha and Abhishek Mishra, "The Indo-Pacific Oceans Initiative: Towards a Coherent Indo-Pacific Policy for India", *ORF Occasional Paper No. 292*, December 2020. https://www.orfonline.org/research/indo-pacific-oceans-initiative-towards-coherent-indo-pacific-policy-india/#_ednref38. Accessed on January 13, 2022.
26. Free and Open Indo-Pacific (FOIP) refers to the all-encompassing Indo-Pacific strategies of nations with mutual interests vis-à-vis this region. This concept was a result of the Japanese and American deliberations on the issues related to the Indo-Pacific region. Japan formally recognised this as a strategy in 2016 followed by the United States recognising it in 2019.
27. Indo-Pacific Oceans Initiative (IPOI) is the joint partnership between Australia and India. The aim of this initiative to shape the maritime cooperation in the Indo-Pacific region to have an open, inclusive, resilient and rule-based maritime order. This was declared by Prime Minister Modi at the 14th East Asia Summit in November 2019. "Australia-India Indo-Pacific Oceans Initiative Partnership", Australian High Commission, New Delhi. https://india.highcommission.gov.au/ndli/AIIPOIP1.html. Accessed on January 12, 2022.
28. Dinkar Peri, "India Looks at Integrating More Countries into Coastal Radar Network", *The Hindu*, December 20, 2020. https://www.thehindu.com/news/national/india-looks-at-integrating-more-countries-into-coastal-radar-network/article33379243.ece. Accessed on January 12, 2022.

29. SAGAR is India's maritime cooperation doctrine in the Indian Ocean region. This was first declared by Prime Minister Narendra Modi in 2015. However, there has been no published official report in this regard.
30. Preethi Amaresh, "India's Emergence as a Leading Global Power and its Role in Indo-Pacific Region", *Diplomatist*, March 15, 2021. https://diplomatist.com/2021/03/15/indias-emergence-as-a-leading-global-power-and-its-role-in-indo-pacific-region/. Accessed on January 12, 2022.
31. Shishir Upadhyaya, "India's Maritime Security Relations with the Gulf Cooperation Council Countries—Prospects Amid Rising Chinese Influence", *Maritime Affairs: Journal of the National Maritime Foundation of India*, 2019, pp. 1-14. https://doi.org/10.1080/09733159.2019.1625224. Accessed on January 13, 2022.
32. Huma Siddiqui, "Indian Navy Projects Power Across IOR, Carries out Drills with Gulf Countries", *Financial Express*, August 13, 2021. https://www.financialexpress.com/defence/indian-navy-projects-power-across-ior-carries-out-drills-with-gulf-countries/2310440/. Accessed on January 12, 2022.
33. Abhijit Singh, "India's Middle Eastern Naval Diplomacy", Middle East Institute, July 27, 2017. https://www.mei.edu/publications/indias-middle-eastern-naval-diplomacy. Accessed on January 13, 2022.
34. Ibid.
35. "Annual Report 2017-2018", Ministry of Defence, Government of India, pp. 170-171. https://www.mod.gov.in/sites/default/files/AR1718.pdf. Accessed on January 13, 2022.
36. Siddiqui, n. 32.

11. Taiwan-India Security Cooperation in the New Indo-Pacific Order

Mrittika Guha Sarkar

Introduction

Ties between India and Taiwan have gained extensive momentum in the recent years. A significant factor contributing to this momentum has been the developing and firming construct of the Indo-Pacific. This regional construct has allowed Taiwan and India to realise the complementarities of New Delhi's Act East policy—aiming to improve relations with the East and Southeast Asian countries, and Taipei's New Southbound policy—purporting to upgrade ties with the South and Southeast Asian states. In particular, the Act East policy and the New Southbound policy have been crucial in charting out India's and Taiwan's Indo-Pacific approaches, respectively, while the synergies between both policy initiatives only reiterate their commitment towards a free, open, inclusive, and rules-based Indo-Pacific order.

However, these policy initiatives between Taiwan and India have primarily benefited the economic, cultural and educational arenas, leaving the crucial area of security largely unexplored and the bilateral relations underutilised. One of the critical reasons for this has been India's hesitant and cautious approach towards Taiwan in a bid to not irk China while adhering to the 'One-China policy', as well as Taiwan's flaccid approach towards India's outreach attempts in the past.

An essential element shaping this development has been the lack of mutual trust in the bilateral relations, the origin of which goes back to 1947. Interestingly, the Chinese Nationalist Party or Kuomintang (KMT) and the Indian National Congress (INC), the mass political organisations in China and India, were the first to pave the way towards bilateral cooperation.[1] It was mainly in the meeting in Brussels in 1927, attended by various representatives of colonies and semi-colonies, where Chinese delegates and Jawaharlal Nehru met post World War 1 to discuss possible cooperation between Nationalist China and India. Subsequently, the cooperative sentiments furthered with significant interactions between the Indian and Kuomintang leaders during the Second Sino-Japanese War (1937-45). The particular, the relations between China and India witnessed further improvement with the visit of Nehru to mainland China, where he was received by Chiang Kai-Shek, as well as the visit by Chiang to India in February 1942.[2] Interestingly, it was during this time, that Chiang became the first major non-European political figure to support the liberation of India.[3] Broadly, China and India shared cordial relations from the 1920s to 1947.

However, differences started occurring in 1947, when divergent perceptions on the McMahon Line and Tibet overshadowed the cordial sentiments between the two powers.[4] In particular, Taiwan, prior to 1990, resolutely considered itself as the legitimate government of the whole of China and stressed conventional borders with India, which overlapped with the latter's territorial claims. As a result, Taipei even condemned India's announcement of Arunachal Pradesh as a state and issued a statement in 1986.[5] The relations between India and Taiwan further deteriorated with the Communist Party of China (CCP) taking over the mainland, while India decided to establish diplomatic ties with the People's Republic of China (PRC) on April 1, 1950, despite the cooperative ties forged between the INC and KMT. In fact, this move by India strained the relationship to a great extent, mainly as India went against Taiwan's interests by supporting the PRC, while ironically, Taiwan had supported India's independence at the cost of its own relations with the British.[6]

Notably, even after India's war with China in 1962 and deteriorating relations between New Delhi and Beijing for 14 years, thereafter, India's Taiwan policy remained restrained and underexplored, guided by India's cautious approach in an effort to not worsen its relations with its northern neighbour, China, and its adherence to the sensitivities of the One China policy. This was underpinned by India's support for the PRC's membership in the United Nations Security Council, subsequently replacing the KMT-led Republic of China in 1971. Besides, India firmly subscribed to the Non-Aligned Movement (NAM) while maintaining closeness with the Soviet Union. But on the other hand, Taiwan closely aligned with the United States and the Western bloc, further preventing Taiwan and India from taking steps to forge closer ties and figure prominently in each other's regional policies.

Nonetheless, considering that Taipei and New Delhi are facing common security threats, sharing democratic values towards national and regional governance, as well as their growing geopolitical significance in the Indo-Pacific, can Taiwan and India explore greater cooperation in security-related areas? To what extent can security cooperation assist Taiwan and India to realise the true potential of bilateral ties? And what are the particular areas under the purview of security that Taipei and New Delhi can explore?

Deteriorating Relations with China: A Rationale for Greater Taiwan-India Cooperation?

A sense of reluctance had shaped Taiwan and India's policy towards each other until 1995, when a channel of communication was created in the form of representative offices under the tenures of Indian Prime Minister P.V. Narasimha Rao and Taiwan President Lee Tung Hui. Thus, the Taipei Economic and Cultural Centre (TECC) and India Taipei Association (ITA) was created in the capital cities of Taipei and New Delhi. Post this development, Taiwan-India cooperation was enhanced to a great extent. However, a significant factor for this, more often than not, had been the deteriorating relations between India and China.

New Delhi and Beijing have shared a complicated relationship; this underpins their cordial relationship until 1956, witnessing a deteriorated bilateral relationship thereafter, resulting in a war in 1962, a freeze in the ties until the 1980s *modus vivendi* between India and China post-1988, with the visit by Rajiv Gandhi, and the gradual crisis in the relations post 2012.[7] Amidst all the phases in their bilateral ties, the boundary dispute between the countries has been a significant thorn in the flesh, while the Sino-Indian War of 1962 still obtains a major spot as a hindrance for both powers to reconcile their differences. Irrespective of both sides' commitment to resolving the border dispute peacefully and many rounds of bilateral talks, incidents of Chinese troops crossing the border illegally or initiating infrastructure construction along the Line of Actual Control (LAC) have become a regular occurrence.

Nonetheless, India has been observing a recent trend of hardening of the Chinese position on the territorial dispute. If anything, the Chinese foreign policy towards India has been witness to a significant change since 2012-13, particularly as a cooperative and development-oriented perspective towards New Delhi gradually gets overshadowed by a more aggressive diplomatic and military posturing. This has been reiterated through several border skirmishes, from Depsang Valley in 2013 to Chumar in 2014, Doklam in 2017, to the recent Galwan Valley border clash in 2020, persisting with tensions in the region. All these point towards a policy transition under Xi Jinping towards India—from viewing New Delhi through the prism of a neighbouring country, to that of a major power, to finally perceiving India as an adversary.[8]

Arguably, such a competing perspective has led to increasing public antagonism towards China in India.[9] Further, such development has also led to a greater demand in the Indian scholarly community to reconsider or alter India's One China policy. For instance, an article in the *Indian Express* argued that India's One China policy should be in tandem with Taiwan's position in the current geopolitics and India's troubles with China. Stating that the decision "should not be made either out of peevishness or fear", the article stressed that New Delhi should analyse the situation based on "apolitical appreciation of the specific technical issues involved." And while the author did not outrightly suggest an alteration of India's One China policy, the article did reflect the growing demand for the same in India.[10]

However, the scholarly community also came across some bold editorials, such as the one in *The Times of India*, which asked the Indian government to "not shy away from supporting Taiwan" while China has seldom taken consideration of Indian interests in the United Nations or other multilateral organisations. The article also suggested that India's support should become an essential aspect of the potential reform of the World Health Organisation (WHO), considering the marvellous efforts by Taipei in controlling the spread of COVID-19 in Taiwan.[11] These voices in India are not new; in 2019, the *The Times of India* published an article titled "Don't be Scared: India should Ignore Chinese Blandishments and Enhance Ties with Taiwan", which argued for greater cooperation between India and Taiwan.[12] Most importantly, such views found a place in an Indian Parliamentary Standing Committee report on India-China relations in 2018, which stressed the irony of China and Taiwan having active trade and investments despite the incrementally worsening political and security ties, while India had been reluctant to strengthen ties with Taiwan overtly, in view of its complex relations with China.[13]

Nonetheless, India's policy towards Taiwan, particularly under the Modi government, seems to be changing with greater pro-activeness. The Modi's government's landslide victory in 2014 generated a greater hope towards improved bilateral ties. This argument is only strengthened by the fact that Modi, the then general secretary of the Bharatiya Janata Party (BJP), in 1999 visited Taiwan. Subsequently, in 2011, as chief minister of Gujarat, he invited an 80-member-high level business delegation from Taiwan.

If anything, the border clashes have played a major role in attracting Indian public support towards Taiwan. Chinese actions along the LAC have reiterated Beijing's disregard for India's territorial sensitivities, while China's increasing aggression has threatened India's interests. Nonetheless, as the Galwan Valley incident between India and China pushed the bilateral relations to a new low since the 1962 War, the border clash also seems to have driven a call for more proactive support towards Taipei, particularly going beyond non-political affairs. This was notably reiterated when the Indian media defied China's displeasure over Indian newspapers publishing advertisements for Taiwan's national day in 2020. The advertisement, which carried a photograph of President Tsai Ing-wen and hailed India as a natural partner to Taiwan, was condemned by China in an email sent to the journalists in India by the Chinese Embassy. However, this time, in contradiction to the Indian government's earlier cautious response towards anything related to its One China policy, Anurag Srivastava, the Ministry of External Affairs (MEA's) spokesperson, stated to the media, "There is a free media in India that reports on issues as it sees fit".[14] Similar instances took place as BJP members of Parliament, Meenakshi Lekhi and Rahul Kaswan, attended Tsai's swearing-in ceremony in 2020, arguably in a move to send a firm signal to China.[15] Further, another important development that marked the solidification of India-Taiwan relations was the revival of the India-Taiwan Parliamentary Friendship Association after a hiatus of three years in October 2020.

India-Taiwan Security Relations in an Emerging Theatre of Strategic Competition in the Indo-Pacific

However, the theme of India-Taiwan security cooperation has generally been met with a pessimistic and reluctant approach by most scholars and practitioners until now, echoing India's apprehensions in stoking the Chinese ire and unnecessarily complicating the already complex bilateral ties going through a thorny phase. Nonetheless, it is crucial for the academic and policy circles to shape India-Taiwan relations beyond the Chinese prism and explore areas, particularly in the field of security, where India and Taiwan could engage and partner constructively without infuriating Beijing.

India and Taiwan hold important strategic positions in the current regional order. However, while Taiwan's strategic location and role in the East China and South China Seas makes it an important regional player, India's emerging position as a security provider in the Indian Ocean makes it a critical power in the regional order. Here, an important role could be played by the construct of the Indo-Pacific, whose emergence has enabled India and Taiwan to chalk out arenas for greater engagement. Further, the revival of groupings such as the Quad 2.0 and the rise of other minilaterals, signalling a shift in the orientations of the regional countries, demonstrates a potential for Taiwan to play a more significant role in the region. More significantly, while despite common security threats, shared democratic values, synergic values towards national and regional governance, India and Taiwan have not been able to establish cooperation in the security areas, the Indo-Pacific has emerged as a possible common ground that holds the potential to generate a greater security partnership between India and Taiwan.

Intelligence Sharing

As suggested by Taiwanese Foreign Minister Joseph Wu in October 2020, one such area can be intelligence sharing. Here, Taipei's knowledge of the Chinese military, its organisation and functioning could be mutually beneficial and synergic to New Delhi's knowledge and experience of confronting the People's Liberation Army (PLA). In fact, there are also possibilities of a trilateral intelligence sharing arrangement among India, Taiwan and Japan to amplify each country's intelligence capabilities in the face of all the countries being at the front line, facing China's military brunt frequently. This becomes further viable as Japan has pro-actively stated its desire to "protect Taiwan as a democratic country".[16] While a call for an intelligence sharing arrangement between Japan and Taiwan is gaining momentum,[17] Japan's seemingly increasing support for Taiwan's sovereignty is only likely to play a greater role in working out a possible arrangement among India, Taiwan and Japan over intelligence sharing.[18]

In terms of India-Taiwan intelligence sharing possibilities, there have been reports suggesting that Taipei and New Delhi have already exchanged intelligence in the past.[19] A possibility of such trilateral cooperation would only relieve pressure on the individual countries' intelligence networks and allow the arrangement to utilise Taiwan's China focussed security establishment, India's superior satellite reconnaissance abilities, and Japan's estimated 19 signals intelligence stations,[20] as well as its extensive underwater surveillance system.[21] Besides, Taiwan is known to have some of the world's best human intelligence assets operating against China, while India is understood to have various types of intelligence systems, such as electronic intelligence, imaging, communications satellites, etc. Thus, such an arrangement is only likely to strengthen the countries' power capabilities, enabling them to attain their national goals and synergise convergent interests with each other. On a broader level, such an arrangement is likely to strengthen India-Taiwan security cooperation in the Indo-Pacific and push the bilateral relations to greater heights, beyond the apprehensions around China.

Partnership in Cyber Security

Another area where India and Taiwan might and must cooperate is soft and hard cyber security. This, in fact, becomes a greater necessity, as cyber attacks by China, to a great extent, seem to have become an instrument to manage its territorial disputes with Taiwan and India. For instance, India recently witnessed a cyber attack in February 2021 with a mega-power blackout in Mumbai, which upheld its suspicions against China, particularly in the backdrop of persistent India-China boundary tensions along the LAC. In fact, India witnessed escalated cyber attacks from Chinese hackers, particularly during the Galwan Valley standoff. This was brought to the forefront when a US-based cyber security firm, Recorded Future, noted that a China-linked hacker group called RedEcho had targeted India's critical infrastructure of the power sector, railway infrastructure, as well as ports since 2020.[22] In a similar vein, CyFirma, a Singapore-based company, noted that a Chinese state-backed hacking group had targeted the computer networks of two Indian vaccine makers, Bharat Biotech and Serum Institute which notably played a very crucial role in driving India's domestic vaccine programme, and were the face of India's vaccine diplomacy.[23] While not publicly attributing them to China, India has been facing sustained cyber offensives from China with greater frequency and bolstered intensity.

On the other hand, cyber attacks are unrelenting for Taiwan. According to the Ministry of Foreign Affairs, cyber attacks seemingly from Chinese source, have increased by 40 times between 2018 and 2020 and surged by 38 per cent in 2021.[24] In fact, according to recent reports, Taiwan witnesses cyber attacks with a frequency of 2,644 per week, forcing it to enhance its resilience against China's cyber offensives which are mounting persistently.[25] Notably, such attacks play a major role in China's hybrid warfare and intimidation campaigns against adversaries. And while Taiwan has been working on defending against such attacks by creating an extensive network of institutions, including the Information, Communications and Electronic Force Command under the Ministry of

National Defence and Cyber Crime Investigation Unit under the Ministry of Justice Investigation Bureau, and India has established dedicated agencies operating under the Ministry of Home Affairs, particularly the Indian Cyber Crime Coordination Centre,[26] greater collaboration would be a necessity in the face of China's growing technological capabilities and the increasingly transnational character of cyber attacks. It is in this context that greater resistance is required against these attacks, which could benefit both with collaboration between India and Taiwan.

These critical issues were mainly discussed during a session on "Cyber Security and Related Research Applications" at the Bengaluru Tech Summit 2021, where Prof. Chin Tsan Wang, director for Science and Technology, Taipei Economic and Cultural Centre in India, stated, "The world is changing in the Artificial Intelligence age, so setting a safe cyber security is necessary". He indicated Taiwan's interest in collaborating with India to enhance its research ability in cyber security. Furthermore, considering Taiwan's high-performing computing platform, partnering with companies from Taiwan would have the potential to build up India's cyber infrastructure effectively, especially by establishing innovation hubs, research organisations and training centres.[27] An encouraging step towards cyber security cooperation was established with the conclusion of a Memorandum of Understanding (MoU) on cyber security cooperation on January 3, 2022, between the National Centre for High-performance Computing (NCHC), Taipei, and the Indian Institute of Technology, Kanpur. With a commitment to bolster bilateral exchange and research, the MoU aimed to provide a platform for both sides to perform "cyber security threat modeling through analysing malware behaviour to understand the impact of malicious programs on systems and networks".[28]

Convergence of Act East and New Southbound through Connectivity

The strategic alignment of India's Act East policy with Taiwan's New Southbound policy makes it a great platform for not just bilateral cooperation between Taiwan and India but also multilateral collaboration with other regional powers. A fertile ground, in this context remains the possibility of cooperation through infrastructural connectivity initiatives. Creating a collaborative platform to export infrastructure construction services and turnkey projects remains an essential element of Taiwan's plan to promote economic collaboration as a part of its New Southbound policy.[29] On the other hand, India too has upped the ante in improving its maritime infrastructure and capability-building efforts, particularly as a part of its Act East policy.[30] In this regard, seemingly synergic goals and interests in the Indo-Pacific, particularly in terms of infrastructure building, could serve as a platform for India and Taiwan to collaborate in the field of infrastructural connectivity in the region. Notably, companies from Taiwan have already demonstrated their infrastructure building capabilities while collaborating with Japan and Indonesia to build Jakarta's first Mass Rapid Transit (MRT) line, which went operational at the end of March 2019.[31] Moreover, Taiwan is also reported to be planning to collaborate with the US to support "quality infrastructure in emerging markets" as convergence between America's Indo-Pacific strategy and Taiwan's New Southbound policy. While no concrete details have been made available on the infrastructural plans or the volume of funding for the projects, such developments signal towards a greater call for lessening dependence on China, while indicating towards a more robust possibility for Taiwan's greater inclusion in the regional architecture.

Here, India could collaborate with Taiwan in infrastructure connectivity in the region under its Act East policy. In addition, India and Taiwan could also collaborate along with the Association of Southeast Asian Nations (ASEAN), a common policy target for both the Act East and Southbound policies. While India has been engaging with the ASEAN countries through connectivity projects such as the Kaladan multimodal project, Taiwan has also been trying to engage with the ASEAN countries, mainly through facilitating cooperation among the shipbuilding industries of Taiwan and Indonesia. Such multilateral collaboration could also be explored with other regional powers, such as the US, Japan, South Korea, and Australia. Furthermore, Taiwan could also engage in the Quad's infrastructure plans under its "quality infrastructure investment" agenda mentioned in the first in-person Quad leaders' summit in 2021[32] by focussing on "high standards infrastructure", in an effort to move away from China's unsustainable infrastructural projects in the region. Notably, Taiwan has already officially iterated its willingness to partner with the Quad. According to reports, Taiwan's representative to the US, Hsiao Bi-Khim, expressed Taiwan's interest in collaborating with the grouping to address the key issues the Quad would aim to tackle.[33] Such a development only encourages the greater potential for a possible infrastructural collaboration between the Quad members and Taiwan in the Indo-Pacific.

Securing the Indo-Pacific: Further, India and Taiwan could play a great role in ensuring the stability of the Indo-Pacific by cooperating in counter-piracy operations, trafficking, fisheries, security of trade, etc. Both Taipei and New Delhi could also coordinate and partner their navies and coast guards for humanitarian and disaster relief missions. Notably, Taiwan has a long and unique history of humanitarianism. Taiwan's International Cooperation and Development Fund has been helping partner countries upgrade public health and medical services, provide overseas humanitarian, disaster relief and technical assistance and manage overseas volunteer programmes. Taiwan played a key role in supplying COVID-19 emergency relief to India while India was reeling under a massive surge in COVID-19 cases in the country during the second wave.[34] At the same time, the Indian military has been playing a significant role in disaster relief operations, as well as partnering with other regional countries in keeping a check on piracy activities, trafficking, etc., in the Indian Ocean. In fact, India was the "first responder" to the 2015 Nepal earthquake while carrying out the largest ever disaster relief operation known as *Maitri*.[35]

Another critical area where Taiwan can underscore its partnership with India is through utilising its Mandarin language capabilities and Chinese culture to teach and train the Indian strategic community, enabling them to benefit by gaining more profound knowledge on China. Taiwan has a better understanding of China's strategic thinking, particularly due to their close geostrategic proximity and shared cultural and linguistic ties. Taiwan has also invested heavily in China studies. Besides, such kind of language training is not a new initiative; in 2013, the O.P Jindal Global University in Haryana, India, conducted a four week training programme in the Mandarin language for Indian Army officers. This programme was attended by 18 senior army officials to augment their verbal communications skills, particularly for bilateral negotiations and in diplomatic fora with the Chinese military during border meetings, and more.[36] Closer cooperation with Taiwan will, thus, enable New Delhi to better understand China's strategic thinking with the assistance of native Chinese speakers with synergic strategic interests. This becomes further important in the face of continuing India-China tensions at the border, and China's increasing unilateral and aggressive military and diplomatic behaviour, and undemocratic activities in the Indo-Pacific posing a security threat.

Security Exchanges and Dialogues: In order to realise the true potential of security cooperation between India and Taiwan, New Delhi and Taipei must also enhance interactions and collaborations between their academic and strategic communities to realise the true potential of security cooperation between India and Taiwan could be to encourage strategic researchers to research on each other's lands, enabling the researchers to utilise the academic resources to better understand the thought processes towards China, as well as towards each other. In this context, another possible arena for cooperation could also be via encouraging think-tanks on both sides to conduct joint research on China and its security affairs. While Taiwan has significantly invested in studying China's strategic affairs, research on China's security developments has increased in India too. Considering the mutual threat concerns for both India and Taiwan, conducting joint research would only assist New Delhi and Taipei in attaining their national interests. Further, both sides could also consider sending their military officials to defence related think-tanks on the other side to facilitate exchange of information, initiate strategic discussions, and deepen understanding on mutual concerns.[37] Moreover, a requirement also remains to renew the Track II and Track 1.5 mechanisms between India and Taiwan, in case Track I dialogues become too sensitive. Notably, such dialogues were conducted by the Institute for Defence Studies and Analyses (IDSA) and Institute of International Relations (IIR), National Chengchi University, in Taiwan, in 2003.[38] However, this mechanism was later terminated.

Considering the increasing relevance of these dialogues to both India and Taiwan, Tracks II and I.5 dialogues should be renewed to utilise the benefits of diplomatic, policy and academic viewpoint exchanges on strategic issues between both sides.

India should also consider sending a defence attaché to Taiwan, to initiate cooperation in areas other than economics and culture. Notably, Taiwan has been stationing its military attaches in its TECC in New Delhi since 2000. In fact, it has gradually being raising the rank of the officer over the years, reflecting the country's intent on forging more profound strategic ties with India. In view of a growing security rationale at the backdrop, sending a military attaché might have its advantages. While the likelihood of sending an attaché still remains at around 50 per cent, considering the concerns of a backlash from China, stationing a military attaché in Taiwan would provide India with the latest intelligence on the development of military facilities in China and a deeper insight into the advancements of the PLA, considering Taiwan's reputation of being one of the best China watchers. In this case, a less controversial way, according to Fang Tien-sze, a less controversial way could be to send retired military officers to fill the attaché positions to avoid irking China.

Security Cooperation through Submarine Building: An important area which is often relatively less discussed is India-Taiwan's collaboration in submarine building is a vital area that is often relatively less discussed. Interestingly, Indian companies have been a part of Taiwan's secret submarine project by providing technology and experts to the programme along with firms from six other countries, namely Australia, South Korea, Spain, the US, the UK and Canada. While maintaining a low profile to evade China's radar, Indian firms, along with companies from other countries, have been aiding the project with cutting edge technology components and experts assisting in designing the submarine. In fact, engineers, technicians and former naval officers from these countries has been working in the shipyards of Kaohsiung, Taiwan. Though India, like other countries, has not collaborated with Taiwan in this project officially, reportedly, the export approvals for critical parts have been approved by the national governments of the countries, only to chalk out greater areas for India-Taiwan security cooperation. This project, if anything, sets the stage for greater India-Taiwan collaboration in submarine building. This comes as a necessity for Taiwan, considering the persistent cross-strait naval threats from China enhancing in the recent years. For India too, while already pursuing initiatives such as the Project 75 submarine plan,[39] collaboration with Taiwan would have its benefits in the face of threats in the Indo-Pacific by China and Pakistan.

Military-Industry Cooperation

While military cooperation between India and Taiwan remains sensitive, military-industry cooperation could be a viable option for collaboration. This comes with Taiwan and India signing a MoU for promoting industrial cooperation in 2017.[40] According to this MoU, India and Taiwan would seek to promote industrial cooperation in areas such as automotive electronics and smart cities. The MoU includes cooperation areas via different business models through Research and Development (R&D), design, engineering, manufacturing and after-sales service sharing to create industrial synergy and establish a value chain to enhance the added value of products and services between both parties. Thing kind of collaboration witnessed a renewed momentum with the MoUs signed between Taiwanese and Indian businesses on industrial partnerships in October 2020.[41] These have optimistically set the stage for possible military-industry cooperation between New Delhi and Taipei, particularly as greater calls for collaboration amongst the military make China's unilateralism in the region a rationale.[42] This was reiterated amidst an online discussion by Indian Air Chief Marshal Vivek Ram Chaudhari and air force commanders in the region on the challenges of distributed logistics and combat deployment while operating in austere locations. Here, the mood of the discussion signalled towards the practicality of collaboration between India and Taiwan on next-generation indigenous fighter jet programmes, in an effort to obtain the much needed mature and stable technology.

While these collaborations might face several challenges before they materialise, such discussions reflect a growing demand for military-industry cooperation between both sides. Taiwan is already considering making major revisions to its Industrial Cooperation Programme (ICP) to support the island's efforts to enhance its defence industrial capabilities and better integrate its industry with the international supply chains. This comes with the requirement of boosting Taiwan's economy via greater local industrial involvement in defence procurement.[43] On the other hand, India is focussing on boosting its defence manufacturing and encouraging foreign companies to invest in India, thus, reducing import dependency, and aiming to increase the value of the Indian defence industry from $1 trillion in 2022 to $5 trillion by 2047.[44] While military-industry collaboration between India and Taiwan might still witness several inhibitions, materialising of the same would only synergise with their national initiatives, and enable them to attain their goals and assist in better integration with the global supply chain. A possibility here could also be the exploration of public-private partnerships, which could relatively reduce the resistance, and enhance the strategic and commercial ties, between India and Taiwan.

The Multilateral Way: On the other hand, while India under the Modi government has been increasing its pro-activeness in participating in groupings like the Quad and minilaterals like Japan-Australia-India, Japan-US-India, and India-Japan-Australia led Supply Chain Resilience Initiative (SCRI), inviting Taiwan to these initiatives, even as an indirect partner, could benefit both Taiwan and the regional powers. The informal nature of these groupings, enables easy adaptations without any obligations. This can prove to be an advantage for Taiwan's integration in the region through a multilateral way, considering an assertive China in the Indo-Pacific. Here, countries like the US, India, Japan and Australia could utilise Taiwan's expertise in areas such as Information and Communication Technology (ICT), semiconductors, artificial intelligence, and more. The Quad grouping has already come together to secure supply chains in critical areas of semiconductors, 5G, and more, in a bid to contain the rising influence of China in strategic sectors. As the US states, "Resilient, diverse and secure technology supply chains—for hardware, software and services—are vital to our shared national interests," and holding Taiwan in a consultative position could benefit the grouping and its major goals while enabling Taiwan to gain a greater regional position and recognition in the face of China's attempts to reduce Taiwan's diplomatic support.[45]

In a similar vein, the SCRI, which hopes to ensure resilient and secure supply chains away from China centred vulnerabilities, could also benefit from Taiwan's expertise. In terms of defence cooperation, there already have been calls for including Taiwan in multilateral naval exercises.[46] For instance, there has been a call for Taiwan to be invited to the Rim of the Pacific (RIMPAC) naval exercises, according to the 2022 defence spending blueprint of the US, signed into law by President Joe Biden in December 2021.[47] While such developments would surely infuriate China, leading it to condemn the act through firm responses, these calls only indicate greater support for Taiwan.

Collaboration through Semiconductor Manufacturing: This would, in turn, allow greater possibilities for India-Taiwan economic security cooperation, particularly while encouraging India to provide greater regional support to Taiwan. In fact, the momentum for the same has already begun as India and Taiwan begin talks on a free trade pact and create a semiconductor manufacturing hub in India in efforts to meet the flourishing demand for chips needed to produce everything from cell phones to cars. Reportedly, officials from New Delhi and Taipei met in October 2021 to discuss a deal to bring in chip plants worth an estimated $7.5 billion to India to supply chips.[48] India is particularly eyeing the potential of attracting Taiwan semiconductor giants like the United Microelectronics Corporation (UMC) and Taiwan Semiconductor Manufacturing Company (TSMC) to set up facilities in India.[49] While setting up a firm in India does prove to be a complicated process due to the competition and accessibility, India's vast and growing market, the improving relations between India and Taiwan, the former's increasingly proactive approach towards the latter and seemingly slowly shedding the reluctance in the face of China's aggression at the LAC do play a major role for India to win the bid. Majorly driven by the strategic significance of the bilateral ties between India and Taiwan, the deal, if materialised, would make India the only country apart from the US to bring in Taiwan's chip manufacturing to a foreign land.

Cooperating through 5G Development: A similar momentum has been witnessed in the area of 5G and the determination of India and Taiwan to enhance their capabilities in the given field. Notably, both sides, in the purview of the current scenario, are lagging behind in 5G development. While Taiwan has the edge over hardware and India has the required software talent, a viable way to utilise their respective qualities would be to combine their key assets and upgrade their ICT industries. A step towards this direction was taken in 2017, when an ICT delegation from Taiwan concluded a four-day visit to India, in order to discuss bilateral cooperation on 5G technology development.[50] Subsequently, the second Taiwan Association of Information and Communication Standards (TAICS) meeting held on June 26, 2018, at the NTUH International Convention Centre, witnessed TAICS and Telecommunications Standards Development Society, India (TSDSI) signing an MoU to collaborate on 5G and Internet of Things (IoT) technology in the future.[51] These developments come in the backdrop of both India and Taiwan seeking to reduce their dependence on China; while New Delhi excluded Huawei and ZTE from participating in its 5G trials in May last year,[52] Taipei, too, excluded Huawei due to national security concerns.[53] It is in this context that a possible collaboration between India and Taiwan in developing a safe and secure 5G network could enhance security cooperation between the two sides.

Conclusion

The possibilities of Taiwan-India security cooperation in the Indo-Pacific have, more often than not, been viewed through reluctance. However, China's aggressive behaviour and assertive posture in the Indo-Pacific and along the LAC vis-à-vis India, coupled with India's mounting capabilities as a critical power in the region have come across as the rationale for India to look towards Taiwan with greater proactiveness. In a similar vein, the gradually increasing importance of Taiwan's geostrategic location and proactive approach in expressing its willingness to engage with the region beyond the US has led to an enhanced momentum for Taiwan to envision India-Taiwan ties beyond economic and cultural relations. This momentum has been increasingly evident in the public domain on both sides and vaguely being witnessed in the official domain in India as well as in Taiwan.

However, it is important to acknowledge that India would continue to demonstrate its apprehensions over infuriating China, and view Taiwan through guarded lenses. Besides, India-Taiwan ties, despite many opportunities and rationales, still underpin robust challenges. For instance, the ties, in their current form, lack a vision, and particularly, a long-term plan. Research on each other still remains nascent, while exchanges and engagement between both sides often remain restrained. While Taiwan needs to diversify its strategic alliances beyond the US and realise the potential of India as a natural partner with shared democratic values, India, too, needs to shape its Taiwan policy beyond the shadows of its complex ties with China.

Nonetheless, with a growing security rationale for India and Taiwan, both sides must consider collaborating via unofficial or multilateral domains, and even within spaces which do not attract unwanted attention from Beijing. Here, partnership in cyber security operations, converging India's Act East and Taiwan's New Southbound policies for collaborating via infrastructural connectivity initiatives, securing the Indo-Pacific by cooperating through counter-piracy operations, trafficking, fisheries, security of trade, as well as partnering their navies and coast guards for humanitarian and disaster relief missions, could be arenas that India and Taiwan could explore. Further, both sides could also explore enhancing security exchanges and dialogues by improving interactions and collaborations between their academic and strategic communities and encouraging the exchange of strategic researchers between think-tanks on both sides.

India and Taiwan could also encourage the think-tanks and organisations on both sides to conduct joint research on China and its security affairs, particularly considering their common threat perceptions. They should also consider renewing the Track II and Track 1.5 mechanisms to bolster engagement among the diplomatic, policy and academic communities, as well as enhance the consideration for India to send a defence attaché to Taiwan. Both sides could also undertake security collaboration through submarine building and facilitate military-industry cooperation. Lastly, both sides could collaborate by participating together in groupings such as the Quad, Quad Plus, and minilaterals like Japan-Australia-India, Japan-US-India, the India-Japan-Australia led SCRI, cooperate in semiconductor manufacturing, as well as in 5G development. Cooperation in these areas would drive the academic and policy circles to view the India-Taiwan relations beyond the Chinese prism and enable them to explore areas, particularly in the field of security, where India and Taiwan could engage without much hesitation.

Notes

1. Wu Chen-Tsai, "Chiang Kai-Shek's Visit to India and the Indian Independence", *Chinese Studies in History*, 1087, 21(1), pp. 2-28
2. Guido Samarani, "Shaping the Future of Asia: Chiang Kai-Shek, Nehru and China-India Relations during the Second World War Period", Lund University, 2005. https://lucris.lub.lu.se/ws/portalfiles/portal/4571404/3128707.pdf
3. Rana Mitter, "Destination Burma", in *Forgotten Ally: China's World War II, 1937-1945* (New York: Harcourt Publishing Company), p. 55.
4. Sana Hashmi, "India-Taiwan Ties: A Case for Stronger Partnership", IFRI, Centre for Asian Studies, No. 125, p. 8. https://www.ifri.org/en/publications/notes-de-lifri/asie-visions/india-taiwan-ties-case-stronger-partnership#:~:text=India%2DTaiwan%20Ties%3A%20A%20Case%20for%20Stronger%20Partnership%20Asie.&text=Its%20carefully%20crafted%20New%20Southbound,friends%20and%20partners%20%E2%80%93%20especially%20India.
5. Mumin Chen, "Taiwan-India Relations Under the Shadow of a Rising China", in G.V.C Naidu, Mumin Chen and Raviprasad Narayan, eds., *India and China in the Emerging Dynamics of East Asia* (New Delhi: Springer).
6. Fan Tuen-sze, "An Overview of India-Taiwan Relations: Why Taiwan Matters?", Institute of Chinese Studies, August 19, 2015. https://www.icsin.org/uploads/2015/09/01/7042b5ce54b618019e0f7af428d215d8.pdf.
7. Shivshankar Menon, "Their Ties Go Back in Time But India, China Were Absent From Each Other's Strategic Calculus", *The Wire*, December 2, 2020. https://thewire.in/external-affairs/india-china-relationship-dates-back-antiquity-mutual-mistrust-dominated-it.
8. Mrittika Guha Sarkar, "Xi Jinping's India Policy—Analysis", *Eurasia Review*, July 14, 2020. https://www.eurasiareview.com/14072020-xi-jinpings-india-policy-analysis/.
9. "News18 China Sentimeter: Here is What Indians Think about China", *News18*, June 20, 2020. https://www.cnbctv18.com/india/news18-china-sentimeter-here-is-what-indians-think-about-china-6175171.htm.

10. Rajeshwari Pillai Rajagopalan, "Calls for India to Play the Taiwan Card Grow Louder", *The Diplomat*, July 9, 2020. https://thediplomat.com/2020/07/calls-for-india-to-play-the-taiwan-card-grow-louder/.
11. "The Taiwan Question", *The Indian Express*, May 18, 2020. https://indianexpress.com/article/opinion/editorials/taiwan-china-united-nations-covid-who-kashmir-unsc-6414739/.
12. "Don't be Scared: India Should Ignore Chinese Blandishments and Enhance Ties with Taiwan", *The Times of India*, January 3, 2019. https://timesofindia.indiatimes.com/blogs/toi-editorials/dont-be-scared-india-should-ignore-chinese-blandishments-and-enhance-ties-with-taiwan/.
13. Committee on External Affairs (2017-18), "Sino-India Relations Including Doklam Border Situation and Cooperation in International Organizations", Ministry of External Affairs, Sixteenth Lok Sabha, September 2018. http://164.100.47.193/lsscommittee/External%20Affairs/16_External_Affairs_22.pdf.
14. "There is a Free Media in India: MEA on Chinese Embassy's Taiwan Guidelines to Journalists", *Indian Express*, October 8, 2020, https://indianexpress.com/article/india/there-is-a-free-media-in-india-mea-on-chinese-embassys-taiwan-guidelines-to-journalists-6716419/.
15. "New Face in Indian Cabinet Attracts Taiwanese MP as Foreign Minister", *news.itn*, July 8, 2021. https://news.ltn.com.tw/news/politics/breakingnews/3596197.
16. "Japan's Deputy Defence Minister says Taiwan Must be Protected 'as a Democratic Country", CNN, June 29, 2021. https://www.cnn.com/2021/06/29/asia/japan-taiwan-defence-intl-hnk/index.html.
17. Kensaku Ihara, "Taiwan Wants Intelligence-Sharing Arrangement with Japan", *Nikkei Asia*, January 26, 2018. https://asia.nikkei.com/Politics/International-relations/Taiwan-wants-intelligence-sharing-arrangement-with-Japan; https://asia.nikkei.com/Politics/International-relations/Taiwan-wants-intelligence-sharing-arrangement-with-Japan.
18. Ryan Ashley, "Japan's Revolution on Taiwan Affairs", *War on the Rocks*, November 23, 2021. https://warontherocks.com/2021/11/japans-revolution-on-taiwan-affairs/.
19. Tien-Sze Fang, "India-China Boundary Dispute: A Taiwanese Perspective", in Jagannath Panda, ed., *India and China in Asia: Between Equilibrium and Equations* (Dew Delhi: Routledge).
20. "Japan's Signals Intelligence (SIGINT) Ground Stations: A Visual Guide", Nautilus Institute, August 6, 2015. https://nautilus.org/napsnet/napsnet-special-reports/japans-signals-intelligence-sigint-ground-stations-a-visual-guide/.
21. Samanvya Hooda and Vinayak Dalmia, "To Check China's Hostility, India, Taiwan and Japan Need an Intelligence-Sharing Alliance", *The Print*, June 26, 2020. https://theprint.in/opinion/to-check-chinas-hostility-india-taiwan-and-japan-need-an-intelligence-sharing-alliance/449031/.

22. Insikt Group, "China-linked Group RedEcho Targets the Indian Power Sector Amid Heightened Border Tensions", *Recorded Future*, February 28, 2021. https://www.recordedfuture.com/redecho-targeting-indian- power-sector/.
23. "Chinese Hackers Target India's Serum Institute, Bharat Biotech: Report", NDTV, March 1, 2021. https://www.ndtv.com/india-news/chinese-hackers-target-india-s-serum-institute-bharat-biotech-report- 2381309.
24. Matthew Strong, "Cyberattacks on Taiwan's Ministry of Foreign Affairs Increased 40-fold in 2020", Taiwan News, March 3, 2021. https://www.taiwannews.com.tw/en/news/4164261.
25. Matthew Strong, "Cyber Attacks on Taiwan Institutions Surged by 38% in 2021", Taiwan News, January 20, 2022, https://www.taiwannews.com.tw/en/news/4416673.
26. Sameer Patil, "The India-Taiwan Imperative for Cybersecurity Cooperation", Gateway House, June 24, 2021. https://www.gatewayhouse.in/the-india-taiwan-imperative-for-cybersecurity-cooperation/.
27. "Cyber Security Collaboration is Significant for India-Taiwan Bilateral Ties: Taiwan Official", *The Indian Express*, November 18, 2021. https://www.newindianexpress.com/world/2021/nov/18/cyber-security-collaboration-is-significant-for-india-taiwan-bilateral-ties-taiwan-official-2385283.html.
28. "Taiwan, India Sign Cybersecurity Cooperation Pact", *Taiwan Today*, January 4, 2022. https://taiwantoday.tw/news.php?unit=2,6,10,15,18&post=213124.
29. "New Southbound Policy Promotion Plan", Bureau of Foreign Trade, Government of Taiwan. https://newsouthboundpolicy.trade.gov.tw/English/PageDetail?pageID=48&nodeID=94.
30. Dhruva Jaishankar, "Acting East: India in the Indo-Pacific", *Impact Series: Brookings*, October 2019. https://www.brookings.edu/wp-content/uploads/2019/10/Acting-East-India-in-the-INDO-PACIFIC-without-cutmark.pdf.
31. Keoni Everington, "Jakarta's first MRT Built with Help from Taiwanese Companies", Taiwan News, February 27, 2019. https://www.taiwannews.com.tw/en/news/3647185.
32. Jonathan E. Hillamn, "The Quad's Strategic Infrastructure Play", Centre for Strategic & International Studies, September 21, 2021. https://www.csis.org/analysis/quads-strategic-infrastructure-play.
33. Jake Chung, "Taiwan Willing to Partner with Quad: Official", *Taipei Times*, September 21, 2021. https://www.taipeitimes.com/News/front/archives/2021/09/25/2003764964.
34. Sophia Yang, "NCKUH Playing Key Role in Taiwan's COVID Emergency Relief to India", Taiwan News, May 7, 2021. https://www.taiwannews.com.tw/en/news/4197386.
35. Saneet Chakradeo, "Neighbourhood First Responder: India's Humanitarian Assistance and Disaster Relief", Brookings, August 18, 2020. https://www.

brookings.edu/research/neighbourhood-first-responder-indias-humanitarian-assistance-and-disaster-relief/.

36. "Indian Army Officers Take Mandarin Course", *The New Indian Express*, September 22, 2013. https://www.newindianexpress.com/nation/2013/sep/22/Indian-Army-officers-take-Mandarin-course-520507.html.
36. Arthur S. Ding, "Cooperation Between Taiwan and India: External Environment, Issues and Format", *Asia Insights*, No. 12, June 2021. https://asiainsightsiir.files.wordpress.com/2021/06/asia-insights-no.12-june-2021.pdf.
38. Fang Tien-sze, "India-Taiwan Relations: A Comprehensive Security Perspective", *Indian Defence Review*, 30(4), October-December 2015. http://www.indiandefencereview.com/news/india-taiwan-relations-a-comprehensive-security-perspective/.
39. "Indian Navy's Fifth Project 75 Submarine Begins Sea Trials", *Naval Technology*, February 3, 2022. https://www.naval-technology.com/news/indian-navy-fifth-project-75/.
40. Juvina Lai, "Taiwan and India Sign MoU on Promoting Industrial Cooperation", Taiwan News, December 15, 2017. https://www.taiwannews.com.tw/en/news/3321435.
41. "Taiwanese, Indian Businesses Sign MoUs on Industrial Partnerships", *Focus Taiwan*, October 23, 2020. https://focustaiwan.tw/business/202010230012.
42. Chang Feng-lin, "Military Cooperation with India Practical", *Taipei Times*, January 27, 2022. https://www.taipeitimes.com/News/editorials/archives/2022/01/27/2003772141.
43. "Taiwan Lines up Revision of Industry Cooperation Guidelines", *Jane's*, July 5, 2021. https://www.janes.com/defence-news/news-detail/taiwan-lines-up-revision-of-industry-co-operation-guidelines_18764.
44. "India's Promising Outlook in Defence Manufacturing", *IBEF*, December 30, 2021. https://www.ibef.org/blogs/india-s-promising-outlook-in-defence-manufacturing.
45. Raghu Krishan, "Quad Alliance Joins Hands to Secure Semiconductor, 5G tech Supply Chains", *The Economic Times*, September 26, 2021. https://economictimes.indiatimes.com/news/india/quad-alliance-joins-hands-to-secure-semiconductor-5g-tech-supply-chains/articleshow/86522479.cms?from=mdr.
46. Neel Vanvari and Alexander C. Tan, "India, Taiwan and the Indo-Pacific: Economic-Security Strategic Partnership and Expected Utility Theory", *Journal of Asian Security and International Affairs*, 8(1), 2021, pp. 98-126.
47. "Invite Taiwan to Massive RIMPAC Naval Exercise, US Defence Act says", CNN, December 29, 2021. https://edition.cnn.com/2021/12/28/asia/taiwan-us-military-rimpac-exercise-intl-hnk-ml/index.html.
48. Shruti Srivastava and Miaojung Lin, "India Accelerates Talks with Taiwan on Chip Plant, Trade Deal", *Bloomberg*, September 24, 2021. https://

www.bloomberg.com/news/articles/2021-09-24/india-accelerates-talks-with-taiwan-on-chip-plant-trade-deal.

49. Rezaul H. Laskar, "India, Taiwan in Talks on Semiconductor Hub, Free Trade and Investment Pacts", *Hindustan Times*, December 16, 2021. https://www.hindustantimes.com/india-news/india-taiwan-in-talks-on-semiconductor-hub-free-trade-and-investment-pacts-101639656166764.html.
50. "Taiwan, India to Cooperate on 5G Technology Development", *The Statesman*, November 20, 2017. https://www.thestatesman.com/business/taiwan-india-cooperate-5g-technology-development-1502531734.html.
51. "TAICS Signed Collaborating MoU with TSDSI of India on 5G and IoT Technology", Taiwan Association of Information and Communication Standards, June 26, 2018. https://www.taics.org.tw/eng/LatestAssForm.aspx?Type=1&Ass_id=6#:~:text=TAICS%20Signed%20Collaborating%20MoU%20with%20TSDSI%20of%20India%20on%205G%20and%20IoT%20Technology&text=TAICS%20and%20TSDSI%20sign%20MoU,at%20NTUH%20International%20Convention%20Center.
52. "India Excludes Huawei and ZTE From Participating in 5G Trials", *Nikkei Asia*, May 5, 2021. https://asia.nikkei.com/Spotlight/5G-networks/India-excludes-Huawei-and-ZTE-from-participating-in-5G-trials.
53. "Taipei Excludes Huawei and Launches 5G Internet with Nokia", *Asianews*, July 1, 2020. https://www.asianews.it/news-en/Taipei-excludes-Huawei-and-launches-5G-internet-with-Nokia-50479.html.

12. Exploring an Indo-Russian Congruence in the Indo-Pacific

Rajorshi Roy

Introduction

Alfred Mahan had presciently stated, "Whoever controls the Indian Ocean, will dominate Asia, the destiny of the world will be decided on its waters".[1] In many ways, Great Britain's rise as a dominant colonial power reflected this prophecy. The British Empire stretched from the "east coast of Africa to Southeast Asia", encompassing what is today increasingly being seen as the Indo-Pacific.

Today, the Indo-Pacific appears to be gaining traction. It has once again emerged as a theatre of great power competition—the key protagonists in this round of contestation being the US and China. This has led to a tussle encompassing ideas, values, rules, laws, partnerships and models of governance.[2]

Crucially, it appears that their ongoing scrimmage will sharpen due to their fundamental differences. Some of the emerging structures in this jostling like the Quadrilateral Security Dialogue (Quad) have polarised opinions. Similar views exist on a "free and open" maritime space and "rules-based order".[3] However, this has complicated options for those having linkages with either Washington or Beijing or both.

In this context, Russia is no exception. As a power that straddles Europe and Asia, with almost 60 per cent of Russian territory being in the latter, the ongoing churnings make Russia a stakeholder in the Indo-Pacific. This is particularly relevant at a time when Russia is seeking a revival of its great power status anchored in its pivot to Asia and Greater

Eurasia concepts.[4] This has seen Russia expand its strategic footprint in the maritime space straddling the Indo-Pacific.

However, Russia's ongoing confrontation with the West has inevitably complicated Moscow's scope for manoeuvre. In fact, the Kremlin has increasingly batted for Beijing.[5] It has supported China's claims of the Indo-Pacific being a Western strategy of containment. Unsurprisingly, Russia has rejected the coinage of "Indo-Pacific" and continues to emphasise on "Asia-Pacific". This despite the fact that the Indo-Pacific could be a strategic opportunity for Russia to strengthen its great power credentials amidst an increasing global bipolarity.

The Russian rejection of the Indo-Pacific has, in many ways, complicated India's foreign policy endeavours. New Delhi has consistently espoused the *raison d'être* of the Indo-Pacific i.e. creation of an inclusive security architecture. Today, New Delhi and Moscow, the two traditional partners, do not appear to be on the same page on the Indo-Pacific.

This was particularly reflected in Russian Foreign Minister Sergei Lavrov's statement of "India being an object of the Western countries persistent, aggressive and devious policy" to "engage in anti-China games by promoting Indo-Pacific strategies".[6] Lavrov's statement possibly highlighted Russia's apprehensions of India's drift towards the West, away from the traditionally strong Indo-Russian strategic partnership.

Therefore, the pertinent questions that this study seeks to examine are:

1. What are the key drivers of Russia's position on the Indo-Pacific?
2. Is Russia's stance on the Indo-Pacific more nuanced than what meets the eye?
3. Can the Indo-Pacific be a strategic opportunity for Russia?
4. Can India and Russia find common ground on the Indo-Pacific?

The present study will proceed with the hypothesis that the Indo-Pacific is a strategic opportunity for Russia in its endeavour to be counted as a global pole despite its aversion to the concept.

Evolution of Russia's Position

Russian practitioners have largely refrained from the terminology of Indo-Pacific. Instead, they have stuck to the concept of "Asia-Pacific". In this light, Foreign Minister Sergei Lavrov's statement that "the Indo-Pacific region is another artificially imposed construct"[7] is an indication of Russia viewing it through the lens of the American strategy of containment. Similar views were expressed by President Putin who termed the Indo-Pacific "un-Asian to begin with and is at odds with the current state of affairs in Asia".[8] When juxtaposed with the Kremlin's stated goal of establishing a polycentric world order,[9] the Russian strategic calculus can be interpreted as looking at the Indo-Pacific through the lens of a zero-sum game in its ongoing confrontation and rivalry with the United States. Any American strategy that strengthens the US global position goes against the Russian grain of global multipolarity.

In this context, it is pertinent to examine the evolution of Russia's policies in the Asia-Pacific.

Historically, as a legacy of Peter the Great, Russian foreign policy had mainly focussed on the West. The Asian part of Russia, comprising two-thirds of its sparsely populated territory, was predominantly seen as a resource basket for developing its European part.[10] While the Soviet Union may have been compelled to tackle two Cold Wars emanating from the West as well as from the East, the existential threat from the US overrode the challenge posed by China. This led to the continuation of Soviet preoccupation with the West.

A similar trend of being Westward focussed was observed during the first few years of Russia's independence. The Russian elite remained pre-occupied in seeking a new *modus vivendi* with the United States.[11] The fact that they were dealing with a weaker hand on account of Russia's military weakness and lack of economic competitiveness had ensured that Russian resources were largely focussed Westwards.[12]

It was only when Russia felt rebuffed by the West in its attempts to seek equality with its erstwhile *bête noire*, did a rebalancing in its foreign policy come about.[13] Led by Foreign Minister Yevgeny Primakov, Russia sought new equations with the fast growing regions of the Asia-Pacific to tap the growth potential of these markets.[14] The Kremlin leveraged its rich reservoir of resources in the Far East, particularly hydrocarbons, to meet the growing energy demands of these economies.[15] This was also the period when Russia sought a rapprochement with China with an objective of securing at least one flank. It led to Russia and China entering into negotiations to resolve their long-festering boundary dispute.[16]

Russia's focus towards the Asia-Pacific Region (APR) was aptly highlighted by President Putin in one of his first speeches since winning the election to the office of Russian Presidency. He stated:

> Russia has always felt itself to be a Eurasian country. We have never forgotten that the main part of the Russian territory is in Asia. Frankly, we have not always made good use of that advantage. I think the time has come for us, together with the Asia-Pacific countries, to move on from words to actions and to build up economic, political and other ties....within a short space of time the countries in the region—above all Japan, China and the ASEAN countries—have seen tremendous changes. Russia has not been left out of the processes taking place here. Russia's full participation in the processes of economic interaction in Asia and the Pacific is natural and inevitable, because Russia is a kind of integration hub that links Asia, Europe and America.... You can judge for yourselves. Russia and China are firmly on course to build an equal and trusting partnership, which has become an important factor of global stability.... In recent years the relations with the Association of Southeastern Asian Nations (ASEAN) bringing together all the countries of this vast sub-region of the APR, have emerged as a distinct area of Russian policy.[17]

The global economic slowdown post-2008 appeared to have fast-tracked Russia's focus on the Asia-Pacific. Notably, this region had weathered the storm more deftly than others. The pinnacle of Moscow's incipient Asia-Pacific approach was crystallised through the 2012 "Asia-Pacific Economic Cooperation" (APEC) Summit that Russia hosted in Vladivostok. The theme of this event—"Integrate to Grow, Innovate to Prosper"[18]—highlighted Russia's game plan of benefitting from the economic dynamism of the region.

However, it was Russia's renewed confrontation with the West in 2014 that provided a real sense of urgency to Russia's Eastward orientation. The standoff over Russia's position on the global stage had in many ways complicated Russia's geopolitical environment.[19] With the West seemingly looking to isolate and contain the Kremlin in its neighbourhood, the need for a more robust rebalancing and readjustment of Russia's foreign policy priorities was acutely felt.[20]

The rebalancing was juxtaposed with the Greater Eurasia concept anchored in Moscow's "historical and cultural heritage of being a bridge between the East and the West".[21] The broad contours of this new identity involved reinforcing Russia's ties with its near abroad—the Eurasian heartland, and underpinning it with a pivot towards Asia (*povrot na vostok*).

In many ways, this realignment reflected Russian philosopher Fyodor Dostoevsky's prophecy of 1881:

> Russia is not only in Europe, but also in Asia. The Russian is not only a European, but also an Asiatic. In Asia, perhaps, we have greater expectations than in Europe. In our future destinies, Asia might be our main outlet.[22]

Some analysts have referred the ongoing recalibration to a vision of Greater Asia, stretching from Shanghai to St. Petersburg.[23] Others have elaborated on a pan-Eurasian integration.[24]

The underlying objective appears to be to build linkages with countries in the Asia-Pacific that follow an independent foreign policy. These countries could also help provide much needed investments and technology against the backdrop of Western sanctions on the Russian economy.[25] In this endeavour, the Kremlin has sought to leverage its energy and defence competitiveness to build new partnerships.[26] The absence of a stable regional security architecture along with a burgeoning energy requirement has enabled Russia to expand its presence in the region.

Crucially, for Russia, the countries that fit the bill of being a source of investment and technology comprise China, Japan, and South Korea. With Tokyo and Seoul being part of the Western camp, Russia has been forced to increasingly rely on Beijing to withstand the ongoing American geopolitical pressure. This, therefore, explains Russia batting for China on the Indo-Pacific as a *quid pro quo*, on what Beijing considers as its core strategic issue.

Moreover, Russia and China appear to be on the same page in their perception of a "rules-based Indo-Pacific" being a Western strategy to bypass international law. This would enable the West to sidestep the United Nations Security Council (UNSC) where Moscow and Beijing are part of the P5. As a show of support to each other, Russia and China have held joint exercises in the South China Sea.[27]

However, there appears to be much more to Russia's opposition to the Indo-Pacific than just merely supporting China. If organisations like the Quad, seen in some quarters as a US attempt to build an Asian North Atlantic Treaty Organisation (NATO),[28] gain traction, Russia could end up in a difficult spot amidst its attempts to diversify its relationships beyond China in the region. This is particularly relevant at a time when Russia remains apprehensive of being the "junior partner" in the Moscow-Being relationship.[29] A polarisation and division into military camps in the Indo-Pacific could upend this Russian calculus.

Additionally, Russia's remains opposed to the Indo-Pacific in the belief that it excludes from its purview not only Africa and the Gulf but also the central position accorded to the Association of Southeast Asian Nations (ASEAN) vis-à-vis the "Asia-Pacific".[30] These are the areas where Russia has recently sought to expand its strategic engagements.

Critical Analysis of Russia's Position

Arguably, the Asia-Pacific does not reflect the spread of economic and political vibrancy to a more boarder region. This includes South Asia as well as Africa and the Persian Gulf. The fact also remains that the concept of the "Indo-Pacific" has been in existence far longer than the "Asia-Pacific". The two oceans were connected even during the colonial times. On the other hand, the Asia-Pacific is largely an artificial construct that connects an ocean with a continent. It is a post-World War II construct linked with the development of economic centres of power.

The exclusion of India from the Asia-Pacific construct too is a glaring anomaly. This is particularly relevant in the context of India's billion plus population, trillion dollar economy and geostrategic location comprising a large coastline. In fact, the proximity of the Andamans to the Malacca Strait accords India a key position in attempts to build a "stable and secure regional security architecture".

Meanwhile, it would be imprudent to look at the Indo-Pacific solely through the lens of being an American construct. The fact remains that it was coined by an Indian and given form and substance by Japan[31]. Similarly, today, a number of countries, whose foreign policies are anchored in strategy autonomy, have adopted the concept of the Indo-Pacific. This includes the ASEAN states, earlier seen as the Asia-Pacific's core. In fact, the ASEAN states, that have been courted by all the key major powers, have been vocal about their recalibration.

The ASEAN "Outlook on Indo-Pacific" acknowledges this shift:

> Southeast Asia lies in the center of these dynamic regions and is a very important conduit and portal to the same. Therefore, it is in the interest of ASEAN to lead the shaping of their economic and security architecture and ensure that such dynamics will continue to bring about peace, security, stability and prosperity for the peoples in the Southeast Asia as well as in the wider Asia-Pacific and Indian Ocean regions or the Indo-Pacific.[32]

Today, given the regional stakeholders' economic interdependence with China, a strategy of containing Beijing appears untenable. In fact, several of them have welcomed the opportunities presented by the Belt and Road Initiative (BRI). These sentiments are also reflected in the Regional Comprehensive Economic Partnership (RCEP) agreement. Its members include China as well as the Quad countries of Japan and Australia.

Today, the broad consensus is on building an inclusive security architecture. With security being indivisible, this would also reflect the reality of the "Indian and Pacific Oceans being interconnected and interdependent".

Notably, regional stakeholders have a shared interest in strengthening developmental partnerships amidst slowing economic growth. They also have a shared concern about China's unilateralism, assertiveness and coercion. China's gaming of globalisation that has seen it emerge as a vital cog in global supply chains has also upped the ante. Similarly, Beijing's clarion call of an "Asia for Asians" is viewed in many circles as an attempt to dominate the continent.[33] Pertinently, these concerns are prevalent even among Russian experts. This is unsurprising given the nature of China's rise and the historical baggage of the Russia-China relationship.

In this context, it appears that the next course of action is to "put diplomatic pressure" on Beijing to ensure "peaceful coexistence". This strategy, however, seems applicable to all, and is not China-specific. Moreover, there also appears to be a consensus on the inclusion of Africa in Indo-Pacific's ambit as well as according centrality to ASEAN.

Meanwhile, the Quad, contrary to Russia's view, is largely a plurilateral dialogue structure. Its objective appears to "complement the Indo-Pacific in building synergies in infrastructure, capacity building, connectivity and tackling non-traditional security threats". Several states are on the same page on these issues. Notably, the Quad Plus structure could alleviate Russia's concerns of "cliques". The recent meetings of the Quad Plus format involving New Zealand, South Korea and Vietnam[34] could help in diluting this perception.

In the light of these developments, Russia's opposition to the Indo-Pacific is, in fact, preventing it from shaping the incipient processes underway in building an inclusive regional architecture.

Russia's Strategic Gains From the Indo-Pacific?

Interestingly, despite Russia's aversion to the Indo-Pacific, its growing regional footprint paints a different picture. Anchored in its "weapons and natural resources diplomacy", Russia has sought new congruence with the regional stakeholders.

This has seen Russia acquire a port in Sudan for a 25-year lease.[35] It is Moscow's first major military toehold in Africa since the disintegration of the Soviet Union. Notably, Port Sudan's geostrategic location overlooking one of the world's most critical lanes of communication in the Red Sea and Gulf of Aden is unmistakable. For a country that has largely focussed on its continental threats since its independence, this acquisition highlights Russia's attempts at playing a more prominent role in regional geopolitics.

The genesis of this calculus, however, dates back to the first Russia-Africa Summit held in October 2019.[36] The summit had laid down the marker for Russia to expand its footprint in Africa, including in the oceanic space. Over the last few years, Russia has emerged as a vector in the regional calculus of Mozambique[37] and Madagascar[38]. The Kremlin has also conducted maritime exercises with South Africa in the Indian Ocean.[39] Besides, Russia is an active participant in tackling piracy off the coast of Somalia.[40]

Similarly, Russia has sought to expand its linkages with ASEAN, at both multilateral and bilateral levels. Russia is an active participant in the "East Asia Summit (EAS), ASEAN Regional Forum (ARF), ASEAN Defence Ministers Meeting Plus (ADMM-Plus), Expanded ASEAN Maritime Forum (EAMF) and ASEAN Plus One mechanisms".[41] The first Russia-ASEAN joint naval military exercise, held in Indonesia in December 2021[42], is a reflection of Russia qualitatively stepping up its engagement with this Southeast Asian organisation. The Russia led Eurasian Economic Union (EEU) has also been negotiating with the ASEAN for a Free Trade Agreement (FTA).

In Southern Asia, Russia has sought new congruence with Bangladesh[43], Pakistan[44], Sri Lanka[45], and Myanmar[46], besides strengthening the *special and privileged* India-Russia partnership. In fact, Russia is constructing a nuclear power plant in Bangladesh in collaboration with India.[47]

Notably, Russia was accorded the status of a "dialogue partner" in the Indian Ocean Rim Association (IORA) in November 2021.[48] This eponymous organisation comprises Indian Ocean littoral states[49], indicating Russia's attempts to be a part of the evolving regional dynamics. Interestingly, Russia was the only major power that was not a part of any major multilateral structure in the Indian Ocean till that point of time.

Foreign Ministry spokesperson Maria Zakharova's statement following Russia's admission as a "dialogue partner" of IORA aptly highlights the Russian calculus:

> This decision confirms broad recognition of Russia's constructive role in strengthening multilateral cooperation based on the norms and principles of international law. It also reflects the high assessment of Russia's tangible contribution to ensuring sustainable dynamics in the development of the Indian Ocean zone.... Russia is attaching much importance to this region. The country consistently supports UN General Assembly Resolution 2832 (passed in 1971) that declared the Indian Ocean a zone of peace. Considering its dense network of sea routes, it is difficult to overestimate its importance for the global economy as well.... Russia intends to continue working (now as an IORA dialogue partner) on strengthening interconnected relationships in the Indian Ocean. Its priorities coincide with the goals and tasks of the forum in such areas as maritime security, resistance to piracy, trade and investment, prompt emergency response, tourist and cultural ties, education, science and technology....... Naturally, one of the priorities is countering the COVID-19 pandemic and other infectious diseases and cooperation on vaccines. Russia is willing to share its groundwork and experience in developing remote territories and expand humanitarian aid programmes. At Southeast Asian summits (a forum close to IORA,) Russia has repeatedly suggested thinking about ways of developing practical cooperation between a system of interstate communication mechanisms that took shape around ASEAN in the Asia-Pacific Region and multilateral associations of the Indian Ocean. This idea is still on the table. Russia is ready to discuss it with all interested parties.[50]

Amidst these developments, Russia's Pacific Fleet's area of operation extends from the Far East to the Persian Gulf.[51] This is an indication of Russia "effectively practising" an Indo-Pacific strategy. Today, the fleet is undergoing a major modernisation.[52] New vessels are expected to be commissioned in the future. This would provide Russia with additional tools to expand its footprint in the Indian Ocean through power projection, joint military exercises and ports of call. These new partnerships could even help achieve Russia's historical endeavour of accessing the warm waters of the Indian Ocean.

Interestingly, Russia's Asia-Pacific advocacy is, at times, at odds with its policies in practice. For instance, Russia has adopted a nuanced position on the South China Sea dispute rather than outright support to Beijing in its core strategic issue. This has seen the Kremlin call for "preventing the dispute's internationalisation".[53] It has also supported "ASEAN's efforts to establish a Code of Conduct for the South China Sea". These sentiments were expressed by President Putin when he stated:

> We believe that interference by any power outside the region will only hurt the resolution of these issues. I believe the involvement of any third-party powers from outside the region is detrimental and counterproductive.[54]
>
> We support and advocate the full observance of the Declaration on Conduct of the Parties in the South China Sea, and speak in favour of a prompt adoption of a Code of Conduct of the parties as a legally binding document.[55]

While Russia has supported China's rejection of the Permanent Court of Arbitration's (PCA) ruling, several Russian experts[56] are of the opinion that this Russian action was driven by the need to use the Chinese precedence to reject any potential PCA ruling on Ukraine's maritime rights in the Black Sea. Russia considers the Black Sea a vital area of operation, with its Black Sea-fleet based in this region. It has assumed even more significance amidst the ongoing Russia-West faceoff.

Russia's position in the South China Sea is, perhaps, emblematic of the need to maintain its strategic autonomy. Notably, Russia remains apprehensive of the equilibrium in the Russia-China relationship shifting towards Beijing. This is reflected in the Kremlin being seemingly forced to accommodate China even in its core strategic space of Central Asia, the Russian Arctic and the Far East. In fact, *Pax Sinica*, marked by China's growing footprint in Eurasia, could upset Russia's comeback in this region. Similarly, exports of top of the line weapons, which Russia had largely refrained from selling to China in the last two decades for fear of reverse engineering, are back on the agenda.

There are also other festering issues. These include Russia and China competing with each other in the lucrative weapons markets of Asia and Africa. The two countries also do not appear to be on the same page on Russia's weapons exports to India. Meanwhile, it is likely that China's aggression and assertiveness on the issue of territory, despite economic interdependence with the opposing side, would have increased Russia's strategic apprehensions. China retains a grouse over the Tsarist takeover of large swathes of the Far East as part of the Unequal Treaties (1860). Also, a bipolar world appears more suited to China than a polycentric one with the latter being a key Russian endeavour.

Amidst these dynamics, Russia has expanded its strategic engagement with regional countries like Vietnam, Malaysia, Indonesia and the Philippines[57] despite these states having ongoing territorial disputes with China.

In this context, Russia is one of Vietnam's key strategic partners. Their relationship encompasses a range of economic and military interests. Russia has even entered into joint weapons production with it.[58] These form the frontline of Vietnam's calculus to preserve its territorial integrity and sovereignty, ostensibly from the challenge posed by China. The two sides have also inked an energy exploration project in the disputed South China Sea.[59] In fact, Russian energy majors Gazprom, Rosneft and Lukoil, apart from the Russia-Vietnam joint venture of Vietsovpetro, are involved in hydrocarbon exploration in the South China Sea.[60]

Similarly, Russia was invited by the Philippines' Rodrigo Duterte in 2019 to explore energy reserves off the country's coast in the disputed South China Sea[61], which Manila refers to as the West Philippines Sea. Interestingly, Philippines has, over the years, relied on the US for its weapons requirements.

Meanwhile, Russia has conducted military exercises with Brunei, Malaysia, Thailand and Japan in the region, even though these were not in the disputed waters of the South China Sea. From these initiatives, it appears that Russia is keeping channels of communication open with majority of the regional stakeholders. This is similar to the Russian playbook in Syria.[62]

Therefore, Russia's strategy appears anchored to deftly balancing China's sensitivities, on the one hand, while maintaining its scope for manoeuvre, on the other.

Opportunity

The Indo-Pacific can be an opportunity for Russia to strengthen its credentials as a global pole. Today, Russia runs the risk of being left behind in the global bipolarity narrative on account of Moscow's relative decline. In fact, Russia appears to be the weakest in the triangle of great powers comprising Russia, China and the US. This calls for Russia to take independent positions.

In fact, "multipolarity and multilateralism" that the Indo-Pacific seeks to strengthen benefits Russia. A "strategic repositioning" could allow Russia to expand the boundaries of its pivot to Asia. This could also help dilute the Western attempts to isolate Moscow.

It, therefore, makes strategic sense to explore congruence with the nuanced Indo-Pacific vision of non-American stakeholders, including the Quad members. Notably, Russia appears to enjoy stable relations with all the key stakeholders, with the exception of the US. This includes Japan, which largely relies on the US security umbrella.[63]

However, this is likely predicated on Russia's willingness to reimagine a new geostrategic maritime role for itself. Russia's unique geographical position of straddling the Heartland and Rimland at a time when the Indo-Pacific's emphasis has been on visualising the continental and maritime areas of the two oceans as a seamless strategic space does seem to provide it the necessary tools.

At a time when Russia is recalibrating its identity from a European to a Eurasian one, its Greater Eurasia construct, envisioned as a harmonious strategic space from Lisbon to Jakarta, seems to aptly complement the Indo-Pacific.

Interestingly, at a fundamental level, there appear to be a number of similarities between Greater Eurasia[64] and the Indo-Pacific. These include the emphasis on having "open and inclusive, developmental partnerships and building connectivity, respecting international law, and eschewing confrontation".[65] The very fact that Russia has envisaged the Greater Eurasia project being open to both Europe and China[66], despite the baggage of history, is a reflection of its inclusivity and openness.

The Russian Far East could be the proverbial "connecting tissue" between Greater Eurasia and the Indo-Pacific. This could allow Russia to tap the expertise of the Indo-Pacific countries, beyond China, to develop this underdeveloped region of Russia. It could also enable Russia to explore synergies of collaboration with the regional stakeholders in the ongoing attempts to build new supply chains. These vectors may perhaps, concomitantly, help Russia to address its Achilles heel i.e. its weak global economic foundation.

Russia appears to be positioning itself to benefit from the emerging opportunities. This was reflected in President Putin's statement:

> There is one more prospective route, the Arctic-Siberia-Asia. The idea is to connect ports along the Northern Sea Route with ports of the Pacific and Indian Oceans via roads in East Siberia and Central Eurasia.[67]

Notably, these nuances could be an opportunity to wean Russia away from China. Moscow's strategic compulsion of an entente with China amidst the Russia-West standoff further strengthens Beijing. As an independent pole, Russia strengthens the trend towards multipolarity.

Exploring an India-Russia Common Ground

Today, the Russia-US confrontation has complicated India's foreign policy options. This includes Russia's geopolitical compulsion of siding with China on the Indo-Pacific. Similarly, it appears that India will benefit from a closer partnership with the US amidst New Delhi's ongoing standoff with Beijing.

With India and Russia seemingly having diverging priorities in this emerging geopolitical landscape, the key challenge will be to find the proverbial sweet spot of collaboration. A break could muddy New Delhi's and Moscow's calculations vis-à-vis their "strategic autonomy" and "regional balance of power".

However, it is likely that India will maintain its policies of multi-alignment and strategic autonomy. The fact remains that the Indo-Russian bilateral relationship is mutually beneficial. The key issue will be to assuage Russia regarding Moscow's apprehension of the dilution of India's independent course of action.

It is, therefore, imperative to remain invested by exploring new areas of congruence. The fact that India and Russia have a similar outlook on a "stable security architecture" apart from "shared concerns over hegemonism" should hold them in good stead. Notably, India's Indo-Pacific outlook emphasises on not just ASEAN's centrality but also inclusion of East Africa within the ambit of this construct. In many ways, it also complements Russia's Greater Eurasia concept as one seamless strategic region that connects the continental and maritime spaces.

As External Affairs Minister Dr. S. Jaishankar had stated in 2019, "Russia is a Pacific power which has Indian Ocean interests" while "India is an Indian Ocean power with very strong and growing Pacific interest".[68]

Notably for India, Russia is no stranger to the Indo-Pacific. The presence of the Soviet Pacific Fleet's armada in the Indian Ocean during the 1971 War is etched in the folklore of the Indo-Russian strategic partnership.[69] The USSR's maritime move had possibly thwarted American designs in the region in support of Pakistan.

Today, a broad structure of New Delhi-Moscow collaboration already exists. This was elaborated by Prime Minister Modi in Vladivostok in 2019 when he launched the "Act Far East" policy. He stated:

> Vladivostok is a confluence of Eurasia and the Pacific. This presents opportunities for the Arctic and the Northern Sea routes. About three quarters of Russia's land is Asia. The Far East reinforces the Asian identity of this great country. India will provide a $ 1 billion line of credit to further contribute to the development of the Far East. This is the first time that we are giving a line of credit to a particular region of a country. My government's Act East policy has actively engaged with East Asia. Today's announcement will prove to be the take-off point of the Act Far East policy and it is my firm belief that this step adds a new dimension to our economic diplomacy. We will be active participants in

> the development of the regions of our friendly countries according to their priorities.[70]

This was seen as the "anchor for harmonising the two countries' strategic outlook". The proposed Chennai-Vladivostok maritime corridor is a key pillar of this objective. This was elaborated by Prime Minister Modi:

> We are about to start a new era of cooperation in the Indo-Pacific region. When the ships will start sailing between Vladivostok and Chennai, and when Vladivostok will become India's springboard in the Northeast Asia market, the India-Russia partnership will further deepen and flourish. Then the Far East will become a confluence of the Eurasian Union, on one side, and the open, free and inclusive Indo-Pacific, on the other. Our relations in this region will have a strong foundation of a rule-based order, respect for sovereignty and territorial integrity and abstaining from interfering in the internal affairs of a country.[71]

Crucially, it appears that both sides remain engaged in exploring congruence. India had strongly backed Russia's application for dialogue partner status in the IORA. This has inevitably opened up new vistas of maritime cooperation. Similarly, the two sides have recently conducted a "joint PASSEX in the Arabian Sea". The "exercise showcased cohesiveness and interoperability between the two navies and included tactical manoeuvres, cross-deck helicopter operations and seamanship activities".[72] The recent signing of the Brahmos Agreement between India and the Philippines[73] would not have taken place without the implicit approval of Russia, on account of India and Russia jointly developing this missile.

The Indo-Pacific also came up for discussion during the annual summit held in December 2021. The joint statement reflected the attempts being made at finding a common ground:

> The sides reaffirmed that the emerging regional security architecture should be free, open, transparent and inclusive, based on universally recognised principles of international law and aimed at maintaining

> international peace and security, developing friendly relations and mutually beneficial cooperation in the region. They agreed to strengthen joint efforts to build an architecture of equal and indivisible regional security. The sides agreed to intensify consultations on complementarities between integration and development initiatives in greater Eurasian space and in the regions of the Indian and Pacific Oceans. They underscored their recognition of the ASEAN centrality in the regional architecture of security and cooperation and reiterated the importance of closer cooperation and consultations in various regional fora and initiatives such as the East Asia Summit (EAS), ASEAN Regional Forum (ARF), ASEAN Defence Ministers Meeting Plus (ADMM-Plus), Asia-Europe Meeting (ASEM), Conference on Interaction and Confidence Building Measures in Asia (CICA), Asia Cooperation Dialogue (ACD), to jointly contribute to regional peace, security and stability.... The sides agreed that safeguarding of global commons including our oceans, outer space and information space should be based on the principles of transparency, accessibility and upholding international law.[74]

India has also expressed interest in "collaborating with Russia on developing the Northern Sea route".[75]

Moreover, President Putin's participation in the UNSC debate on maritime security[76] chaired by Prime Minister Modi in August 2021 was seen as Russia's tacit support to India's vision of the Indo-Pacific. In a meeting skipped by the Chinese premier, the event focussed on building a stable regional security architecture.[77] This debate was inherently critical of China's regional maritime playbook. Similarly, Russia's weapons exports to India, despite reported Chinese objections in the aftermath of the Galwan incident, are an indication of the Kremlin not letting Beijing have a veto over its foreign policy. These dynamics highlight Moscow's abiding interest in an enduring partnership with India.

Meanwhile, new mechanisms could also be explored. These include a trilateral comprising Russia-India-Japan. Notably, India's and Japan's Indo-Pacific visions seem to be the "closest to Russia's strategic comfort".[78] This is particularly relevant at a time when Tokyo has sought to build new equations with Moscow. Notably, Japan remains a key investor in the Russian Far East.

Needless to say, the key test of the "special and privileged" India-Russia partnership will be to "harmonise each other's viewpoints". A white shipping agreement along with a logistics sharing pact could provide the necessary ballast.

Notes

1. Alfred Mahan, *The Influence of Sea Power upon History 1660-1783* (Boston: Little Brown and Company, 1890).
2. Sujan Chinoy, "AUKUS Could Rock China's Boat in the Indo-Pacific", *The Hindu*, November 8, 2021. https://www.thehindu.com/opinion/op-ed/aukus-could-rock-chinas-boat-in-the-indo-pacific/article37372664.ece.
3. "Foreign Minister Sergey Lavrov's Remarks at the General Meeting of the Russian International Affairs Council, Moscow, December 8, 2020", The Ministry of Foreign Affairs of the Russian Federation, December 8, 2020. https://archive.mid.ru/web/guest/evropejskij-souz-es/-/asset_publisher/6OiYovt2s4Yc/content/id/4470074?p_p_id=101_INSTANCE_6OiYovt2s4Yc&_101_INSTANCE_6OiYovt2s4Yc_languageId=en_GB.
4. "Vladimir Putin's Annual News Conference", *President of Russia*, December 23, 2021. http://en.kremlin.ru/events/president/news/67438.
5. "Foreign Minister Sergey Lavrov's Remarks and Answers to Questions at a Plenary Session of the Raisina Dialogue International Conference, New Delhi, January 15, 2020", The Ministry of Foreign Affairs of the Russian Federation, January 15, 2020. https://www.mid.ru/ru/foreign_policy/news/-/asset_publisher/cKNonkJE02Bw/content/id/3994885?p_p_id=101_INSTANCE_cKNonkJE02Bw&_101_INSTANCE_cKNonkJE02Bw_languageId=en_GB.
6. "Foreign Minister Sergey Lavrov's Remarks at the General Meeting of the Russian International Affairs Council, Moscow, December 8, 2020", The Ministry of Foreign Affairs of the Russian Federation, December 8, 2020. https://archive.mid.ru/web/guest/evropejskij-souz-es/-/asset_publisher/6OiYovt2s4Yc/content/id/4470074?p_p_id=101_INSTANCE_6OiYovt2s4Yc&_101_INSTANCE_6OiYovt2s4Yc_languageId=en_GB.
7. "Foreign Minister Sergey Lavrov's Remarks and Answers to Media Questions During the Russia-Vietnam Conference of the Valdai Discussion Club", Valdai Discussion Club, February 26, 2019. https://valdaiclub.com/a/highlights/foreign-minister-sergey-lavrov-remarks/.
8. "Valdai Discussion Club Session", *President of Russia*, October 3, 2019. http://en.kremlin.ru/events/president/news/61719.
9. "Conversation with President of China Xi Jinping", *President of Russia*, June 28, 2021. http://en.kremlin.ru/events/president/news/65940.

10. Dmitri Trenin, "Post-Imperium", Carnegie Moscow Centre, 2011. https://carnegieendowment.org/pdf/book/post-imperium.pdf.
11. Alexander Lukin, "Russia in a Post-Bipolar World", *Survival*, 58 (1): pp. 91-112; and Alexander Lukin, "Russia's Pivot Toward Asia: Myth or Reality?", *International Affairs* (Moscow), 62 (3), 2016, pp. 60-77.
12. Ibid and Fyodor Lukyanov, "Break-up of the Soviet Union: Russia's Obsession and Turning Point", *Moscow Defence Brief*, 2016. https://mdb.cast.ru/mdb/2-2016/item1/article1/.
13. Alexei Tsygankov, *Russia and the West from Alexander to Putin* (New York: Cambridge University Press, 2012).
14. Yevgeny Primakov, "Perception of Russia in the World," *Russia in Global Affairs*. http://eng.globalaffairs.ru/number/Perception-of-Russia-in-the-World-15926.
15. Dmitri Trenin, "Russia Leaves the West", *Foreign Affairs*, 87 (4), 2006, pp. 81-89.
16. Vladimir Lukin, "Post-Soviet Russia in Search for Identity: Foreign Policy", *International Affairs* (Moscow), 63 (2), 2017, pp. 164-181.
17. Article by Russian President Vladimir Putin, "Russia: New Eastern Perspectives", *President of Russia*, November 9, 2000. http://en.kremlin.ru/events/president/transcripts/21132.
18. "Russia Announces APEC's Priorities for 2012", Asia-Pacific Economic Cooperation, December 13, 2012. https://www.apec.org/press/news-releases/2011/1213_isom.
19. Fyodor Lukyanov, "Everything on Display", *Russia in Global Affairs*, 3, 2019, pp. 5-6.
20. Alexander Lukin, *Pivot to Asia: Russia's Foreign Policy Enters the 21st Century*, (New Delhi: Vij Books India Pvt Ltd., 2017).
21. Vladimir Petrovsky, "The Greater Eurasian Partnership Project: Challenges and Opportunities", *International Affairs* (Moscow), 63 (4), 2017, pp. 13-24.
22. Hans Kohn, "Dostoevsky's Nationalism", *Journal of the History of Ideas*, 6 (4), 1945, pp. 385-414.
23. Dmitri Trenin, "20 Years of Vladimir Putin: How Russian Foreign Policy Has Changed", *The Moscow Times*, August 27, 2019. https://www.themoscowtimes.com/2019/08/27/20-years-of-vladimir-putin-how-russian-foreign-policy-has-changed-a67043.
24. Mikhail Titarenko and Vladimir Petrovsky, "Russia's Neo-Eurasian Identity", *International Affairs* (Moscow), 62 (3), 2016, pp. 120-141.
25. Dmitri Trenin, "Russia's Changing Identity: In Search of a Role in the 21st Century", Carnegie Moscow Centre, July 18, 2019. https://carnegiemoscow.org/commentary/79521.
26. V. Petrovsky, "Outlines of Security for the Greater Eurasian Partnership", *Far Eastern Affairs*, 46 (4), 2018, pp. 35-42.

27. "Iran, Russia and China Begin Naval Drill", *The Hindu*, January 21, 2022. https://www.thehindu.com/news/international/iran-russia-and-china-begin-naval-drill/article38304811.ece.
28. Andrey Dikarev and Alexander Lukin, "Russia's Approach to South China Sea Territorial Dispute: It's Only Business, Nothing Personal", *The Pacific Review*, January 2021. https://doi.org/10.1080/09512748.2020.1866652.
29. Dmitri Trenin, "Russia and China in the Arctic: Cooperation, Competition, and Consequences", Carnegie Moscow Centre, March 31, 2020. https://carnegiemoscow.org/commentary/81407.
30. "Valdai Discussion Club Session", *President of Russia*, October 3, 2019. http://en.kremlin.ru/events/president/news/61719.
31. "Confluence of the Two Seas" Speech by H.E. Mr. Shinzo Abe, Prime Minister of Japan at the Parliament of the Republic of India", Ministry of Foreign Affairs of Japan, August 22, 2007. https://www.mofa.go.jp/region/asia-paci/pmv0708/speech-2.html.
32. "ASEAN Outlook on the Indo-Pacific", *ASEAN*, June 23, 2019. https://asean.org/asean2020/wp-content/uploads/2021/01/ASEAN-Outlook-on-the-Indo-Pacific_FINAL_22062019.pdf.
33. "Xi Jinping's 'Asia for Asians' Mantra Evokes Imperial Japan", *South China Morning Post*, July 14, 2014. https://www.scmp.com/comment/insight-opinion/article/1553414/xi-jinpings-asia-asians-mantra-evokes-imperial-japan.
34. "Focus on Covid in Quad Plus Meet", *The Times of India*, May 13, 2020. https://timesofindia.indiatimes.com/india/jaishankar-discusses-covid-19-with-counterparts-in-us-5-other-countries/articleshow/75702875.cms.
35. "Russia Set to Establish Naval Logistics Base in Sudan", *TASS*, November 11, 2020. https://tass.com/defence/1222673.
36. "Russia-Africa Summit", *President of Russia*, October 24, 2019. http://en.kremlin.ru/events/president/news/61893.
37. "Mozambique, Russia Sign Energy, Security Deals", *France 24*, August 22, 2019. https://www.france24.com/en/20190822-mozambique-russia-sign-energy-security-deals.
38. "Russia, Madagascar Sign Agreement on Military Cooperation", *TASS*, October 5, 2018. https://tass.com/defence/1024770.
39. "China, Russia and South Africa Team up for First Joint Naval Drill", *South China Morning Post*, November 27, 2019. https://www.scmp.com/news/china/diplomacy/article/3039469/china-russia-and-south-africa-team-first-joint-naval-drill.
40. "UN Security Council High-Level Debate on Maritime Security", *President of Russia*, August 9, 2021. http://en.kremlin.ru/events/president/news/66352.
41. "ASEAN-Russia Dialogue Partnership Overview", Mission of the Russian Federation to ASEAN. https://asean.mid.ru/en_GB/dialogue-partnership.

42. "Russia, Southeast Asia Conclude First Joint Naval Exercise", *Reuters*, December 4, 2021. https://www.reuters.com/world/asia-pacific/russia-southeast-asia-conclude-first-joint-naval-exercise-2021-12-04/.
43. "Russia to Deliver 2 Mi-171A2 Multirole Helicopters to Bangladesh in 2023", *TASS*, November 19, 2021. https://tass.com/defence/1363931.
44. "Russian Foreign Minister Arrives in Islamabad on Two-Day Visit—First in 9 Years", *Dawn*, April 6, 2021. https://www.dawn.com/news/1616752.
45. "Interview of Foreign Minister Sergey Lavrov with the *Daily News,* Sri Lankan newspaper, Published on January 13, 2020", The Embassy of the Russian Federation to the United Kingdom of Great Britain and Northern Island", January 14, 2020. https://www.rusemb.org.uk/article/586.
46. "Russia to Step up Military Cooperation with Myanmar—Deputy Defence Minister", *TASS*, August 26, 2021. https://tass.com/defence/1329011.
47. "India, Russia, Bangladesh Sign Pact for Rooppur Atomic Plant", *Live Mint*, March 1, 2018. https://www.livemint.com/Industry/QD5ex7YkwRkooAmYgWPVHK/India-Russia-Bangladesh-sign-pact-for-Rooppur-atomic-plant.html; and "Russia Extends $11.38 bln Loan to Bangladesh to Build Nuclear Power Plant", *TASS*, January 13, 2017. https://tass.com/economy/925025.
48. "Russia to Promote Development of International Ties as IORA Partner—Statement", *TASS*, November 18, 2021. https://tass.com/politics/1363251.
49. "Dialogue Partners", *IORA*. https://www.iora.int/en/about/dialogue-partners.
50. "Comment by Foreign Ministry Spokeswoman Maria Zakharova on the Granting of Dialogue Partner Status to Russia by the Indian Ocean Rim Association (IORA)", The Ministry of Foreign Affairs of the Russian Federation, November 18, 2021. https://archive.mid.ru/en/foreign_policy/news/-/asset_publisher/cKNonkJE02Bw/content/id/4946409.
51. "Pacific Fleet", Ministry of Defence of the Russian Federation. https://eng.mil.ru/en/structure/forces/navy/associations/structure/forces/type/navy/pacific/about.htm.
52. "Russian Pacific Fleet's Resurgence Sets off Alarm Bells in Washington", *Russia Beyond*, February 6, 2017. https://www.rbth.com/blogs/continental_drift/2017/02/06/russian-pacific-fleets-resurgence-sets-off-alarm-bells-in-washington_696366.
53. "Chinese Foreign Ministry Commends Lavrov's Stance on South China Sea", *TASS*, April 13, 2016. https://tass.com/world/869259.
54. "Answers to Journalists' Questions", *President of Russia*, September 5, 2016. http://en.kremlin.ru/events/president/news/52834.
55. "Press Statements Following Russian-Vietnamese Talks", *President of Russia*, September 6, 2018. http://en.kremlin.ru/events/president/transcripts/58474.

56. Vasily Kashin, "The Ukrainian Crisis: Impact on Sino-Russian Relations", *RSiS*, October 14, 2016. https://www.rsis.edu.sg/wp-content/uploads/2016/10/CO16257.pdf.
57. "Arms Trade Fuels Russia's Inroads into Southeast Asia", *The ASEAN Post*, February 19, 2018. https://theaseanpost.com/article/arms-trade-fuels-russias-inroads-southeast-asia.
58. "Russia, Vietnam Aim for Further Promotion of Partnership—Statement", *TASS*, December 1, 2021. https://tass.com/politics/1368907.
59. Andrey Dikarev and Alexander Lukin, "Russia's Approach to South China Sea Territorial Dispute: It's Only Business, Nothing Personal", *The Pacific Review*, January 2021. https://doi.org/10.1080/09512748.2020.1866652.
60. "Commitments Made for Expansion of Russian Ties", *Vietnam Investment Review*, October 5, 2021. https://vir.com.vn/commitments-made-for-expansion-of-russian-ties-88201.html.
61. "Courting Russia with South China Sea Oil is a 'Dangerous Gamble' for Duterte", *South China Morning Post*, October 8, 2019. https://www.scmp.com/week-asia/politics/article/3031980/courting-russia-south-china-sea-oil-dangerous-gamble-duterte.
62. Dmitri Trenin, *What is Russia Up To In The Middle East?* (Cambridge: Polity Press, 2018).
63. "Japan-Russia Summit Telephone Talk", Ministry of Foreign Affairs of Japan, October 7, 2021. https://www.mofa.go.jp/erp/rss/northern/page1e_000359.html.
64. "Expanded Meeting of the Foreign Ministry Board", *President of Russia*, November 18, 2021. http://en.kremlin.ru/events/president/news/67123.
65. Sergei Karaganov, "From Eastward Pivot to Greater Eurasia", *International Affairs* (Moscow), 63 (4), 2017, pp. 1-12.
66. "Valdai Discussion Club Session", *President of Russia*, October 3, 2019. http://en.kremlin.ru/events/president/news/61719.
67. Ibid.
68. "External Affairs Minister's Conversation with Valdai Discussion Club, Moscow on 27 August 2019", Ministry of External Affairs, Government of India, October 19, 2019. https://www.mea.gov.in/Speeches-Statements.htm?dtl/31957.
69. "Calling the US' Bluff in 1971", *The Hindu*, December 19, 2019. https://www.thehindu.com/opinion/op-ed/calling-the-uss-bluff-in-1971/article30341831.ece.
70. "Translation of Prime Minister's Speech in Plenary Session of 5th Eastern Economic Forum", Ministry of External Affairs, Government of India, September 5, 2019. https://www.mea.gov.in/Speeches-Statements.htm?dtl/31798/translation+of+prime+ministers+speech+in+plenary+session+of+5th+eastern+economic+forum+september+05+2019.

71. "Translation of Prime Minister's Speech in Plenary Session of 5th Eastern Economic Forum", Ministry of External Affairs, Government of India, September 5, 2019. https://www.mea.gov.in/Speeches-Statements.htm?dtl/31798/translation+of+prime+ministers+speech+in+plenary+session+of+5th+eastern+economic+forum+september+05+2019.
72. "Indian Navy Passex With Russian Navy", Press Information Bureau, January 16, 2022. https://pib.gov.in/PressReleaseIframePage.aspx?PRID=1790311#:~:text=Indian%20Navy's%20indigenously%20designed%20and,2022%20in%20the%20Arabian%20Sea.
73. "Indo-Russian BrahMos Missile Deal Worth USD 374 Million Sealed with Philippines", *Financial Express*, January 28, 2022. https://www.financialexpress.com/defence/indo-russian-brahmos-missile-deal-worth-usd-374-million-sealed-with-philippines/2418367/ .
74. "India- Russia Joint Statement Following the Visit of the President of the Russian Federation", Ministry of External Affairs, Government of India, December 6, 2021. https://mea.gov.in/bilateral-documents.htm?dtl/34606/India_Russia_Joint_Statement_following_the_visit_of_the_President_of_the_Russian_Federation#:~:text=The%20Leaders%20welcomed%20the%20signing,term%20supply%20and%20pricing%20arrangements.
75. Ibid.
76. "UN Security Council High-Level Debate on Maritime Security", *President of Russia*, August 9, 2021. http://en.kremlin.ru/events/president/news/66352.
77. "Issuing Presidential Statement, Security Council Underlines Importance of Maritime Safety, Safeguarding Oceans for Legitimate Use", United Nations Security Council, August 9, 2021. https://www.un.org/press/en/2021/sc14598.doc.htm.
78. "Towards Free and Open Indo-Pacific", The Government of Japan, November 2019 at https://www.mofa.go.jp/files/000407643.pdf And "Address by Prime Minister Shinzo Abe at the 4th Eastern Economic Forum Plenary Session", Ministry of Foreign Affairs of Japan, September 12, 2018. https://www.mofa.go.jp/erp/rss/northern/page4e_000898.html.

13. Europe's Interest in the Indo-Pacific and the Rise of AUKUS

Mahima Duggal

Over the past few years, the Indo-Pacific region has swiftly risen as a global focal point. The region is home to not only some of the world's largest militaries, but also the world's largest economies—including the US, China, Japan, and India to name a few. With 50 per cent of the world's total trade—equivalent to roughly 62 per cent of the global Gross Domestic Product (GDP)[1]—transiting through the Indo-Pacific annually, the region has replaced the Atlantic as the world's busiest (and most important) trade corridor. In particular, the European Union (EU) holds significant economic interests in the region's sea lanes since it accounts for not only 1.5 trillion euros in goods trade (as of 2018),[2] but also over 35 per cent of Europe's total exports.[3] In other words, the Indo-Pacific represents Europe's largest market—especially for export-focussed economies like Germany—and unimpeded trade via the region's maritime trade corridors has a direct impact on Europe's security and prosperity. Such economic interdependence has made Europe a key stakeholder in the region. (See Fig 13.1 for a brief summary of the interdependency between the two geographies.) In April 2021, the EU issued a "Strategy for Cooperation in the Indo-Pacific",[4] which indicated a clear intention on the EU's part to reorient its outlook and enhance its existing activity in the region. On September 16, 2021, the EU released a "Joint Communication to the European Parliament and the Council" that detailed the EU's rationale, principles, approach and vision for building deeper partnerships in the Indo-Pacific.[5] With European engagement with the Indo-Pacific growing steadily, there must be a greater study of the opportunities and limitations for Europe's interactions and cooperation with the region. In particular, the EU's strategy must be considered in the context of its broader foreign and security policies. What is the EU's strategy and vision to enhance its engagement with the geopolitical Indo-Pacific concept? How does the EU's strategy complement those of the European powers, France, Germany and the Netherlands?

Fig 13.1: EU and the Indo-Pacific: An Economic Connect

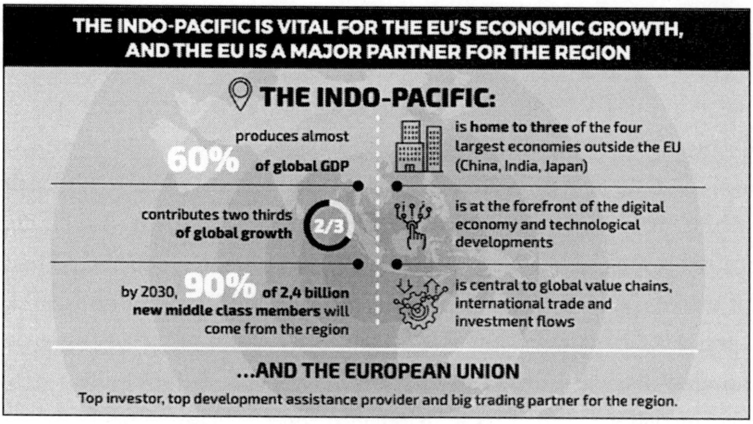

Source: European Commission[6]

Interestingly, the release of this document coincided with (and was overshadowed by) the announcement of the creation of the AUKUS trilateral—[Australia-United Kingdom (UK)-United States (US)]. A by-product of the emerging trilateral and minilateral associations in the Indo-Pacific, the tripartite "enhanced" security pact made a massive splash and gave rise to a vigorous debate on the value and strategic implications of the grouping.[7] Under AUKUS, the UK and US plan to help Australia build eight nuclear-powered submarines, thereby transferring the US' prized nuclear propulsion technology to help Australia boost its maritime security capabilities. The UK, thus far the only recipient of this technology (and that too, at the height of the Cold War) will help provide technical expertise and its nuclear submarine hull technology to support the process. This is expected to enhance interoperability among the three powers and enable them to collaborate militarily and leverage their collective strength for positive outcomes in the region, especially vis-à-vis China. With this view, AUKUS also looks to address key areas like advanced and critical technologies (including military technology), which will define the geopolitical competition and warfare in the times to come. Importantly, the establishment of the grouping cemented not only Washington's, but also London's presence in the region. In essence, as the UK's National Security Advisor, Sir Stephen Lovegrove, stated, AUKUS marks "the most significant capability collaboration anywhere in the world in the past six decades".[8]

On the other hand, the AUKUS announcement caused a major rift in trans-Atlantic ties—especially US-France and French-Australian relations. The signing of the pact directly led to Canberra abruptly cancelling the 2016 Franco-Australian submarine deal; not only was this a massive financial blow to France's defence manufacturing industry, but also a diplomatic breach of trust between Paris and Canberra (alongside Washington).[9] Despite reassurances by US President Joe Biden, negotiations on AUKUS remained secret, with France and the EU being kept out of the loop. For France (and the EU), this decision undermined its policy towards the Indo-Pacific and came as proof of Washington's continued disregard for its partners, and wavered confidence in the US' leadership ability and trust as a reliable partner. Although US-Europe ties have long been a solid foundation of international politics, the trans-Atlantic relationship deteriorated under President Trump's 'America First' approach that forced the EU to seriously consider 'strategic autonomy'. In this context, despite an increased and more active British presence in the region, AUKUS places further strain on Europe's Indo-Pacific engagement plans, which were increasingly driven and shaped by France in its capacity as an Indo-Pacific resident power. Considering that the France-Australian submarine deal was a key cornerstone of French engagement, questions remain about how AUKUS and the resulting tensions will impact the geopolitical dynamics of the Indo-Pacific. How will the establishment of the AUKUS trilateral impact Europe's approach towards the Indo-Pacific? This chapter looks to discuss such questions in reference to Europe's focus on the Indo-Pacific region.

EU's Indo-Pacific Strategy: Connecting Distant Geographies

The Indo-Pacific region has no geographical boundaries and exists more as a geopolitical concept that is bound together by shared principles of fostering a free, open, inclusive and rules-based regional order that is rooted in international law and democratic values. This positive vision—encoded in the Quadrilateral Security Dialogue's (Quad's) first joint statement[10]—has emerged as a driver of the Indo-Pacific concept. In other words, the essence of the Indo-Pacific is "more consequential" than the technical (or geographical) contours.[11] Such a flexible definition of the regional geography has opened the doors for the engagement of distant stakeholders, including the European powers. An increasingly assertive—if not aggressive—and rising Chinese power; the emergence of India as a global power that can balance China; and the decline and uncertainty of US engagement amidst the possibility of a return to the Trump era are some of the key factors driving Europe's interest and involvement with the Indo-Pacific. In essence, the economic and political weight of the region has forced the EU to hastily reassess its Indo-Pacific engagement strategy—going from barely using the term to developing a full-fledged policy for cooperation in the region.[12] (See Fig 13.2 for a timeline of the EU's recently growing engagement with the Indo-Pacific.)

Assessing EU's Indo-Pacific Policy

Europe's Indo-Pacific policy opens by categorically declaring that "the futures of the EU and the Indo-Pacific are inextricably linked", making them natural partners.[13] At its core, the EU's aim is to build "principled and long-term" engagement with the region that will help strengthen Europe's "strategic reach and security and... the resilience of its supply chains".[14] For this, the EU will seek to defend the rules-based international order by promoting inclusivity, multilateralism based on shared values of respecting democracy, the rule of law and human rights. This would involve extending its role as a 'defender of human rights' to the Indo-Pacific via tools like diplomatic dialogues and consultations, trade preference policies, and mainstreaming of human rights in all of the bloc's policies and programmes. Further, the EU will also look to promote a fair trade environment, further Sustainable Development Goals (SDGs), achieve climate objectives under the Glasgow Climate Pact,[15] support inclusive policy-making processes, encourage multilateral cooperation via the Association of Southeast Asian Nations (ASEAN)-centric institutions, and economic growth and connectivity.[16]

Fig 13.2: Key EU Policy Advances in the Indo-Pacific

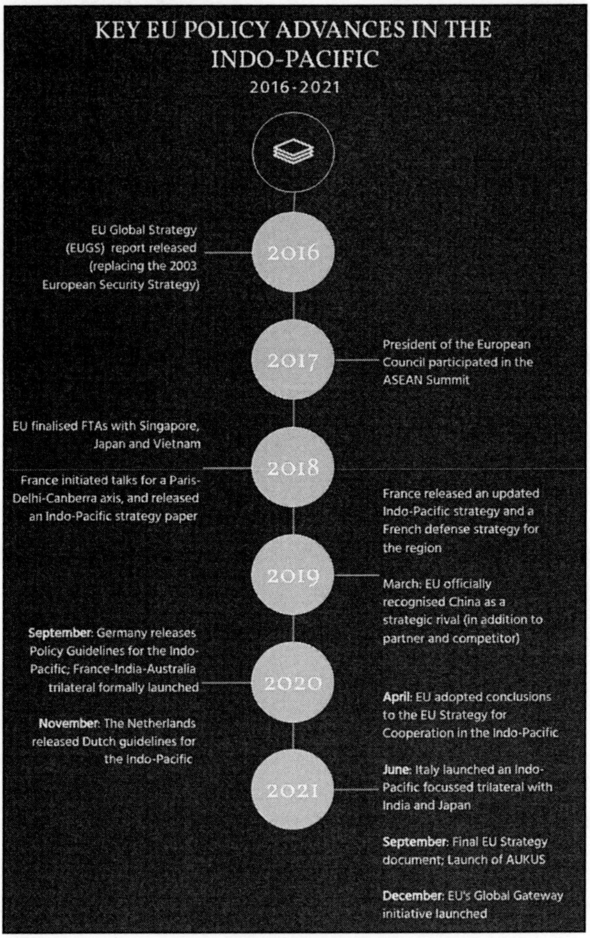

Source: Prepared by the author

To realise such a vision, the EU aims to deepen and reinforce its cooperation with Indo-Pacific partners like ASEAN, Australia, New Zealand, India, Japan, South Korea, the US and the UK. This will not only include launching concrete initiatives on a bilateral level, but also at the regional level via minilateral groupings such as the Quad. Considering its economic interests in the region, the EU sees the Indian Ocean—the most important passage to the Indo-Pacific—as a gateway to the region; safeguarding stability and freedom of navigation by building strong partnerships are, thus, a key priority. In particular, the EU strategy highlights Brussels' interest in becoming a Regional Economic Communities partner of the African Union (AU), supporting the Indian Ocean Commission, and forging and bolstering new Economic Partnership Agreements (EPAs) in the region. Further, it also looks to underpin its already dynamic partnership with ASEAN by explicitly supporting ASEAN centrality, ASEAN's position in negotiating an effective and substantive Code of Conduct with China, and expanding consultations on security issues through existing fora like the ASEAN Regional Forum (ARF). Similarly, it also seeks to further strengthen its relations with the Pacific region, via the Organisation of African, Caribbean and Pacific (ACP) states, Pacific Island Forum (PIF), Pacific Community, and Council of Regional Organisations of the Pacific. At the same time, considering the regional dynamics, the EU strategy also looks to pursue "multifaceted engagement"[17] with China in order to collaborate and devise solutions to shared challenges. It hopes to use its influence to push back against China's gross human rights infrigements and other areas of disagreement (like unfair trade practices and structural trade issues), while encouraging Beijing to play a more active and positive role in achieving shared objects vis-à-vis issues like climate change.

In particular, the strategy identifies seven priority areas for action: "sustainable and inclusive prosperity; green transition; ocean governance; digital governance and partnerships; connectivity; security and defence; and human security" (see Table 13.1). The pandemic was a critical event highlighting the importance of resilient and diversified supply chains and a green socioeconomic recovery. Brussels aims to build on its reputation as a responsible donor and business partner to champion environmental, human and labour rights related causes. To ensure its economic security, the EU is deeply focussed on building sustainable and resilient global value chains that are inclusive of the developing and underdeveloped countries; and concluding and implementing new trade agreements with partners like Australia, New Zealand, Indonesia, Japan, South Korea, Malaysia, Philippines, Thailand, and India, as well as investment deals with Vietnam and Singapore. Over 2020 and 2021, Europe has increasingly emerged as a leader and standard-setter of best practices in these sectors: the European Green Deal, for instance, has been defined as Europe's "man on

Fig 13.3: EU's Seven Areas of Priority Engagement in the Indo-Pacific

Sustainable and Inclusive Prosperity

- Cooperate with Indo-Pacific partners to reinforce stronger and more diverse supply chains, finalise and implement free trade agreements with focus on greater economic collaborations in strategic sectors
- Cooperate with regional partners to reinforce international trade laws and norms, so as to prevent unfair trade practices, coercive behaviour, and technology or intellectual property threats

Security and Defence

- Protect and promote a rules-based regional security architecture via an increased naval pesence and deployments in the Indo-Pacific - including a particular focus on securing sea lines of commnication (SLOCs)
- Supporting maritime capacity-building efforts of the EU's Indo-Pacific partners as well as in other areas (like cyber crime)

Connectivity

- Promote increased connectivity between Europe and the Indo-Pacific by supporting financing efforts under a strong regulatory environment

Digital Governance and Partnerships

- Expanding and building new digital partnerships with strategic Indo-Pacific partners (similar to the Green Alliance with Japan)
- Bolstering joint collaboration in areas like research and innovation (such as via Horizon Europe initiative)

Green Transition

- Collaborating with regional partners to achieve international climate targets, and taking steps to adapt to climate changes (such as by devising and implementing solutions to issues like loss of biodiversity and pollution)

Ocean Governance

- Working with like-minded partners to ensure maritime activities in the region abide by international laws, including the United Nations Convention on the Law of the Sea (UNCLOS)
- This involves expanding and implementing Sustainable Fidsheries Partnership Agreements and collaborating to address issues like illegal, unreported and unregulated (IUU) fishing

Source: Prepared by the author based on the EU's Indo-Pacific Strategy

the moon moment";[18] it has emerged as a significant and comprehensive strategy to enable a sustainable transformation of the environment, climate and society.[19] The Conference of Parties (COP 26) proved to be a medium achievement at best; more than anything, it highlighted the need for not only effectively linking post-pandemic recovery to the climate crisis and devising an internationally-accepted roadmap. Under these circumstances, the European Green Deal—the first of its kind—

has become a model for green recovery, and initiatives under the deal, like sustainable transportation, biodiversity loss, deforestation, renewable energy and circular economy (see Fig 13.4). In May 2021, Brussels signed a Green Alliance with Japan,[20] and wants to build similar partnerships in the Indo-Pacific covering sustainable finance, green supply chains, renewable energy transition, and targeted investments under the 'Global Europe'[21] scheme.

Importantly, what stands out in the EU's Indo-Pacific strategy is its new focus on security and defence in the geographically distant region. Although the EU has long been present and active in the Indo-Pacific region, this has largely been in an economic or developmental capacity. The strategic and security dimensions of the region have been of little concern; its new strategy, however, is a clear-cut indication that the bloc is now viewing the Indo-Pacific through a security lens.[22] Despite the EU's strong trade ties with China—and perhaps even because of them—Brussels has found it necessary to embrace the Indo-Pacific as a strategic concept, and become more involved in security sectors like supply chain resilience, emerging technologies, protecting the Sea Lines of Communication (SLOCs), countering disinformation and cyber crime (see Fig 13.3). As China's expansionist tendencies lead to its growing footprint not only in

Fig 13.4: Key Areas under the European Green Deal

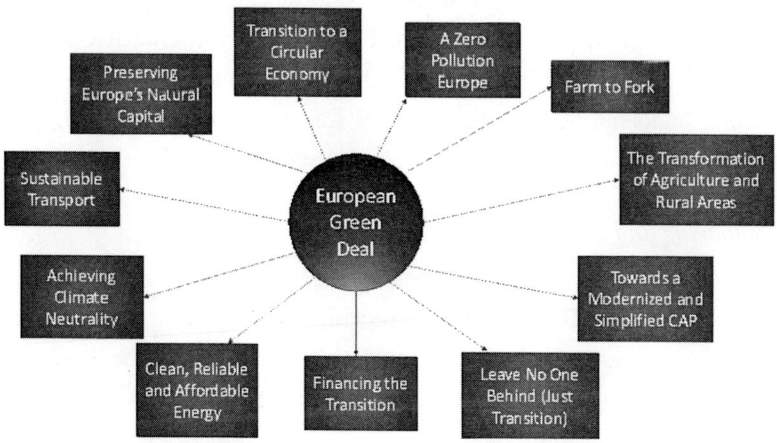

Source: Prepared by the author

the Indo-Pacific, but also Western Asia and Eurasia,[23] Europe has become directly impacted by China's rise. Thus far, Europe's relationship with China maintained a fine balance between a cooperation partner, economic competitor and 'systemic rival'.[24] However, Beijing's 'wolf warrior' style of diplomacy and wilful disinformation campaigns amid the coronavirus pandemic have somewhat "shattered" the EU's China perception, chilled ties, and tilted the balance of their relationship in favour of rivalry.[25]

An example of the EU's efforts to balance China's growing clout is its Global Gateway initiative, launched on December 1, 2021, which aims to "boost smart, clean and secure links in digital, energy and transport and strengthen health, education and research systems across the world".[26] It pledges to mobilise €300 billion via a European model for a sustainable global recovery and resilient growth. Widely perceived as a competitive venture to the Belt and Road Initiative (BRI),[27] the Global Gateway presents the EU as a trusted partner over China; it purports a "values-based approach", "transparency", "good governance", "democratic values" and "links, not dependencies"[28]—thus, standing in stark contrast to the BRI, which is frequently criticised for lax transparency, environmental and governance standards, and 'debt trap'[29] diplomacy. The Global Gateway comes in addition to a myriad other financing initiatives (including the Build Back Better World, of which the EU is a part via the G7) that have emerged as an answer to the BRI. Whether it can succeed in such an objective, considering the massive scale of easily accessible funding available under the BRI remains to be seen. Yet, the Global Gateway will be integrated within the EU's Indo-Pacific strategy, and with other existing regional and national ventures for complementary action,[30] to enable maximum impact in the region vis-à-vis the BRI.

Comparing and Contrasting National Initiatives

The EU's Indo-Pacific policy has been driven by the stakes and increasing interests of key European powers, especially France,[31] Germany[32] and the Netherlands[33]—all of which published their own Indo-Pacific strategies (see Fig 13.2). Paris and Berlin, in particular, have been key forces driving an independent EU outlook towards the Indo-Pacific, as a way of further strengthening its strategic autonomy at a time of turbulent trans-Atlantic relations under US President Donald Trump's 'America First' approach that included publicly rallying against, and threatening to pull out of, the North Atlantic Treaty Organisation (NATO). Notably, the outlooks of all three countries find congruence on three points: they have an inclusive approach to the region; they highlight ASEAN centrality and align closely with the ASEAN Outlook on the Indo-Pacific (AOIP); they tend to focus less on the US and more on regional partners like Japan, India, South Korea and ASEAN. Further, the three approaches also have much in common in regards to the key trends and issues in the Indo-Pacific, European priorities, and an overall objective to enhance Europe's profile in the region.[34]

Yet, all three countries' documents vary in terms of their positions, the government institutions involved, the level of details specified, and have vastly different starting points. France's strategy is based in the fact that it views itself as a resident Indo-Pacific power; not only does it hold island territories spanning the eastern African coast to the South Pacific and the western coast of Central America, but also the world's second-biggest Exclusive Economic Zone (EEZ), over 1.6 million citizens and 7,000-strong military presence in the region.[35] Germany and the Netherlands, in contrast, have no such natural role in the region and their interest is primarily based on trade, ensuring open sea lanes and sustaining a rules-based order. While the French strategy provides a broad geographical definition of the region, in keeping with its expansive territorial presence, the German and Dutch documents are less specific. The German paper acknowledges the numerous delineations of the region by various actors, but identifies it as the aggregate of the Indian and Pacific Oceans, where "strategic projections compete with each other and global value chains are intertwined". For the Netherlands, the region extends from Pakistan to the Pacific islands, including the South and East China Seas.

Importantly, while France's documents (released by both its Foreign Affairs and Defence Ministries) were explicitly titled 'strategies'—thus, showing the strategic importance of the Paris Accords to the region in its strategic outlook—the German and Dutch papers were labelled 'guidelines'—pointing to much more cautious approach. Germany has been more reluctant to adopt an outrightly confrontational approach towards China, possibly because of the economic significance of China. Since 2015, China ranks as Germany's largest trading partner with almost $260 billion trade in 2020; it accounts for almost 50 per cent of total European exports to the country, including cars, chemicals and precision machinery.[36] In 2021, Beijing imposed sanctions on several European officials critical of China; this has forced Berlin to separate economics from politics, avoid taking sides in the bifurcation of global politics into pro-China and pro-US camps, and not antagonise China. Germany is one of the few European states that has officially recognised Taiwan as a part of China.[37] In this regard, the EU's Indo-Pacific policy is based heavily on the German approach. Germany taking over the G7 Presidency in 2022 will provide a further opportunity for close coordination with like-minded partners and further shape the EU's outlook. Moreover, now, with a new German government post-Merkel, Berlin's 'pro-China' outlook may undergo a more radical shift and become more critical, in line with its public opinion.[38] At the same time, France has also been a major power shaping the EU outlook. For instance, France is the only country so far that has created an ambassadorial position for the Indo-Pacific; the EU followed Paris' example by appointing a special envoy for the Indo-Pacific in September 2021. Beyond these states, the UK's 2021 Global Britain report outlined a clear 'tilt' towards the Indo-Pacific, and Italy too—despite being a part of the BRI—has shown overtures towards the region by initiating a maritime security focussed trilateral with India and Japan.

The AUKUS Conundrum

While President Joe Biden announced AUKUS as "always together; never alone,"[39] it was a "stab in the back"[40] that detracted from efforts of enhancing trust and cooperation between democracies, according to French Foreign Affairs Minister Jean-Yves Le Drian. The EU, however held vastly divided views on the development, for example, in regards to whether it will empower Australia or reduce its sovereignty by furthering reliance on the US.[41] It also raised questions about the internal coherence of the EU, as well as its external relevance in the Indo-Pacific, where it stands as an important stakeholder. The EU High Representative,

Joseph Borell, bemoaned the "lack of consultations and communication" between the trans-Atlantic partners, which "created real difficulties" and gave the impression of a disunited and fragmented West—particularly due to the unfortunate timing of the announcement.[42] With Russia and China already escalating their campaign to undermine European unity, the AUKUS revelation's timing could not have been more awkward—even embarrassing—for Brussels. In this context, for the EU, AUKUS was indicative of the low regard Biden held for the US' long-time trans-Atlantic partner and the continued, deep-seated cracks in their partnership even post-Trump.

From the US perspective, Washington and Canberra are far more strategically aligned in their Indo-Pacific interests; this gives the US immense confidence in Australia which made AUKUS possible. In contrast, the US and Europe have divergent stances and policies on China. On the whole, Brussels has been reluctant to outrightly counter China in line with US expectations. The conclusion of the EU-China Comprehensive Agreement on Investment (CAI) in December 2020, under Berlin's leadership as EU president, despite opposition from member states like Poland, was not received well by the incoming President Biden. For the Biden camp, which urged the EU to refrain from rushing things and engage in early trans-Atlantic consultations on China's economic practices ahead of finalising the CAI,[43] the agreement was not "neutral" vis-à-vis allied cooperation on China.[44] Notably, EU initiatives like the Global Gateway too, while they may have ambitions to counter Chinese influence, are not explicitly aimed at Beijing but rather to strengthen European presence via values-driven financing in the Indo-Pacific. In essence, notwithstanding Biden's statements on deepening cooperation with democratic allies to ensure the US' global leadership,[45] the EU's decision to take forward the trade pact with China came as a confirmation for him that the White House will likely not see eye-to-eye with Brussels on China. Unlike Trump, Biden has sought to frame US ties with China through a prism of intense competition (or rivalry) over conflict and promoted a multilateral and minilateral approach for a same; the EU would be a natural partner in this regard as the White House's historically close ally. However, the CAI incident was undoubtedly damaging to the US-EU partnership and the potential for their cooperation as allies against China; the EU's exclusion from the AUKUS discussions may be a sign of lukewarm times to come.

Even so, considering their rapidly growing interest and stake in the Indo-Pacific, Washington's decision to entirely exclude European powers like France, Germany, and the EU, was a serious breach of trust. For France's political class particularly, the move was reminiscent of "Trumpian unilateralism, Australian two-facedness, and the usual British perfidy".[46] Notably, French Prime Minister Emmanuel Macron received Australian Prime Minister Scott Morrison on June 15, 2021, where Morrison applauded the Franco-Australian deal as a pillar of the partnership and trust between them.[47] In August 2021, a joint communique released post a meeting of the French and Australian defence ministers' reiterated the importance of their submarine programme in underpinning their cooperation.[48] Therefore, to Paris, the loss of the submarine defence contract with Australia without any forewarning despite France-US and France-Australia consultations shortly prior to the announcement was an indication of Washington's lack of trust in France when it comes to sensitive matters like nuclear technology. Furthermore, Biden's mishandled and haphazard withdrawal from Afghanistan—a NATO operation—only added to doubts and uncertainties about whether the US was truly back under Biden.

The EU's Strategic Autonomy Debate

Europe has become increasingly wary of being caught in the Sino-American rivalry. The vastly diverging standpoints of EU member states on both China and the US have resulted in the EU's lack of a concrete policy to deal with either. As EU High Representative Borrell stated in 2019, intensifying geopolitical competition has made it necessary for the EU to step up its global presence and become an international political player, rather than being limited to its own backyard. In this context, AUKUS has served to highlight the debate on strategic autonomy within the EU.

The strategic autonomy discourse emerged in the EU over the past few years with French President Emmanuel Macron calling for developing a conscious European sovereignty and German Chancellor Angela Merkel arguing that Europe must take control of its own destiny and no longer rely on the US for its security needs.[49] The changing security landscape—with Brexit and its impact on European security, the EU's defence capabilities,[50] lack of a US-China war, a changing threat calculus from Russia, the COVID-19 pandemic and its social, economic and health repercussions—have forced Brussels to reset its strategic compass. The end of the Pax Americana era and the rise of China (and Asia at large) have spurred focus on the EU as an independent geopolitical actor. The question of Europe's autonomy is not one between the EU with the US or going at it alone—but rather of Europe taking greater responsibility for its security by enhancing its military capabilities and contributions. The EU is already a veritable global power in the economic realm, but not in security and defence. Proponents of strategic autonomy argue that in order to protect, defend and enhance its interests, the EU must be capable of acting on its own. Such ambitions, to imbibe, if not absolute, then at least a greater degree of autonomy, were only highlighted due to AUKUS.

Hours prior to Biden's AUKUS announcement, European Commission President Ursula von der Leyen appealed for strategic autonomy in her annual "State of the European Union" speech to the EU Parliament. In particular, she made a case for a European Defence Union—a joint military force formed by the EU member states—and a unified defence strategy.[51] The German foreign minister emphasised that the AUKUS was a "sobering" moment for the EU and called for developing an independent position on critical matters to reflect "European sovereignty".[52] Brussels release of its Indo-Pacific strategy was a step in this direction. Not only did it project the EU as a significant stakeholder in a distant (but vital) region, but its focus on security illustrated Brussel's desire to play a more active role in the Indo-Pacific as a global power. Further, the tone of the strategy, carefully balanced vis-à-vis China, points to the EU's intent to follow an independent stance, away from the US, in keeping with its interest. Most recently, in January 2022, France (a long-time advocate of strategic autonomy) assumed the EU Presidency under the motto "recovery, strength, belonging"; amongst its many agendas, strengthening strategic autonomy ranks at the top.[53] Such pointed focus on the concept by Paris, and support by major European powers like Germany, has solidified the case for European sovereignty and strategic autonomy.

Looking Ahead: Trends, Opportunities and Challenges

Going forward, Europe will need to look at several factors to shape its threat perception, strategic thinking and Indo-Pacific strategy. AUKUS is not merely a French issue—as it is often perceived to be due to France's 'resident' Indo-Pacific power status and the impact of the cancellation of the submarine deal—but one that must be considered at the European level. AUKUS' focus is broad-based, from nuclear to critical military technologies to value chain management; accordingly, its impact will be trans-sectoral and deeply influence the geopolitics and strategic environment of the region. While it is by no means opposed to the EU's strategic objectives in the Indo-Pacific, as laid out in its strategy, AUKUS will force the EU and EU member states to make strategic choices of key significance.

Expanding Europe's Empire of Norms

Although cracks in the trans-Atlantic partnership are likely to persist despite US attempts to mend ties,[54] Washington and Brussels do share fundamental commonalities that could see convergence in the Indo-Pacific and give a new normal to their ties. Most importantly, Europe sees itself as a guardian of fundamental values of democracy, freedom, the rule of law, and human rights.[55] Its aims include promoting such European values and interests beyond its borders, and contributing to global peace, security, sustainable development, solidarity, free and fair trade, and human rights.[56] Conceptualised as a powerful normative empire,[57] the EU has sought to export its values and practices beyond its borders—such as through its ties with states on its immediate vicinity—that has helped serve its security and economic interests. In other words, the EU's norm-based behaviour has helped it construct a normative identity while also being a "utility-maximising strategy" to further its interest-based policies.[58] Now, with its Indo-Pacific policy, the EU can extend its norm-based behaviour and normative power beyond its neighbouring states via its aim to protect and promote a rules-based order in the Indo-Pacific.

In recent times, Lithuania, an outspoken critic of China's human rights record, has stood as a unique example of a small state standing up to China; it allowed Taiwan to open a representative office in its capital Vilnius to enable a more "intense economic, cultural and scientific relationship" with Taipei.[59] If such a small country can challenge China, the EU—in its capacity as a major economic and normative power—can make a great impact. Lithuania's actions have, however, not been without cost, with China downgrading diplomatic ties and inflicting economic repercussions in tens of millions of dollars (as of January 2022).[60] Moreover, in a sign of aggressive wolf warrior diplomacy, China further escalated the issue by targeting German firms. Whether the Chinese tactics will work, and Lithuania is pressured into changing its stance (thus, compromising its sovereignty) will depend on the extent of support that Lithuania will receive from Europe. In other words, China's tactics have shifted the issue from a bilateral one to one requiring a European answer.[61] While Lithuania could withstand only so much pressure, the EU has stood in solidarity to reinforce its values in the face of Chinese coercion by coming together to take the issue up at the World Trade Organisation and statements of support from fellow states.[62]

Profits vs Principles Calculus

The case with Lithuania exemplified the key debate that the EU will be faced with in the coming times—that of prioritising profits or principles. Countries like Germany that share deep trade ties with China have long held the hope that increasing trade would bring a change to Beijing; such thinking is now facing a reality check as China under Xi continues to solidify its socialist roots. In 2021, Xi accelerated the drive for 'common prosperity' through the introduction of several new policy guidelines that put the private sector on a tight leash; Xi's aim was essentially to strengthen his hold on Party politics and ensure that people do not rise up in rebellion, in a retrogression to the Mao era.[63] In Europe's own periphery too, the China challenge has become increasingly concerning. In June 2020, Brussels recognised China (alongside Russia) as a source of disinformation on COVID-19, attempting to sow divisions within the EU.[64] In many ways, the politics of the Indo-Pacific has a direct bearing on Europe. Some argue that the EU must prioritise its immediate security needs—both economic (via continued trade with China) and traditional (by focussing its limited defence resources in its proximity, that is, in Eurasia, Middle East and Africa). However, with China's growing economic coercion over its partners and increasing influence in Europe's backyard through ties with Russia and presence in Eurasia, playing a role in the Indo-Pacific and helping tackle regional issues has become a necessity for safeguarding European security. Montenegro's €1 billion loan to construct a highway that has snared the country in a debt trap illustrates Beijing's growing clout on the EU's periphery.[65] Such developments indicate that it has become ever more important for the EU and its member states to deliver on a values-based policy despite China's economic allure.

To some extent, this shift is already visible in several EU countries. China has already lost the battle for any soft power influence in Europe. A 2020 survey found that although all the European countries view China as the leading global economic power, they have no confidence in Xi's China; in Germany, the UK, Sweden, and Spain, negative views on China have reached historic highs.[66] Further, the public opinion in Europe values ties with the US over those with China. Overall, the unfavourable perceptions of China in 2021 are at least 20 points higher than those in 2006[67]—demonstrating a trend of declining ties between the two actors.

Interestingly, despite its reliance on, and positive ties with, China, Berlin has also sought to present a stronger stance vis-à-vis China while juggling a delicate profit versus principles balance. Apart from its release of the Indo-Pacific guidelines (which were admittedly soft on China), and driving the EU's Indo-Pacific strategy, Germany deployed the *Bayern* frigate to traverse the Indo-Pacific for over six months, via the South China Sea (SCS). More than anything else, the visit comes as a sign of Berlin's commitment to the Indo-Pacific. Its aim was not to provoke China, but act as a mode of outreach to regional partners—such as through the German naval chief's dialogues with partner states in which the *Bayern* docked. Speaking to the strategic community in New Delhi, Vice Admiral Kay-Achim Schönbach emphasised that the frigate's deployment was a form of strategic communication;[68] since Berlin is viewed as its key friend and the "bell weather" of EU-China cooperation in Europe,[69] the fact that Germany sent a ship to the region for the first time in almost 20 years—an action entirely out of the norm—signifies the strain in their ties. For Beijing, the downturn in their ties is a message that it has failed to effectively communicate and conduct diplomacy with Europe. Furthermore, Schönbach stressed that the deployment was a national endeavour, and not in concert with either the US or the EU. Although Germany's actions are largely embedded in the EU framework, it is also looking to expand its bilateral partnerships with states like Japan, India and Singapore; its focus on inclusivity means that Berlin's goal is not to prevent China from becoming a world power, but setting and upholding norms in the region. Nevertheless, Berlin is aware of China's efforts to hinder EU (and NATO) unity, and the importance of resisting such efforts. Germany's case demonstrates its changing perception of China—despite their trade ties—and points to Europe's commitment to the Indo-Pacific, even if its priorities may be different compared to the regional actors or AUKUS states.

Navigating Stumbling Blocks

In this context, the EU's engagement in the Indo-Pacific will not be without its challenges. *First*, although the rise of the Indo-Pacific has been accompanied by the formation of a myriad trilaterals and minilaterals, these associations have varied objectives, priorities and perceptions, especially on how to incorporate the white elephant that is China. Within the EU too, the differences in priorities between the French security-driven Indo-Pacific strategy and German economic-driven Indo-Pacific guidelines suggest a long-standing issue on how to prioritise objectives in the face of difficult choices. The EU strategy itself lays out seven areas of engagement but gives little clarity on how they may be prioritised when one comes at the cost of another. A key solution to confront such differences (or dissonances) is via regular, frank and transparent discussions—like the India-led Indian Ocean Naval Symposium (IONS)[70]—on sensitive security-related matters to help change the perceptions of the regional states. Such dialogues can help forge congruence in the stakeholders' policies and strategies and move them towards greater collaborations.

Second, China's reaction will persist as a key problem in forming and implementing any position on the Indo-Pacific. The EU's approach to the Indo-Pacific, and for that matter the approach of regional actors like India, stresses inclusivity as a core value for building a rules-based multipolar order and recognises that Beijing has a role to play in combatting shared global challenges like climate change and nuclear non-proliferation. Nevertheless, Beijing is likely to continue to view the Indo-Pacific concept as a US-driven anti-China construct. As China continues to adhere to aggressive and unscrupulous diplomatic tactics vis-à-vis Europe (like with Lithuania), Brussels will find it exceedingly difficult to sustain a fine balance between China as a partner, a competitor, and a rival. The EU will, thus, need to be prepared to reevaluate its priorities and make hard choices.

Third, and perhaps the most crucial challenge to the EU's Indo-Pacific strategy will be actualising it through effective implementation. This will only be possible with a "sustained political will" and "considerable financial, material and human resources" to adequately fulfil the ambitious commitments made, and perform as per the expectations of the EU's regional partners.[71] To ensure that the EU's Indo-Pacific focus sustains and its strategy is effective in the long term, it cannot merely be driven by the France-German engine. The EU is characterised by a multi-level governance system that necessitates internal convergence and (although it is a shared point of concern), China has become a point of competing interests and policy divergence between EU member states. These factors will make implementation exceedingly complicated—yet more critical than ever before.[72] While France, Germany and the Netherlands have the security capabilities and willingness to project these in the service of the EU's interests in the region, for several EU states, the Indo-Pacific remains a distant concern with little traction despite its growing centrality in global affairs. These differences are evident in a European Council on Foreign Relations study, which found that for 10 EU states, the Indo-Pacific was a way to respond to the China challenge alongside economic benefits; for 13 states, it was merely a tool to further European economic interests.[73] Similarly, while 11 member states view the EU engagement as a way of asserting European strategic autonomy without US support, eight states perceive it as a strategy to "manage" trans-Atlantic ties by "keeping the US engaged", and six others see it entirely as a step to align more closely with Washington.[74]

The EU has repeatedly rejected making a choice in the emerging US-China binary in global politics. Yet, achieving a common position and moving towards a collective recognition of strategic autonomy has been a struggle. In the light of such differences, it will be up to states like France and Germany to convince their fellow member states, consolidate unity, and ensure that the EU presents a common, coherent and autonomous front in implementing its Indo-Pacific strategy. One way to do this is to focus on areas like climate change, technology and maritime security, where the EU has much to contribute. Brussels can support capacity building for deterrence across the Indo-Pacific through visible projects implemented via coalitions that clearly exhibit its presence and intent in the region. As modern geopolitics moves away from traditional security to focus on human-centric issues like climate change, Europe can have a great impact. It can, for instance, work with island states in the Western and Southern Indian Ocean to help them adapt to climate change. However, only a united EU—with a shared vision, collective political will, and greater capabilities—can be an effective partner and vital strategic asset in the Indo-Pacific.

Implications for India

India features prominently in the EU's Indo-Pacific outlook amongst regional partners with which Brussels must expand its ties. Both France and Germany share positive ties with New Delhi and have highlighted the critical role India plays in their perceptions and policies towards the Indo-Pacific. This was highlighted by the German Ambassador to India, Walter J. Lindner, who stated that regardless of changes in the German government, India's strategic importance for Germany (and the world) was increasingly obvious owing to its pivotal position in the Indo-Pacific.[75] On the other hand, for India too, Germany is India's most important trading partner in the EU, particularly in the development cooperation sector.[76] Similarly, France and India share traditionally close relations; both regard the other as one of their closest strategic partners based on their shared interests in the Indian Ocean, a common vision of a "truly multilateral" order,[77] and a strong defence partnership (especially in defence manufacturing, with India procuring the Rafale jets from France). India is a neighbouring state to French island territories in the Indian Ocean, and accordingly forms a "top priority" for both Paris and Brussels.[78] France's and Italy's outreach to India through trilateral formats offers further testament to India's importance, and its own growing interest in, and synergy with, the European partners.

Beyond Germany and France, EU member states are of tremendous significance to India. Nordic states like Denmark, Sweden, Finland and Norway, which are leaders in the green sector, can contribute much to India's sustainable, economic and technological transformation.[79]

India's External Affairs Minister, S. Jaishankar, outlined the country's diplomatic agenda: to "engage America, manage China, cultivate Europe, reassure Russia, bring Japan into play, draw neighbours in, extend the neighbourhood and expand traditional constituencies of support".[80] Under such an all-out diplomatic agenda, cultivating the EU as a special strategic and global partner can help New Delhi enhance its economic power and active posture globally, thus, forging a favourable balance of power in the region. Estonia, a small EU state, boasts of a highly sophisticated e-government system with reliable digital identities and is regarded as a cyber security hotshot;[81] as India looks to finesse its own e-governance structure and bolster cyber security amid a highly contested cyber space in the Indo-Pacific, Estonia could be an ideal partner. Similarly, Luxembourg's immense financial clout, Norway's expertise in maritime technologies, and the role of Eastern European countries like Slovenia and Poland as a commercial gateway to Europe are merely a few examples of how India and the EU can tap into still unrealised potential for cooperation. Notably, as India looks to develop a digital rupee (as mandated in its 2022 budget),[82] cooperation between the Reserve Bank of India and the European Central Bank, which also launched a digital euro project in July 2021,[83] can be another point for cooperation to limit China's dominance in this space.[84] In this context, the EU-India partnership holds immense potential in the Indo-Pacific.

The EU's Indo-Pacific policy explicitly reflects its hope for greater engagement with New Delhi. Under France's EU presidency in 2022, working with India to ensure transparent and green financing to small states in the region—so as to limit China's use of its economic heft as a tool for gaining influence—has emerged as a priority.[85] In this context, the EU's interest in the Indo-Pacific, and focus on India amid a disconnect with its trans-Atlantic partner post-AUKUS, presents a window of opportunity for India. Partnering with an economic stalwart like the EU can help New Delhi compete with China's BRI in its backyard and prevent it building a 'string of pearls' (that is, strategically located naval facilities encircling India). Further, India and the EU share the vision of an inclusive regional order, and a closer alignment with Brussels over Washington can be an opportunity for New Delhi to balance China's growing influence without relying on the US (which could further complicate India-China tensions), while also expanding its regional and global standing. Unlike the US, the Asian powers (including China) do not perceive the EU with strategic suspicion, making it a more acceptable and valuable partner. Its limited military projection in the Indo-Pacific and focus on the economy add to such a perception. Building on this, India must capitalise on the EU's pivot to the Indo-Pacific, and welcome its entry as an opportunity for greater mutual gains. While much will undeniably depend on how EU member states manage their China engagement and tackle the stumbling blocks they are faced with in the region, welcoming the EU's entry to the region—with its greater economic muscle, technological prowess, and normative power—must be a priority for India to strengthen its posture and achieve its goals for the region.

Notes

1. "Keynote Address by Secretary (East) at the Special Session of the 1st edition of the Indo-Pacific Business Summit," speech, Ministry of External Affairs, July 6, 2021. https://mea.gov.in/Speeches-Statements.htm?dtl/33982/Keynote_Address_by_Secretary_East_at_the_Special_Session_of_the_1st_edition_of_the_IndoPacific_Business_Summit.
2. This number represents the total value of trade between Europe and Asia. See Ana Neves, "Explained, the Economic Ties between Europe and Asia," World Economic Forum, May 14, 2019. https://www.weforum.org/agenda/2019/05/ways-asia-and-europe-together-connected/.

3. European Commission and High Representative of the Union for Foreign Affairs and Security Policy, *Joint Communication to the European Parliament and the Council: The EU Strategy for Cooperation in the Indo-Pacific* (Brussels: European External Action Service, September 16, 2021). https://eeas.europa.eu/sites/default/files/jointcommunication_2021_24_1_en.pdf.
4. General Secretariat of the Council, *EU Strategy for Cooperation in the Indo-Pacific—Council Conclusions,* 7914/21 (Brussels: Council of the European Union, April 16, 2021). https://data.consilium.europa.eu/doc/document/ST-7914-2021-INIT/en/pdf.
5. n. 3.
6. European Commission, "(Factsheet) EU Strategy for Cooperation in the Indo-Pacific," September 2021. https://eeas.europa.eu/sites/default/files/eu-indo-pacific_factsheet_2021-09_final.pdf.
7. The White House, "Joint Leaders Statement on AUKUS," Press release, September 15, 2021. https://www.whitehouse.gov/briefing-room/statements-releases/2021/09/15/joint-leaders-statement-on-aukus/.
8. Stephen Lovegrove, "Sir Stephen Lovegrove Speech at the Council on Geostrategy," Cabinet Office, September 16, 2021. https://www.gov.uk/government/speeches/sir-stephen-lovegrove-speech-at-the-council-on-geostrategy.
9. Mahima Duggal, "France, Indo-Pacific Outlook and AUKUS Tensions: Assessing India's Position," Centre for Air Power Studies, November 11, 2021. https://capsindia.org/france-indo-pacific-outlook-and-aukus-tensions-assessing-indias-position/.
10. The White House, "Quad Leaders' Joint Statement: 'The Spirit of the Quad'," Press release, March 12, 2021. https://www.whitehouse.gov/briefing-room/statements-releases/2021/03/12/quad-leaders-joint-statement-the-spirit-of-the-quad/.
11. C. Raja Mohan, "India and the Indo-Pacific: Trade, Aid and Security," panel discussion event, Brookings Institution, December 12, 2018. https://www.brookings.edu/events/india-and-the-indo-pacific-trade-aid-security/.
12. Garima Mohan, "Assessing the EU's New Indo-Pacific Strategy," LSE, September 24, 2021, https://blogs.lse.ac.uk/europpblog/2021/09/24/assessing-the-eus-new-indo-pacific-strategy/. Also see Garima Mohan, *A European Approach to the Indo-Pacific?* (Berlin: Global Public Policy Institute, December 2019). https://www.gppi.net/media/Mohan_2019_A_European_Approach_To_The_Indo_Pacific_final.pdf.
13. n. 3.
14. Ibid.
15. The Glasgow Climate Pact was concluded at the COP21 in 2021. See UN Climate Change Conference, *COP26 The Glasgow Climate Pact* (Glasgow: UK Government, 2021). https://ukcop26.org/wp-content/uploads/2021/11/COP26-Presidency-Outcomes-The-Climate-Pact.pdf.

16. n. 3.
17. Ibid.
18. Ursula Von der Leyen "Special Address at the World Economic Forum Annual Meeting 2020," January 22, 2020. World Economic Forum, Davos, Sweden, video, 1:14, https://www.youtube.com/watch?v=hZBjwMQhL0k.
19. The European Green Deal was first presented in December 2019, with the tools to deliver it announced in July 2021. See "Communication From the Commission: The European Green Deal," European Commission, December 11, 2019. https://eur-lex.europa.eu/legal-content/EN/TXT/?qid=1588580774040&uri=CELEX:52019DC0640; "Delivering the European Green Deal," European Commission, January 7, 2021. https://ec.europa.eu/info/strategy/priorities-2019-2024/european-green-deal/delivering-european-green-deal_en.
20. Directorate-General for Climate Action, "The EU and Japan Commit to a New Green Alliance to Work Towards Climate Neutrality," European Commission, May 27, 2021. https://ec.europa.eu/clima/news-your-voice/news/eu-and-japan-commit-new-green-alliance-work-towards-climate-neutrality-2021-05-27_en.
21. European Union, *Regulation (EU) 2021/947 of the European Parliament and of the Council of 9 June 2021 establishing the Neighbourhood, Development and International Cooperation Instrument—Global Europe, amending and repealing Decision No 466/2014/EU and repealing Regulation (EU) 2017/1601 and Council Regulation (EC, Euratom) No 480/2009,* Official Journal of the European Union L209/1, June 14, 2021. https://eur-lex.europa.eu/eli/reg/2021/947/oj.
22. Premesha Saha, "What does an EU Indo-Pacific Strategy Entail?," Observer Research Foundation, September 17, 2021. https://www.orfonline.org/expert-speak/what-does-an-eu-indo-pacific-strategy-entail/.
23. See reports like: Philippe Le Corre, "On China's Expanding Influence in Europe and Eurasia," testimony before the House of Representatives Foreign Affairs Committee, Carnegie Endowment for International Peace, May 9, 2019. https://carnegieendowment.org/2019/05/09/on-china-s-expanding-influence-in-europe-and-eurasia-pub-79094; Tom Harper, "China's Eurasia: The Belt and Road Initiative and the Creation of a New Eurasian Power," *The Chinese Journal of Global Governance*, 2019, pp. 99-121. http://doi.org/10.1163/23525207-12340039; Serafettin Yilmaz (Yao Shifan) and Liu Changming, "Remaking Eurasia: the Belt and Road Initiative and China-Russia Strategic Partnership," *Asia Europe Journal* 18, 2020, pp. 259-280. https://doi.org/10.1007/s10308-019-00547-1; Daniel S. Markley, *China's Western Horizon: Beijing and the New Geopolitics of Eurasia* (Oxford: Oxford Scholarship Online, 2020). https://doi.org/10.1093/oso/9780190680190.001.0001; Erik Brattberg, Philippe Le Corre, Paul Stronski, and Thomas De Waal, "China's Influence in Southeastern Central, and Eastern Europe: Vulnerabilities and Resilience in Four Countries," China's Impact on Strategic Regions, Carnegie Endowment for International Peace, October 13, 2021. https://carnegieendowment.org/2021/10/13/china-

s-influence-in-southeastern-central-and-eastern-europe-vulnerabilities-and-resilience-in-four-countries-pub-85415.

24. The EU first identified China as a 'systemic rival' in a March 2019 EU strategy document, which marked a turning point in their ties. See European Commission and High Representative of the Union for Foreign Affairs and Security Policy, *Joint Communication to the European Parliament, the European Council and the Council: EU-China—A Strategic Outlook* (Brussels: European External Action Service, March 12, 2019). https://ec.europa.eu/info/sites/default/files/communication-eu-china-a-strategic-outlook.pdf.
25. Philippe Le Corre and Erik Brattberg, "How the Coronavirus Pandemic Shattered Europe's Illusions of China," Carnegie Endowment for International Peace, July 9, 2020. https://carnegieendowment.org/2020/07/09/how-coronavirus-pandemic-shattered-europe-s-illusions-of-china-pub-82265.
26. European Commission, "Global Gateway: Up to €300 Billion for the European Union's Strategy to Boost Sustainable Links Around the World," Press release, December 1, 2021. https://ec.europa.eu/commission/presscorner/detail/en/ip_21_6433.
27. See David Hutt, "CEIAS Considers: Can EU's Global Gateway Compete with China's BRI?," Central European Institute of Asian Studies, December 6, 2021. https://ceias.eu/ceias-considers-can-eus-global-gateway-compete-with-chinas-bri/; Andreea Brinza, "The Global Gateway Joins the Competition Against the BRI," *China Observers,* December 1, 2021, https://chinaobservers.eu/the-global-gateway-joins-the-competition-against-the-bri/.
28. n. 26.
29. 'Debt trap' diplomacy refers to offering of financing or loans with unsustainable conditions attached that make it too difficult for the borrowing countries to repay. This ensnares them in a trap, which forces them to make political or economic concessions. See Brahma Chellaney, "China's Debt-Trap Diplomacy," Project Syndicate, January 23, 2017. https://www.project-syndicate.org/commentary/china-one-belt-one-road-loans-debt-by-brahma-chellaney-2017-01.
30. Office of the Spokesperson, US Department of State, "EU-US: Joint Press Release by the EEAS and Department of State on the High-Level Consultations on the Indo-Pacific," Press release, December 3, 2021. https://www.state.gov/eu-u-s-joint-press-release-by-the-eeas-and-department-of-state-on-the-high-level-consultations-on-the-indo-pacific/.
31. Ministère de l'Europe et des Affaires étrangères, *The Indo-Pacific Region: A Priority for France* (Paris: Directorate for Asia and Oceania, France Diplomacy, updated April 2021). https://www.diplomatie.gouv.fr/en/country-files/asia-and-oceania/the-indo-pacific-region-a-priority-for-france/.
32. Federal Foreign Office of Germany, *Germany-Europe-Asia: Shaping the 21st Century Together: The German Government Adopts Policy Guidelines on the Indo-Pacific Region* (Berlin: Federal Foreign Office, September 1, 2020). https://www.auswaertiges-

amt.de/blob/2380514/f9784f7e3b3fa1bd7c5446d274a4169e/200901-indo-pazifik-leitlinien--1--data.pdf.

33. Ministry of Foreign Affairs, Indo-Pacific: Guidelines for Strengthening Dutch and EU Cooperation with Partners in Asia, AVT/BZ-201002-011A. The Hague: Ministry of Foreign Affairs, November 2020. https://www.government.nl/binaries/government/documents/publications/2020/11/13/indo-pacific-guidelines/Indo-Pacific+Guidelines+EN.pdf.
34. For a detailed study on the similarities and differences between the French and German approaches, see Felix Heiduk and Nedim Sulejmanovic, "Will the EU Take View of the Indo-Pacific? Comparing France's and Germany's Approaches," Working Paper NR. 01, Research Division Asia, Siftung Wissenschaft und Politik (SWP), January 2021. https://www.swp-berlin.org/publications/products/arbeitspapiere/WP_EU_Indopacific_Heiduk_Sulejmanovic.pdf; Gudrun Wacker, "Europe and the Indo-Pacific: Comparing France, Germany and the Netherlands," ARI 9/2021, Real Instituto Elcano, March 9, 2021. http://www.realinstitutoelcano.org/wps/portal/rielcano_en/contenido?WCM_GLOBAL_CONTEXT=/elcano/elcano_in/zonas_in/asia-pacific/ari29-2021-wacker-europe-and-the-indo-pacific-comparing-france-germany-and-the-netherlands.
35. On France's stake in the Indo-Pacific, see Mahima Duggal, "France's Indo-Pacific Strategy in 2021: Characteristics, Capabilities, Challenges and Opportunities," *Air Power Journal*, 16, No. 4, Winter 2021, pp. 121-149.
36. Max J. Zenglein, "Mapping and Recalibrating Europe's Economic Interdependence with China," *China Monitor*, Mercator Institute for China Studies, November 17, 2020. https://merics.org/en/report/mapping-and-recalibrating-europes-economic-interdependence-china.
37. Rohan Sinha and Stefan Talmon, "Germany Confirms Non-Recognition of the Republic of China (Taiwan)," Universitat Bonn, December 18, 2019. https://gpil.jura.uni-bonn.de/2019/12/germany-confirms-non-recognition-of-the-republic-of-china-taiwan/.
38. Ruairi Casey, "In Germany, Debate on Trade with China Grows as Merkel Nears Exit," *Al Jazeera*, September 17, 2021. https://www.aljazeera.com/news/2021/9/17/in-germany-debate-on-trade-with-china-grows-as-merkel-nears-exit.
39. Jules Darmanin and Zoya Sheftalovich, "'Stab in the Back': France Slams Australia, US Over Move to Ditch 50B EUR Submarine Deal," *Politico*, September 16, 2021, https://www.politico.eu/article/france-slams-australia-us-e50b- submarine-deal/.
40. The White House, "Remarks by President Biden, Prime Minister Morrison of Australia, and Prime Minister Johnson of the United Kingdom Announcing the Creation of AUKUS," speech, September 15, 2021. https://www.whitehouse.gov/briefing-room/speeches-remarks/2021/09/15/remarks-by-president-biden-prime-minister-morrison-of-australia-and-prime-minister-johnson-of-the-united-kingdom-announcing-the-creation-of-aukus/.

41. Zsuzsa Anna Ferenczy, "The EU and AUKUS: The View from Brussels," in Niklas Swantröm and Jagannath Panda, eds., *AUKUS: Resetting European Thinking on the Indo-Pacific?* (Stöckholm: Institute for Security and Development Policy, October 2021). https://isdp.eu/content/uploads/2021/10/AUKUS-Resetting-European-Thinking-on-the-Indo-Pacific-9.11.21.pdf.
42. Joseph Borrell, "United Nations General Assembly: One Week in New York," Europe External Action Service, September 25, 2021. https://eeas.europa.eu/headquarters/headquarters-homepage/104654/united-nations-general-assembly-one-week-new-york_en.
43. Eleanor Mears and Girgio Leali, "EU-China Investment Deal hits a Snag as US Exerts Pressure," *Politico,* December 22, 2020. https://www.politico.eu/article/eu-china-investment-deal-no-show-us-forced-labor/.
44. Nicholas Vinocur, "Why Europe's China Deal will Poison Transatlantic Relations," *Politico,* January 14, 2021. https://www.politico.eu/article/why-europe-china-investment-deal-will-poison-transatlantic-relations-joe-biden/.
45. Joseph R. Biden, "Why America Must Lead Again," *Foreign Affairs,* March/April 2020. https://www.foreignaffairs.com/articles/united-states/2020-01-23/why-america-must-lead-again.
46. Patrick Wintour, "Aukus Deal Showing France and EU that Biden is not all That he Seems," *The Guardian,* September 16, 2021. https://www.theguardian.com/world/2021/sep/16/aukus-deal-showing-france-and-eu-that-biden-not-all-he-seems.
47. Ibid.
48. *Ministère de l'Europe et des Affaires étrangères*, "Inaugural Australia-France 2+2 Ministerial Consultations: Joint Statement," *France Diplomacy*, August 30, 2021. https://www.diplomatie.gouv.fr/IMG/pdf/210830_-_australia-france_2_2-_joint_statement_cle4a1241.pdf.
49. For a note on recent discussions on the topic, see "The EU Strategic Autonomy Debate," briefing, European Parliament, March 30, 2021. https://www.europarl.europa.eu/RegData/etudes/BRIE/2021/690532/EPRS_BRI(2021)690532_EN.pdf.
50. Although, European countries spend over €223 billion on defence annually, its output in this regard has remained somewhat stagnant amid poor efforts on inter-Europe cooperation outside NATO on defence matters. While initiatives like Permanent Structured Cooperation have been launched to this end, they presently lack direction and have shown little progress. See EDA, Defence Data 2017-2018. Key Findings and Analysis, December 16, 2019. https://www.eda.europa.eu/info-hub/publications/publication-details/pub/defence-data-2017-2018; Dick Zandee, "More European Military Capabilities for a More Autonomous Europe," Ester Sabatino, Daniel Fiott, Dick Zandee, Christian Mölling, Claudia Major, Jean-Pierre Maulny, Daniel Keohane and Domenico Moro, eds., *The Quest for European Strategic Autonomy—A Collective*

Reflection (Rome: Instituto Affari Internazionli, December 2020). https://www.clingendael.org/sites/default/files/2020-12/_IAI_Quest_ESA_2020_0.pdf.

51. David Hutt, "EU's New Indo-Pacific Strategy: What are the Objectives and Challenges?," *DW,* September 17, 2021. https://www.dw.com/en/eus-new-indo-pacific-strategy-what-are-the-objectives-and-challenges/a-59210529.
52. "German Foreign Minister Urges EU-US Cooperation in Indo-Pacific," *DW,* September 23, 2021. https://www.dw.com/en/german-foreign-minister-urges-eu-us-cooperation-in-indo-pacific/a-59287758.
53. "France Takes Over EU Presidency with Push for 'Strategic Autonomy'," *DW*, January 1, 2022. https://www.dw.com/en/france-takes-over-eu-presidency-with-push-for-strategic-autonomy/a-60308915.
54. "Biden: We were Clumsy over France Submarine Row," *BBC,* October 29, 2021. https://www.bbc.com/news/world-us-canada-59085806.
55. See Article 3 of: European Union, *Charter of Fundamental Rights of the European Union,* Official Journal of the European Union 2012/C 326/02, October 26, 2012. https://eur-lex.europa.eu/legal-content/EN/TXT/?uri=celex:12012P/TXT.
56. "Aims and Values," European Union. Accessed January 20, 2022. https://european-union.europa.eu/principles-countries-history/principles-and-values/aims-and-values_en. Also see Article 3 of the Lisbon Treaty: European Union, *Treaty of Lisbon Amending the Treaty on European Union and the Treaty Establishing the European Community*, Official Journal of the European Union 2007/C 306/01, December 17, 2007, https://eur-lex.europa.eu/legal-content/EN/ALL/?uri=OJ%3AC%3A2007%3A306%3ATOC.
57. On the EU's normative power, see Ian Manners, "Normative Power Europe: A Contradiction in Terms?," *Journal of Common Market Studies* 40, No. 2, 2002, pp. 235-258. https://doi.org/10.1111/1468-5965.00353.
58. Raffaella A. Del Sarto, "Normative Empire Europe: The European Union, its Borderlands, and the 'Arab Spring'," *Journal of Common Market Studies,* 54, No. 2, 2016, pp. 215-232, DOI: 10.1111/jcms.12282.
59. Joseph Yeh, "Minister Praises Lithuania for 'Moral Courage' in Allowing Taiwan to Open Office," *Focus Taiwan,* November 22, 2021. https://focustaiwan.tw/politics/202111220010.
60. See interview with Lithuania's Foreign Minister, Gabrielius Landsbergis: Anthony Faiola, "Lithuania is Learning the Cost of Standing up to China. Without EU Backing, it may be Forced to Sit Back Down.," *The Washington Post,* January 14, 2022. https://www.washingtonpost.com/world/2022/01/14/lithuania-china-foreign-minister-landsbergis/.
61. Ibid.
62. Katharina Rosskopf and Milda Seputyte, "Europe Seeks United Front in Lithuania's Trade Feud With China," *Bloomberg,* January 14, 2022. https://

www.bloomberg.com/news/articles/2022-01-14/europe-seeks-united-front-in-lithuania-s-trade-feud-with-china.

63. Mahima Duggal, "China's Frantic Scramble for 'Common Prosperity': Premise, Promises and Problems," Organisation for Research on China and Asia, September 30, 2021. https://orcasia.org/chinas-frantic-scramble-for-common-prosperity-premise-promises-and-problems/.
64. Mark Scott, Laura Kayali and Laurens Cerulus, "European Commission Accuses China of Peddling Disinformation," *Politico*, June 10, 2020. https://www.politico.eu/article/european-commission-disinformation-china- coronavirus/.
65. The highway project, initiated in 2014 under the BRI through a Chinese contractor, concerns a 25-mile section of the 270-mile highway that remains incomplete as of 2021 and is expected to have little utility. Montenegro expects the loan for the project will sink the country into debt for several generations to come; if it is unable to pay back the loan on time, the Chinese state-owned bank will have the right to seize land in Montenegro. See Rob Schmitz, "How a Chinese-Built Highway Drove Montenegro Deep Into Debt," *NPR*, June 29, 2021, https://www.npr.org/2021/06/28/1010832606/road-deal-with-china-is-blamed-for-catapulting-montenegro-into-historic-debt.
66. Laura Silver, Kat Devlin and Christine Huang, "Unfavourable Views of China Reach Historic Highs in Many Countries," Pew Research Centre, October 6, 2020, https://www.pewresearch.org/global/2020/10/06/unfavorable-views-of-china-reach-historic-highs-in-many-countries/.
67. Laura Silver, Kat Devlin and Christine Huang, "Large Majorities Say China Does Not Respect the Personal Freedoms of Its People," Pew Research Centre, June 30, 2021, https://www.pewresearch.org/global/2021/06/30/large-majorities-say-china-does-not-respect-the-personal-freedoms-of-its-people/.
68. Kay-Achim Schonbach, "Germany's Indo Pacific Strategy," January 21, 2022, video, talk by Vice Admiral Kay-Achim Schonbach, Chief of the German Navy, Manohar Parrikar Institute for Defence Studies and Analyses (MP-IDSA), https://www.youtube.com/watch?v=ODmkoGQw1TU.
69. "Xinhua Commentary: Stronger China-Germany Partnership for a Better World," *Xinhua*, December 22, 2021, http://www.xinhuanet.com/english/20211015/C9A4B2E98350000121BF1A301E60AF20/c.html.
70. "About IONS," IONS, updated June 24, 2021, https://www.ions.global.
71. Wacker, n. 34.
72. Ferenczy, n. 41.
73. Frédéric Grare and Manisha Reuter, "Moving Closer: European Views of the Indo-Pacific," European Council on Foreign Relations, September 13, 2021, https://ecfr.eu/special/moving-closer-european-views-of-the-indo-pacific/.
74. Ibid.
75. Nayanima Basu, "India's Importance Getting More Obvious, New Govt Won't Change Ties: Germany Envoy Lindner," *The Print*, September 27, 2021, https://

theprint.in/diplomacy/indias-importance-getting-more-obvious-new-govt-wont-change-ties-german-envoy-lindner/741305/.

76. Federal Foreign Office, "Germany and India: Bilateral Relations," September 16, 2021, https://www.auswaertiges-amt.de/en/aussenpolitik/india/218838.
77. "France to Work with India to Promote 'Truly Multilateral' Order," *Al Jazeera,* September 18, 2021. https://www.aljazeera.com/news/2021/9/18/france-work-with-india-promote-truly-multilateral-order.
78. "EU Wants India to Join in Financing Initiative for Indo-Pacific to Counter China: French Diplomat," February 2, 2022. https://economictimes.indiatimes.com/news/defence/eu-wants-india-to-join-in-financing-initiative-for-indo-pacific-to-counter-china-french-diplomat/articleshow/89303126.cms.
79. Dattesh D. Parulekar, "India-Nordic Engagement: A Veritable Strategic Partnership in Reimagine and Configure," Institute for Security and Development Policy, September 2021. https://isdp.eu/content/uploads/2021/09/India-Nordic-Engagement-FA-07.09.21.pdf.
80. S. Jaishankar, *The India Way: Strategies for an Uncertain World* (New Delhi: HarperCollins, 2020), p. 10.
81. "How Estonia Became a Global Heavyweight in Cyber Security," e-Estonia, June 14, 2017. https://e-estonia.com/how-estonia-became-a-global-heavyweight-in-cyber-security/; Damien McGuinness, "How a Cyber Attack Transformed Estonia," April 27, 2017. https://www.bbc.com/news/39655415.
82. Sneha Kulkarni, "Digital Rupee to be Introduced by the RBI: Budget 2022," *The Economic Times,* February 2, 2022. https://economictimes.indiatimes.com/wealth/personal-finance-news/digital-rupee-to-be-introduced-by-the-rbi-budget-2022/articleshow/89267150.cms.
83. "Eurosystem Launches Digital Euro Project," Press release, European Central Bank, July 14, 2021. https://www.ecb.europa.eu/press/pr/date/2021/html/ecb.pr210714~d99198ea23.en.html.
84. Mahima Duggal, "The Dawn of the Digital Yuan: China's Central Bank Digital Currency and Its Implications," Institute for Security and Development Policy, June 2021. https://isdp.eu/publication/the-dawn-of-the-digital-yuan/.
85. n. 78.

14. Making Capital of Quad Plus

Jagannath Panda

Emerging as a need-of-the-hour mechanism in response to the 'black swan'[1] COVID-19 pandemic, the abstract Quad Plus grouping has remained a point of strategic conjecture. Under the umbrella of the Quadrilateral Security Dialogue (Quad)—comprising the US, India, Japan and Australia—the idea of the Quad Plus originated as an extended version of the Quad framework, with doubt over its potential materialisation into a more concrete grouping. However, with developments in the Quad itself including the release of formal joint statements and a leaders' summit, revisiting the Quad Plus framework becomes significant.

As the Quad itself becomes an institutionalised part of Indo-Pacific diplomacy, the Quad Plus framework has been left behind as a momentary vector. At the height of the pandemic in 2020, it was the inclusion of New Zealand, South Korea, and Vietnam in the then weekly Quad meetings of Foreign Ministry officials, initiated[2] by former US Deputy Secretary of State Stephen Biegun in March 2020, that marked the beginnings of the Quad Plus mechanism. This was followed by a higher-level meeting organised[3] by former US Secretary of State Mike Pompeo in May 2020, which saw the further addition of Brazil and Israel, indicating grander global strategic intent. The Quad Plus emerged with the aim to discuss an international response to the pandemic. However, in the post-COVID order, the scope for cooperation and convergence among the 'Quad Plus' nations emerges as a geopolitical reality. As highlighted in the joint statement of the Quad, the world's "shared futures will be written in the Indo-Pacific" and the grouping seeks to now "not only deepen our cooperation in these critical areas, but we will broaden it to new ones".[4]

Framing the Quad Plus

The Quad Plus grouping can be framed best as a 'conjectural alliance'[5] that imbibes universalism, the rule of law, democratic ideals with free and open maritime domains. Ultimately, the idea of the 'Quad Plus' is a minilateral engagement in the Indo-Pacific that draws from the Quad to include other crucial emerging economies. At the same time, it offers a multipolar lens through which we can view, analyse and assess the strategic multilateral growth of the nations involved. Hence, it is not necessary to view the Quad Plus as an extension of the Quad; while the former has largely focussed on creating a cooperative framework to tackle pandemic induced economic and public health concerns, the Quad has remained a dialogue that has looked at maritime, technological, infrastructural and health challenges through the lens of security. Concurrently, the need to view the 'Plus' framework in isolation is equally incorrect, especially post the release of the "Spirit of the Quad"[6], which highlighted the Quad's own growing focus on avenues such as global health, vaccination, infrastructure, critical technologies and climate.

Rather, it becomes important to view the Quad Plus as a format that can bridge the gap between the Quad and the world. As the Quad's admission remains—defined and restricted within its namesake as well—limited to the four founding members, the 'Quad Plus' allows them a platform to link with other emerging powers and ventures in the region on an extended (rotational) attachment basis. Such outreach would provide an amalgamation of the East and the West within the Quad's famous 'like-minded' dimension, providing a linking of major, middle and developing powers together. The 'Quad Plus' would further the Quad's pluralistic outlook and inclusive nature by building a participatory framework that allows for shared leadership and distribution of power on avenues like health, infrastructure, climate and technology, linking to the Quad's new working groups[7] as well. The pandemic has been a devastating event, yet a crucial indicator that regional and global issues cannot be solved by a small grouping of countries, such as the Quad alone. Areas such as critical technology, vaccine expertise, sustainable climate-oriented action, blue economy, financial connectivity and supply chain strengthening are vital avenues of cooperation between the Quad (and its overtures) and the

Quad Plus, and they require cooperation[8] among as many countries as possible. The Quad Plus framework would also help serve as a framework against the common security threats[9] that many regional countries see in China and North Korea, but are unable to challenge on a bilateral basis, for example, New Zealand.

Such cooperation can be furthered multilaterally, bilaterally and within trilaterals. For instance, with the addition of Vietnam as a 'Plus' country, multiple avenues of cooperation emerged such as the creation of an India-Japan-Vietnam trilateral in the post-COVID order; multilateralism driven inculcation with the Supply Chain Resilience Initiative (SCRI)[10] and the strengthening of the specific bilateral relationships.[11] For example, strengthened India-Vietnam ties under the aegis of Quad Plus would draw on the Association of Southeast Asian Nations' (ASEAN's) centrality,[12] capacity building and connectivity outreach to create a post-COVID supply chain network that is 'inclusive'.[13] As actors such as the UK and Europe look towards supply chain diversification with a focus on Asia, the SCRI-Quad Plus connect is one that must be developed with strategic determination. The UK's Global Britain[14] and the European Union's (EU's) new Global Gateway[15]—as both London[16] and Brussels[17] launch their individual Indo-Pacific driven strategies—will find in the Quad Plus a valuable partner that will allow them a seat at the table. The basis of the potential formalisation of the framework will be via rotational membership and building their entry into the Asian markets by finding a trilateral with the Quad Plus and SCRI via their specific Indo-Pacific focussed initiatives.

While the Quad is often perceived to be a coalition of democracies driven by the US to contain China and preserve the US' hegemonic status in the regional order, the Quad Plus is unlikely be an extension of this. Rather, the essence of the Quad Plus is to preserve the existing rules-based, liberal international order and promote multipolarity in the Indo-Pacific. In contrast to the Quad 2.0, it will focus less on the idea of upholding 'democratic values', which are not only much harder to define[18], but their weight would immediately isolate and challenge China on many fronts, such as with regards to human rights issues in Xinjiang, which members will be cautious to do. If democratic principles were to be a criterion for inclusion within the Quad Plus, the grouping would likely lose members such as Vietnam, which participated heavily in the Quad Plus framework while it was utilised during the pandemic. Instead the Quad Plus framework may represent a grouping of 'like-minded' countries, Eastern and Western, developed and developing, which are committed to preserving the status quo and wish to reinforce the liberal order in the Indo-Pacific.

By going beyond the China trope while accepting realistic national security threats, a 'Quad Plus' system allows the participating nations to create a strategic alignment that might indicate a growing, or temporary, embrace of a US-led order in the Indo-Pacific region while still not becoming part of a set 'alliance framework'. It is important to remember that it was the COVID-19 pandemic that catalysed the forming a 'Quad Plus' mechanism, with the inclusion of countries like South Korea, New Zealand and Vietnam being supported due to their success in handling the pandemic within their borders.[19] The emergence of the 'Quad Plus' dialogue as China-centric is not a goal that most of the participating nations would like to openly espouse, with almost all the participating nations having elaborate economic ties with Beijing. Regardless of the fact that nations are aiming to create newer, more sustainable and diversified supply chains and that economic ties with China have witnessed a redaction in the post-COVID order, China remains deeply embedded within the world economy, with globalisation here to stay.[20] Hence, tagging the Quad Plus as a China-centric framework is not conducive to the grouping's growth. This temporary alignment with the US is unlikely to shift the focus of the framework towards a China-centric dialogue, nor an anti-China alliance, and, thus, the Quad Plus would remain a pillar to reinforce the liberal international order.

In many ways, the Quad Plus can fill a gap that the Quad has failed to cover; it can build on the Quad's work by projecting a truly holistic approach, thereby strengthening its rules-based inclusivity outlook. It can also provide the link that delineates the structural limitations of the SCRI which requires, at present, linkage with other economic initiatives to truly reach its full potential—and enables a partial decoupling from China in the globalised world order by creating a sense of collective economic security.[21] Vis-à-vis the Quad's own China angle, while the grouping has not imbibed an overtly anti-China outlook, its focus on limiting China's aggression across the region is clear, both as a grouping and via the members' individual foreign policies. With regards to the 'multipolar Asia' proposition, the 'Quad Plus' would also emerge as a variable that can manoeuvre the contours of the US-China rivalry and prevent a Thucydides Trap creation.[22] For instance, with meticulous implementation and the recognition of China's role as a key economic actor in the globalised world order, the Quad Plus rotational association could potentially also make room for Beijing, providing a much needed new and modern avenue of dialogue between the US and China in the presence of Asian economies, as they fight over the future of dominance in Asia and the Indo-Pacific.

How Quad Members View 'Quad Plus'

The implementation of national initiatives by Quad partners has enhanced the sphere of influence they wield individually and as a grouping in the Indo-Pacific. By way of the Quad Plus narrative, an expansion of the outreach of ventures like Japan's Expanded Partnership for Quality Infrastructure (EPQI), US-led Group of Seven (G7) venture 'Build Back Better World' (B3W), India's Indo-Pacific Oceans Initiative (IPOI), SCRI and Australia's Pacific Step-Up can and must be promoted with countries like Vietnam, New Zealand, Brazil, Israel, South Korea and further 'Plus' state additions. Furthermore, in the aftermath of the Australia-UK-US (AUKUS)[23] partnership's blow to trans-Atlantic ties and Europe's growing demands for strategic autonomy[24], the 'Quad Plus' emerges as an expansion—not necessarily extension—of the Quad, permitting the creation of a "continental connect" and "corridor of communication" that will allow independent and direct links to the Asian economies for the EU, beyond a US-led entry.[25]

Japan: Quad Plus as Promoting FOIP

Japan views the Quad Plus with great potential to promote Tokyo's view of the Free and Open Indo-Pacific (FOIP). Former Prime Minister Abe

Shinzo developed a strategic vision of the Indo-Pacific and the role that the regional democracies of Japan, India and Australia, plus the US, would have to play in defending freedom, peace and stability in the region.[26] Although Abe's launch of 'FOIP' pre-dated the Trump Administration's Indo-Pacific policy released in 2017, the similarities in their visions have contributed to the strong relationship that Japan and the US share. The relationship is largely a consequence of the high threat perception that Tokyo and Washington share of Asian powers such as China and North Korea, and is why Japan considers the US an indispensable security ally to secure its national interests. Overall, Japan's feeling of 'ownership' of the FOIP has led the country to undergo a fundamental shift from security bilateralism to security multilateralism,[27] in order to use frameworks such as the Quad to preserve the rules-based order. Current Prime Minister Fumio Kishida appears to be continuing the policies of Abe,[28] but with an understanding that there is a limit to the extent that the Quad alone is able to promote FOIP. While the extent of Kishida's foreign policy is yet to be uncovered, thus far it bodes well for the facilitation of Japanese diplomatic engagement within the Quad Plus. Kishida has vowed to strengthen Quad cooperation to achieve FOIP,[29] an unsurprising sign of the continuation of Abe's foreign policy legacy, considering Kishida's history of earlier holding the post of foreign minister. It has led to Japan's support to the expansion of the Quad through the Quad Plus framework. Abe was clear that he wanted the Quad to partner with states that share similar views of the international order so that the objective of the Quad Plus would always be the maintenance of a rules-based order in the Indo-Pacific, and not become an anti-China coalition. For example, Japan has indicated that the UK and France would be good candidates for the Quad Plus because their Indo-Pacific strategies align with that of Tokyo. Japan has also vocalised support for alignment between the Quad and ASEAN[30]—endorsing the ASEAN outlook on the Indo-Pacific, and promoting ASEAN centrality—thus, opening the door for the ASEAN's and ASEAN member states' involvement with the Quad Plus.

Australia: Quad Plus as Enhancing Inclusivity

Australia's attitude towards the Quad Plus has been positive, promoting inclusivity and a wider grouping with the same commitment to the Indo-Pacific construct that Canberra endorses separately. Australia was largely blamed for the break-up of the Quad 1.0 because it was not willing to compromise its relations with China. However, in the interim years, before the formation of the Quad 2.0, Australia became increasingly aware of China's assertive behaviour and embraced the construct of the FOIP. China's rather aggressive economic coercion tactics only pushed bilateral ties to an all-time low. During this time, Australia also strengthened its partnerships with fellow Quad members. For example, in January 2022, Australia and Japan signed a 'breakthrough'[31] defence pact to enhance their security ties against the backdrop of China's rising aggression. The COVID-19 pandemic has also been considered a wake-up call to the coercive behaviour Beijing is capable of projecting and targeting on individual economies with lasting effect, and is a contributing factor to why Canberra encourages the inclusion of other regional actors in the Quad.[32] Effectively, Australia feels that the Quad Plus will be a step towards a wider acceptance of the Indo-Pacific construct, and appears to be welcoming the inclusion of the Republic of Korea, Vietnam and New Zealand because of the strong relationships it already shares with these countries.

US: Quad Plus as Addressing the China Challenge

While the Biden-Harris Administration began with a reversal of many Trump-era policies, it has chosen to continue to view China and the Indo-Pacific with the same stance and vigour. To the US, the Quad is foundational to American policy[33] in the Indo-Pacific and it views it as its primary security framework[34] in the region, which is why it has been the Quad member that has most forcefully pushed to use it as an 'anti-China' group. This mindset has led China to view the Biden's Administration as adopting a 'Cold War'[35] like stance towards ensuring the containment of China. Trump's Administration focussed on investing in like-minded partners in the Indo-Pacific that would help the US hold China accountable and promote a rules-based order. Stemming from this policy, the Quad Plus framework is, thus, a way to develop further coalitions[36] and strengthen the Quad's ability to preserve the liberal international order, which is why the Biden Administration views the Quad Plus as a positive prospect. The US initiated the Quad Plus efforts in 2020 in response to the global security concerns of the COVID-19 pandemic, but it was also motivated to mobilise the Indo-Pacific states around the US' leadership by incentivising them to address concerns over China. For example, with regard to economic decoupling with China, the US is trying to promote moving production out of China and wants other countries to follow suit especially after the supply chain concerns that the pandemic revealed. The Quad Plus umbrella could act as a way for its members to diversify their supply chains away from China and work together to strengthen their respective presence within the framework of global supply chains. While decoupling from the Chinese economy is the first step towards avoiding being hit by a full-scale supply chain crisis for the US, engaging with other manufacturing nations through the set-up of the Quad Plus would be the ideal next step towards diversifying its supply chain routes.

Overall, worsening perceptions of China have led the Quad members to recognise the potential that the Quad Plus holds to achieve their objectives and they have, therefore, come to align with the US. For the US, the Quad Plus represents a way to reinvigorate its hegemonic power in the Indo-Pacific and presents an avenue to challenge the growing narrative[37] of the US' decline.

India: Quad Plus for Greater Regional Outreach

The Quad Plus framework complements India's Indo-Pacific vision and is thus, viewed as a format worth pursuing. New Delhi has expressed its view of a free, open and inclusive Indo-Pacific and particularly that it wishes to harness it as an opportunity to expand its presence[38] in the region, in the context of its capability constraints. India's main focus, however, continues to revolve around the Indian Ocean; building a thriving 'blue economy'[39] and ensuring regional security and prosperity. The Quad 2.0 has fallen under India's 'pointed alignment strategy',[40] to build partnerships with like-minded countries in order to enhance India's power by pooling resources and capabilities to face transnational challenges in the

Indo-Pacific and its own strategic interests. Unlike its other Quad partners, India has chosen to pursue a balancing policy within the Indo-Pacific, attempting to focus on regional inclusivity and not isolating China, whilst enhancing partnerships. India's 'pluralistic' approach has made it cautious of the 'China-centric' element of the Quad pushed by the US, and the perception of the grouping becoming an 'Asian NATO'.

First, India's Indo-Pacific strategy indicates compatibility with the Quad Plus framework in regard to promoting an inclusive, 'multi-polar Asia'.[41] The Quad Plus is an opportunity for New Delhi to further strengthen its alignment with countries that adhere to the same view of the Indo-Pacific as India: rules-based, democratic, free and open. Not only would it deepen the ties that India shares with the Quad 2.0 partners, strengthening defence, economic and security prospects in the process, but it would also promote new ones with partners such as Vietnam and South Korea. The Quad Plus mechanism would be an ideal platform to enable India to pursue its goals of asserting strategic autonomy, especially within the realm of being considered a key emerging power to partner with in the Indo-Pacific. A Quad Plus framework would further enable pointed alignment for India with countries such as Israel, Brazil, New Zealand and Vietnam. Despite increased bilateral ties with India and the respective powers, expanded multilateral engagement could further defence, economic and political collaboration, which currently leaves much to be desired. Specifically, in the defence sector, increased synergy between India and partners such as Israel and France would help further initiatives such as "Make in India".[42] Enhancing strategic autonomy through the avenue of the Quad Plus will enable India to position its interests well within multilateral institutions currently overcome by great power rivalry. Engaging with the Quad Plus powers will, in turn, cement India's position as a key strategic partner within a multipolar world order.

Additionally, Quad Plus could complement the modified approach[43] that India has adopted towards China post the Galwan Valley clash in 2020. The skirmish has led to India recognising China as more of a challenger and competitor than a partner, and has, therefore, influenced New Delhi's foreign policy to focus on further strengthening India's capabilities. This has already started to occur with regard to the Quad, in the form of embracing stronger military, economic and security ties with partners. This could also be promoted and developed through frameworks like the Quad Plus. India will be looking to retain its multilateral ventures alongside China [Brazil, Russia, India, China, and South Africa (BRICS)], Russia-India-China (RIC), Shanghai Cooperation Organisation (SCO), Asian Infrastructure Investment Bank (AIIB), etc., maintaining its commitment towards working alongside China on certain global governance issues of importance. However, by participating actively with other Quad Plus members on issues of economic importance, China's belief of indispensability vis-à-vis India will reduce.

Identifying Potential Quad Plus Partners

As Quad Plus enters into a new, post-pandemic era, it will undoubtedly look to reinvent itself from being a conjectural alliance to a broader forum involving other key, like-minded powers. Strategic consultations with Quad partners are vital for the Quad to play a more effective role in the region and achieve its set objectives in the security, economic and health spheres. In this context, in addition to New Zealand, South Korea, Vietnam, Brazil and Israel, the following states could emerge as potential partners under the Quad Plus format.

UK: Actualising Global Britain's 'Tilt' to the Indo-Pacific

The idea that the UK could become a 'Plus' country and would be a worthy addition to the grouping has been recognised by the Quad members, such as Japan. Although all countries that have been associated with the Quad Plus, thus, far are located within the Indo-Pacific, the UK's geographic location should not discount it as a potential partner. The UK has a keen interest in the Indo-Pacific as well as the potential to be a significant asset to the Quad. Historically, Britain, as a naval superpower, was a guarantor of free and open waters, or *mare liberum*[44] as it was known, and today the UK continues to have a presence in the Indo-Pacific. British military bases such as in Singapore are not simply relics of the Empire but functioning facilities that continue to support the presence of the Royal Navy because the UK has security interests in the region. For example, China's claims in the South China Sea are a threat to the UK's national interests, given that 12 per cent of British trade[45] travels through these waters. Ultimately, the UK has demonstrated its willingness to respond to China's assertive behaviour in these contested waters in a way which could bolster the strength of the Quad Plus and the Quad. In 2018, the UK was the only country aside from the US to challenge China over the Paracel Islands, and more significantly, the HMS *Queen Elizabeth*[46], the most powerful vessel ever constructed by the Royal Navy, is currently on a long-term deployment in the South China Sea to uphold the international rules-based order in the Indo-Pacific. It is also worth noting that the UK is a nuclear power[47] and its addition to the Quad Plus would further serve as an added deterrent against China, alongside the other nuclear powers, the US and India.

It is not only that the UK could offer the Quad Plus military strength, but also that the UK is looking to enhance its presence in the Indo-Pacific. The new national strategy 'Global Britain in a Competitive Age: The Integrated Review of Security, Defence, Development and Foreign Policy' was unveiled in March 2021 and was promised by Prime Minister Boris Johnson[48] to be the "deepest review of Britain's security, defence and foreign policy since the end of the Cold War". The strategy does confirm the UK's 'tilt' towards the Indo-Pacific and highlights its aim to be the "European partner with the broadest and most integrated presence in the Indo-Pacific".[49] It also touches on strengthening dialogue with ASEAN, championing free and fair trade, strengthening defence and security cooperation (particularly maritime), and redirecting the Official Development Assistance (ODA) to achieve its goals in the region.[50] This in particular can be inferred as an attempt to counter China's Belt and Road Initiative (BRI). While there is no explicit mention of the Quad or Quad Plus in the strategy, it does confirm a key strategic goal of the UK to be involved in the Indo-Pacific, and there have been signs elsewhere of the UK's interest to join the framework. For example, remarks[51] from the British high commissioner to India suggested that the UK was open to joining the grouping if membership was ever expanded, adding to which, the UK invited Australia, India and South Korea to join the G7 conference this year.[52] However, a potential setback to the UK joining the Quad Plus may be that there are already other groupings the UK values within the

Indo-Pacific. These include the Five Power Defence Arrangements with Australia, Malaysia, New Zealand and Singapore,[53] and the 'Five Eyes' intelligence sharing alliance with Australia, Canada, New Zealand and the US. The UK has also applied to join the Comprehensive and Progressive Agreement for Trans-Pacific Partnership (CPTPP), and is championing the idea of the 'D10' to replace the G7.[54]

The EU: Projecting EU Presence via Issues-Based Cooperation

The announcements of the Indo-Pacific strategies of EU member states, France and Germany, and subsequently the EU's own strategy, indicate synergy between Europe and the strategic powers in the region. These strategies reveal that the EU and its members are committing more to the Indo-Pacific than ever before,[55] recognising it as both a construct and a geostrategic reality that they must engage with. However, the divergences between the Indo-Pacific strategies of its member states may impede the EU as a whole from becoming a part of the Quad Plus framework and result instead in key individual members states adopting a place.

For example, Germany and France have presented incompatible approaches,[56] making cooperating together under the EU within the Quad Plus framework challenging. Germany's Indo-Pacific guidelines indicate a reluctance to align with the US and a desire to promote inclusivity through cooperation with China. France, however, has a vision for the Indo-Pacific that aligns more closely with that of the Quad members, leading states such as Japan to view Paris as a viable partner. Initially France did not appear interested in the idea of the Quad, believing it to be too antagonistic towards China. However, the idea of the Quad Plus as a cooperative mechanism that has the potential to work on other causes—including matters related to climate change, blue economy and health security—has proved to be more enticing. In April 2021, France looked to be on its way to joining the Quad Plus as relations between France and the Quad members were at an all-time high following the joint naval war games, La Pérouse, held in the Bay of Bengal.[57] This type of exercise with other Quad members held a key strategic message that France wishes to project itself as an important player in the region with the same vision as the Quad, and was a further nudge to other European powers to follow suit.[58]

Since then, however, France's bilateral relations with Quad members, the US and Australia, have been significantly tarnished by the trilateral security partnership, AUKUS, signed in October 2021 among the UK, US and Australia.[59] The French felt betrayed by Australia's decision to join AUKUS and scrap an agreement between them. It may, therefore, take a while before France is again ready to consider being a part of the Quad Plus. France's positioning vis-à-vis the Quad has obscured post the AUKUS snub, considering the fact that the US and Australia are two of the main parties to the grouping. However, through an extended Quad, France may find ways to engage with the key developing powers in the region, not necessarily through a mandate stipulated by the US. The Quad Plus provides an opportunity for smaller powers in the Indo-Pacific to present, and take ownership of, what they can offer to the EU powers looking to collaborate within the region. While AUKUS recently emerged as a powerful grouping looking to reinforce Western protective alliances in the Indo-Pacific region, France could capitalise on being left out by engaging directly with key Indo-Pacific powers on security issues. Filling a potential gap that the US has left by failing to provide as a security guarantor for powers in the region, France may find a way to posture itself as an important defence partner for the Indo-Pacific nations through the Quad Plus. Notably, Japan has already hinted heavily that France would be a promising candidate in an expanded Quad Plus, as well as an extended Quad grouping.[60]

ASEAN: Furthering ASEAN Centrality

The Quad 2.0 was revived at the sidelines of an ASEAN meeting in 2017 and, thus, ASEAN can be considered to have facilitated the rise of the Quad in regional politics. Despite this, there is caution from ASEAN over whether both groupings can coexist and complement each other in the Indo-Pacific, or whether the Quad jeopardises the relevance of ASEAN. However, the Quad has asserted its commitment to the centrality of ASEAN. The Quad recognises that many challenges that it wishes to address cannot be dealt with by the Quad alone, which the pandemic revealed, and were critical to the establishment of the Quad Plus framework in the first place. Nonetheless, Vietnam agreeing to be part of the Quad Plus during the pandemic is not an indication of consensus among the ASEAN countries towards the Quad, as a majority remain suspicious of where ASEAN is placed within the order,[61] as well as the US-led anti-China rhetoric behind it. There is also concern regarding the overlapping security challenges and members the two coalitions would share, and without a clear division of labour.[62] Since the COVID-19 pandemic, ASEAN does appear to have welcomed efforts to expand the Quad as a source of public good in Southeast Asia and the Indo-Pacific, such as with the vaccine roll-out and coordination to reduce the pandemic's impact on the regional economies.[63] While it is unlikely that ASEAN would join as a 'Plus partner', the member states may consider it if they are able to see the two as equally important and complementary as they possibly coexist. It is instead probable that ASEAN will remain a close partner of the Quad with the potential for communication and exchange over a broader range of issues to be implemented through dialogues such as the 'ASEAN Working Group on Climate Change'.[64]

Ultimately, the 'capital' of the Quad Plus mechanism is one that requires serious study and focus, especially as it remains largely unrecovered and unutilised. By paving the way for the 'Quad Plus' inclusive future, the Quad could both move away from China's characterisation of the dialogue as an "exclusive clique"[65] while allowing the quadrilateral nations room to build their multilateral and bilateral links with the Indo-Pacific and Asian powers, starting with areas beyond security, but ultimately encompassing the same.

Summing Up: India's Interest in an Expanded Quad Plus

Therefore, as the Quad Plus looks to expand into a larger format comprising actors such as the EU, ASEAN and the UK, India has much to gain. India's primary aim in its diplomatic agenda moving forward is to pursue a form of energetic and conscientious outreach to a myriad actors. As New Delhi grapples with an increasingly serious China challenge, it is no longer enough to build strategic partnerships within the Indo-Pacific region. In other words, India's outreach cannot be limited to the Quad, through a focus on engaging with America, bringing Japan into play, and building a stronger comprehensive partnership with Australia. Rather, as India looks to enhance its global profile, it must look to enhance its ties with actors beyond the Quad, both within and outside the Indo-Pacific, including Vietnam, ASEAN, South Korea, Israel, Brazil, New Zealand, the UK and the EU. The Quad Plus gives India an opportunity to bring together such powers alongside the Quad states and, therefore, move towards its vision of a truly inclusive and multipolar regional (and global) order.

A direct expansion of the Quad—at least at this stage—is highly unlikely. Although moving towards an institutionalised format, the Quad is still in its nascent stages and only just beginning to define itself as a concrete pillar in the foreign policies of the four member states. Amid such dynamics, an abstract 'Quad Plus' framework is where 'Plus' partners interact with the Quad powers on specific issues. At the same time, as a press report from the Indian Ministry of External Affairs explicitly stated, the forum can be an "attempt to keep the Quad-plus countries within a certain sphere of influence and strategic direction".[66] India is already making attempts at such wider outreach through its newly established fora like the IPOI; the Quad Plus can be an additional mechanism for greater outreach in concert with India's Quad partners. States and actors involved in an expanded Quad Plus forum can build synergy based on shared perceptions and values of a rules-based order for peace, security and stability in the region. In this context, it can be a pragmatic pathway for not only India, but the other powers involved as well, to pursue greater comprehensive cooperation, particularly in areas like vaccine delivery and climate change where much alignment already exists. An expansion will by no means be an easy feat; yet concerted efforts in this direction by India and its Quad partners can yield immense gains in devising solutions to shared or similar concerns, not the least through burden sharing of common problems.

Notes

1. John Drake, "Was Covid-19 A Black Swan Event?", Forbes, November 11, 2021. https://www.forbes.com/sites/johndrake/2021/11/11/was-covid-19-a-black-swan-event/?sh=506b3634bd36.

2. "Foreign Secretary's Conference Call with Counterparts from Indo-Pacific Countries," Ministry of External Affairs—India, March 20, 2020. https://mea.gov.in/press-releases.htm?dtl/32592/Foreign+Secretarys+Conference+Call+with+counterparts+from+ IndoPacific+Countries.

3. "Meeting on the Novel Coronavirus Disease among Foreign Ministers of Interested Countries, Hosted by the United States," May 22, 2020, Ministry of Foreign Affairs of Japan. Accessed January 16, 2022. https://www.mofa.go.jp/press/release/press4e_002806.html.

4. "Joint Statement from Quad Leaders," The White House, September 25, 2021. https://www.whitehouse.gov/briefing-room/statements-releases/ 2021/09/24/joint-statement-from-quad-leaders/.

5. Jagannath Panda, "JIPA QUAD PLUS SPECIAL ISSUE, Vol. 4 No. 3," Journal for Indo-Pacific Affairs, 2021. https://media.defence.gov/2021/Feb/06/2002577570/-1/-1/1/JIPA_QUAD_PLUS_SPECIAL_ISSUE.PDF.

6. "Quad Leaders' Joint Statement: 'The Spirit of the Quad,'" 2021, The White House, March 12, 2021. https://www.whitehouse.gov/briefing-room/statements-releases/2021/03/12/quad-leaders-joint-statement-the-spirit-of-the-quad/.

7. "Fact Sheet: Quad Summit," 2021, The White House, March 12, 2021. https://www.whitehouse.gov/briefing-room/statements-releases/2021/03/12/fact-sheet-quad-summit/.

8. Hideshi Tokuchi, "The Quad Plus in the Security of Asia: Its Significance and Outlook", Society of Security and Diplomatic Political Studies, 2021. http://ssdpaki.la.coocan.jp/en/proposals/79.html.

9. Rajeswari Pillai Rajagopalan, "Towards a Quad-Plus Arrangement," Observe Research Foundation (ORF), May 2020. https://www.orfonline.org/research/towards-a-quad-plus-arrangement-65674/.

10. The Trade Ministers of India, Japan and Australia have formally launched the Supply Chain Resilience Initiative (SCRI), aiming to create a virtuous cycle of enhancing supply chain resilience, in a bid to eventually attain strong, sustainable, balanced and inclusive growth in the Indo-Pacific. https://www.meti.go.jp/press/2021/04/20210427004/20210427004-1.pdf.

11. Jagannath Panda, "Making 'Quad Plus' a Reality," January 13, 2022. https://thediplomat.com/2022/01/making-quad-plus-a-reality/.

12. ASEAN centrality is defined as ASEAN's role in the regional security architecture, regional order, and the power dynamics between and among external powers that have interests in the region.

13. "Quad Leaders' Joint Statement: 'The Spirit of the Quad,'" 2021. Ministry of External Affairs, India. March 12, 2021. https://mea.gov.in/bilateral-documents.htm?dtl/33620/Quad+Leaders+Joint+Statement+The+Spirit+of+the+Quad.

14. "Global Britain in a Competitive Age: The Integrated Review of Security, Defence, Development and Foreign Policy," March 2021, GOV.UK. Accessed January 16, 2022. https://www.gov.uk/government/publications/global-britain-

in-a-competitive-age-the-integrated-review-of-security-defence-development-and-foreign-policy.

15. "Global Gateway: Up to €300 Billion," December 2021, European Commission. Accessed January 16, 2022. https://ec.europa.eu/commission/presscorner/detail/en/ip_21_6433.
16. Louisa Brooke-Holland, "Integrated Review 2021: The Defence Tilt to the Indo-Pacific," January 2022. https://commonslibrary.parliament.uk/research-briefings/cbp-9217/.
17. "EU Strategy for Cooperation in the Indo-Pacific," September 2021, Text, European Commission. Accessed January 16, 2022. https://ec.europa.eu/commission/presscorner/detail/en/QANDA_21_4709.
18. Panda, n. 5.
19. Vijay Gokhale, "On the Quad, Define the Idea, Chart a Path" *The Hindu*, October 1, 2020. https://www.thehindu.com/opinion/lead/on-the-quad-define-the-idea-chart-a-path/article32735780.ece.
20. "China's Role in the Next Phase of Globalization: McKinsey" n.d. Accessed January 16, 2022. https://www.mckinsey.com/featured-insights/china/chinas-role-in-the-next-phase-of-globalization.
21. Jagannath Panda, "'China Plus One': Supply Chain Resilience Initiative and Beijing in Indo-Pacific", Manohar Parrikar Institute for Defence Studies and Analyses, IDSA, July 2021. https://www.idsa.in/issuebrief/china-plus-one-beijing-indo-pacific-jpanda-260721.
22. Graham Allison, "The Thucydides Trap", *Foreign Policy*, June 9, 2017. https://foreignpolicy.com/2017/06/09/the-thucydides-trap/.
23. AUKUS refers to the trilateral security pact among Australia, UK and the US announced in September 2021. Under the pact, the US and UK are said to help Australia procure nuclear-powered submarines. The announcement of the pact came as a big blow to the trans-Atlantic partners due to the lack of consultation, especially to France, whose USD 56 billion submarine deal with Australia was abruptly cancelled.
24. Henry Foy and Sam Fleming, "European Defence: The Quest for 'Strategic Autonomy,'" *Financial Times*, September 27, 2021. https://www.ft.com/content/f14c3e59-30bb-4686-8ba3-18ff860647e7.
25. "India's Continental Connect on Indo-Pacific and Quad 2.0," 2018, East-West Centre, September 25, 2018. https://www.eastwestcenter.org/publications/indias-continental-connect-indo-pacific-and-quad-20.
26. Aurelie George Mulgan, "2021 in Review: Abe's Lasting Strategic Legacy in the Indo-Pacific—Australian Institute of International Affairs", December 23, 2021. https://www.internationalaffairs.org.au/australianoutlook/abes-lasting-strategic-legacy-in-the-indo-pacific/.
27. Ibid. https://www.internationalaffairs.org.au/australianoutlook/abes-lasting-strategic-legacy-in-the-indo-pacific/.

28. William Sposato, "Japan's New Prime Minister Fumio Kishida Tries Economic Populism," *Foreign Policy*, January 11, 2022. https://foreignpolicy.com/2022/01/11/japans-new-prime-minister-takes-on-abenomics-legacy/.
29. "Japan PM Kishida Vows to Strengthen Quad Alliance and China Ties", *Asia Nikkei*, October 2021. https://asia.nikkei.com/Politics/Japan-PM-Kishida-vows-to-strengthen-Quad-alliance-and-China-ties.
30. Tokuchi, n. 8.
31. "Japan, Australia Sign Defence Pact for Closer Cooperation", Reuters, January 6, 2022. https://www.reuters.com/world/asia-pacific/japan-australia-sign-defence-cooperation-pact-2022-01-06/.
32. Paul Karp, 2020, "China's Coercive Behaviour a 'Wake-up Call', Australia's Former Top Public Servant Says", *The Guardian*, May 7, 2020. https://www.theguardian.com/australia-news/2020/may/08/chinas-coercive-behaviour-a-wake-up-call-australias-former-top-public-servant-says.
33. "Passing the Baton 2021: Securing America's Future Together", United States Institute of Peace, January 2021. https://www.usip.org/events/passing-baton-2021-securing-americas-future-together.
34. "The Quad: Contrasting Chinese and US Perceptions", *The Asan Forum* (blog), June 10, 2021. https://theasanforum.org/the-quad-contrasting-chinese-and-us-perceptions/.
35. Ibid.
36. Jagannath Panda and Akriti Vasudeva, "US-China Competition and Washington's Case for 'Quad Plus,'" *The National Interest*, Centre for National Interest, September 28, 2020. https://nationalinterest.org/feature/us-china-competition-and-washington%E2%80%99s-case-%E2%80%98quad-plus%E2%80%99-169751.
37. Thomas O. Falk, "Decline No Longer a Choice for Fading US as China Rises to Power", *South China Morning Post*, January 13, 2022. https://www.scmp.com/comment/opinion/article/3162981/decline-no-longer-choice-fading-us-china-rises-power.
38. Darshana Baruah, "India in the Indo-Pacific: New Delhi's Theater of Opportunity", Carnegie Endowment for International Peace, June 2020. https://carnegieendowment.org/2020/06/30/india-in-indo-pacific-new-delhi-s-theater-of-opportunity-pub-82205.
39. Natasha Jha Bhaskar, "India's Developing Economic Ties with the Indo-Pacific". Observer Research Foundation, April 26, 2021. https://www.orfonline.org/expert-speak/india-developing-economic-ties-indo-pacific/.
40. Ibid.
41. Jagannath P. Panda, and Ernest Gunasekara-Rockwell, *Quad Plus and Indo-Pacific: The Changing Profile of International Relations*" (Taylor and Francis Group, December 29, 2021). https://www.taylorfrancis.com/books/edit/10.4324/9781003206408/quad-plus-indo-pacific-jagannath-panda-ernest-gunasekara-rockwell.

42. Make in India is an initiative by the Government of India to make and encourage companies to develop, manufacture and assemble products made in India and incentivise dedicated investments into manufacturing. India's extensive modernisation plans, with an increased focus on homeland security and growing attractiveness as a defence sourcing hub have led it to engage countries in choosing to manufacture defence equipment in India.
43. Panda, and Rockwell-Gunasekara. n. 41. https://www.taylorfrancis.com/books/edit/10.4324/9781003206408/quad-plus-indo-pacific-jagannath-panda-ernest-gunasekara-rockwell.
44. Panda, n. 5. https://media.defence.gov/2021/Feb/06/2002577570/-1/-1/1/JIPA_QUAD_PLUS_SPECIAL_ISSUE.PDF.
45. See n. 40.
46. "UK's First Carrier Continues Long Deployment in South China Sea," *The Maritime Executive*, October 12, 2021. https://www.maritime-executive.com/article/uk-s-carrier-strike-group-exercises-in-south-china-sea.
47. Dr Anil Kumar Lal, "Quad Plus and Beyond: Blue Print for Operationalisation—Part 2," *The Times of India*, March 12, 2021. Accessed January 16, 2022. https://timesofindia.indiatimes.com/blogs/rakshakindia/quad-plus-and-beyond-blue-print-for-operationalisation-part-2/.
48. See n. 12.
49. See n. 12; n. 44.
50. See n. 12; n. 40; n. 44.
51. Jeff M. Smith, "The Future of the Quad is Bright," The Heritage Foundation, March 2021. https://www.heritage.org/global-politics/commentary/the-future-the-quad-bright.
52. See n. 8.
53. "The Quad: An Emerging Multilateral Security Framework of Democracies in the Indo-Pacific Region", Think-Tank, European Parliament, March 18, 2021. https://www.europarl.europa.eu/thinktank/en/document/EPRS_BRI(2021)690513.
54. Erik Brattberg, "Britain's D-10 Summit of Democracies Beats a Moribund G-7," June 2020. https://foreignpolicy.com/2020/06/10/g7-d10-democracy-trump-europe/.
55. See n. 8; n. 12.
56. Mathieu Duchatel, and Garima Mohan, "Franco-German Divergences in the Indo-Pacific: The Risk of Strategic Dilution," Institut Montaigne, October 20, 2020. https://www.institutmontaigne.org/en/blog/franco-german-divergences-indo-pacific-risk-strategic-dilution.
57. Xavier Vavasseur, "Australia, France, India, Japan and the United States Take Part in Exercise La Pérouse," *Naval News* (blog), April 6, 2021. https://www.navalnews.com/naval-news/2021/04/australia-france-india-japan-and-the-united-states-take-part-in-exercise-la-perouse/.

58. "France and Sailing Toward the 'Quad-Plus'", *The New Indian Express*, April 6, 2021. Accessed January 16, 2022. https://www.newindianexpress.com/opinions/2021/apr/06/france-and-sailing-toward-the-quad-plus-2286408.html.
59. Dhruv Nilkanth, "Has AUKUS Ended All Hopes of a Quad Plus France?" *Diplomatist*. October 12, 2021. https://diplomatist.com/2021/10/12/has-aukus-ended-all-hopes-of-a-quad-plus-france/.
60. Sandeep Dikshit, "Japan for Expanding Quad; France Could be First Addition," *Tribune India,* October 6, 2020. https://www.tribuneindia.com/news/nation/japan-for-expanding-quad-france-could-be-first-addition-151873.
61. Jonathan Stromseth, "ASEAN and the Quad: Strategic Impasse or Avenue for Cooperation?" Brookings, September 23, 2021. https://www.brookings.edu/blog/order-from-chaos/2021/09/23/asean-and-the-quad-strategic-impasse-or-avenue-for-cooperation/.
62. See n. 18.
63. See n. 57.
64. See n. 57; n. 59.
65. "Foreign Ministry Spokesperson's Remarks," Embassy of the People's Republic of China in Solomon Islands, May 12, 2021. https://www.fmprc.gov.cn/ce/cesb/eng/fyrth_17/t1875292.htm.
66. Indrani Bagchi, "India Joins Hands with NZ, Vietnam, S Korea to Combat Pandemic," *The Times of India,* March 21, 2020. https://timesofindia.indiatimes.com/india/india-joins-hands-with-nz-vietnam-s-korea-to-combat-pandemic/articleshow/74740424.cms.

Conclusion

Mapping the Future of India's Indo-Pacific Strategy

Mahima Duggal

Over the past few years, the 'Indo-Pacific' has risen as a new geopolitical concept with several states, including India, which has adopted the 'Indo-Pacific' concept as an integral part of its foreign policy. While the rise of the Indo-Pacific was a steadily emerging trend prior to COVID-19, the pandemic has proved to be a 'black swan' event that has thrown the region (if not the entire world) into uncertainty and geopolitical flux. The rise of China across the Indian and Pacific Oceans, which has been belligerent rather than peaceful, has challenged the security and stability in the region and accelerated the conceptualisation and acceptance of the Indo-Pacific as a new geopolitical space. Although the region is often looked at through a dominant lens of US-China competition (or confrontation), India's perception and conceptual construct of the region is vital to understanding how regional politics takes shape in the coming times.

Pragmatism and Pointed Alignment in India's Indo-Pacific Outlook

Faced with its own territorial conflict with China, India has rapidly expanded its engagement with the region as a way to secure its position and geopolitical, geoeconomic and geostrategic environments. In fact, as the only member of the Quadrilateral Security Dialogue (Quad)—comprising India, Japan, Australia and the United States (US)—to share a land border with China, as well as the only Indian Ocean power amongst the group, India's role in the Indo-Pacific is vital. Over the past year, New Delhi has made maritime security in the Indo-Pacific a central part of its foreign and security policy. This has involved a calculated adjustment in foreign policy engagements to expand its focus from its immediate South Asian neighbourhood to the broader Indo-Pacific and a strategic shift in India's security calculus from a neutral, non-aligned position to one of pointed alignment (meaning, a focus on like-minded partners).

This change in the regional dynamics and India's outlook is evidenced by the growing and pragmatic focus on Indo-Pacific trilateral partnerships and increased involvement with the Quad. In 2020, for the first time, India invited Australia to the annual India-Japan-US naval exercises, making it a true Quad endeavour. Australia's involvement has continued in 2021 and can become a regular occurrence moving forward. Further, India has also helped elevate the Quad from a ministerial level dialogue to a state leader level consultation, with an in-person meeting planned for later in 2021. In essence, after briefly emerging as a tentative grouping in response to the 2004 tsunami in India, the Quad was reformed in 2017 and has since become a formal part of India's strategic thinking; New Delhi is now looking at the institutionalisation of the grouping, demonstrating the clear changes in India's engagement with the Quad as a way of balancing China's increasing assertiveness.

Even if India is not yet considered a major player east of the Malacca Strait and in the Western Pacific, it is a significant power of the Indian Ocean and, therefore, an anchor of the Quad's promoted free, open, prosperous, and inclusive Indo-Pacific strategy. Considering India's centrality in the rapidly bolstering Indo-Pacific conceptualisation, as well as the changes in New Delhi's own strategic thinking, this book delves into India's role in the region to better understand its strategy, challenges and opportunities.

Key Takeaways

The selection of chapters in this edited volume have provided a comprehensive and broad-ranging overview of the Indo-Pacific region, while keeping India at the centre. In an attempt to make a thorough investigation into India's role and posture in the Indo-Pacific, and the implications of the regional dynamics on India's policy and outlook towards the region, this volume is divided into three distinct sections:

India's Emerging Power and the Rise of the Indo-Pacific, which highlights the various aspects of India's policy and strategy towards the Indo-Pacific; *India as a Critical Link in the Quad Diamond,* which explores India's bilateral partnerships with its Quad partners and the dynamic evolution and institutionalisation of the grouping in relation to China; and lastly, *Moving Beyond the Quad,* which examines the Indo-Pacific policies and activities of various extra-regional powers, including West Asia, Russia, Association of Southeast Asian Nations (ASEAN), Taiwan, and Europe, as well as the emerging 'Quad Plus' grouping (including Israel, Brazil and South Korea).

Beginning with a chapter on the US-China strategic competition in the Indo-Pacific, the book sets the background and context for the discussion that follows. The US' weakening global position, and the simultaneous rise and expanding military reach of China under an overt desire to dominate the Indo-Pacific, has forced India to reevaluate its challenges and options in the new era. Not only does the presence of a politically and militarily formidable China vying for greater influence and absolute dominance over the region make it difficult for India to engage in a power parity relationship with Beijing, it also makes negotiating on equal terms vis-à-vis their boundary dispute difficult. China's growing presence in the Indian Ocean, and increasingly assertive actions at the disputed Line of Actual Control (LAC) in Ladakh and Arunachal Pradesh, further force India to reassess its threat calculus and accordingly commit greater sums to bolster its defence capacity.

In this context of the intense challenges that India faces in the Indo-Pacific, the book presents the following five key takeaways for the future of India's Indo-Pacific strategy.

1. Enhancing Engagement with the Western Pacific

India's drive to become an active player in the Western Pacific region stems from its desire to expand its footprint beyond its traditional domain, the Indian Ocean, and effectively contain Chinese expansionism here, as well as ensure uninterrupted access to regional waters. Yet, despite its security dynamics in South Asia being inherently tied to the Western Pacific, India's formal military-based engagement with the region is sorely lacking.

Moving forward, the Indian Navy must look to enhance its blue water naval capabilities so as to enable it to project its power in distant waters beyond the Indian Ocean. This must be accompanied by a clearer turn towards the Western Pacific under its Act East policy through military arrangements; as India looks to become a responsible Indo-Pacific power, maintaining peace and security beyond its neighbourhood is vital to securing its economic and political interests and military security. While New Delhi must obviously account for the China threat, India's policy towards the region must be independent and look to convert already existing cultural linkages into political and strategic ones. Most states in the region are reliant on the US for their security needs, which have only grown in the face of belligerent Chinese power; however, should the US' security guarantee fail—which is no longer an entirely unlikely scenario—these states may be forced to fall in with China. Considering this, India's must look to position itself as an alternative pillar for security in the region that is capable of leading a coalition to balance (if not counter) China in the Western Pacific, and by extension, the Indo-Pacific.

2. Overhauling Maritime Strategy and Bolstering Naval and Air Power Capacity

India's economic well-being is inextricably linked to the seas, and accordingly, the Indian Navy will need to be prepared to tackle challenges in the maritime domain. This includes traditional and non-traditional threats like state conflicts, maritime terrorism, piracy, Illegal, Unreported and Unregulated (IUU) fishing, and climate change among others. Chapter 3 argues how India, despite being a naval power to be reckoned with, still lacks as a manifest maritime power. Inadequate government support has thus far prevented it from transforming its natural potential—based on its central geographical positioning in the Indian Ocean, over a 1,000-mile-long coastline, and a young, vibrant coastal populace—into maritime power.

Accordingly, India's foremost priority must be capacity building in the Indian Ocean, which remains its primary domain of interest, via instruments like bilateral ties, minilateral engagements, military diplomacy, and, most importantly, perhaps, naval engagement with foreign powers for a well-coordinated approach to tackle oceanic security challenges. To some extent, such a shift in India's strategy is already visible with its move away from goodwill naval operations to overseas deployments aimed at enhancing its operational footprint in the region. The Indian Navy has grown by leaps and bounds since independence; a full spectrum capability force, it is now focussing on power projection and sea control, strategic deterrence abilities, undersea warfare, developing formidable surface warfare and naval aviation capabilities, streamlining logistic supply chains, and enhancing indigenisation capacity. This indicates that India is already standing at the cusp, emerging as a phenomenal maritime power. To realise this vision, the government must ensure that the navy has all the requisite resources and can be agile and flexible in the tech-driven battlespace of a swiftly changing security environment.

In congruence with its naval capacity, India must also revisit its air power capabilities, considering air power's immense potential as a national policy tool to become a balancing force in the region. Air power offers diverse utility and can be critical in areas ranging from intelligence and reconnaissance to aerial denial operations and deterrence. India must, therefore, look to establish air superiority in the theatre during periods of armed hostilities to ensure that China's People's Liberation Army Air Force (PLAAF) and People's Liberation Army Navy (PLAN) cannot dominate the region. This will necessarily require India to join forces with other like-minded powers, but, more importantly, invest heavily in enhancing its capacity; this would include investments in next-generation technologies like hypersonic weapons and Unmanned Combat Aerial Vehicles (UCAVs) and greater military engagement with the Quad partners.

3. Continued Focus on Quad Partners

Moving forward, the Quad partners will continue to feature heavily in India's pragmatic foreign policy. While New Delhi has already built strong and comprehensive ties with Japan, Australia and the US, several areas have much scope for cooperation. With Japan, India must look to further cooperation in defence technologies and their transfer to India, and develop greater understanding vis-à-vis the Asian security landscape that improves their network operations in conflict situations. Similarly, with Australia, India can build greater collaborations and synergies in areas like cyber norms and security, hydrogen energy, establishing critical mineral and rare earth supply chains, and critical and emerging technologies (particularly 5G and undersea communication cables). Further, Delhi and Canberra can focus on cooperation and innovation in defence technology, and enhanced defence interactions in areas where their strategic interests overlap, such as the Eastern Indian Ocean and Southeast Asia, via joint patrols, joint exercises, defence-related information sharing and establishing secure military-to-military communication channels. At the same time, India's engagement with the US should remain calibrated. While the China threat looms large, the US is a pivotal actor and net security provider in the Indo-Pacific. Although several gaps persist between New Delhi and Washington, especially while the US perceives China through a great power rivalry, the Indo-Pacific is central to both their foreign policy outlooks, and greater interaction to enhance mutual understanding, navigate their differences and increase synergy is crucial.

Simultaneously, New Delhi must also persist with its focus on the Quad grouping and utilise the platform it provides to further the security-growth-prosperity nexus in the region. The Quad has rapidly become an institutionalised forum in the Indo-Pacific strategies of its constituent members, with a comprehensive agenda, from climate change, vaccine delivery and semiconductor supply chains to critical technologies, and cyber, space and maritime security—and it holds immense prospects for the future. In the post-pandemic order, it is vital that the Quad maintain its progressive trajectory and explore avenues like a Quad trade deal to balance Chinese economic dominance, addressing the nuclear proliferation in the region such as vis-à-vis North Korea, amplifying renewable power generation capacity (including clean hydrogen) to meet climate targets, sustainable infrastructure development in the region, and the Taiwan issue. With a look towards the future, India must make sure it can effectively use the Quad's immense potential as a strategic construct to sustain regional peace.

4. From East to West: Broadening ASEAN Ties and Emphasising the Persian Gulf Connection to the Indo-Pacific

Importantly, India's definition of the Indo-Pacific stretches from the western coast of the US to the eastern coast of Africa. A natural point of focus within this region and India's eastward outlook is ASEAN; ASEAN's centrality—which implies placing ASEAN values and mechanisms at the centre of regional engagement—continues to be a critical factor in India's (and indeed its Quad partners') Indo-Pacific policy. While economic drivers have been a constant in India-ASEAN ties, there remains significant scope for expanding geoeconomic engagement, particularly in areas like rare earth element supply chains where China enjoys a veritable monopoly.

On the other hand, as part of its broader, more inclusive outlook, India is increasingly strengthening its connect with the Persian Gulf states—such as through the Quad II (India, Israel, the UAE and the US). As it looks to alter the existing balance of power equations in the Indo-Pacific, India is looking to establish itself as a security provider in both the Persian Gulf and Indo-Pacific regions, and, therefore, closely connecting the two under a geopolitical vision. While there is much focus on the Eastern Indian Ocean, it is vital that India also project itself as a reliable partner in the Western Indian Ocean to achieve strategic maritime pre-eminence and great power aspirations, and this demands a greater connect with West Asia through bilateral, minilateral and multilateral modes.

5. Cultivating Partnerships with 'Plus' Partners and Extra-Regional Actors like Russia and Europe

Alongside continued focus on the Quad, ASEAN, and increasingly, Western Pacific and West Asia, achieving its goals and aspirations in the Indo-Pacific requires India to pursue an all-out diplomatic approach that includes extending outreach to partners like the European Union (EU), reassuring Russia, and drawing in other extra-regional partners like Israel and Brazil. While any such engagement will not be without challenges, especially considering that there will be gaps between India's and the external actors' Indo-Pacific outlooks, greater engagement with key partners can help India promote inclusivity (a key pillar of its Indo-

Pacific policy) and, therefore, strengthen cooperation to safeguard a rules-based order. In Europe, India shares strong economic and security ties with Germany, France, and the UK as well as great potential for a green partnership with the Nordic states. Further, the EU's interest and focus on the Indo-Pacific—particularly as it recalibrates its outlook post the formation of Australia-UK-US (AUKUS)—make it a vital partner in the region. India must build on shared democratic values and perceptions with the EU for greater engagement that helps New Delhi enhance its regional and global profile.

At the same time, Russia is a key defence partner for India, making exploration of common ground vis-à-vis the Indo-Pacific an important aspect of their bilateral relations. Although both countries have profound differences when it comes to their perceptions of the West and China, there are several existing and potentially new areas for congruence—including defence trade and cooperation in multilateral forums. Considering the importance India allocates to Moscow, New Delhi will need to make sure that its future engagement with the US and Europe does not alienate its 'special and privileged' partner Russia.

To bring together such a varied set of external partners into the Indo-Pacific, India will need to expand and utilise platforms like the conjectural Quad Plus alliance, or even the Delhi-led Indo-Pacific Oceans Initiative (IPOI). While a direct expansion of the Quad remains unlikely, an abstract or ad hoc framework that provides an Indo-Pacific focussed platform for stakeholders to come together and collaborate on shared issues can yield immense gains; it must, therefore, be a priority as India looks to tie together its diplomatic channels.

Summing Up

India is faced with an incredibly difficult and continuously changing security landscape in the Indo-Pacific. To be able to effectively adapt to this new theatre of geopolitical rivalry, India's foreign and security policy will need to be equally flexible and quick to adjust. This will require not only constantly calibrating our threat perception in an evolving environment but also regularly revisiting our foreign policy imperatives and priorities and significantly strengthening our national security structures, including military capacity. New Delhi must be cognisant of the fact that India can no longer attempt to stay neutral in geopolitical rivalries, even as it looks to maintain an independent foreign policy and strategic autonomy. Rather, to assert India's voice on the global stage and pursue greater growth, development and prosperity, New Delhi must be open to building greater synergy, be more accepting of pointed alignment arrangements, and initiating new collaborative ventures (whether bilaterally or minilaterally) that help bolster its own capabilities and capacity. In other words, even as New Delhi stays away from alliances, it must actively seek greater alignments with like-minded powers to further shared goals, especially securing and safeguarding the strategic autonomy of all regional powers in the face of formidable Chinese power that is increasingly employing its economic weight to gain strategic influence over smaller states. Such synergetic alignments need to be built via regular, substantive, and holistic high-level and institutional-level security dialogues with like-minded powers in the Indo-Pacific, that address, at their core, ways to protect the rules-based regional and global governance system, the freedom of navigation and the free flow of commerce through the maritime domain of the Indo-Pacific—so as to ensure mutual security and prosperity.

In geopolitics, the past never dies, but the future is where we look. If the Chinese had not shown territorial aggression, they could have remained important stakeholders in the system. The prevalent disputes in the region are a heady mix of history, law, morality, and expediency. The Indo-Pacific requires responsible stewardship. The Quad members will be central to peace and stability in the region. Other free world democracies would have to resolve to expand and deepen the strategic partnership between the countries and advance common objectives. These objectives would include combatting terrorist threats, promoting stability across the Indo-Pacific region, increasing free and fair trade, and strengthening energy linkages.

Editors and Contributors

EDITOR

Air Marshal **Anil Chopra** PVSM, AVSM, VM, VSM (Retd), is a fighter pilot, test pilot, and a pioneer of the Mirage-2000 fleet, who has commanded a Mirage 2000 Squadron and the Flight Test Centre, Aircraft and Systems Testing Establishment (ASTE) of the Indian Air Force (IAF). He was the Team Leader of the MiG 21 Bison Upgrade project in Russia. He has commanded operational air bases in both the Western and Eastern Sectors. He was head of the IAF in Jammu and Kashmir (J&K), and head of Operational Inspections of the IAF. He retired as the Air Officer Personnel. He has been a member of the Armed Forces Tribunal, Lucknow Bench, and member of the Executive Council of Jawaharlal Nehru University (JNU). He has also been an advisor on a committee of the National Green Tribunal. In addition to the four Presidential awards, he is recipient of the Gandhi Family Peace Medal for his work in J&K.

An avid writer, Air Marshal Chopra has more than 600 articles published in various magazines, newspapers and books. He has recently written a book titled *China, The Rising Aerospace Power: Implications for India*, and was also the co-editor of a book titled *The 1971 Indo-Pak Air War: Reflections and Projections*. Air Marshal Chopra is presently the Director-General of the Centre for Air Power Studies (CAPS) and runs "Air Power Asia" (airpowerasia.com), a website that puts Asia's aviation and military power into the correct perspective.

ASSOCIATE EDITORS

Air Commodore **Savinder Pal Singh**, VSM (Retd), was commissioned in the fighter stream of the Indian Air Force (IAF) in December 1985.

He has flown more than 3,000 hours on various fighter aircraft including the MiG-21 Bison and SU-30. He is a Qualified Flying Instructor, Fighter Combat Leader and Instrument Rating Examiner. He commanded a Fighter Squadron and later a SU-30 Fighter Flying Operational Base. He has held several prestigious appointments, including Air-1, Western Air Command, Principle Director (Air Def and Weapon Sys) Air Headquarters, with two tenures at the Strategic Force Command.

He is an alumni of the prestigious National Defence College (NDC), Army War College (AWC) in Mhow, and Defence Services Staff College (DSSC) in Ooty. He is also a recipient of the Presidential award and commendation by the Chief of the Air Staff (CAS). Post retirement, he has worked as a strategic analyst and advisor and has written many articles on various issues covering air poower, theatre command, China and Pakistan. He has covered a series of podcasts on various combat assets of the IAF, which were recorded by BharatShakti.com. Presently, Air Commodore SP Singh is working at the Centre for Air Power Studies (CAPS) as a Senior Research Fellow and is heading the team for research and analysis on Indo-Pacific issues.

Ms **Mahima Duggal** is a Research Associate with the Centre for Air Power Studies (CAPS) in New Delhi. Her research is focussed on the changing balance of power and security issues in the Indo-Pacific region. Ms. Duggal has written extensively on subjects like Indian foreign policy, India-China ties, East Asian security dynamics, US alliances and partnerships in the Indo-Pacific, and Europe's interest in the Indo-Pacific for both national and international platforms, including *The Diplomat*, *Asia Times*, *South Asian Voices*, *9DashLine*, *Council on Geostrategy* (UK), and the *Canon Institute for Global Studies* (Japan). She has authored several peer-reviewed journal articles (including for the *Journal of Indo-Pacific Affairs*, *Journal of Indian Ocean Studies* and *Air Power Journal*) and numerous individual and co-authored chapters in edited volumes published internationally. Ms. Duggal is also an Associated Research Fellow at the Stockholm Centre for South Asian and Indo-Pacific Affairs (SCSA-IPA) of the Institute for Security and Development Policy

(ISDP) in Sweden, and the Editorial Assistant to the Series Editor for Routledge Studies on Think Asia.

CONTRIBUTORS

Dr **Joshy M. Paul** is a Research Fellow at the Centre for Air Power Studies (CAPS), New Delhi, focussing on the Chinese Navy. He has fifteen years of research and academic experience in issues like Asian security, East Asian affairs and maritime security of the Indo-Pacific. Before joining CAPS, he worked as an Assistant Professor at the Department of International Studies, School of Law, Christ University (Bangalore) and also with the premier naval think-tank, the National Maritime Foundation, New Delhi. He has published a number of articles in reputed journals, including *India Review*, *South Asian Survey*, *International Studies*, *Air Power Journal*, and *Maritime Affairs*. He was the RSIS MacArthur Associate Visiting Fellow (Singapore) in 2010, NIDS Visiting Research Fellow (Japan) in 2011, and Salzburg Global Seminar Fellow in 2009, 2015 and 2021. He earned an MPhil and PhD in International Politics from CIPOD, School of International Studies, Jawaharlal Nehru University, New Delhi.

Commodore **Anil Jai Singh** is the Vice President of the Indian Maritime Foundation, the country's leading maritime Non-Governmental Organisation (NGO), the Senior Vice President of a leading European Multinational Corporation (MNC) in India and has formerly co-chaired the Defence and Aerospace Committee of the Associated Chambers of Commerce and Industry (ASSOCHAM), a leading industry association. A naval veteran, he served for over three decades as a submariner and had the privilege of commanding four submarines and a fleet ship. He also served as India's Naval Advisor to the United Kingdom and his last appointment was in the Integrated Defence Staff of the Ministry of Defence (MoD). A post-graduate in Defence and Strategic Studies, he takes keen interest in maritime matters and writes and speaks extensively on the subject in India and abroad. He has been a part of numerous Track 1.5 Expert Group workshops on maritime security in the Indian Ocean Rim Association (IORA), East Asia Summit (EAS), Bay of Bengal

Initiative for Multi-Sectoral Technical and Economic Cooperation (BIMSTEC), etc. and has also participated in various study groups on the subject.

Dr **Shamshad Ahmad Khan** is an Assistant Professor of International Relations at the Department of Humanities and Social Sciences, BITS Pilani Dubai Campus, UAE. After completing his PhD in International Relations from the School of International Studies, JNU, New Delhi, he had researched at Indian and Japanese institutes. He was associated with the Indian Council of World Affairs, Institute for Defence Studies and Analyses, Institute of Chinese Studies, and Department of East Asian Studies, University of Delhi. He had been associated with various Japanese think-tanks, including the Policy Research Institute, Keio Research Institute, Japan Institute of International Affairs, Institute for Developing Economies, Slavic and Eurasian Research Centre, Hokkaido, as a visiting researcher. Before assuming his current position, he taught as Visiting Assistant Professor at the Department of International Relations, University of Sharjah, UAE. He got the Nakasone Yasuhiro award in 2011 from the International Institute of Policy Studies, Tokyo, for his research on Japan-India relations.

Dr **Peter Layton** is a Visiting Fellow at the Griffith Asia Institute, Griffith University, a RUSI Associate Fellow and a Royal Australian Air Force Reserve Group Captain. He has extensive aviation and defence experience including flying fast jets and maritime patrol, force development, and as a defence attaché. For his work at the Pentagon on force structure matters, he was awarded the US Secretary of Defence's Exceptional Public Service Medal. He has a doctorate from the University of New South Wales on grand strategy and has taught on the topic at the Eisenhower School for National Security and Resource Strategy, US National Defence University. For his academic studies, he was awarded a Fellowship to the European University Institute, Fiesole, Italy. He contributes regularly to the public policy debate on defence and foreign affairs issues and is the author of the book *Grand Strategy*. He is co-authoring a new book, *Warfare in the Robotic Age*.

Dr **Stuti Banerjee** is a Research Fellow at the Indian Council of World Affairs, New Delhi, where she is engaged in research on North America and Latin America and the Caribbean, the Indo-Pacific and the Polar region. Her areas of interest include international relations with emphasis on US and Indian foreign policy, as well as issues of strategy and security and nuclear security and risks. She is also engaged in writing policy recommendations papers for the concerned departments.

Dr **Hina Pandey** is a Research Analyst, working on nuclear issues, including nuclear non-proliferation, nuclear energy politics, nuclear strategy and security. She has also written on issues related to the US foreign policy, the Indo-Pacific, India's foreign policy, etc. Some of her work has been published by the Diplomat, Institute for Security and Development Policy (ISDP), The Japan Forward, Nuclear Asia, Stimson Centre, Pakistan Politico, Kalinga Institute of Indo-Pacific Studies (KIIPS) and Institute for Peace and Conflict Studies (IPCS). Earlier, she has worked with the Centre for Air Power Studies (CAPS), New Delhi, as an Associate Fellow. She holds a PhD from the American Studies Division School, JNU.

Ms **Neha Mishra** is a Research Associate (Indo-Pacific Group) at the Centre for Air Power Studies (CAPS). Her research interest focusses on India-China Geoeconomic Engagement or Competition, Role of Energy or Resource Strategy in International Politics, and China's Resource Diplomacy. Before joining CAPS, she worked as a Research Intern at the Institute of Chinese Studies (ICS) and then in the Indian Council of World Affairs (ICWA). Ms Mishra has an M.Phil and a Master's degree in Political Science from the Department of Political Science, University of Delhi. She is pursuing her PhD from the University of Delhi on 'India-China Geoeconomic Engagement'.

Ms **Anu Sharma** is an Associate Fellow with the Centre for Air Power Studies (CAPS), New Delhi. Her core interest areas include area studies, foreign policy and defence politics of the West Asian region. She has published and presented various papers on the foreign and domestic politics of Iran and the broader West Asian region, both nationally and internationally. She also published a book titled *Through the Looking Glass: Iran and its Foreign Relations* (2020). She graduated from Delhi University in Journalism and Mass Communications and has credible experience as a freelancing journalist with a New Delhi-based newspaper, *The Statesman*. She holds Master's and M.Phil degrees from the Jawaharlal Nehru University (JNU) and is a PhD candidate at the Centre for International Politics (CIP) of the University of Gujarat.

Ms **Mrittika Guha Sarkar** is a scholar at the Chinese Language Centre, National Chengchi University, Taipei, Taiwan. She is also a Research Scholar at the Centre for East Asian Studies, School of International Studies, Jawaharlal Nehru University (JNU), New Delhi. She is further associated with the Series Editor for the Routledge Studies on Think Asia and the *Journal of Indo-Pacific Affairs* (*JIPA*), and the Air University, USA, as a researcher and writer. Earlier, she worked for the Centre for Strategic Studies and Simulation, United Service Institution of India (USI) and the East Asia Centre, at the Manohar Parrikar Institute for Defence Studies and Analyses (MP-IDSA) as a Project Assistant. Her area of focus mainly encompasses China's foreign policy and strategic affairs.

Dr **Rajorshi Roy** is an Associate Fellow at the Manohar Parrikar Institute for Defence Studies and Analyses. His areas of research and analysis cover the foreign, defence, security and domestic policies of Russia and the Central Asian countries. He has written extensively on these issues. He was a member of the Institute's web editorial team during 2019-20. He was the Secretary for the Indian side of the Eminent Persons Group for Nepal-India Relations (2016-18), set up by the Governments of India and Nepal, to recommend ways to strengthen bilateral relations. He is an alumni of St. Stephen's College, University of Delhi.

Dr **Jagannath Panda** is the Head of the Stockholm Centre for South Asian and Indo-Pacific Affairs (SCSA-IPA) at the Institute for Security and Development Policy (ISDP), Sweden. He is also the Director for Europe-Asia Research Cooperation at the YCAPS, and an International Research

Fellow at the Canon Institute for Global Studies (CIGS) in Japan. Dr Panda is the Series Editor for Routledge Studies on Think Asia. Dr Panda is the author of the book *India-China Relations* (Routledge, 2017) and *China's Path to Power: Party, Military and the Politics of State Transition* (Pentagon Press: 2010). Dr. Panda's recent work includes *Quad Plus and Indo-Pacific* (Routledge, 2021); *Scaling India-Japan Cooperation in Indo-Pacific and Beyond 2025* (KW Publishers, 2019), and *The Korean Peninsula and Indo-Pacific Power Politics: Status Security at Stake* (Routledge, 2020).

Index